THE COMPUTER ESTABLISHMENT

THE
COMPUTER
ESTABLISHMENT

:·;

Katharine Davis Fishman

McGraw-Hill Book Company
New York St. Louis San Francisco Bogotá Guatemala
Hamburg Lisbon Madrid Mexico Montreal Panama Paris
San Juan São Paulo Tokyo Toronto

For Joe

Portions of this work originally appeared in *The Atlantic Monthly*.

Reprinted by arrangement with Harper & Row, Publishers, Inc.

First McGraw-Hill paperback edition, 1982

1234567890FGFG8765432

ISBN 0-07-021127-2

Library of Congress Cataloging in Publication Data

Fishman, Katharine Davis
   The computer establishment
    1. Computer industry—United States—History.
2. International Business Machines Corporation—History
I. Title.
HD9696.C63U51646   1981   338.4'7621381958'0973
ISBN 0-06-011283-2   80-8202
    0-07-021127-2 (PBK)   AACR2

Designer: Sidney Feinberg

Acknowledgments

It is probably not original to note that journalists, like Tennessee Williams's Blanche Du Bois, must always depend on the kindness of strangers. Any harried worker who is willing to pause for an hour to chat with an outsider is, of course, performing a kindness (not diminished by the fact that most of us, at least occasionally, find it fun to take a break, talk about our work, and try to bring our views to public attention); thus I'm indebted to everyone who sat still for an interview. A number of computer people, however, performed the extra kindnesses that turn strangers into friends, some for a brief but noteworthy period, others for several years, still others throughout the decade I worked on this book.

Among them, they gave many hours of additional interview time; remained accessible on the telephone to review difficult technical material "once more" until I got it right; acted as sounding boards for my wilder ideas and listened to the odd paragraph that it might become less odd; supplied bales of documents I wouldn't have seen otherwise; introduced me to hosts of new people, opened long-closed doors and helped me navigate bureaucratic shoals. The most unusual of these kindnesses came from the Atanasoffs, who entertained not only me but my family, immobilized by a balky car, for the better part of a weekend; the most extensive from the two former-strangers who reviewed the entire manuscript for accuracy. I thank everyone equally, in alphabetical order, so that those who gave the most help are not implicated in my sins (a smaller group of people, not mentioned here, are those I think would prefer total anonymity; I hope they'll silently add their names to the list): J. V. and Alice Atanasoff, Alex Bernstein, A. G. W. Biddle, Dick Brandon, Robert Braudy, J. Chuan Chu, Philip Dorn, Edward Goldstein, Herbert Grosch, Sam Harvey, George Hsieh, Michael Joyce, H. A. Kinslow, Charles Lecht, William R. Lonergan, Sema Marks, the late John W. Mauchly, Edwin S. McCollister, Theodore B. Merrill, David Mordy, John Morrissey, Janet L. Norman, Anthony Oettinger, James Peacock, Louis Robinson, Maxine Rockoff, John Rothman, Aran Safir, Oscar Schachter, Roger Schank, Naomi Seligman, John Siegel, Gordon Smith, Theodore Stein, Oscar Tang, Norman Taylor, S. S. Tyler, Joseph Weizenbaum, Alan Westin, Frederic G. Withington and Daniel Wright.

There is another group of people whose assistance came more in the line of official duty and, to boot, in the context of a largely adversary relationship. I'm speaking, of course, of the corporate press officers, and anyone who thinks they should be dispensed with is welcome to try setting up a day of interviews with a chairman and four vice-presidents so as to get out on the six o'clock plane; in addition, the press departments exhumed archival pictures, paleolithic speeches and the specifications of long-defunct machines; and did their best to answer arcane questions whose purpose was not revealed but might well get them into trouble. The best press officers are knowledgeable and conscientious and do a thankless job with good grace. Accordingly (in the jobs in which they helped me) I salute J. Bradley Stroup of Honeywell and then Data General, Sandy Lanzarotta and Tom Abbott of Xerox, James Fullam, Harry Wulforst and Michael Maynard of Sperry Univac, William Friis and Kenneth Bilby of RCA, Charles Truax of NCR, William Shaffer, Jim Bowe and the late Gordon Wise of Control Data, Don Young and Richard Brady of Burroughs, Edwina Mays and John McDonald of Digital Equipment, Ed Kanarkowski and Jim McDevitt of ADP, Chad Jewett of Cray Research, and George Capsis of The Singer Company and earlier, the Association for Computing Machinery.

At IBM the press officers come in phalanxes, each rotated in when its predecessors become exhausted; among these good soldiers were J. R. Young, Richard Whalen, Daniel Burnham, Kenneth Allen, Kenneth Foege, Edward Nanas, Victor Macdonald, Fred Steinberg, Steve Huben, Traug Keller, Richard Miller, Dan Udell, Jeannette Maher and Charles Watson. Few of these people would have been permitted to help much at all without the good offices of Jane Cahill Pfeiffer, who persuaded her colleagues that since I wasn't going to go away, they might as well learn to live with me.

For patience, wisdom and support I am immeasurably grateful to my editors, past and present: Genevieve Young, who got me to start the book, and Edward L. Burlingame, who got me to finish it; and to Frances Lindley for helpful suggestions on taming the beast. Ellen Royer displayed the qualities most desirable in a copy editor, a sharp eye and a gentle disposition; Winifred Osborn provided administrative solicitude.

I thank Joe, Maggie and Nancy Fishman for sharing with me the highs and lows of this lengthy project; and Joe Fishman one more time for sound advice and supplementary venture capital.

Finally, I am indebted to all the computer establishment for ten years of fascination and challenge, and for introducing me to a world I would never have expected to know.

Contents

Contents

PART V : THE TECHNOLOGY

PART VI : CONCLUSIONS

PART I

PROLOGUE

1

The Way Things Are

———

THE OBSTETRICS department of a large metropolitan hospital keeps a computer file of discharge summaries. As each patient leaves the hospital, the history of her labor and delivery, the drugs she has taken, and the sex, size and health of her baby are stored in the computer. The summaries, like written medical records, are used by the staff to look up a particular case; they have also become the basis of much statistical research done by the hospital. The computer's ability to retrieve and analyze data quickly and cheaply has encouraged staff members to carry out studies they might never have undertaken without it.

Soon after the file was set up, the director of obstetrical service was troubled by a spurt in the incidence of respiratory diseases among newborn babies delivered at the hospital. In studying the discharge summaries, he learned that many of these babies were premature; that is, they weighed less than twenty-five hundred grams. Then the director decided to check a hunch.

There had also been a growing trend toward induced labor. Both doctors and patients were becoming reluctant to wait for the midnight twinge and the two A.M. dash to the hospital. Successful urban obstetricians often are overloaded with work, and some may yearn for a "normal" life of charity balls, poker games and trips to Europe; mothers want to clear their desks before taking maternity leave, or know when to hire the nurse. And so medical policy toward induced labor had become more permissive, although many doctors were still reluctant to undertake it simply for convenience. (If an induced birth produces a premature child who develops difficulties, the doctor and the hospital are liable to malpractice suits.)

The director asked the statistician for the discharge summaries of all recent cases of induced labor in which the baby weighed less than twenty-five hundred grams. What he found was a high correlation between induced labor, prematurity and respiratory diseases—and also an inordinate number of premature babies with respiratory complaints whose birth had been induced by one particular doctor. The doctor was promptly taken to task, and the hospital introduced stricter regulation of induced delivery.

As patients, we are grateful to computer technology for developments like this one, and we might tend to anthropomorphize and call the computer the hero of the piece. But our gratitude is less fervent when this sort of hero appears in our own offices. No development of modern technology has aroused such ambivalence as the computer.

It was Pascal who said, "Man is a reed, the weakest in nature, but he is a thinking reed"; but Pascal himself did not consider the ability to calculate a sacred property of the thinking reed. At the age of about twenty he devised a simple machine for adding and subtracting which he hoped would be useful to his father, a government official who was revising the local tax system. The gears and wheels of the Pascal machine and other primitive models that followed it were not seen by society at large as threatening. But when *Fortune* reported, in 1966, that the newest supercomputer could multiply every number in the Brooklyn and Manhattan telephone books by the number that followed it, add the products of all the multiplications, divide the total by any other number and print the answer in less than two seconds, the reader was understandably humbled. And by that time, we had been worrying about the more modest accomplishments of the Giant Electronic Brain for nearly twenty years.

For a time, Giant Brain stories nourished our fears of automation-generated unemployment and omniscient robots' takeover of the world. If the computer could devour, digest and spit out all those numbers in the time it took us to say "um" there was clearly a risk that it could become our master. Meanwhile, the machine became a seductive promotional aid ("every one of our parts is carefully checked by computer"; "our computer will have a rental car ready before you hang up the phone") as well as a convenient scapegoat: if the customer's reservation was garbled, if his bill was inaccurate and illegible, the computer was to blame. And when this happened the customer, the thinking reed, despite his frustration, was triumphant.

This is not the place to itemize the many aspects of our lives now touched by the computer. It has entered the classroom and the sick-room, and we will confront it more often at work and perhaps at home. As computer technology permeates our lives, we have the right not to be mystified by it. We need to learn something about the machine itself, and, in order to understand how fast and how far the computer will change the way we live, we must get to know the sprawling, vigorous, eccentric industry it created barely thirty years ago.

The room is invariably windowless, shutting out the steamy New York summer noon, the last russet leaves of Massachusetts autumn, the copious moonlit drifts of Minnesota snow, the azalea-pink spring mornings of Charleston. Nothing smells, unless the boss is permissive about cigarette butts; if the clock were broken, the overflowing ash-trays and abundant Styrofoam coffee cups would not offer a reliable clue to the time. The clock, the calendar and the map have no in-trinsic meaning here; they only mark the deadlines for the work, the source of the input, the destination of the product. It is super-cool in the room. The floor and ceiling are façade, white squares that float within the structure of the building. The massive steel boxes, French blue with accents of Oriental red, form a Mondrianlike arrangement of squares and rectangles not unpleasing to the eye, although the calculated pleasantness might itself prove wearying. The people here tend to be young.

This place, so utterly free of context, is the computer room. Whether it is used to help sell furniture or track down taxpayers, the machine and its surroundings look the same (the colors vary accord-ing to the manufacturer). Generally, the room is closed to outsiders for reasons of efficiency and security which are quite understand-able but do not build rapport between computer people and civil-ians, and which only deepen the mystery of the machine. While computer rooms don't have windows overlooking the landscape, some sport a large glass wall which gives on the office corridor and serves as a vitrine to display the ultramodern curios within, allowing top management to walk visitors by with a wave of the hand toward the evidence that the company is properly with it. And so many laymen who work in and visit offices—and others who go to the movies and see some spotless actor pressing the buttons of the con-sole and carefully studying the screen—are familiar with what computer rooms look like, and for this reason may feel even more set apart from them.

Certainly the room makes a good symbol of computer people's isolation from the rest of the world; whether it helps to cause it is not clear. Most of the workers here are computer operators, technicians at a low level in the company hierarchy. For them advancement is impossible without more schooling; they are the real button-pressers. While programmers working on special projects may spend much time in the computer room, they generally have offices nearby which look like any other offices, and the higher up they move in the organization the less their jobs require actual contact with the machine. Today's computers are programmed from a terminal which could be down the hall or across the country. But this is the womb that nurtured them, to which they often return (for reasons that are complex and not completely explicable); and they have a special family feeling for the people who work here.

Anyone smart enough to drive a car can learn what is necessary to start feeling comfortable about computers. Just like human beings, the machines perform five functions in solving a problem: input, storage, control, calculation and output. First you look up the pertinent facts (that's *input*); then you *store* them in your memory; then you decide on the sequence of steps you will use to solve the problem (that's *control*); then you solve it *(calculation)*; and finally you record the answer *(output)*.

Each of the boxes in the computer room is designed to perform one or several of these functions; they are all connected to each other by cable beneath the false floor. The large rectangular boxes are the computer's mainframe or central processing unit: they handle the control and calculation and also contain some storage, or memory. There is a low square box which has a screen and keyboard and usually a chair in front of it; this is the console, where the operator sits, presses the keys or buttons which work the machine, and receives progress reports on the screen.

All of the other boxes in the room are called peripheral equipment, or just peripherals: they perform input, output and some storage. The programs which tell the computer what to do and the data it uses to solve problems are recorded on punched cards, magnetic tape and magnetic discs; some of the boxes in the room are input devices which scan this material and feed it to the central processor.

Outside the computer room are other input-output devices called *terminals* which send and receive computer data over telephone lines, often via a combination of keyboard and screen. Several of the peripheral boxes are auxiliary storage devices; they are the computer's equivalent of bookshelves or filing cabinets, holding amounts of data beyond the main memory's capacity to retain. The most familiar of these is the tape drive, the rectangular box with the glass window at the top that reveals two spinning reels of magnetic tape; the tape drive is often used as a graphic symbol of the computer itself, and in almost any filmed scene of a computer room there are plenty of tape drives in evidence. The one that looks like a jukebox is the disc drive. The best-known output device is the high-speed printer, which accounts for the clacking noise you hear in the computer room.

If you opened a computer mainframe you would first notice a beautiful thick network of multicolored wires connecting the machine's circuitry, giving precise access to each of the hundreds of thousands of switches inside. A computer is just a collection of switches. Imagine a roomful of light bulbs, in which the pattern made by the bulbs that are on and those that are off is meant to convey a message; the switches move on and off very rapidly, altering the pattern to change the message. This is a code. Programming is the breaking down of any solution into a series of minute steps which can be represented—or coded—as reading, adding or subtracting. A program tells the computer what switches to turn on or off; programmers are said to write code; the verb for translating information into the form the machine requires is *encoding*. (Today, when much of the data the computer receives is confidential, there is another level of coding meant to disguise the data. This is done inside the machine or terminal, and is called *encryption;* any programmer can read code, but only the computers of the sender and the recipient, at least in theory, can read encrypted data.)

The computer reads the code by detecting the presence or absence of an electronic pulse which opens or closes a particular series of switches; it does this, for example, by sensing whether a tiny spot on a reel of tape is magnetized, or whether there is a hole in a punched card through which current can flow.

The code, then, takes its form from the properties of the machine: on-off, yes-no, right-wrong (there are no maybes in computing). It is called *binary code* (what today's schoolchildren learn as the base-2 system). In the decimal system, when you move a number one place to the left it is worth ten times as much; in the binary system, it is worth twice as much. This allows you to represent all numbers by combinations of ones (on) and zeros (off), as follows:

Decimal	Binary
0	0
1	1
2	10
3	11
4	100
5	101
6	110
7	111
8	1000

But binary notation is tedious and time-consuming for the programmer, and one of the first tasks for programming researchers back in the fifties, when computers came into general use, was to devise higher-level languages in which the programmer could write instructions for the computer. The languages—FORTRAN for scientific use and COBOL for business computing are the most popular—consist of English words for commonly used instructions ("move" and "go to," for example). A program called an *assembler* or *compiler* translates these instructions into the binary code that the computer understands.

Think of the computer's memory as a series of mailboxes, with each box holding an instruction or an item of data. The instruction "add" might be stored in one mailbox; the programmer tells the computer to add (mailbox 1) the number stored in mailbox 12 to the number stored in mailbox 13 and to store the sum in mailbox 14.

All the central processing unit is really able to do is read, add and subtract; multiplication is repeated addition, and division is repeated subtraction. The next simple operations that arise from reading, adding and subtracting are comparing and branching: if the number in mailbox 12 is greater than the number in mailbox 13, follow the instruction in mailbox 2; if it is less, then follow the instruction in mailbox 3.

If all this has led you to the conclusion that computers can't do very much, you are both right and wrong. It is surprising how many mental processes can be represented as reading, adding and subtracting. For example, in a program developed at MIT the computer reads children's stories and then answers questions about them. It contains the sentences "Jack was in the house. Some time later he was in the kitchen." The procedure outlined by the programmer for answering the question "Is Jack in the house?" goes this way:

> To establish that PERSON is not at location LOC
> Find out where PERSON is, call it X,
> If X = LOC, then theorem is false so return "No."
> If X is part of LOC then return "No."
> If LOC is part of X, then try to find a different x.
> Else return "Yes."

The ability of the computer to solve a particular problem depends on whether the programmer can break down the problem in this manner without distorting the solution, and also on whether the coding of the problem requires more steps than the computer's memory can store. The second factor suggests that as technological improvements allow computers to house more mailboxes, their versatility increases; the first factor indicates that the computer's performance depends on programming skill.

The greatest limitation of the computer is that it is wholly literal-minded. If the president of a company asks a human personnel director to find him a French-speaking engineer with ten years' experience, the personnel director may remember that the boss has an irrational dislike of fat men and will act accordingly. But if the boss planned to search for his engineer in the company ranks by pressing the buttons on a computer terminal he must, theoretically, have told the programmer to record employees' heights and weights and must have submitted the standards for fatness, procedures which few company presidents are likely to follow. Thus the computer would send in John Falstaff, and the boss would conclude that computers are no good at finding the man for the job. For practical purposes, he would be right: some decisions are made for emotional reasons that people can't (or won't) identify. Technically, however, he would be wrong.

A failure in the workings of the machine can be observed by the operator at the console; that kind of mechanical miss is not the cause of errors in billing or inaccuracy in predicting the course of the economy. The latter occurs because someone has given the literal-minded computer incorrect or inadequate data or has failed to devise an effective way of breaking down the problem so that the machine can solve it. The former failure—a three-million-dollar residential electric bill or a deluge of dunning letters which continues despite the customer's notification that the bill was paid two months ago—occurs because someone was stupid, lazy or cheap: a programmer made an error in instructing the machine, a keypuncher entered the wrong data or the company president didn't want to spend money on refinements that would make the billing system responsive to customers' needs. To attribute such failures to "computer error" is about equivalent to blaming surgical malpractice on "scalpel error."

The boxes in the computer room are known as *hardware,* and technological improvements in hardware are often described in terms of generations. The key factor in distinguishing each generation of computers is the type of circuitry it uses—vacuum tubes for the first generation, transistors for the second, integrated circuits for the third. Each generation of circuitry has made computers faster, more compact and less expensive, allowing the user (among other advantages) more mailboxes per dollar and thus increasing the number and variety of jobs the computer can do. The newest development in circuitry, the microprocessor, has made it practical to manufacture computers for home use.

Without the programs that tell it what to do, a computer is obviously a useless pile of metal. The programs are known as *software;* the two basic types are systems software and applications software. The systems software (or operating system) is a set of general instructions which tell the machine how to go about accepting input, storing it in various mailboxes and processing it; as computers have acquired more mailboxes and become capable of executing several programs at a time and accepting input from many remote terminals, the job of scheduling all this work, which is what systems software does, has become increasingly complex and has itself required more mailboxes. The assemblers and compilers mentioned above can also be classed as *systems software.*

The ones and zeros of binary code are known as *bits.* Bits are assembled into groups of six or eight called *characters* or *bytes,* each of which represents a number or letter, and into larger groups called *words*. The number of bits in a byte or a word is peculiar to the architecture of the machine, and this is one of the factors that make it impossible to run the same program on two different computer models without a little or a lot of rewriting.

Systems software is usually furnished by the manufacturer; its price is often included in the price of the machine. *Applications software* is the set of instructions telling the computer how to process a payroll (or, more specifically, company X's payroll), predict the weather or book airplane reservations. Much of this is prepared by the customer (computer customers, like heroin customers, are known as *users*).

Whether it is the systems or the applications variety, programming is a brutal discipline. There are innumerable opportunities for error: the omission of a parenthesis from one instruction in a string of thousands can lead to chaos. The machine says "right" or "wrong"; it never says "nice try." Often it is difficult for the programmer to determine just where he went wrong; debugging is a long, frustrating procedure. A good programmer needs a strong ego and must be the sort who trusts nothing to fate. "A compulsive skeptic" is the way one man who heads a software company describes the programmer, and he goes on to note that while a civilian summoning an elevator in an office building will simply press the button and wait, the programmer will press the button again and again until the elevator arrives.

The assumption that computers are arcane and temperamental engines best left to a fraternity of experts—a misconception held not only by laymen but by many of the experts themselves—is responsible for much of our past disappointment with computer technology. There is a useful lesson in the true story of two executives we shall call Ira and Bob. Ira is the Harvard-educated son of a well-known figure in a branch of the fashion industry. A man in his late forties, he is the chief operating officer of the family business, which he expanded from a mom-and-pop store to a multimillion-dollar corporation with sales all over the world. Ira is smart, competent and well respected. He is a man without airs and generally candid.

One day in 1969, a reporter investigating the computer business called Ira to inquire about his company's experiences with data processing. "Don't ask," said Ira. "That computer system has been the worst trial of my business career. Everything in the company has always run smoothly—the machinery in the plant, everything. But the computer is—the road to Calvary. I've had three data processing managers and three controllers on it, each one worse than the last."

"Can I talk to the dp man you have now?" asked the reporter.

"Sure," said Ira. "As long as *I* don't have to talk about it."

Before hanging up, the reporter asked Ira if he'd ever tried one of the computer courses for businessmen. He answered, "I've sent most of my key executives to computer school. Since there are people who are interested, it saves me the trouble and it's one of the things that ought to be delegated."

So the reporter called Bob, Ira's data processing manager, at the plant, which sat in a potato field at the outer reaches of Long Island. Bob had been prepared for her call and suggested they have lunch in New York at the currently fashionable French restaurant across the street from corporate headquarters. "I only get into New York a couple times a year, so I don't know much about gourmet dining," said Bob. "But Ira tells me it's a nice place."

And so they met. Bob was a short, thickset man in a limp suit, scuffy shoes and short socks. When the waiter approached with a menu Bob waved him aside: "If you have shrimp cocktail and veal parmigiana I don't need to see that," he said.

Over drinks, they talked computer hardware; then, after a couple of whisky sours, Bob felt loose enough to recount what turned out to be a classic horror story featuring a series of consultants, the arrival of IBM, the dismissal of IBM, the arrival of an independent service bureau, the dismissal of the independent service bureau, the return of IBM, and the procession of managers and controllers already described by Ira. At the end of the story Bob leaned over his canteloupe and said, "If you want to know who's really driving me crazy, it's Ira."

Although the company had a computer-operated order-processing system for ordinary orders and another for priority orders, every day Ira would go out to lunch with Andrew Goodman of Bergdorf's or Gerry Stutz of Bendel's, and somewhere between the café filtre and the handshake or cheek-peck, Ira would promise to give the store's order priority treatment. Then he'd go back to the office and hassle the controller, who would hassle Bob. "Ira is still running this business like a boutique," Bob said. "Everything is handled personally. He can't delegate."

The truth was that neither Bob nor Ira understood that computers are meant to serve people, not the other way around. Bob thought of himself as a computer man, not a fashion executive, and had not learned that the fashion business—perhaps more than any other—runs on personal rapport, on promises sealed with pecks on the cheek. The company was successful because Ira, before the computer arrived, had been able to introduce Harvard-style efficiency without losing the personal flavor of the fashion industry. But Ira had not thought to educate Bob on the nuances of the business he was entering; moreover, Ira had bought himself a complex and expensive tool and neglected to learn how it could be used to serve the unique requirements of his organization.

After a while it was easy to pick out the Iras-who-couldn't-be-bothered and the tunnel-vision Bobs. They included Iras sitting in the Pentagon or practicing medicine in the ghetto and a bearded academic Bob who spoke Oxbridge, quoted Piaget and had no patience for explaining computers to any layman over the age of twelve.

In 1958, just before the second generation of computers was introduced, American users spent less than $1 billion on data processing; in 1980 they spent more than $55 billion. Of that total about a third went to the machines themselves, the hardware. About 6½ percent went to software and services—programs and computer power purchased from outside suppliers. A substantial $26¼ billion—13 percent more than the hardware costs—was paid out in salaries to the people who fed and tended the machines. Some 3 percent went to the telephone lines and equipment that enable computers a continent apart to talk to each other, and 4½ percent went to punched cards, magnetic tape and other supplies.

Computer stocks and industry entrepreneurs have been the darlings and the pariahs of the financial community. Whatever the quarterly vagaries of IBM stock, the investor who ventured $20,600 for a hundred shares in 1951, two years before the company delivered its first electronic computer, could have seen the value of his holdings grow to over $1 million by March 1980; he would have received $437,500 in dividends. On the other hand, the stocks of young computer companies that were magic in the late sixties were poison in the early seventies. The stock figures reflected Wall Street's reaction to the balance of power in the computer business.

In 1980, IBM machines accounted for 62½ percent of the dollar value of new American-made general-purpose computers; IBM equipment represented more than 69 percent of the dollar value of American-made general-purpose computers already installed around the world. The rest of this market was divided principally among Honeywell Information Systems, Sperry Univac, Burroughs Corporation, National Cash Register and Control Data Corporation. These companies, along with General Electric and RCA, who closed down their computer operations in the early seventies, were known in the industry as the Seven Dwarfs. Xerox Corporation, which both bought into and opted out of the industry during the seventies, and Digital Equipment Corporation, the leading manufacturer of minicomputers, have sometimes been classed with the dwarfs. At the end of 1976, before IBM began a costly expansion of its factories and increased its operating expenses in other ways, it held a reserve of cash and marketable securities surpassing $6 billion, making it in effect one of the largest banks in the United States. While none of the dwarfs was a piddling concern—most brought in more than $1 billion in data processing revenues in 1976—IBM, using its reserves, could have bought out Honeywell, Sperry Rand, Burroughs, NCR and Control Data at book value and still have had $400 million in loose change lying around in the cash drawer.

IBM's supremacy is explained through a combination of factors, including historical circumstance, financial acumen, marketing know-how, managerial genius, esprit de corps and brute force. While the company's equipment is of good quality, its dominance is almost never credited to consistently better products or technological leadership (indeed, IBM was not the first large company to enter the computer business; that distinction belongs to Remington Rand, Sperry's ancestor, which soon lost its early lead). Still, decisions made by IBM management have steered the course of the industry. The dwarfs—as well as the several thousand companies who supply peripheral equipment, minicomputers, software and other computer-based services—are justifiably paranoid about "Big Brother." (Hardly anybody calls IBM "Snow White." It doesn't seem to fit, and computer people are uninhibited about mixing metaphors.)

Certain economic factors peculiar to the computer industry help to explain the solidity of IBM's position. The first one is: *until recently, most computers were not bought outright; they were rented from the manufacturer.* The corollary to that is: *when you start out in a rental business, the better you do, the worse you do.* A dramatic illustration of this was offered by Eugene Collins, a securities analyst, in his 1974 testimony before the Senate Subcommittee on Antitrust and Monopoly. Here is a paraphrase of Collins's example.

Consider a hypothetical company, the Smith Company, which sells its computers outright. In its first year of operation, Smith ships $100 million worth of equipment and records this money as revenue. The company's manufacturing costs are $35 million; when these are subtracted, there is a gross profit of $65 million. From this figure it deducts its operating expenses: $25 million for marketing, $10 million for research and development, and another $10 million for general and administrative costs, totaling $45 million and leaving a net profit before taxes of $20 million.

Now compare Smith with an imagined Jones Company, whose engineers and programmers are equally inventive, whose salesmen are just as compelling and whose management is every bit as tough-minded, efficient and courageous. The proof is that Jones, like Smith, has also been able to place $100 million worth of equipment in customers' computer rooms. Unlike Smith, however, Jones rents its machines. Since rented computers take four years to earn out the full purchase price, the Jones machines generate only $25 million worth of revenue in their first twelve months of installation. Moreover, Jones doesn't place all its computers on January 1. If we assume its installations are evenly distributed throughout the year, the machine sold on December 1 will yield only one month's rent by the end of the year, and Jones will have taken in just $12½ million.

In a rental business, manufacturing costs are recorded as capital assets and depreciated over the life of the equipment, which means subtracting $4.4 million from the $12.5 million revenues in the first year, leaving a gross profit of $8.1 million. When the operating expenses are then subtracted—the cost of the inventive engineers and programmers, the compelling salesmen and the tough-minded, efficient and courageous management, which comes to the same $45 million that the Smith Company spent—unlike Smith, the Jones Company is left at the end of the first year with a $36 million loss.

How might the Jones Company get through the next year? It could, perhaps, decide to design, manufacture and rent no more new computers, fire most of its employees and sit waiting for the $25 million from the computers it rented last year to come in. While this strategy would allow Jones to show a profit in the second year, it is commonly known as liquidation. The alternative would be to try to raise capital to cover its expenses. It could borrow money, provided it could find a bank willing to lend to a company with an operating loss and a negative cash flow. Or it could sell stock or try to attract venture capital from private investors willing to risk their money on a company which is shipping more computers every year but is consequently spending more money on salesmen, engineers and executives.

The Jones Company's losses increase till they reach a peak—in Collins's simulation the peak occurs after five years—and then they begin to decline until the company breaks even, after about ten years, when it ships enough computers to realize economies of scale in manufacturing and product development. By then the rented machines contribute enough gross profit to cover the fixed costs. Collins's estimate of ten years to break even is, however, a deliberate oversimplification. It assumes that management makes no big mistakes, that there are no recessions to slow the company's shipments, that it can raise the necessary capital every year, and that a larger company doesn't use its greater resources to render the Jones computers obsolete before they have recovered their costs. Remington Rand entered the computer business in 1950; it was 1966 by the time its descendant, Sperry Rand, broke even on computer operations. NCR's computer business did not show a profit until 1973.

For a solidly entrenched company, however, leasing is more profitable than outright sale, provided the machines stay out on lease long after they have paid for themselves. The rule then is: *in a rental business, introduce new products only when you are forced to;* otherwise you make your own equipment obsolete prematurely. In 1979, IBM spent one billion three hundred sixty million dollars on research and development—notably more than Sperry, Honeywell, Burroughs, Control Data, NCR and Digital Equipment *together* invested in r & d. In view of this expenditure, one would expect IBM to be technologically light-years ahead of its major competitors; it isn't. The investment is essentially a wager on all the promising technological innovations at every stage from basic research through product development. If a competitor—perhaps a young company with no substantial rental base—brings out an innovative product that might woo customers away from IBM, there is a strong chance that somewhere in the laboratories of the industry giant are engineers working on a similar product whose development can be accelerated to meet competition. (Other circumstances may also force IBM to introduce new products: when the market for a specific computer is so saturated that demand for it drops, it is time to bring out a new line. And sometimes the necessary revenue growth can be provided by a new *kind* of machine that reaches an untapped market, such as an automated supermarket checkout terminal.)

Renting offers another advantage to the established manufacturer: this is called *account control*. When a computer is bought outright, the salesman and the customer shake hands and say goodbye until the customer needs a new machine. If the computer is rented, however, the customer has a continuing relationship with the supplier, and the liaison is the salesman, who returns regularly to see that everything is going right and incidentally to suggest new applications for the equipment. The more applications, the more equipment the customer will need—more memory, additional peripherals and ultimately a larger mainframe. The salesman gets to know the customer's data processing manager, is quick to pick up signs of discontent and has the inside track on any new plans the customer may have. The salesman is helped in servicing the customer by the systems engineer, a programming expert who works for the manufacturer's marketing division and helps design applications for the customer. Before 1969, IBM's systems engineering services were "bundled" or included in the price of the machine, allowing the company to offer additional help to customers whose own programming staffs were small or unsophisticated or who, as industry cynics and antitrust opponents observed, might be leaning toward competitive equipment.

Renting, not at all incidentally, offers obvious benefits to the customer. An annual expenditure of $250,000 for four years is usually easier to justify than an initial outlay of $1 million. An additional advantage to the user is that *in renting, the risks of technological obsolescence are borne by the manufacturer*. If the customer sees a shinier toy, if his needs change or if he simply doesn't like the product or service he gets from IBM or Univac, he can simply return the machine. Indeed, the riskiness of this arrangement would be insupportable for manufacturers were it not for one factor: each manufacturer's machine has a different way of manipulating the ones and zeros, and *software written for an IBM computer is largely incompatible with a Univac machine.* The customer's outlay for software is sizable, and it is expensive and time-consuming to have one's programs rewritten. Thus the decision to replace the supplier is not made lightly.

The story of the computer is the newest chapter in the two-hundred-year-old tussle between men and machines. Engineers building a medium-sized computer have a hundred thousand functioning (or malfunctioning) elements to design. The software system that drives the computer contains perhaps a million instructions (any of which could be erroneous). The people who decide how to design, manufacture and market this incredibly complex piece of machinery must be courageous and resilient; they do battle with a formidable opponent.

The producers and the users form the computer community. To understand the machine, then, we must learn about that community and its origins.

2

How It Began

THE SEARCH for mechanical aids to computation is an ancient one: the first digital computer was the abacus, devised in various forms by the Egyptians, Greeks, Romans and Chinese. (A *digital* computer is a device which works by counting, in contrast with an *analog* computer, which operates by measuring the relationship between different lengths or sizes that represent, and are thus *analogous* to, different numbers; the best-known example of an analog computer is the slide rule.) In the seventeenth century Leibniz as well as Pascal invented a calculating machine, and Leibniz also conceived the notion of a calculator that would use binary code. However, historians, mathematicians, engineers, programmers and computer executives trace their heritage to Charles Babbage, an Englishman who in the early nineteenth century devised most of the principles on which modern computers are based. Unfortunately, like his predecessors, he did so in an age in which neither the need nor the technology was sufficiently developed to make the most of his ideas.

While in his early twenties Babbage envisioned the possibility of automating the calculation of mathematical tables. By 1822 he had devised the Difference Engine, a small machine for computing polynomials (algebraic expressions with many terms); he then applied, successfully, to the Chancellor of the Exchequer for funds to build a bigger version of the engine, and thus received one of the first recorded government research grants.

Babbage spent ten frustrating years on the second Difference Engine but was never able to complete it, and in 1833 he conceived a better idea. While the Difference Engine had been what would now be called a special-purpose computer, a machine built to do only one job, Babbage then decided to construct a general-purpose machine which could solve virtually any mathematical problem. All of his machines were, of course, mechanical—elaborate combinations of gears, wheels, barrels and levers, to be operated by steam, the contemporary power source. But there was no way such engines could move fast enough to change the nature of computation, and engineering methods were inadequate to build the gears and wheels with the precision Babbage needed. It is the sophisticated organization of Babbage's new machine—the Analytical Engine, it was called—to which modern computer designers now pay homage.

The Analytical Engine was inspired by the Jacquard loom, which had revolutionized weaving in the early part of the century. The loom was actually programmed by punched cards: that is, the warp threads were pulled down through holes in the cards which were arranged to produce a predetermined pattern. In Babbage's machine the punched cards controlled a set of levers which moved several barrels, each of which held an arrangement of studs representing a particular number or command; the studs were organized in eighty vertical columns, just like the IBM punched-card apparatus we all know, devised sixty years later.

Like the modern computer, the Babbage machine had a punched-card input and output, a storage, a control mechanism and an arithmetic unit. It had separate cards for programs and data; among its features was feedback operation through which the machine could alter its behavior according to the results of earlier calculations, a procedure incorporated in computers today. One scholar notes that "the earliest program-controlled computers . . . were conceptually hardly a match for Babbage's engine."

The machine, alas, was never built: the Chancellor of the Exchequer, presumably reluctant to throw bad money after good, offered no further research contracts, and Babbage, who spent the rest of his life tinkering with parts of the engine and thinking up ill-fated schemes to raise the funds to build it, died an embittered man. While a few other men tried to build automata or calculating machines following Babbage's model, his work was largely forgotten until modern inventors, embroiled in computer projects of their own, stumbled on their extraordinary antecedent.

One more early inventor deserves mention. Herman Hollerith was nineteen in 1879 when he got a job as an assistant in the U.S.

Census Office, which was then planning the 1880 tabulation of vital statistics. He was encouraged by his superior to look into developing a mechanized tabulating system for future efforts. The tabulating system he invented, which was ready before the 1890 census, used holes in punched cards to indicate sex, race, age and so forth; the cards were passed under contact brushes which completed an electrical circuit whenever a hole was present, and the system included a card-punching machine and a sorter which dropped the cards into bins according to the holes sensed by the electric current.

The equipment proved enormously successful, allowing the census figures to be released more quickly than ever before, and Hollerith began to improve it for commercial use in accounting as well as tabulating. In 1896 he left the Census Office to found the Tabulating Machine Company, which he subsequently sold to the primitive conglomerate that later became IBM. Descendants of the Hollerith machines continued to form the basis of IBM's business until the computer era as we know it.

In the United States three men have claimed credit for inventing the electronic digital computer. John Vincent Atanasoff, born in 1903, was the son of a Bulgarian immigrant who had worked his way through Peddie and Colgate and become an electrical engineer; Atanasoff's mother, a schoolteacher, had a fondness for mathematics which she passed on to her precocious son (when the old lady was well into her nineties she could still do algebra in her head). At ten, Atanasoff learned to use his father's slide rule and began to teach himself calculus, radio theory and physics. "I was happy to play baseball for one hour and then come back and study all this for three hours," he remembers. "When I got intensity of purpose I just kept it up."

After getting a Ph.D. in theoretical physics at the University of Wisconsin, Atanasoff began teaching at Iowa State in the early thirties. There he encountered the same difficulties that plagued many mathematicians and physicists of the period: most of the problems they were studying required the solution of complex equations with many variables. None of the available aids was adequate in precision or speed, and each of Atanasoff's graduate students had computation problems. By 1935 he decided something had to be done. During his teenage years as an omnivorous student he had read encyclopedia articles on computing machines and knew something about Babbage and Pascal; he had made a hobby of radio electronics since his youth.

The designer of an electronic computing machine had to make a multitude of choices in determining the circuitry and its arrangement and the method of calculation the machine would use. "I commenced to go into torture," Atanasoff says. "For the next two years my life was hard. I thought and thought about this. Every evening I would go off to my office in the physics building. One night in the winter of 1937 my whole body was in torment from trying to solve the problems of the machine. I got in my car and drove at high speeds for a long while so I could control my emotions. It was my habit to do this for a few miles: I could always gain control of myself by concentrating on driving. But that night I was excessively tormented, and I kept on going until I had crossed the Mississippi River into Illinois and was 189 miles from where I started. I knew I had to quit; I saw a light, which turned out to be a roadhouse, and I went in. It was probably below zero outside, and I remember hanging up my heavy coat; I started to drink and commenced to warm up and realized I had control of myself." In the tavern, he testified in court nearly forty years later, "things seemed to be good and cool and quiet," and there he resolved the problems which had been tormenting him.

He had toyed with the idea of building a machine that would operate on the binary system, which would mean you had only ones and zeros to represent, thus conforming perfectly to the "on" and "off" of an electrical circuit. A punched card could carry more information if digits were represented only by the presence or absence of a hole. In all, a binary machine would be far simpler and cheaper than one using the ten digits of the decimal system, but Atanasoff had been afraid users would have trouble mastering the two-number code. That night in the tavern he decided the benefits of binary outweighed the disadvantages.

Machines then in use accomplished addition by a process called *ratcheting*, in which the command to add 9 and 4 would cause a wheel to rotate through ten positions, turn another wheel through one position, and then move through three more. Human beings don't add by ratcheting, and in the tavern Atanasoff thought of a way to design and connect the circuits so as to avoid this process and at the same time handle large numbers by what is called *serial calculation*.

Finally, he faced the problem of choosing a cheap and simple memory device. There were five alternatives (one that Atanasoff discarded because it was too expensive was similar to the magnetic core developed some years later at MIT, which became the basis for modern computer memories). The circuit he preferred could hold an electrical charge for only a short time, but that same night he conceived of a procedure through which the machine would detect the charge and regenerate it before it leaked away.

The four ideas that crystallized that night—binary code, nonratcheting logic, serial calculation and regenerative memory—made it possible for Atanasoff to formulate the first electronic digital computer. He spent about a year working out the details, and at last he applied to the Iowa State Research Council for money to construct his invention. An initial grant of $650 bought him the part-time assistance of Clifford Berry, a graduate student in engineering (Atanasoff gives Berry equal billing as co-developer of the Atanasoff-Berry Computer, known as the ABC), and the materials to build an operating "breadboard" model. When this was completed in the fall of 1939, the inventors received two more grants from the college, bringing the total up to $1,460. In late 1940 they received another $5,000 from a private foundation.

In December 1940 the second claimant to electronic digital computer fame met Atanasoff at a meeting of the American Association for the Advancement of Science. The late John W. Mauchly, born in 1907, had dismantled an adding machine during his boyhood in Chevy Chase, Maryland, and was never far from a calculator after that. Mauchly's father had been a physicist at the Carnegie Institute in Washington, and young Mauchly worked as a research assistant for fifty cents an hour while earning his physics degree at Johns Hopkins. Both his studies and his job required extensive measuring and calculating, and he experimented with methods for doing the calculations faster than the desk machines then available. In 1933, he became head of the physics department at Ursinus College near Philadelphia. There his research in atmospheric electricity required extensive statistical data on weather; to get it, he hired some students (also at fifty cents an hour) and by 1937 had gotten far enough to realize it would take a lifetime to do the calculations he needed on existing equipment. Colleagues were using vacuum tube devices for atomic research, and although this did not involve computing, it seemed obvious to Mauchly that if one had the money, one could find a way to speed up computation electronically. He hadn't the money, so he built a small analog computer and went to the AAAS meeting to deliver a paper describing it.

At this point Mauchly's and Atanasoff's stories begin to conflict. Mauchly said he had also assembled some rudimentary counting circuits at Ursinus, tinkering with vacuum tubes (which were fast but expensive) and gas tubes (which were slow but cheap). Atanasoff asserts that Mauchly never mentioned his work with digital devices, and had no reason to conceal it; their subsequent relationship was completely open. At any rate, the two struck up a conversation during which Atanasoff told Mauchly about the machine he was building and invited his new acquaintance to see it.

In was June 1941 before Mauchly—who, like Atanasoff, was making about $2,000 a year—could hitch a ride to Ames, Iowa. When he arrived he was Atanasoff's house guest for five days, which he spent discussing computing with his host, watching the ABC operate and reading a description of the machine which Atanasoff had prepared for his fund-raising proposal. At the time the ABC could solve up to twenty-nine simultaneous equations with twenty-nine variables, and Berry was still working on the binary card punch and reader which provided input-output and slow memory for the machine. Mauchly said many years afterward, "What I saw was a small piece of electronic gear which if you pushed the buttons caused a binary addition, and a light went to signal carry-over."

Mauchly did not seem to dispute the thoroughness of Atanasoff's description of the machine, nor a 1973 court ruling that this description was adequate to enable "one of ordinary skill in electronics" to make and use an ABC computer. What he did dispute was the value of all this to him: "I feel I got nothing out of the visit to Atanasoff except the royal shaft later," he said. Still, at the time Mauchly found Atanasoff's work interesting enough to describe in a letter to a colleague shortly after his return from Ames.

That summer of 1941, with our entry into the war imminent, the University of Pennsylvania's Moore School of Engineering scheduled, at the government's urging, special courses to train engineers in electronics. Mauchly signed up for one. The laboratory instructor was a young graduate student named Pres Eckert.

J. Presper Eckert, twelve years Mauchly's junior, was the only child of well-to-do parents. At Penn Charter, the toughest private school in Philadelphia, he swiftly polished off his regular courses and zipped through two years of college math. He also made a hobby of electronics; he bought a castoff experimental television set from RCA to tinker with, worked one summer at Farnsworth Electronics, and earned several hundred dollars in his spare time installing sound systems which played church bells in cemeteries. After Penn Charter he enrolled at the Moore School, and when he had exhausted the available math courses, studied business administration at Wharton.

Today Eckert is a trim, urbane man with a sharp tongue, an entrepreneurial mind and an air of impatience. Mauchly—who acted as if he had all the time in the world—was rumpled, soft-spoken and discursive, with somewhat abstracted academic calm. The differences in temperament were always there, and while in later life they kept the engineer and the physicist apart except for the ceremonial duties of fighting patent suits and receiving medals, there was a time when it seemed that all of Eckert's and Mauchly's previous lives had been a preparation for meeting one another, and their very differences seemed felicitously complementary.

Mauchly found Eckert a sympathetic listener. "When I'd done the experiments for the course, Pres and I would sit on a bench and talk about computers," he remembered. "I thought he was the most rational man I had ever met. He convinced me that the things I was dreaming were possible." By the end of September Mauchly had joined the Moore School faculty and was sufficiently excited about computers to write Atanasoff:

> A number of different ideas have come to me recently anent computing circuits—some of which are more or less hybrids, combining your methods with other things, and some of which are nothing like your machine. The question in my mind is this: Is there any objection, from your point of view, to my building some sort of computer which incorporates some of the features of your machine? For the time being, of course, I shall be lucky to find time and material to do more than merely make exploratory tests of some of my different ideas, with the hope of getting something very speedy, not too costly, etc.
>
> Ultimately a second question might come up, of course, and that is, in the event that your present design were to hold the field against all challengers, and I have got the Moore School interested in having

something of the sort, would the way be open for us to build an "Atanasoff Calculator"... here?

Atanasoff answered that while he didn't mind having told Mauchly about the ABC, he wanted to keep the machine under wraps until a patent application could be filed. His agreement with Iowa State called for the college to get the patent and divide the royalties equally with Atanasoff.

But Iowa State never did file a patent application for the ABC. In 1942, when Atanasoff left Ames to join the Naval Ordnance Laboratory and Berry went out to Pasadena to work for Consolidated Engineering, the electronic portion of the machine was working but the card reader had not been perfected. For some years afterward Atanasoff tried to persuade the college to act on his patent application; ultimately he gave up. His defeat was not unlike Babbage's; in Atanasoff's case, the timing was a little bit off. And he was at the wrong college.

Mauchly was luckier. For a man looking to build an electronic computer, there was no better place to be during the war than the Moore School of Engineering. The school was engaged in a joint project with the U.S. Army Ordnance Department's Aberdeen Proving Ground, which specialized in ballistics research, to compute all the Army and Air Corps artillery firing tables. The field offered an interesting challenge to mathematicians and physicists, who sought the best formula for calculating the effects of gravity, air movement, and the size and material of the weapon and the shell on the path of a projectile; the goal was a more precise firing table, which would direct the gunner's aim. The amount of math required to compute a firing table was monumental, and the Army was desperate: it took thirty days to complete one table on the most advanced equipment available—an analog machine invented by Vannevar Bush—and this was fifty times faster than a human with a desk calculator. The Moore School did the rough calculations on the Bush machine and then gave them to a hundred frenzied WACs to smooth out.

In the laboratory, Mauchly worked at combining Atanasoff's ideas with his own and then set down his conclusions in a memo circulated around the Moore School, while Eckert was boning up on counting circuits. It was not surprising that Mauchly's ideas found a hospitable reception from Lieutenant Herman Goldstine, the young mathematician who was serving as a liaison officer between Aberdeen and the university. Goldstine got the Ordnance Department interested in funding the development of an electronic digital computer, and on April 9, 1943, Eckert's twenty-fourth birthday, the two men were told to proceed with the project. Shortly afterward, the proposed machine was christened ENIAC, the Electronic Numerical Integrator and Computer.

In comparing ENIAC with the ABC it is interesting to note the comparative cost of producing the two machines. Atanasoff, as we remember, received just under $6,500 for his efforts. According to Goldstine's account of the ENIAC project, it was first estimated that the computer would cost $150,000 to develop; by the time it was completed, it had run up a bill of $486,804.22. Discrepancies on this scale have marked the development of large computers ever since.

The idea of using vacuum tubes for computing was not in itself completely novel; military researchers had considered it several years earlier but had concluded that electronic equipment was not yet reliable enough. Here is Goldstine's explanation of the risks involved in building ENIAC:

> . . . we should realize that the proposed machine turned out to contain over 17,000 tubes of 16 different types operating at a fundamental clock rate of 100,000 pulses per second . . . once every 10 microsecond an error would occur if a single one of the 17,000 tubes operated incorrectly; this means that in a single second there were 1.7 billion . . . chances of a failure occurring. . . . Man had never made an instrument capable of operating with this degree of fidelity or reliability, and this is why the undertaking was so risky a one and the accomplishment so great.

Thirty years after the ENIAC was completed, Eckert described the design philosophy that had guided the project: "If you have a radical idea . . . for God's sake don't be a radical in how you carry it out as well. Be as conservative as you can. Become a right-wing conservative in carrying out a left-wing idea."

Every aspect of the design and testing of the ENIAC circuitry was notably cautious and thorough. In particular, Eckert decided to operate the circuits at unusually low voltages, opting for longer life instead of maximum power. Moreover, to make the computer as independent as possible of the varying quality of its components, he decided to represent numbers by the simple presence or absence, rather than the magnitude, of an electrical pulse. It was the same on-off principle that Atanasoff had used several years earlier, but while Atanasoff had carried the idea to its logical conclusion by representing numbers in binary code, Mauchly (who held sway over the methods of computation) thought binary a bad idea for the user, and so ENIAC was a decimal machine; Mauchly also rejected Atanasoff's technique of serial calculation. Partly for these reasons ENIAC was more ungainly than it needed to be.

The next set of advances in computing technology—and of complications in the story of who invented what—followed the arrival on the ENIAC scene of John von Neumann, the brilliant and colorful Hungarian mathematician. Von Neumann, then based at Princeton's Institute for Advanced Study, was also consulting for Aberdeen, Los Alamos and the Naval Ordnance Laboratory. Herman Goldstine ran into von Neumann on the railroad platform at Aberdeen one summer day in 1944 and told him about the ENIAC project; in Goldstine's account, "the whole atmosphere of our conversation changed from one of relaxed good humor to one more like the oral examination for the doctor's degree in mathematics."

Von Neumann began to consult with the Moore School group, and as ENIAC moved into the construction stage its designers started discussing a second machine with which they might solve at leisure some of the unsettled problems presented by the first. ENIAC, which occupied 15,000 square feet, had little storage capacity and was programmed by plugging and replugging some 6,000 switches. The plugboards covered three walls, and, as Mauchly remembered, every time a visitor came in for a demonstration someone would make a mistake in resetting the switches and garble the program. Obviously the plugboards had to go, and Eckert, Mauchly, von Neumann and others talked of ways to store the programs internally.

The new machine was to be called the EDVAC—Electronic Discrete Variable Calculator—and in June 1945 von Neumann wrote a 101-page paper headed "First Draft of a Report on EDVAC." The paper, which is considered a landmark in computing theory, laid out the requirements for the design of a computer from the logical rather than the engineering point of view, mapping the organization of the machine as dictated by the jobs it would have to do. Moreover, von Neumann advocated binary code, serial calculation and a method of operation that more closely resembled that of the human nervous system—ideas that had, of course, occurred to Atanasoff in the tavern and had, in primitive fashion, been built into the ABC, a machine of which von Neumann had heard nothing. For more than three decades, despite dramatic changes in technology, all computers have followed the von Neumann model. Only the most recent developments have permitted designers to start thinking in other directions.

Von Neumann, through the oversimplifications of easy history, was given full credit for the stored program and the other ideas in the EDVAC paper, and Eckert and Mauchly felt slighted; mostly they blamed Goldstine, with whom they were on chilly terms ever afterward (von Neumann died in 1957). Yet Goldstine's latest account, written in 1972, seems reasonably fair. He observes:

> . . . all members of the discussion group shared their ideas with each other without restraint and therefore all deserve credit. Eckert and Mauchly unquestionably led on the technological side and von Neumann on the logical. It has been said by some that von Neumann did not give credits in his *First Draft* to others. The reason for this was that the document was intended by von Neumann as a working paper for use in clarifying and coordinating the thinking of the group and was not intended as a publication.

In 1943, when Atanasoff was head of the acoustics section of the Naval Ordnance Laboratory at Silver Spring, Maryland, Mauchly began part-time work as a statistician in that section. According to Mauchly he came at Atanasoff's suggestion, while Atanasoff says Mauchly wanted to work for him. At any rate, in 1945, when the war was over and ENIAC was nearing completion, the Bureau of Ordnance decided to have another computer built at the Naval Ordnance Laboratory. Having heard that Atanasoff had a background in computers, the bureau gave him more than $100,000 to begin the job. But Atanasoff was then working on an acoustic mines project and complained he couldn't do two things at once. He put the computer on the back burner, asking Mauchly and other aides to write job descriptions for employees needed to staff the effort and letting other assistants do some work on memory devices. After a year or so, the project was dropped for lack of progress. "My boss was critical of me for not doing anything on computers, but my hands were full with other things," Atanasoff says.

As for ENIAC, it was first used in a calculation for Los Alamos Laboratories in December 1945, was formally dedicated with considerable hoopla in February 1946, and except for a nine-month period of dismemberment while the machine was in transit between the Moore School and Aberdeen it served the government well until 1955, when it was turned off and sent to its current resting place in the Smithsonian Institution.

The most distinctive feature of the ENIAC had confronted the greatest shortcoming of the ABC, which had instructions for solving one particular type of problem soldered into it. The ENIAC user could change the instructions without resoldering, just by resetting the switches. The EDVAC, the most advanced of all, would run on software, which might be fed to the machine on punched cards, paper tape, magnetic tape or wire, or film.

As early as 1944, Eckert and Mauchly had begun sounding out prospective commercial customers at government agencies. They left the Moore School on March 31, 1946 after quarreling with the university about patent rights, and founded the Electronic Controls Corporation, soon afterward rechristened the Eckert-Mauchly Computer Corporation. The company had two major projects: one was a machine called the BINAC for the Northrop Corporation, and the other was the Univac (Universal Automatic Computer) to be developed for the National Bureau of Standards and delivered to the Bureau of the Census, with contracts for two more Univacs to be sold to corporations.

Slowly Eckert-Mauchly began to expand and moved to quarters in Philadelphia which had, prophetically, a cemetery on one side and a junkyard on the other. The company struggled: prospects came to find out all about computers and then decided to try building their own; the BINAC was delivered in 1948 but didn't meet the customer's needs; at some time during those early McCarthy days it was revealed that Mauchly's secretary had been involved with a man who went to Communist meetings, and the company lost its security clearance and $2 million worth of government contracts; and the Univac was a more expensive and ambitious undertaking than anybody had dreamed. Nearly broke, Eckert-Mauchly sold 40 percent of its stock to American Totalizator, the company that makes racetrack tote boards.

But in Norwalk, Connecticut, headquarters of the Remington Rand Company, an engineer named Arthur Draper had been charged by the company's chairman, James H. Rand, Jr., to keep watch over several interesting technological companies spawned by the war, among them Eckert-Mauchly. Rand was himself an inventor-entrepreneur: in 1915 he had devised the Kardex system and had then bought out his father's ledger company, Remington Typewriter, and a string of office-equipment concerns. Draper embraced his new assignment with gusto: he notified Remington Rand's Philadelphia sales office that whenever Eckert-Mauchly needed typewriter repairs, he would accompany the service man. "I told Eckert," Draper remembers, " 'Look, new companies are my business and sooner or later you're going to be in financial trouble. When the time comes, just call me.' "

A year later, in 1950, the man who'd been running American Totalizator was killed in a plane crash, leaving the owners with a piece of a company about which they knew little and cared less, and Eckert and Mauchly at the end of their rope. At some time during their struggles, they had visited Thomas J. Watson, Sr. "He gave us a sermon for fifteen or twenty minutes," Mauchly recalled, "the gist of which was that there was no such thing as invention, just discovery. He was playing down the value of patents. Then he shook hands and turned us over to someone else who offered us each a lab and a small salary and a chance to work for the greater glory of IBM. So we turned them down."

They had also tried NCR and Addressograph-Multigraph, and now it was Art Draper or nothing. "Eckert and Mauchly came up to Norwalk and spent the whole day chatting about typewriters," recalls Draper. "At four o'clock I said the hell with it and started to close the meeting, and then they brought up their problem."

It is not known how much Rand shelled out in total, but Eckert and Mauchly each got about $40,000 for their equity shares and another $40,000 in royalties under the pending patents. Remington Rand delivered its first computer, Univac I, to the Bureau of the Census on June 14, 1951 (the price was somewhat higher than had originally been announced). Eckert and Mauchly went to work for Remington Rand, and as the industry grew the community it spawned paid them the respect properly due inventors. Outside the community they received more scanty recognition, but their reputations, however small, were secure, and they complained only about not receiving proper credit from von Neumann for the stored program. Hardly anyone had heard of Atanasoff. Then came the lawsuit.

The ENIAC patent application had been filed in 1947, but it was 1964 before the patent was actually awarded. The delay was due to the resolution of patent interferences (proceedings held by the Patent Office to establish which of several claimants is entitled to priority of invention), in particular between Sperry Rand, the product of a 1955 merger between Remington Rand and Sperry Corporation, and Bell Telephone Laboratories.

A few months after the issuance of the ENIAC patent, Sperry Rand, through a subsidiary specially created to collect ENIAC royalties, sent notices of patent infringement to a number of computer and peripherals manufacturers, excluding IBM, with which Sperry had already negotiated a royalty settlement in 1956. The notices offered to license these companies at 1½ percent of the selling price of equipment covered by the ENIAC patent. Since the royalties amounted to considerable sums of money, none of Sperry's offers were accepted, and in May 1967 Sperry decided to start by suing Honeywell for patent infringement. On the same day Honeywell brought suit against Sperry for violating the antitrust laws in enforcing a fraudulently obtained patent. The two cases were consolidated, with Sperry as the defendant.

In 1968 a delegation of lawyers from Honeywell and Control Data (which was also preparing a case against Sperry) visited J. V. Atanasoff. Atanasoff says he had not realized before that the ENIAC was derived from the ABC: "I thought I'd missed something that Eckert and Mauchly had found," he says. Atanasoff and the lawyers went around the country speaking to former associates who remembered the ABC and Mauchly's visit, and an electronics specialist was assigned to help Atanasoff reconstruct sections of the ABC according to the proposal he had written in 1940. (It was Atanasoff's greatest pleasure to sit in court and press the buttons of the reborn ABC and to watch the judge's fascination as the lights lighted and the machine added and subtracted.)

In 1973 the judge invalidated the ENIAC patent. He did so for several reasons, some of which had nothing to do with Atanasoff, but he also ruled significantly on the ENIAC and the ABC.

Eckert and Mauchly had made an exhaustive claim for the

ENIAC, and it was this most of all that got them into trouble. The judge ruled that Sperry was bound by its representation that the invention claimed in the ENIAC patent is "broadly 'the invention of the Automatic Electronic Digital Computer.'" Next, said the judge, "Eckert and Mauchly did not themselves first invent the automatic electronic digital computer, but instead derived that subject matter from one Dr. John Vincent Atanasoff." Even the more detailed claims for the ENIAC, he ruled, were not patentable over the subject matter derived from Atanasoff. Finally, he observed, "The Court has heard the testimony at trial of both Atanasoff and Mauchly, and finds the testimony of Atanasoff with respect to the knowledge and information derived by Mauchly to be credible."

The judge noted that Mauchly "may in good faith have believed that the monstrous machine he helped create had no relationship to the ABC or Atanasoff," and cited an account Mauchly wrote in 1944, which called the ABC "very ingenious, but . . . not by any means what I had in mind." In this and other areas the judge stopped short of finding deliberate fraud and held only that the derelictions were sufficient to render the patent invalid. Thus he managed to rule so that neither corporation would have to pay anything to the other.

Mauchly, not surprisingly, said he had been unfairly treated. He claimed that the full evidence of his work on vacuum tube computing at Ursinus was not introduced in the case. Moreover, when asked whether the claim that he and Eckert invented "the automatic electronic digital computer" wasn't a bit grandiose in view of Atanasoff's work, he replied that the standard procedure in patent applications is to make sweeping claims which will be modified when the Patent Office resolves the interferences with other applications. In the case of the ABC, however, no application was filed—but Mauchly said he didn't know that.

In Mauchly's defense, it should be said that the notion of an electronic digital computer was not unique to Atanasoff: engineers and mathematicians in other parts of the country (and around the world) had considered the idea since the thirties. Atanasoff's achievement was that he was the first to figure out how to do it and make it work, and also that his design incorporated some advanced concepts that did not reappear in the Moore School work until the second machine on which Eckert and Mauchly collaborated with von Neumann. As for ENIAC, its general-purpose nature was an advance over the ABC; the accomplishment of getting a machine with more than 17,000 vacuum tubes to work and the attendant contributions to engineering knowledge of reliability are significant; and the ENIAC project trained a number of young engineers who went on to contribute much to computing.

Neither Eckert nor Mauchly was notably enriched by the invention of ENIAC: according to Mauchly, each received about $300,000 over a period of ten years, including the money from the sale of their company to Remington Rand and additional royalties awarded to the two inventors after Sperry's settlement with IBM. Mauchly left Sperry after his contract expired and started a small consulting firm which followed the boom-and-bust cycle common to software houses in the mid-sixties and early seventies; he died in 1980. Eckert is still a vice-president of Sperry; in the style of corporate vice-presidents he lives in a handsome house in Gladwyne, a suburb of Philadelphia, and spends much time on his power boat.

In 1952 Atanasoff started a company that designed automated systems for various government agencies; four years later he sold it to Aerojet General for enough money to ensure him a comfortable life. He lives on a farm near Frederick, Maryland, in a house he designed himself, which includes an elaborate machine shop; the air-conditioning system, the rain gauge, the kitchen cabinets and all the other fittings and fixtures are also Atanasoff-designed, and he and his wife produce their own food. In Mauchly's accurate characterization, he is "a small Jefferson." In 1975 Atanasoff had a stroke, but he is still surprisingly vigorous and is keen on a Shavian scheme to devise a new alphabet. His pleasant life is marred only by a feeling that history has passed him by. He wants a place in the encyclopedias and textbooks his grandchildren will read, and he wants to sit on the dais at more of the commemorative dinners the industry is always giving. The only government award Atanasoff has ever received is the Bulgarian Order of Cyril and Methodius, First Class.

As for Clifford Berry, in 1963 he was found dead in bed with a plastic bag over his head. His death was ruled a suicide.

II

There is perhaps no more dramatic illustration of the changes wrought during the computer era than the story of how that era

minute, muttered "the sonofabitch" and moved on.)

Some specialists consider Aiken to be the father of modern-day computing because the Mark I had been revolutionary in its organization, incorporating many of Babbage's concepts; but it was still an electromechanical machine, composed of standard IBM parts which were electrically controlled. The appearance of the all-electronic ENIAC made the Mark I obsolete almost immediately (although capable of performing successfully for fifteen years afterward). But Watson was vengeful, and in 1948 he came up with what was, in essence, a faster electromechanical machine. The Selective Sequence Electronic Calculator sat in the showroom at 590 Madison, fascinating passersby and doing computing work for the government, universities and industry at $300 an hour. A profitable tangent, but a tangent nevertheless. "Watson thought the SSEC would be the last word in electromechanical equipment, and that, unfortunately, is just what it was," says one IBM alumnus.

In 1946, Watson hired a former Sunday editor of the New York *Herald Tribune* for a low-profile job with responsibility for press relations. Until then, there had been no executive in the corporation whose full-time mission was to deal with the press, an estate which Mr. Watson deeply distrusted: he was his own publicity man, a function he performed by instinct and brilliantly. But during the late forties, Eckert and Mauchly were receiving increasingly awestruck coverage in the newspapers; universities were beginning to design their own computers; and other companies, new and old, were dipping their feet into computing. The first computer experts from the universities and from government agencies, such as the National Bureau of Standards, were gathering at conventions of the newly formed Association for Computing Machinery, and they tended to characterize IBM as a stodgy company shackled to obsolete technology. Their comments were not lost on the securities analysts. More particularly, they rankled young Tom. In 1949 Tom asked the ex-*Tribune* man, who had been upgraded to advertising manager, to bring in one of the better young salesmen and assign him the task of securing favorable mention in the popular press.

But Tom was beginning to understand that the new technology would require more than image-polishing from IBM. Back in the thirties, some progressive engineers had tried without success to push the company into electronics. After the war, they resumed their experiments with vacuum tubes. Tom's experiences with radar as an army pilot had whetted his interest in electronics, and when he came upon the laboratory prototype of a vacuum tube calculator, he ordered the machine to be built. The result was IBM's first electronic product. The calculator—which was miles ahead of Remington Rand's accounting machines—proved enormously successful and was followed by two more sophisticated models, which found a substantial market in the scientific and defense communities.

Nonetheless, the IBM electronic calculators, however advanced, could not challenge Eckert-Mauchly's newly announced (but still uncompleted) Univac. The IBM gear carried out simple instructions conveyed by punched cards fed in by a human operator; the Univac would handle a complex sequence of commands recorded on magnetic tape without manual intervention. Competitively Univac's chief disadvantage was that it was being sold first by technical men from Eckert-Mauchly and then by Remington Rand, which failed to integrate the new computer people with its regular salesmen. Univac customers were given free access to the producers' engineers, who tended to answer anxious questions a bit too frankly, whereas IBM dealt with users exclusively through its sales force, whose minds were not cluttered with unnecessary technical details.

Furthermore, IBM developed intelligence networks in customer corporations, who would inform the IBM salesman whenever the Univac team paid a call. An IBM delegation would then swoop down on the user, painting gory pictures of what would happen when the Univac monster broke down. If the horror stories failed to make an impression, the IBM man would suggest that the potential user set up a task force to make a study before investing in a piece of equipment as costly as the Univac. "The study idea bought us at least six months with every account we tried it on," says a former branch manager. "If we had had Univac equipment," he says, "we'd have told a big customer like the Naval Aviation Supply Depot to buy an extra computer for backup, but Remington Rand never thought of that."

Meanwhile, the IBM engineers who had designed the calculators had been yearning to produce a more sophisticated machine. In particular Ralph Palmer, an electronics enthusiast who had spent the war years doing top-secret work on cryptographic computing machines, had returned to IBM even more eager to develop electronic computers. Palmer's group began experimenting with different types of memory, which they tried out by hooking them up to a monstrous homemade machine called the test assembly. Soon their experience with memory technology and building the test assembly encouraged them to propose the design of a tape processing machine for commercial use.

One of IBM's important customers was Metropolitan Life, whose chief executive had told the Watsons his company was drowning in punch cards and so he wanted to explore tape machines. Tom asked a group of the brightest salesmen in the field to look into the prospects for tape processing. After some study, the group concluded that tape machines would never sell. They argued that information stored on punched cards could be fished out as you needed it, while tape had to spin and spin until you got to the place you wanted. The salesmen had no real conception of how fast the tape would whirl.

But there were two men whose influence on Watson acted as a counterweight to these conclusions. James Birkenstock, Watson's executive assistant, was responsible for looking at future requirements, keeping alert to outside developments in electronics and administering the company's patent operations. Birkenstock was impressed both with Palmer's efforts inside IBM and with the work of various small companies which were getting into computing. "Also," he says, "with my patent hat on I became increasingly worried about the growth of important technology in the outside world that was novel and thus patentable and the comparative lack of emphasis on it in IBM. The number of engineers we had working on electronics was relatively small." And Birkenstock had a "very uncomfortable feeling" about the validity of the sales group's findings. "I told Tom," he remembers, "if we didn't change our whole attitude, enter into a real research effort and hire a lot of Ph.D.'s in electronics we'd be second to last. He said, 'Birkenstock, come up and tell this to my father.' Mr. Watson, Sr. was not happy. I was told that engineering people were far more capable of advising in this area."

Birkenstock had a valuable ally in Dr. Cuthbert Hurd, who came to IBM from the AEC laboratories at Oak Ridge. By this time Watson senior was beginning to give Tom his head, and Tom seemed unable to get his mind off electronics. He set Hurd to hiring the engineers. In fact, Hurd remembers, "Every day or two Tom would say, 'Cuthbert, have you signed von Neumann yet?' and I would say no, and Tom would say, 'I'm losing confidence in you.' It shows Tom had a lot of insight. He knew what was important—he had no technical knowledge whatsoever but he had a feeling ENIAC was important, von Neumann was important, electronics were important."

Between the good offices of Hurd and Birkenstock and Tom's natural bent, Palmer's group got the money to continue work on the tape processing machine. Then the Korean War struck. Watson senior, in Europe at the time, sent President Truman the customary telegram placing the resources of IBM at the government's disposal. When he returned, Watson senior told Birkenstock to repeat IBM's pattern of mobilizing in World War II. And then, Birkenstock remembers, "Tom said, 'I have something further to add. Jim, this is our real opportunity to get government support for a highly sophisticated electronics program.'"

At first it was assumed that IBM would obtain government contracts to design several computers custom-tailored to the needs of individual defense agencies. Birkenstock and Hurd visited twenty-two such agencies. They went to Los Alamos; they went to Cocoa Beach; and, of course, they went to Washington. "We spent several days walking around the Pentagon," says Hurd. "Every time we passed a door that said 'General' we'd go in." And as Birkenstock remembers, "It dawned on us that while all of them had different requirements they varied not that much. Probably one scientific computer wouldn't answer one hundred percent of the problems of each agency, but it would solve ninety percent of them. I was particularly anti doing anything that required giving away all our rights and data to the government and not having a solid patent position. I said to Tom, 'Why not build a production lot with IBM's own money?' Tom said it was quite a gamble; a three-million-dollar gamble seemed awfully big."

Birkenstock and Hurd talked with various technical people in the company, all of whom had different ideas about the type of computer that should be designed. By January 1951 they had arrived at specifications, which they presented at a large meeting in Tom Watson's office. Palmer brought a block diagram on a sheet of typing paper, showing the different parts of the system, its speed and its memory capacity. As Tom Watson remembers, "Hurd, Palmer and Birkenstock put their briefcases on the table and took out the drawings of the Defense Calculator. I was having pressures from all over the place—the antitape people were putting on pressure. I saw this machine which was a black box with the number of calculations per second. It was all highly confusing, because mainly I was an airplane pilot."

According to Hurd, the product planning people believed the machine would never sell. Learson, then general sales manager, was noncommittal, and Al Williams, the treasurer, was uneasy about the cost estimates. "Finally Tom says, 'Go out and see if you can get any orders for this.' I said, 'I have to have a price.' So that afternoon we had a tube count on the thing. Probably the tubes would cost three times as much as the tubes on the 604 [calculator]. So we did the multiplications and got a rental of fifty-two hundred dollars a month. Williams said, 'Let's round it off to eight thousand dollars a month.' I made forty photostats of Ralph's diagram and toured the country with them."

Birkenstock also went out prospecting, and between them they brought in, by Hurd's account, about thirty letters of intent from aircraft companies and government agencies. But as soon as the engineers began to build the Defense Calculator, it became evident that $8,000 a month was a ludicrously low estimate. The financial men suggested that $22,000 a month would be more realistic, while Hurd insisted that you couldn't tell people a machine was going to cost $8,000 and then raise it to $22,000. Finally a compromise figure of $15,000 was reached, and Hurd and Birkenstock were told to deliver the news.

Hurd remembers that "the meeting with the Douglas [Aircraft] vice-president, was the single worst experience. . . . There were four or five of these vice-presidents, and they said: 'Look, we've put our jobs on the line, based on what we could do for eight thousand dollars a month, and now you want fifteen thousand dollars.' But they finally swallowed it, and they went back and met with Donald Douglas, Jr., and finally the number disintegrated from thirty orders to about twelve, and then gradually crept up to eighteen, and we then made a nineteenth one. By that time, we could have sold twenty-five, but the machine was underpriced, obsolete. . . ."

Douglas, in fact, took two. IBM sold eight machines to aircraft companies, four to government agencies, three to Atomic Energy Commission laboratories, one to the Rand Corporation, and two to commercial customers for scientific use; the company itself kept one.

The Defense Calculator was not the tape processing machine Palmer had proposed; Palmer's machine, geared to commercial use, had been rejected as inadequate for the needs of the scientific computing required for defense purposes. Jerrier Haddad, now an IBM vice-president, who led the team that built the new machine, says, "From then on every computer would be cost-oriented. This was just 'get it built and make it work.' It hadn't been done before and it was needed. Our cost estimates were blown by a factor of two, our schedule by two, and still we were heroes. We had a lot of fun doing new things—there had never been an electronic machine this large built in a factory. We had to invent packaging techniques. I thought we would have to move this machine down the hall and up in the elevator and in through the door, so we made it in units to be independently tested, shipped and moved." In fact Hurd—who has long since left IBM—believes that Haddad's key contribution, one which "revolutionized the computer business," was the apparently simple one of building a machine that was easy to ship and install.

By 1953, when the Defense Calculator was first delivered, it had been rechristened the 701, and it was what IBM had on hand to keep at bay the competition from Univac. In those days computer people believed that the scientific user fed in a few long numbers and waited for the machine to perform a large number of complex calculations and provide the answer; he presumably would trade relatively slow input and output for enormous calculating speed. The commercial customer, on the other hand, fed great quantities of information into the computer, which then performed some fairly simple processing operations on each item. As computers came into wider use, their manufacturers discovered that many of the differences in their customers' requirements were illusory: there were more input and output in scientific computing than expected, and a good deal of calculation involved the storage and retrieval of numbers, while business uses were often more complex than anticipated.

If one were to draw a genealogy chart of IBM's computers, it would show two separate families, the scientific and the commercial, developing through two generations and marrying in the third, producing a brood of computers some of which tended ever so slightly to favor the father and some of which leaned a bit toward the mother.

The ancestor of the commercial line was the old Palmer machine, now named the 702, which had been slowly developing through the efforts of a small crew while the company's major energies were focused on the Defense Calculator, 701. But when a task force of salesmen and engineers reviewed the incipient 702 and labeled it clearly inferior to the Univac, Tom Watson ordered another machine to be designed and produced immediately. Learson remembers, "In ninety days I had a new machine announced. The boys worked around the clock. I had engineering people on the manufacturing line. I said no testing, no one knows how to test, and saved a lot of time, and we got away with it. The new machine chewed up the market."

In particular, the new machine—the 705—featured the new magnetic core memory developed at MIT, which used tiny doughnut-shaped cores that could be magnetized to the left or the right to signify a one or a zero in binary code. The 705 is generally acknowledged to be Learson's first great triumph. Ironically, it had been partly a "penalty-box" assignment. Watson and Learson had quarreled; Watson nevertheless recognized Learson's effectiveness; the 705 project would have a first-rate czar, and it would keep Learson out of sight at the factory.

Through all the frenzy, uncertainty and rumor-spreading of those days, Watson senior, in his personal style, helped sustain the traditional spirit of the company. At one meeting, when a marketing executive had prepared little pink slips for each account recently lost by IBM salesmen and was explaining the reason for each disaster ("machine didn't work," "faulty maintenance," etc.), Watson watched for a time and finally cut in. "I wonder," he asked, "if I might say a few words. This," he said, "is a meaningless exercise. There is only one reason for losing an account . . . neglect."

After the old man's death, the company faced a late delivery crisis on its current scientific model, partly because thousands of tubes had to be soldered, and the first thirty machines already delivered to the customers had been soldered badly. "It's ten o'clock," Tom Watson told the director of engineering. "I want every man on your staff out with a soldering iron this afternoon." The machines were fixed in three days, and as an alumnus remembers, "The poor bastard with the broken machine saw six senior engineers walk into his office with soldering irons, and he never forgot it."

Univac salesmen, well primed in the special features of their equipment, visited company presidents and talked learnedly of dual circuitry, metal tape and mercury delay lines; IBM salesmen promised that their computer would get the payroll out two days early and save vast sums of money in the process; and there was no question whose argument was more persuasive. For commercial customers, IBM developed a team of industry specialists, familiar with the particular requirements of utilities, media or insurance companies. Scientific users were approached by teams of salesmen and IBM-trained programmers with degrees in math or physics who developed their own kind of spirit.

Univac continued to announce better machines but was late in delivering them. As month after month went by, more customers switched to IBM. In August 1955, according to a contemporary *Fortune* report, Univac had thirty large computers installed while IBM had twenty-four. One year later, IBM had seventy-six of its big machines installed to Univac's forty-six, with three times as many machines on order. And IBM's middle-sized computer led all competitors in the field. That year IBM had 84.9 percent of the domestic market, while Sperry had 9.9 percent.

III

Between 1956 and 1967, the Univac division of Sperry Rand lost $250 million. For this considerable accomplishment, IBM does not deserve all the credit; a stream of worthy executives at Sperry helped.

In 1969 Professor Saul Rosen of Purdue wrote in a publication of the Association for Computing Machinery:

> The first Univac was delivered on June 14, 1951. For almost five years after that it was probably the best large-scale computer in use for data processing applications. Internally, it was the most completely checked commercial computer ever built. . . . Remington Rand was launched into the computer field with a product that was years ahead of any of its competitors.

It was, then, a considerable technological lead that Remington Rand and its successor, Sperry Rand, allowed to evaporate during the days when the general public referred to computers as "Univacs." The joke about the company's poor performance—"Univac snatched defeat from the jaws of victory"—became one of the industry's most durable clichés, describing a failure widely credited to indecision, mismanagement and corporate intrigue.

Remington Rand had entered the tabulating business in 1927 with the acquisition of the Powers Accounting Machine Company. By the thirties, in the government's very first antitrust suit against IBM, IBM and Remington Rand, its only significant competitor, were charged with dividing up the market for punched cards and tying in the sale of the cards with the rental of their tabulating machines; the government won, and these practices were prohibited. By the time Remington Rand bought Eckert-Mauchly, it was manufacturing a full line of office equipment as well as electric shavers. To James Rand, the company's chief executive, the tabulating equipment was the least important of the company's products, and he always regarded computers as something of a sideline.

This attitude prevailed in Sperry Rand's top management until 1965. As one former Univac man observes, "In trying to avoid risk, Univac created risks. IBM took calculated risks." When Remington Rand merged with the Sperry Corporation, Rand retired and Sperry's Harry Vickers, a hydraulic engineer, became chief executive. According to a former executive, William R. Lonergan, whenever he and his superiors submitted a proposal to Vickers, "he would say, 'Leave it, we'll look it over.' He never turned anything down, and he never approved it."

In 1952, Rand had had the additional shrewdness to buy another small computer company, Engineering Research Associates, a St. Paul firm employing some of the industry's brightest technical talent. The leader of the ERA group was William R. Norris. What Rand didn't know—could not have known beforehand—was that in Norris and Presper Eckert he had also managed to acquire two of the crustiest men in the business. Besides the inevitable personality clash, there were ideological differences: "The ERA principals had the philosophy of using today's art, and Eckert wanted to push back frontiers," says Norris. A series of organization changes, mostly to Norris's disadvantage, made things worse. By 1957 he had had a bellyful and left to form Control Data Corporation, taking most of the ERA group with him and leaving Univac's St. Paul facility badly demoralized. It took many years after their departure to bring about reasonable harmony between Philadelphia and St. Paul. Lonergan observes, "Univac engineers spent twenty percent of their time working on design problems and eighty percent working on each other."

In the late forties and early fifties, says Gordon Smith, who left IBM for Univac, a Remington Rand branch manager in a big city like Chicago made $65,000 to $80,000 a year in commissions and sat like a ward boss with a big cigar, distributing patronage plums—the best territory, the most sympathetic quota—to his favorite aides. Naturally, he spurned promotion and had no enthusiasm for computers; one could do much better selling the machinery one knew to the customers one knew. There was no rapport between the new "Eckert-Mauchly kids with Ph.D.'s and sneakers and the salesmen with the waxed mustaches and no education. Univac had a traveling team which would get the customers in each city all worked up about computers, but nobody in the branch office followed through."

After Vickers took over, a succession of presidents tried to shape up the Univac operation; as each president was counted out, vestigial groups of his disciples would try to sabotage the next team. In 1959 Vickers, paying tribute to IBM's success in the computer business, brought in Dause L. Bibby, a dethroned IBM vice-president, to refurbish the division with Watsonian spirit, techniques and alumni. It was the first time an IBM detail had tried functioning in the outside world, and they found the Univac milieu shocking. Smith, a new marketing executive, asked one of his colleagues to take him on a tour of the branch offices. "At one branch," he recalls, "they hadn't had a visit from the home office in seven years." And, according to Lonergan, "at IBM, Bibby would press a button and a thousand guys in pin-striped suits would come out and salute; when he pressed the button at Univac, nothing happened. Mobilizing an effective organization takes one kind of talent; breathing life into a dead one takes another."

Another observer adds that Bibby, a sales executive, didn't understand production. "In an engineering company if you grow more than twenty percent in sales you have to build new production facilities and train extra technical people," he says. "Bibby built up a great big sales force that Univac couldn't support."

One engineer who left the company was asked by his new boss to analyze the Univac situation. His memo, written in 1965, notes that engineering, programming and marketing expenses nearly tripled between 1958 and 1961. Reorganization in the engineering department spread the talent too thin; manufacturing management "was composed of a group of old-timers whose business was to manufacture typewriters and shavers"; and the marketing organization, having overcommitted the engineers, had to bring in expensive subcontractors. Nor was finance exempt from blame: bad inventory control and careless bookkeeping led to sizable shortages of parts and raw materials.

Univac is seldom faulted for the quality of the products it designed during all this chaos; often they were superior to IBM's. The Livermore Atomic Research Computer, ordered in 1956 by the Atomic Energy Commission, exemplified the company's considerable engineering talent. Advanced architecture made the LARC extremely powerful for its time: in its first performance test the machine did twenty-eight billion operations in two days.

However, the LARC was developed under a fixed-price contract with the AEC, and the development costs far exceeded that price. Two LARCs were delivered, for total revenues of $6 million, but by the time Univac killed the project, it had spent $26 million on it. Some Univac alumni still believe the machine would have made money eventually; so do the champions of all extravagant failures, and no one can prove them wrong. IBM experienced a similar loss on a supercomputer contemporary with LARC. But IBM's other computer operations were showing a hefty profit, and Sperry Rand's were losing money.

Though far outpaced by IBM, Univac managed to maintain a weak second position. It took a strong new management, introduced in the mid-sixties, to make the division profitable at last.

PART II

IBM

3

Chieftains

THE PAST DECADE has brought significant changes to IBM. In 1970 the company was still ruled by a dynasty of entrepreneurs; by 1980 it had evolved into a mature corporation run by professional managers. The transition spanned the stewardship of four men: Thomas J. Watson, Jr., T. Vincent Learson, Frank T. Cary and John Opel, who became chief executive in January 1981. These men have shaped the goals and set the tone of IBM—and through it, the computer industry. The mid-seventies was the last period when all four were deeply involved in the company: Cary was chairman; his predecessors were on the board of directors; his heir, Opel, was president.

I

> There is a reason for my success. You know it. . . . I want you to know that I know it. Made unusually good choice of father so I always had a friend in the firm. . . .
>
> I have never claimed to be a great salesman . . . but I do claim to be the son of one of the greatest salesmen that ever lived. I appreciate the honor you do him today in recognizing me. The IBM Company is his monument and any sales sense that I have has come from him.
> —Notes for speech by Thomas J. Watson, Jr. to New York Sales Executives Club, September 10, 1957

The skis are still out in the hall. Thomas J. Watson, Jr., just back from Davos, off to Antigua tomorrow, has joined the band of fortunates who take their text from Ecclesiastes: to everything there is a season. On this day in mid-February 1974, the boss's son has been in retirement for six weeks, having served thirty-one years with the company his father built, having multiplied that company's revenues, during his own fifteen years as chief executive, by more than thirteen times, having nearly quintupled the number of employees. He has vowed not to visit corporate headquarters for the first hundred days of his retirement, and so he sits on the sun porch of the house in Greenwich surrounded by portraits of an apparently limitless supply of Watson daughters in bridal dress. The only son practices law in Boston; the dynasty is ended.

Watson, a rangy, elegant-looking man, is dressed in what must be his freedom clothes. His jacket is of an assertive plaid, the shirt of the former IBM chairman is emphatically pink, and black boots peek out beneath grey flannel trousers. ("I revel in these boots.") But he is sixty now and looks it, the survivor of a heart attack which forced him to relinquish the chairmanship two and a half years earlier, staying on to head the executive committee until his official retirement. Despite the skis in the hall, his step seems a trifle slow.

At the age of five, Tom Watson took his first walk down an IBM assembly line; at twelve, he first addressed an IBM meeting. In youth he was a proper princeling, hard-drinking, an indifferent student at Brown, able to buy himself a small plane over the objections of his father, then coming to work at IBM, a world in which obstacles, not surprisingly, melted away. President of his class at sales training school; in his first year on the job, member of the Hundred Percent Club, for salesmen who achieve quota; the next year's quota passed on January 2. Accolades to build the confidence of any young man other than the chief executive's son, who might not have been studious but was also not stupid. And so the son defiantly continued to carouse, while the father waited.

The obstacles one meets as an army pilot do not melt away; they are faced and overcome. The princeling emerged from World War II a lieutenant colonel with a distinguished record earned far beyond the borders of his father's dominion. Like many other men, he came home more serious, ready to get on with it; shortly before his return he wrote his father, "My affinity for night clubs, at its peak in 1939, has dropped to the point where in the past year I have been in two and failed to enjoy either."

And so Tom Watson was apprenticed to Charles Kirk, a harddriving forty-three-year-old comer who had led manufacturing at IBM during the war. Now Kirk was executive vice-president, and the younger Watson's chair was pulled up to his desk. They worked and traveled together for a year, until late one night at a hotel in

Lyons there came a pounding on Tom's door. Mr. Kirk was dying. He was beyond help.

During that first year the two Watsons took one of their frequent walks through corporate headquarters. In the patent development office, young Watson saw some engineers working with a gang-punch machine hooked up by a thick wire to a frame with tubes in it. The punched cards were feeding in payroll information, rates and hours and social security deductions. "What's this?" Tom asked, and the engineers answered, "We're multiplying with radio tubes." Fascinated by the gadgetry, eager for IBM to have a "first," he ordered the engineers to develop the machine and put it into production. It became IBM's first electronic product, the 603 calculator.

The former chairman borrows a match to light the fire, points out a model of Pascal's adding machine and settles down to remember. "My father and I had terrible fights," he says. "He seemed like a blanket that covered everything. I wanted to best him but also to make him proud of me. I really enjoyed the ten years with him. I used to tell Olive I wouldn't go back another day—he'd call me in the middle of the night, and Olive would pass me notes to keep my temper. The old gent must have known before that he would die soon, and he made me chief executive in 1956. That was better than having it fall to me after his death.

"I've always been terribly modest about my own intellectual abilities. I thought I'd do better to hire the best people. They wouldn't push me out of my job since I was the boss's son and had some security. I had high goals: von Neumann, the mathematician, had important ideas and articulated them well. We had him come every two months to talk to our engineers. It meant a lot to IBM. I think he needed money, so it was good for him.

"By all odds Al Williams, who became president of the company in 1961, was the most helpful to me. He was an interesting individual from Harrisburg. His father was a coal miner. Al had been a trumpet player to work his way through school. One day he read a headline saying, 'Thomas J. Watson, Sr., the chairman of IBM, makes a thousand dollars a day.' Al said 'That's where I want to work,' and he came up to us.

"Al was sought after in the business community. My father never had much interest in finances. He liked earnings per share, but not the details. Father gave Williams all the tough financial jobs.

"Al was a CPA and he had the annual reports on IBM and other companies. He said we were spending three percent of gross on research and development and other companies spent six or eight or nine percent, so we ought to be spending more. We had less than forty engineers in my father's day. We got one of our men who was an MIT graduate to come down to New York and hire thousands of engineers. My father wasn't particularly concerned about electronics, though we'd have gone in without me. He had people he had faith in who told him we were fine—maybe they told him what he wanted to hear. I went in and told him our engineering department was a farce and unless he supported my hiring the engineers we'd go down the tubes.

"In father's day progress had been so slow—he had groups of three people who developed new machines. I learned that competition among technical people brings discipline to the company. If we get any segment of IBM into one group of engineers' hands the discipline is gone. So the engineers competed. Mechanical engineers had a taint—the prestige was in electronics. When one machine was picked and the others not it took a dinner or two to handle the morale of the losing group.

"Vin Learson had been on my list as a terribly competent salesperson from the first few months I was at IBM. In 1947 we had a personal disagreement and I told him, 'Don't mess around with a problem like this because you're headed for the top or near it.' I never saw a salesman to equal him. He had a forceful personality and some people got on the bad side of it, but the better side was his strong salesmanship.

"The secret I learned early on from my father was to run scared and never think I had it made. We got highly excited over things that were not that important. I never felt I was completely adequate to the job and always ran scared. In June 1957, a year after my father died, I said, 'By golly, Olive, I've made it through twelve months.' I never had great concern about my ability to tell everyone what to do but I was concerned about the balance sheet and being judged by the board of directors."

The younger Watson's reign was bracketed by antitrust suits. His accession to power came in 1955, on the day he stormed off to the Federal Courthouse to accept a consent decree settling a four-year-old government suit against IBM, leaving the adamant old man raging behind him. (Later that morning the internal weather of the father changed, and he called a messenger and sent his son a note expressing confidence, appreciation, admiration and love.) In 1969, the government sued IBM once more; this time both sides held firm through Tom Watson's retirement, and long past it.

"After the 1956 consent decree we had serious talks about how to run IBM, and we learned to live with the decree. We had a team of lawyers lecture on antitrust law and what we couldn't do, and we had signoffs on that. I think it's sad that the government is not more specific in laws governing business. Antitrust law could be made to read more specifically. You work hard for thirty-odd years, have admiration, get bigger, and then various people start suing you and you look like a torn old coat. If we used Department of Commerce and Labor statistics to define the size of any industry, we could set up a committee to decide how much of the industry a company can have before it's illegal. Pick fifty-five percent or twenty-five percent, and say the law gives you thirty-six months to divest. Then as you're developing you make a new company.

"There are half a dozen decisions I regret about how to meet competition. Now that I see we've survived and are admired, it would have been nicer to make a different decision, but at the time we wondered if we were going to last another three years. When RCA and GE went into computers Al Williams said the thing to worry about was GE—they were a well-managed company and understood electronics. The fundamental reason for our success was running scared. I've seen us go by companies whose chief executives used to make me shake in awe.

"If you look back over history, what stands out is individual human beings. I don't think we can get down to a scientifically managed gadget. You need a central authority who is vivid, exciting and reachable.

"Do you know what I'd like to do? Write a book about Captain Cook, the way he managed men. Cook had five hundred men and took them on two- or three-year voyages. He never had a mutiny and the men always re-enlisted."

When a man is in the prime of his power, he runs scared. Later, when that time is over, he thinks of his place in history. If any of the men Tom Watson managed had a fondness for Shakespeare, they might have observed that he began his career as Prince Hal and ended it by giving his kingdom prematurely to a man named Lear-son. In retirement, Watson was beginning to sound like his father.

II

A government building in White Plains: July 18, 1973. Justice Department lawyers are taking the deposition of Thomas Vincent Lear-son, who followed Tom Watson into the chairmanship of IBM and then, being one year older, preceded him into retirement. He is a giant man, deeply tanned and dressed in a white linen suit; he sits sucking a sourball and fiddling with a matchbook, looking as comfortable as a caged beast. If an ingenious Mikado were to devise a particularly fiendish punishment for Vin Learson, it would be to sit forever in this stuffy crowded room listening to lawyers split hairs and answering questions of considerable legal significance but little other interest ("What is a computer?" "Does IBM make and sell computer systems?"), particularly on a beautiful breezy sailing day.

The former chairman answers questions in a stage whisper unless asked to speak up, when he produces a ringing baritone. The quality of nervous energy, the first thing one notices in a room that contains—or almost contains—Vin Learson, is more striking for being pent-up. The next thing one notices is his Boston accent; perhaps, like the brogue of the late Michael Quill, the labor leader, it has become more pronounced over the years in proportion to the speaker's distance from the source. The flat a's punctuate the sentences: here is a man who will not choose the word "capricious" when he can use "ahbitrary." Like Tom Watson, he is a man mindful of his origins.

Two exchanges seem particularly pertinent today. Learson is asked to read and comment on a memo from a branch manager describing the federal government as a market for computers. "This is a sales statement made by a salesman trying to puff himself up," he says. "This is good poetry. This is all the good poetry of the salesman." Later, when the IBM lawyer accuses the government lawyer of harassing the witness, Learson interrupts: "Mr. Schwarz uses the word 'unfair' and he used it in one context. I would use it in another context . . . all you are doing is bringing delaying tactics into this whole proceeding and at twenty dollars a day, I think it's unfair. That is all I am getting for it. . . . I'm on your payroll today."

Vin Learson is famous for his low tolerance of poetry and his keen appreciation of the dollar value of his time. In the quintessential Learson story—which has many variations—an underling comes into Learson's office with a forty-page presentation he has taken a month to prepare and expects to spend two hours delivering. Learson sits impassive as the first chart rolls over, but before the young man can begin his speech, Learson calls out, "next page." It takes ten minutes to run through the forty pages, and Learson has not taken a single note. When the ten minutes are over, he announces that the material on pages 3, 8, 10, 16, 17, 22, 38, 35 and 39 is questionable and the underling had better get in tomorrow with supporting documentation. It is a chastening experience, particularly since the young man later discovers that six out of the nine pages picked up by Mr. Learson do indeed contain errors.

Nearly a year after Learson's deposition in the White Plains government office, in a small room that IBM has provided for the use of its former chairman, a visitor asks Learson if it is true that he, son of a ship's captain and a schoolteacher, worked his way through Harvard pumping gas.

"I didn't pump gas. I pahked cahs. We lived in a nice neighborhood in the suburbs, but we weren't wealthy. I had a hell of a good father and a hell of a good mother. My mother was the taskmaster; my father was easygoing. The work ethic was drilled into me early. I had a younger brother who died at thirty-two—he had a rheumatic heart and he was close to death for a long time. But he went to school part-time to receive his degree from Harvard at twenty-eight, married, had a child and taught high school. I got a kick out of seeing him make it against tremendous odds.

"I went to Boston Latin; my subject was math. Fifty was the passing mark, and they loved to give you forty-nine. Harvard was a lead-pipe cinch after Latin. I enjoyed sports but never excelled in them. I was a severe asthmatic.

"Some kid at IBM asked me to what I attributed my success. I said pure luck. When IBM was under the old man he had a system of picking people. It was very arbitrary—sometimes it was successful, sometimes not. If he liked the cut of your jib you might move up. The first year I made a speech at the Hundred Percent Club meeting—I was fourth in the company and treasurer of the Club—the son of an IBM director was also making a speech. I'm on the elevator, and the director and a crony stepped in. The crony says 'That was a good speech your boy made,' and the director said 'That tall, lanky guy from Boston did better.' I recognized that it wasn't his idea—he had heard the old man.

"Today I lecture on identification of high-potential people. We ask management to recognize a fellow four or five years in the business that they believe will go all the way and we follow him. Today it's very formalized but when I began there was no such formal thing.

"I was not a great salesman. I was by no means spellbinding. A salesman at IBM is not an ordinary peddler, though I use the term to bring the salesmen down to earth, to remind them what their job is. We attract the best because selling a computer is sophisticated. Our people become management-oriented as salesmen—these young kids, twenty-five or -six, call on treasurers and vice-presidents and see them living with their problems and making decisions—that develops a man. You are a businessman getting MBA training on the job. Now, of course, the fellow who's been to B-school is the type who'll run the business in the future.

"A salesman will write and cry and exaggerate, he'll be gentle with the facts—that's life. There are two or three serious points to make in a presentation and all the rest is window dressing. The engineer will exaggerate too, but generally engineers are more factual. The financial men are the most factual of all but they're so factual they get lost in numbers. I was not a report man. Reports may obfuscate the main issue of what you were doing, where you want to go. I hated the flip chart mentality. People are enamored of charts and numbers. Managing technology is the key to the business. I started knowing the market but knowing nothing about technology, and relating the two is what makes the IBM Company. I've spent the largest share of my life working with engineers and manufacturing people in the lab. It's what I enjoyed most. I wasn't creative but it was the creative area of the business. Not being technical I never understood the fine points of materials, circuits, programming—I didn't have to. I had to listen, give assignments, and always hold some one fellow responsible. Protect him from diversions in other areas. With the System 360 project, I was there to feed it, let it grow, protect the men doing the job. They'll say I was the worst s.o.b. because I kept challenging them.

"We've never stuck with anything—it's the excitement, the gamble, move, move, move. In the 360 there were flaps about the circuitry not being advanced enough—it was the most advanced for its time. What you worry about is that you're making a decision in 1962 for 1964 to '68—the components lead the machine by two years. Success is having good men around you, and I was fortunate. I had my own staff brought in, hot guys, John Opel and Havens, an engineer who had developed the NORC computer which was famous for having the least number of circuits. He was not part of the establishment; he was an offset to the troops.

"We have a bureaucracy, no question about it, but the fellows who were winning would cut right across it. John Opel goes where the action is, Frank Cary the same. They're tops intellectually. You spot doers and give them a job: some fail, some win. The troops can pick hot men; talent shows.

"All these fellows had guts, plain guts. They were willing to risk their jobs on any decision. I can remember Frank Cary would come to a meeting and we'd pull one of his people apart. We couldn't get away with it unless we were right. Frank would move right in and protect him. Protecting your people when they fall apart under pressure is a sign of guts. If Frank's man was wrong, he'd say 'We're sorry.'

"Tom did his job well, and with grace. He knew his limitations and relied on others. Tom was more interested in personnel and morale and the management team and the organization. I was interested in product. I had no plan or strategic program—all I wanted was to do a job in a pretty decent way."

About the antitrust suits, Learson says, "I think what we did was legal as the devil. I lived through the decisions on pricing and leases. If I were to relive it I would do precisely what we did. It was right. This is a capital-intensive business, and the little guys have tough sledding.

"I'll tell you one more story. If IBM had been more efficient in the early days I wouldn't be here today. In 1935 I first reported to work at Endicott. That summer I'd been sick as a dog with asthma. I took a train from Boston to Grand Central to catch the sleeper to Endicott. While I was in the Lackawanna station I had an attack of asthma and staggered into a little Greek restaurant. Only the owners were there. I said, 'May I go into the back room, and would you boil some water, I have to give myself a shot of adrenalin.' I gave myself a humdinger, boarded the train, and couldn't sleep all night—my heart was keeping pace with the wheels. I staggered in all shaky the next morning. But they didn't give me a physical till a few days later. If they'd given it that morning I'd have flunked."

Perhaps the asthma was itself adrenalin for Learson, providing the obstacle for a hard-driving young man to overcome; but Learson, skeptical not only of poetry but of easy psychology as well, will not speculate on this. Nor does he dwell on the story of the princeling and the Boston commoner, yoked together in uneasy union for three decades, each needing the other and knowing it, each giving the other his due—but only his due.

III

There is something executorlike in Frank Cary's manner. If one had inherited the company one's father built, and if one had spent one's career raising that company to a stature in American industry that conformed with, perhaps even surpassed, the vision of its founder, and if one finally had to pass the company on to someone outside the family, Frank Cary seems just the man one would pick, a man who would neither squander the inheritance by rash decisions nor let it diminish through excessive caution. And despite his conservative demeanor, Cary proved not to be an overcautious chairman: he wasn't afraid to split the stock or borrow a billion dollars or get the company into satellites, when he thought that was the wise course to take. He was a man to keep the inheritance growing and preserve its dignity, to show respect for the corporate tradition by not trying to superimpose his own too-dominant or colorful personality.

Cary is bald and bespectacled and smiling, a pleasant Humpty-Dumpty–looking man—and among IBM's top management he is the one who looks most comfortable in a vest. Learson and Al Williams once had a bloody battle over him, Learson wanting Cary in a line position reporting to him, Williams insisting Cary was "a born staff man" and fierce to place him on the corporate staff. Williams won, but Cary got the line job a few years later. In retirement, both Watson and Learson seem to claim Cary as their personal discovery.

In a small private dining room off the employee cafeteria at corporate headquarters in Armonk, Cary reminisces. "I was born in

1921," he says, "and when I was two we moved to a small town in California called Inglewood, which was the site of the LA airport. There were a couple of hangars in the airport in my youth and flying was so unusual we used to go out on Sunday to see the planes take off. There were about twenty thousand people in Inglewood and no smog so that you could look across the valley and see the mountains from the ocean.

"My mother's people came from farm communities in Iowa. As a youngster I went to Iowa picnics in Long Beach, where you'd see thousands of people divided up by the county in Iowa they'd come from. My family were very religious Protestants, especially my mother. My father, a doctor, was also from a farm community in Wisconsin. His parents came over from Ireland. There were eleven children and several of them worked their way through college.

"I started as premed, but my father died my sophomore year and I couldn't afford all that schooling, so I switched to prelaw. Then I went into the service, and got a little antsy when I came out; business school only took half as much time as law school so I enrolled at Stanford Graduate School of Business. I knew nothing about IBM, but one of my friends had a job there and he was always talking about it. Those were very rapid-growth days for punched card accounting machines. They had proven their value to government and big industry during the war. I had great success when I was on quota. When the first large electronic computers arrived there was a surprisingly insatiable appetite for them among the aerospace companies.

"If I were to select one single business practice that was most important to our success in the early days it would be that we only leased equipment. This put a discipline on the business that was excellent. It motivated IBM people and it built a great relationship of trust between the customer and the company. The customer knew he had leverage, and the manager could motivate the salesmen, whose pay depended on their ability to help the customer get results.

"Selling in IBM or anywhere is a gregarious activity. While I wouldn't describe myself as very gregarious, what I liked was selling a product with a high intellectual content. It was not a pitchman operation. It was very professional. Every situation was different, the personalities were different. There was almost infinite variety. When you study the prospect requirements and come up with a system proposal and get the order, there's satisfaction, but the real satisfaction is when you install it and it performs as proposed.

"I had little to do with product development until 1966, a lot to do with it after that. In general you always have to manage the differences between the engineers and the salespeople and be aware of their natural biases. You have to know when to rub them together and what the sparks mean, and you have to do it without producing personal conflict. Von Neumann laid out the concept of the computer, and it hasn't changed too much—most computer organizations are based on the von Neumann concept. New things come from the development portions of the product divisions and from research. In 1966 I separated out the components division—in those days it was difficult to understand the interface between the engineering and the manufacturing of components, which were fairly discrete. With the technology coming down the road today the interface disappears—you have an entire computer on a chip, so where does the component begin and end?

"Some aspects of bureaucracy are terrible, but some are essential. We have changed the organization every couple of years—changed the approval procedures and so forth. If you leave the structure in place you can endanger it. We don't change the organization just to be doing it—we change because our problems change and we need different leverage.

"My attitude is that I feel responsible for everything that goes on. I am pretty active. I'll stick my nose in to a problem in some depth. I tend to be thoughtful and I don't perhaps react quite as emotionally as some people, but I'm just as intense. Maybe I just have a slower fuse."

Frank Cary was a division president by the age of thirty-eight, having held six jobs—starting with sales trainee—in eleven years. He was chief executive officer at fifty-one. One cannot make such a steep climb without intensity somewhere in one's temperament. But if Cary was driven by inner demons, they did not make themselves apparent, and he remained—if only by default—the perfect professional manager, the negotiator, the nest-egg protector.

IV

Of all the men who have headed IBM, John Opel has had the most varied background, having held jobs in marketing, manufacturing, product development and finance, and having served as administrative assistant to both Watson and Learson; he even spent a reportedly uncomfortable year as director of communications, the chief liaison between IBM and the press. The only anomaly in Opel's career is that until 1972, when he was being groomed for the presidency, he hadn't actually headed a division.

A former colleague of Opel's says of him: "John is the most brilliant guy in the business, but with the brilliance comes a little intellectual autocracy. Learson and Cary both wanted him to be president, but John wasn't ready at the time Cary took over. John had jumped—he had never really run anything, he was always the second man, the staff man. So in 1972 they let him run the product development complex. There was a resistance to John among the older management because he was considered too arrogant. He had respect for Watson, but not great respect. So he was told to cool it. Frank Cary is not charismatic, but John can get the engineers to do almost anything because they like his intellect."

Opel is dark-haired and clean-cut and wears horn-rimmed glasses. "I had a very ordinary but idyllic middle-American childhood in Jefferson City, Missouri," he says. "My father owned a hardware store, and mostly sold fishing tackle and sporting goods—I fished all the time. The town was somewhat immune to the problems of larger cities. There was one school. There was a heterogeneity of economic strata and the subordinate social structure was governed by the fact that there was one of everything, and you had to come to terms with that. You could walk from one end of town to the other. It's different from what my kids have—there's a sameness to where they live, no cross-section. In Jefferson City you knew the price of corn and the yields per acre and the batting averages in the major leagues.

"When I started as a salesman at IBM my territory was a poverty-stricken district in the Ozarks. The territory was empty before me—I started with thirteen customers and an annual revenue of thirty-six thousand. The territory contained the greatest fishing holes in the world. Then, when Learson was sales manager, he didn't like the way manufacturing operations were run. He put four of us into Endicott to document all procedures, to try to understand how the process worked and see if we could simplify it. I was the only one with experience in production, from business school. We installed different procedures and learned a lot of new techniques.

"Early in life, as a kid, I learned if you do your homework you're going to know more than most of the other kids because most of them won't read the books. You set a goal and energize yourself to achieve it. I think I'm an i-dotter and t-crosser but all good line executives are as well. The really successful ones are capable of finding where the sand is. At lower jobs it's good to have an automatic quarterback who does what you say without thinking, but it only works for platoon leaders. Above that, you need thinkers.

"My role in the System 360 project was supporting Learson. This was a revolution—the marketing people had their own views and the development people were out of patience with them. I had to rationalize the differences and see what was doable and not be a patsy. The development engineers trusted me—I'd grown up with them. I had to get at what was the truth. Those were days of polarization. There were constant arguments about machine architecture. I'd get into them and take a position. People thought the world would come to an end if we brought in the thirty-two-bit word; if we had push-down accumulators, gravity would stop.

"I went into manufacturing when the 360 was late. We set up a troika of managers at every site, development engineering, manufacturing and field engineering, and Vin said to make decisions ourselves, if it boils up it better be important. For example, when you're releasing a new product out of the lab into manufacturing and then shipping it to the customer you have reliability specifications about how often the machine can be down. The field maintenance engineer says the machine was either designed wrong or manufactured wrong. The manufacturing man says it wasn't designed right and those idiots in the field don't read the training manuals. The engineer says the machine was overdesigned, an ape could manufacture it the way it was designed. Often it's a little bit of everything. You need seasoned people at the functional interfaces—you need patience and an unforgiving management.

"There's no way to avoid revolutions in our business. We're a vertically integrated company and that's a profound thing. I don't know any like it. It's revolutions in packaging at three levels—from the raw silicon through the machine architecture to the delivery of systems and applications in customers' offices. You can't put new component technology or new applications concepts on an old device. This industry and technology are so untapped it's absurd to think we've done it all.

"I do have deep emotional feelings about IBM, but they're different from Tom's, and that's understandable. He is the son of the man who was the symbol of the beginnings of the business. I haven't been a very spectacular person in my life. The thing in my career in IBM was the interdisciplinary assignments, getting into the business management of the company early in my career, into operating sides other than marketing. I was fortunate enough to get assignments at crucial times in IBM history where a lot depended on how well I did my job. A lot depends on opportunity. I have a broader depth of experience than most people of my vintage. I was the chief financial officer with control over all the financial men from here to Timbuktu.

"Some people are played up as one kind of person or another, but most businessmen are pretty intense on their jobs. I consider myself pretty intense."

4

"The Higher the Monkey Climbs the More He Shows His Ass": Winning and Losing at IBM

———

I believe the real difference between success and failure in a corporation can very often be traced to the question of how well the organization brings out the great energies and talents of its people. What does it do to help these people find common cause with each other? How does it keep them pointed in the right direction despite the many rivalries and differences which may exist among them? And how can it sustain this common cause and sense of direction through the many changes which take place from one generation to another?
— THOMAS J. WATSON, JR., *A Business and Its Beliefs*

IBM is an institution. As such, it compares favorably with the U.S. Army and the Catholic Church, and I'll say this: before or since, I've never been surrounded by such a collection of first-rate people as I found during the twelve years I worked at IBM.

One of the older men I got friendly with, in his fifties, had this forty-two-foot yawl. We were on the boat one day, and I was running my fingers over the wood, and I said, "God, you live well." "I'd give it all up to be your age again!" he told me. "What would you do?" I asked, and he answered, "Get the hell out of IBM."

The loneliest day in your life is the day you leave IBM.
— Comments of IBM alumni

TOM WATSON'S distaste for panoply is reflected in the 727 sales offices, 20 plants and 19 laboratories of IBM in the United States and the 675 sales offices, 23 manufacturing plants and 11 laboratories of the corporation's two major international subsidiaries in 122 countries around the world. They were furnished to present what one architect called "the appearance of conspicuous economy." Similarly when Watson, during his years as IBM chairman, visited one of these locations to instill a sense of common cause, it was understood that the atmosphere was to be business-as-usual.

The thirty-two-year-old district manager who was to shepherd Watson on one such visit was aware of this; he hoped to see a lot of Watson's familiar boyish grin as they walked through the office together and the chief executive delivered verbal pats on the head and reassured everyone that IBM respects the individual. But the district manager had also heard that on certain unpredictable occasions, Watson's smile would suddenly vanish and his tanned face turn white with anger. The district manager had had three promotions in the past six years, moving his wife and three kids from Houston to Chicago to Atlanta, and he didn't want it to be for nothing. Watson would arrive at the airport at two o'clock, to be met by the district manager in his Buick and sped without fanfare to the office, and he would never know—unless, of course, the Buick should develop a flat tire—that the manager had ordered a backup car to follow discreetly three blocks behind.

At the district office, Watson asked about local morale. Perhaps, suggested the manager, the chairman would like to chat with a group of systems engineers who had returned from calling on customers. The ingenuous crinkly smile lit Watson's face. "They didn't hang around just to talk to me?" he asked.

Some years later, removed by time and venture capital from the orbit of Watson's humors, the former district manager sat in the head office of his own company and recalled the episode: "Hell, no, they didn't hang around. They were shackled together and locked in a room till Watson got there."

In recent years many of IBM's internal documents—minutes recording the deliberations of its management committees, interoffice memos, task force reports—have been used as plaintiff's exhibits in antitrust suits against the company. As such, they are in the public domain. While the layman would find their combination of computerese and fuzzy, prolix management jargon tolerable only in small doses, the documents provide the professional IBM-watcher with solid evidence of the way company executives thought during the sixties and early seventies. Without the live reminiscences of IBM'ers of the period, however, they are of limited use; reminiscences need documentation, and the documents need insight. Besides the jargon they contain subjective words like "commitment," "leadership," "prestige," "excellence," and even "maturity," and phrases such as "the homework had not been done," which also suggest values.

The values of IBM as a society affect the decisions its executives make, and these decisions do much to shape the course of computer technology: not only does the rest of the industry work around or react to IBM, but the company exerts indirect leadership through thousands of former employees, trained at the Watsons' corporate knee, who permeate the computer industry. *The IBM Alumni Directory* published by ex-IBM'er Robert W. Grath contains some twenty-five hundred names gleaned from trade journals and former colleagues. Of those listed in the directory, nearly a thousand hold the title of vice-president or above, mostly with computer-oriented companies.

The IBM whose values thus affect so many is Tom Watson's company, a society shaped by his substance and his style, his dreams and his whims, his standards for admiration and ostracism, his notions of winning and losing. The men now in upper and middle management are his creatures: he was their first symbol of IBM, in his own words "a central authority who is vivid, exciting and reachable." As chairman, he was an odd—but princely—mixture of compassion and capricious cruelty; the compassion was most often displayed toward the foot soldier, while the officers felt the cruelty. Above all, like his father before him, he was a consummate showman, an actor who built his performance from telling details and never acted out of character with an incongruous word or look or gesture so long as he was on stage and within earshot.

An aide who often found himself in the chairman's path during the fifties and sixties recalls Watson's appearing in Los Angeles to dedicate a large computer installation at UCLA. After the ceremony there was a luncheon at the Bel Air Hotel, at which the dean of the university's business school, in a lighthearted tribute to Watson, declared, "Here is a man of true humility. Just the other day we were sitting around the pool of the Palm Springs Racquet Club, and Tom Watson raised his sunglasses, looked around him and said, 'Where are the celebrities?' Can you imagine Thomas J. Watson, Jr. looking for the celebrities?"

Several other speakers embroidered this theme, until at last the chairman of UCLA's board of trustees, a snowy-haired Scotsman who also headed a large mining company, got up and observed dryly, "I have always wished my business affairs were in good enough shape so that I could sit by the pool of the Palm Springs Racquet Club and watch celebrities." Watson's aide, a sharp-eyed man who was sitting at a table with a good view of the dais, saw his boss's face cloud over. "His next stop," says the aide, "was a visit to our Western Regional Headquarters, and I knew the vice-president there was in for it, so I ducked out early, commandeered one of the extra limousines, and went ahead to warn him."

The Western Regional Office, which Watson would be touring for the first time, was a new creation whose appearance of economy was less conspicuous than usual: in particular, the cathedral-ceilinged foyer with its avant-garde sculpture and the serpentine employee cafeteria could be called sumptuous. The manager at each IBM site had some autonomy under corporate guidelines and was held finally responsible for his building. The aide went into the vp's office and said, "There is no time for explanation. Watson is in about as tough a mood as I have ever seen him. Get ready for a very rough ride. To start with, you'd better have a list of the prices of everything in this building."

Watson arrived and the vice-president, disregarding the warning, began his tour with a long-winded discussion of the foyer and the cafeteria. Watson remained silent through the first fifteen minutes of the tour and then said in a most pleasant tone of voice, "This is all very interesting, Mr. Clark. Tell me, is there a *work* area in this building?"

For the next couple of hours, says the aide, "He was up one wall and down the other. What's this, what's that, how much did it cost, what's the price of carpeting per square yard, everything I'd said he'd do. We ended up in Clark's office, where Watson's eye lit on the wastebasket—he picked it up and turned it over. Two balls of crumpled paper and a shiny new clip tumbled out. On the bottom of the wastebasket was stamped, 'Handcrafted in Sweden.' Watson looked up and said, 'Handcrafted in Sweden, Mr. Clark. That is elegant.' Then he put the basket down, replaced the two balls of crumpled paper, picked up the shiny new paper clip, examined it very carefully, put it in his pocket and walked out."

Yet it must be said that Watson's anger was often provoked by lapses more substantial than an overdecorated sales office. In 1963 Control Data Corporation, then a fledgling enterprise, brought out the mightiest computer on the market. Watson sent a memo to seven of his ranking generals, including his brother, Al Williams, Vin Learson and Emanuel Piore, the company's chief scientist. "I understand," he noted, "that in the laboratory developing this system there are only 34 people, 'including the janitor.' Of these, 14 are engineers and 4 are programmers, and only one person has a Ph.D., a relatively junior programmer." Contrasting Control Data's effort with IBM's vast development activities, Watson wrote, "I fail to understand why we have lost our industry leadership position by letting someone else offer the world's most powerful computer." IBM responded to Watson's anger with marketing practices it is still defending in the courts.

But despite his occasional outbursts, Watson is mostly remembered as a benign figure because he understood the need for sensitive gestures to repair morale among the troops. Often these were made in consequence of IBM's traditional Open Door policy, through which any employee who feels he has been treated unfairly by his boss or his boss's boss can appeal directly to the chairman, have his complaint investigated and, if justified, receive redress. The story is told of an engineer who had been granted permission to deliver a paper at an important symposium and then had the permission retracted by a higher executive who decided the paper was humdrum. The engineer wrote Watson, whose aides determined that the higher executive was right; nonetheless, the engineer was allowed to deliver the paper because Watson felt IBM's reputation would survive it and that the engineer should not be humiliated before his wife, his colleagues and his friends.

On another occasion Dr. Enrico Clementi, a distinguished scientist and the manager of large-scale scientific computations at the San Jose research lab, wrote a highly emotional memo to the chairman, protesting the cancellation of a major project in his field. Ironically, the project was a supercomputer, the same sort of machine that Control Data had launched six years earlier. Clementi's memo, in characteristic IBM style, was headed "Why Plan to Be Only Second Best?" and asked, "Has IBM decided not to be ready with the computers needed to solve our urban problems (pollution), our scientific and defense problems (nuclear, atomic, molecular, biological, meteorological applications)?"

What Watson did was bring Clementi from San Jose to Armonk

for a personal explanation of why the machine had been canceled. In his deposition in the government antitrust case, Watson recalled, "I was impressed by his intestinal fortitude to write directly to me . . . in expressing his dissatisfaction with a corporate decision, and out of courtesy to the man and corporate morale, I invited him to New York . . . he was not fully satisfied with this answer, but I think he was flattered with the fact that I would take some time out to chat with him, and I believe that was the end of the matter, as far as Mr. Clementi and I went." As for Clementi's machine, it stayed canceled.

Whatever the solid business explanations for IBM's success, the observer who studies the company carefully is bound to conclude that business explanations go only part of the way. One encounters something else, something unique and preposterous and anachronistic and impossible to ignore. It is the IBM esprit de corps, an elusive quality emanating initially from the Watsons, which, like certain delicate wines, has been found not to travel well. That it exists in apparently equal measure among Ph.D.'s like Enrico Clementi (9 percent of IBM's domestic employees have postgraduate degrees), among those who service the customer's machines, and among the salesmen (whose gung-ho attitude is more predictable) seems particularly significant. In fact, it does not seem extravagant to suggest that IBM's business practices have been effective largely because of the spirit with which they have been employed.

IBM marries business goals with military style. Its celebrated policies toward dress and drinking—as well as certain other precepts and ceremonies that may seem bizarre to the outsider—become comprehensible when one remembers both style and purpose. That a salesman's clothes should not distract the customer from his presentation, and that it is difficult to demonstrate a complex piece of equipment after a three-martini lunch are sensible business axioms to which most companies would subscribe; only IBM has carried them out with a fervor and pervasiveness that attracts particular attention. It does so as part of a discipline that includes parades, spit-and-polish and a code of conduct becoming to young officers.

What the discipline suggests is that of a West Point–trained cavalry of the turn of the century, ready to charge up San Juan Hill. IBM'ers refer to their company as "The Business" in the same tone that West Pointers use to speak of The Academy (outsiders may feel disoriented, at first, when an alumnus working for a software house is described as having "left the business"). A salesman in a pink shirt—the same mufti that Tom Watson wore so elegantly on his sun porch in Greenwich—is like a lieutenant with dingy boots, a discredit to the service. The civilian who thinks the sole purpose of a uniform is to stifle the wearer's individuality underestimates the cleverness of the Watsons. In Scott Fitzgerald's World War I tale of the last southern belles, Ailie Calhoun falls in love with a handsome lieutenant garrisoned nearby. After the war the lieutenant, product of a northern mill town, returns to visit Ailie:

> His hat was green, with a radical feather; his suit was slashed and braided in a grotesque fashion that national advertising and the movies have put an end to. Evidently he had been to his old barber, for his hair bloused neatly on his pink, shaved neck . . . in these clothes even the natural grace of that magnificent body had departed . . . from the moment he came back into her world on its own terms he must have known it was hopeless.

IBM is not opposed to drinking, it is opposed to drinking On Duty. Alcohol is forbidden on company premises, and officially it is also taboo at outside functions staged under company auspices. Still, an IBM salesman can have a drink with a customer at lunch, although he is not supposed to visit other prospects in the afternoon. The reason for allowing him to drink at lunch is that good manners—and good sense—supersede abstemiousness. For the same reason there will be liquor at some informal hotel or restaurant dinners for outsiders: IBM recognizes that its guests grow thirsty at the end of the day, nor does it expect them to drink alone.

Many of IBM's mores are, of course, deeply rooted in the past: Tom Watson's great strength was as a renovator and remodeler. As an enthusiastic young couple might refurbish an old house, altering the façade and making certain internal structural changes to fit the rooms for modern living while remaining aware that no one builds walls like those any more, Tom took the discipline his father had used to build a successful company and adapted it to the needs of a new technological era. Among the principles and the techniques are some that are admirable and others we might properly question, but there is no doubting the skill that developed them.

The elder Watson was himself a synthesizer, and vestiges of his experience can be detected in the most cherished tenets of IBM.

Born in 1874, he had begun his career as an itinerant peddler, visiting the towns around his home village of Painted Post, New York, in a bright yellow wagon loaded with pianos, organs and sewing machines. His business was part cash and part barter, and he learned to make a shrewd bargain without losing the goodwill of the customer; he would, after all, be back again. He moved on to Buffalo, selling first sewing machines and then stock in a building and loan company; big-city salesmen were a rootless, hard-drinking bunch, and Watson, according to his official biographer, "learned the price they paid, and the instruction burned into his mind."

He also learned the importance of appearances from a well-tailored colleague named Charles Barron, who eventually made off with his employer's money. Watson was impressed with Barron's flair for grand gestures, his strategy of checking into the best hotel in town, buying and ostentatiously smoking an expensive cigar, and spending his last dollar to tip the bellboy to have himself noisily paged in the dining room. Many years later Tom Watson, Jr., addressing the Public Relations Society of America, observed,

> . . . why did IBM'ers wear blue suits and stiff collars? Simply because my father had the feeling that, if we could look the part of a successful corporation . . . if we could look the part of intelligent corporate businessmen . . . then we would slowly and inevitably become known in the eyes of the public as a smart corporation with intelligent, dignified, above-average personnel . . . and this, I submit, came to pass. Clothes don't make the man—but they go a long way towards making the successful businessman. . . .
>
> Long before we really had enough money to get off Broadway, we established an unusually fine showroom on Fifth Avenue. If we were to decorate a showroom today and use as much of our income to do it as we did relatively in those days, our Directors would tell us we were crazy . . . yet, we were again carrying the corporate image far out in front of the size and reputation of the corporation in order to increase the velocity of its growth.

When Thomas J. Watson, Sr. went to work for the National Cash Register Company, John H. Patterson, the redoubtable, eccentric father of modern salesmanship, was already evolving the policies which Watson, two decades later, would use to build his own company. A master at employing the carrot and the stick, Patterson was the first to offer his salesmen the security of a guaranteed territory, whereas other companies allowed their men to roam at will in self-defeating competition with one another; he satisfied their competitive urges by holding sales contests with diamond stickpins as prizes. He paid handsome commissions and originated the quota system, conferring membership in the Hundred Point Club on salesmen who brought in thirty thousand dollars' worth of business for the year.

As for the stick, it amounted to strict supervision and perpetual fear of dismissal, made vivid by the spectacle of a succession of banished colleagues. From his own boss at NCR, Watson learned the technique of "ripping a man apart and sewing him up again"; when a man was down you lit into him unmercifully, but then, because he could not do his job unless you raised his spirits, you got into the buggy and made sales calls with him, letting him benefit from your experience. To this day, that is how it is done at IBM.

The cash register business was a brutal one at the turn of the century, and no company was as rough as Patterson's in harassing competitors and intimidating customers. In 1912, thirty NCR executives, including Watson, were indicted under the criminal provisions of the Sherman Antitrust Act. Among the abuses charged to company officials were stealing competitors' salesmen, disparaging and even tampering with their machines, and the use of patent infringement suits to perpetuate their monopoly. The NCR officials were convicted and Watson was sentenced to a year in jail, but ultimately the conviction was set aside and a new trial granted because the judge had not allowed NCR to support the claim that rivals had infringed its patents. Before the second trial could take place, the suit was settled with a consent decree—which Watson refused to sign because he felt, as he would feel some forty years later, confronting IBM's own antitrust suit, that to sign was to admit guilt.

While the case was still on appeal, Patterson fired Watson—a few months before Watson's fortieth birthday. Cast adrift with a new wife and a child on the way, he decided that nothing less than greatness was in store for him in the second half of his life. Of the several opportunities open he chose the most obscure, because it offered him the chance to take over an unprofitable company—the Computing-Tabulating-Recording Company—and build it to preeminence, earning a portion of the profits for himself.

In 1914, when Watson arrived, CTR was a lackluster union of thirteen small firms that made butcher scales, time clocks and rudimentary accounting machines. It had 1,200 employees and annual revenues of $4 million. It was still a small enterprise in 1923, the night Watson announced to his family that he was changing the company's name to "International Business Machines Corporation." Young Tom was nine at the time, and thirty-five years later he observed, "I thought that this was a pretty big name for something that didn't impress me very much. But the name itself was another indication of the early public relations consciousness of the Corporation. ... The dignity of 'International Business Machines' opened far more doors than did the 'Computing, Tabulating and Recording Company.'"

Watson's task was to build esprit de corps among the ragtag, listless, suspicious rabble of employees he now commanded. To do so he drew on the techniques of Patterson, adding to these his own qualities of moral fervor and family spirit. He believed that "joining a company is an act that calls for absolute loyalty in big matters and little ones." Slogans, pep talks, rallies and company training programs developed that loyalty; a carefully engineered structure of rules, benefits and punishments maintained it.

As many now know, IBM spirit was kindled by song in the old man's time. Every member of the IBM family had a copy of the IBM Songbook, which, in its 1940 edition, contained forty-seven pages of fight songs dedicated to the company at large and to executives ranging from assistant secretary up to Watson himself. "Ever Onward IBM," the employees chorused ("Our products now are known in every zone, Our reputation sparkles like a gem"). One characteristic entry was headed, "To Professor T. H. Brown, IBM Board of Education, Professor, Statistics, Graduate School of Business Administration, Harvard University, Tune: 'Let Me Call You Sweetheart.'" It ran:

> Theodore H. Brown, Professor so well-known,
> At our schools in Endicott his seeds are sown
> In the minds of students of the IBM,
> Helping them develop into greater men.

The songbooks were a source of some embarrassment to Tom Watson, who eliminated them as soon as he could tactfully do so. By 1957, as one alumnus who had been Song Leader of his class at IBM Sales School later wrote to one of the trade publications, "They were collected very carefully at the end of each class, and we were cautioned not to talk of them to 'outsiders.' "

One evolving ceremony that originated in Watson's days at NCR is the annual Hundred Percent Club meeting, a three-day military parade for salesmen who have made 100 percent of quota. A mainstay of early IBM inspirational technique, it met first at various New York hotels (working up from the Pennsylvania to the New Yorker to the Waldorf as the company prospered) and then reached its baroque phase during the forties, when company warriors encamped in tents on the grounds of the IBM Country Club in Endicott, New York. The festivities included band music, displays of flags and fireworks, awards for gallantry in commercial combat, and endless St. Crispin's Day speeches by company brass. Those salesmen whose records were most heroic became officers and directors of the club and saw huge pictures of themselves displayed on the dais at the final banquet, which featured such pertinent guest speakers as Generals Marshall and Eisenhower. Gordon Smith, an alumnus whose enlarged 1948 likeness now gathers dust in his cellar, remembers, "There was surprisingly little cynicism. You worked hard to get in. If you hadn't made quota in late November or December people pitched in and helped you. When I was district manager I spent one Christmas driving through the snow in Grand Rapids, Michigan, to help find new business for one of my branches."

Today there are too many crack salesmen to fit on the old campground and ostentation is out, so the club has for some years been divided into several branches, which meet in convention hotels without fireworks. The branch managers no longer equip their men with striped blazers or straw hats labeled "first in district 3"—but in these sophisticated times the Hundred Percent Club pin is no less coveted a badge of merit.

Thomas J. Watson, Sr. had eliminated piecework in 1934, and in 1958 his son decreed that factory workers, like white-collar employees, would be paid a weekly salary instead of an hourly wage. While salary and length of service affect vacation time and retirement pay, other IBM largesse is distributed equally: whether the worker is an assembler at the Fishkill plant or John Opel himself, the company will help him shoulder the burdens of psychiatric care, root-canal work or adoption fees. The benefit program, however, follows the norm for major corporations: it would be bad form to outdo one's best corporate customers. But the stock option goes only to some seven hundred executives who, in Frank Cary's words, "have a material effect on the profit performance of the business." Of these about sixty also receive bonuses tied to the performance of their particular divisions, and the top dozen IBM executives get extra rewards commensurate with corporate profits.

IBM's employee education programs, which began in 1916, now cost more than $100 million a year, according to a *Business Week* estimate. At the lowest level, they enable the company to retrain surplus production and administrative workers for positions in sales and customer engineering where more manpower is needed; this helps to perpetuate a long-standing policy of avoiding layoffs, which is one good reason why there are no unions at IBM.

Whatever the position, IBM employees are perpetually being schooled. A new computer salesman receives some thirteen months of education, including classroom instruction, computer-aided study, and on-the-job training with senior salesmen; afterward, each man spends about three weeks a year learning updated computer applications and selling techniques. A less formal but equally abundant program of courses, lectures and seminars keeps technical people current, and the best engineers and software designers are rewarded with a semester of graduate level study at the company's Systems Research Institute, which has its own full-time staff and imports additional instructors from universities and industry. IBM'ers can even improve themselves after working hours through the company's voluntary education program, which includes basic computing studies and such how-to-cope courses as defensive driving, corporate and personal finance, practical psychology and effective speaking.

The most elaborate syllabus, however, is for the managers who will exemplify the IBM spirit and instill company values in the junior employees. With each promotion, the new manager gets a week at corporate school, and another week's refresher course is laid on every three or four years; among the curriculum topics are "people-managing skills," "IBM beliefs applied to current environment," "managing managers" and "translating top management decisions to employees." By the time a man reaches senior middle management, the courses grow meatier, covering the effects of political, social, economic and technological changes on the computer business.

The *crème de la crème* among new executives are treated to a three-week management development course which for many years was held at a lavish estate in Sands Point, Long Island (it is now given at a new corporate school building at Armonk). The course attacks business problems through case studies, lectures and operational gaming; as one graduate says, "You knew you were meeting the people who'd go higher. If you made enemies they'd stick with you. There was a bit of genteel aggression—you tried to be loose enough to be with it but not so free you'd jeopardize your career. Then of course the instructor was making notes on little sheets of paper, and it wouldn't do to have him say you alienated the whole group."

In all, the obvious purpose of the training program is to provide both indoctrination and opportunities for self-betterment. Mere attendance at one of the loftier corporate schools—for which candidates are chosen on the basis of their records—in itself suggests that a man has a bright future. But one ex-salesman points out another by-product of frequent attendance at corporate schools: "The training program breaks the cadence of being with your family. The people who do well at IBM learn to get fun out of problem-solving, not playing with their children."

To deal with the downside of this fun, in 1946 the company instituted family dinners at which wives could digest some company spirit along with the roast beef. One branch manager in the forties frequently dropped by the front porches of complaining wives to talk things over. But while IBM still holds a number of functions for employees' families, this sort of direct intervention would be frowned on today. "We have sensitized managers to the way their actions could be interpreted," says Cary. "Employees have a personal life separate and apart from their business life." At any rate, the company's gestures to preserve domestic tranquility are sometimes as effective as treating a compound fracture with mercurochrome. "By the time I left IBM," observes a not-unique alumnus, "I needed two divorces, one from the company and one from my wife."

As the senior Watson's era drew to a close, Tom junior began his revamping with the physical premises, calling in Eliot Noyes, the architect, who had done consulting work for IBM since the late forties. First Noyes attacked the corporate headquarters building at 590 Madison Avenue. "I was appalled by the total look of it," he remembered many years later. "The ground floor exterior showed the trademark thirty times on Madison Avenue. The showroom had a marble floor and Persian carpets and a coffered ceiling. There was oak paneling and those bumpy plastered walls you find in Italian restaurants, with corporate photographs and Think signs everywhere. When you finally got to the machines, they were cast iron on Queen Anne legs. It was absolutely schizophrenic—you thought 'who's running this, what are they selling here?'"

Noyes persuaded Tom that all IBM architecture, design and graphics should be "avant-garde and technological and precision and make you believe in it." From then on everything from computers to typewriter-ribbon boxes, booklets that explain corporate policy to employees, and "No Exit" signs was coordinated under the late architect's direction. In 1964, a corporate headquarters building, designed by Skidmore, Owings and Merrill, was erected in an apple orchard in Armonk, New York. The culmination of Noyes's new look, it is an austere white structure built around two Noguchi gardens. It reflects Noyes's order that "Nobody should say 'did they ever spend a wad of dough on that!'" In the eastern United States, the only IBM building that displays its wad of dough is the Saarinen-designed Thomas J. Watson Research Center at Yorktown Heights, a sweeping semicircular building of smoke-grey glass and local stone, in which advanced work on subjects such as crystallography and numerical analysis goes on. It was built when IBM was trying to increase its prestige in basic research and has always been somewhat isolated from the hub of corporate activity.

What goes on inside IBM's well-decorated rooms is more difficult to coordinate. In the elder Watson's time, as Tom later observed, the company's organization chart, had it existed, would have shown thirty lines leading into the chairman's office. Within a few months after his father's death Watson called his top hundred executives together for a three-day conference in Williamsburg, Virginia, which produced the more formal, decentralized staff-and-line organization typical of mature corporations. All subsequent reorganizations have been guided first by IBM's system of checks and balances, which plays group against group, turning natural ambitions and political interests to the company's advantage (this principle has unfailingly dictated separate engineering and marketing divisions in the main computer portion of the business). Within this rule, individual groups can undergo fission and consolidation, so that as the company grows it can be rearranged into manageable units reflecting the current technogical trend. A components division, for example, was born in the early sixties when IBM, in developing System 360, first began to manufacture its own circuitry; by 1972, when advances in large-scale integrated circuits dictated a closer alliance between components and mainframe development, this division was swallowed whole by the one that made central processors.

The map of IBM's divisions, being both ephemeral and complex, need not be drawn here, but a few important facts are worth remembering. The divisions are clustered into three Groups, and the vice-presidents who head the Groups are the ranking line executives in the company. The company's international business, which now accounts for more than half its sales, is carried on by two subsidiaries, the daughters of the old IBM World Trade Corporation, once the fiefdom of Tom Watson's younger brother, Arthur K. "Dick" Watson (who served as Ambassador to France and died in 1975). There is one division that doesn't make or sell computers—Office Products, which markets typewriters, copiers and dictating equipment—and an educational publishing subsidiary, Science Research Associates. Finally, there have been innumerable reorganizations within the divisions. Task forces are continually at work revising managerial responsibilities, and the organization charts are rapidly outdated.

Explosive postwar growth and the company's entry into the computer field brought in legions of technical men, math majors and physicists, city boys raised in the Depression and educated on the G.I. Bill. These men were, of course, attracted by good pay, enlightened personnel policies and the chance to work on the technology of the future. But oddly enough (and while they were sheepish about it), many of them lapped up the IBM spirit. "The first Christmas," recalls one of the initial batch of programmers, "I saw the lounge on the second floor all fixed up as an auditorium. On each folding chair was a piece of paper with the IBM song and some Christmas carols. Mr. and Mrs. Watson, senior, led the singing. I was sort of embarrassed to discover that all I'd heard was true, but there was tremendous warmth. Old Watson was tall and lean and impressive, and at Christmas he walked through and shook everybody's hand and thanked them for a job well done."

The comment tells much about the source of IBM's appeal. Even among the salesmen there are relatively few prep-school men in the corporation. Opel's father owned a hardware store; Cary's father was a doctor, but a small-town doctor who came from a farm and had worked his way through school. To many IBM people the company offered the chance to move up in the world. It didn't care who your parents were, and it taught you what clothes to wear, and some day it might get you a house in Darien. With all this, who could object to a few fight songs, which weren't half bad once you got used to them?

Whatever the shape of the organization, its beliefs are eternal. Their cornerstone is still a combination of security and fear. "It's a greased pole," says one former employee. "They move you as fast as they can until you slip, and then they see if you can come back again." One will probably never be fired, but one may be banished at any moment. "The higher the monkey climbs, the more he shows his ass" was the way Tom Watson himself put it.

Like the water in the pools of the Noguchi gardens at Armonk, IBM employees are constantly being recirculated. The official biography of Thomas J. Watson, Sr., *The Lengthening Shadow*, notes that "Watson believed in promotion within the company, and he developed a technique of firing within also, known as the lateral promotion—movement without advancement." Lateral promotions are as old as organizations themselves, and the term is now part of the common business vernacular, but the procedure has been finely honed at IBM. Because the company believes in developing versatility in its managers, it is not always easy to detect the significance of certain new appointments. As an example, some IBM'ers cite the prestigious IBM Fellowship, the highest award a technical man can receive, enabling him to "pursue professional objectives of his own choosing for a period of five years." If a man is under fifty, they say, the Fellowship is an honor; if he's over fifty, it's an honorable lateral. But they have occasionally been proved wrong.

An interesting career to study is that of Francis G. "Buck" Rodgers, the IBM vice-president with staff responsibility for worldwide marketing. For four years in the late sixties Rodgers headed the Data Processing Division, the marketing division, an elite group whose identity has remained sacred and thus intact despite the reshuffling that goes on around it. It harbors the phalanxes of sincere, persuasive, hard-driving young salesmen for whom the company has always been famous, and from whom its top management ultimately emerges. Almost anyone who worked in DPD under Rodgers will tell you there is no finer gentleman than Buck. He joined the company in Cleveland in 1950; between 1957 and 1967, when he was made division president, he received seven promotions. Then came four eventful, competitive years of heading DPD until he was removed, in October 1970, to a position on the corporate staff.

One of Rodgers's last official duties as division president was to officiate at the announcement ceremonies for System 370. A financial reporter had an early deadline and asked if he could see Buck early. "We'll bring him to your shop," said the IBM pr man, and on a sweltering summer afternoon Rodgers and the flack arrived at the magazine's offices. "It was a hundred degrees," the reporter remembers. "Buck appears in a winterweight pin-striped suit with a vest. The air-conditioning in the office is broken, and everyone is sitting around in limp rolled-up shirt sleeves mopping their foreheads. My editor invites Buck to take his jacket off; Buck says 'No, thank you.' So Buck sits there for forty-five minutes in his wool suit and vest and his impeccable white shirt and he doesn't sweat, not a drop."

Rodgers kept cool through most of 1970, as the 360 ended its cycle and the recession began to hit IBM. But by October, when the salesmen were running at 65 percent of quota, he was laterally promoted to corporate Director of Marketing. IBM is a civilized organization; one doesn't get one's epaulets ripped off for not making quota in a recession, but one understands the code. Was Buck, in IBM parlance, "sitting in the penalty box"? At the time, no one was quite sure; meanwhile, Rodgers held on, diligently pursuing his assignment to study the needs of the marketplace but lacking the power to "make things happen," resisting the opportunities to leave the company that had nurtured him and now kept him financially secure. Other IBM executives have been benched and returned; one can find such a hiatus in the printed biographies of most of the company's leaders, including Learson. What happened to Rodgers? In 1974 he was made a corporate vice-president, but having first suffered movement without advancement, he now experienced advancement without movement. The vice-presidency did not change his duties: even in 1980 he was still doing what he did in late 1970. Perhaps he exhibited the traditional failing of marketing men who reach their plateau: not "deep" enough. (The technical man tops out because he is not "broad" enough.) His career is not over, but one might assume that the vice-presidency was IBM's medal for a faithful old soldier.

Vice-presidents rarely lose their titles, and men who have topped out at a slightly lower level may learn another way in which IBM takes care of its own. When an important customer happens to mention that he needs a vice-president for information systems, the corporation will be glad to send him one—a highly capable executive whose IBM horizons have proved to be limited.

There are, of course, some outright demotions, and even a lateral may send ripples through the organization. When Buck Rodgers became director of marketing, the man who had been in that spot was reassigned to his old job. And after announcing that he welcomed "this opportunity to greet the men and women of the Eastern Region on the occasion of my return to the post of regional manager," he left to work for RCA. Generally, however, lateral promotions have delivered a clear message. One of the young men of the fifties, who often absorbed demoted executives into his department, recalls, "They'd tell me I was getting a man with great experience. They wouldn't cut salaries even if people weren't producing, so I'd have men working for me for much more money than I was making. All of us lived with it, and we thought, 'he's being taken care of, I will be some day.'"

In this climate of constant movement up, down and sideways, just a touch of fear applied directly can have remarkable effect. One young manager watched his superior under pressure: "I started to see little bottles of pills in his desk drawer. He was a big, athletic, hirsute man, and he developed the habit of twisting his watch around. After several months I noticed that all the hair was worn off his left wrist. Finally he asked to be transferred to a branch office out west." Indeed, as the IBM spirit stays with alumni long after they have left the company, so does the IBM fear. Many former IBM'ers will not talk with reporters at all; some are notably guarded in their reminiscences; still others require assurance not only that quotes will be kept off the record, but that their identities will be carefully disguised. And the apocryphal literature of fear persists. One alumnus who had risen quite high in the company told a reporter—in dead earnest—that Frank Cary keeps the heat turned off in his office so that subordinates will automatically shiver in their chairs.

There are two kinds of people in IBM; those who aspire to run the company and those who don't. The second category probably outnumbers the first by a small margin, and the men in it don't take pills or twist their watches. Living is easy for the physicist ambling down the Yorktown corridor licking an ice cream cone, the public relations man with red sideburns and a fuchsia tie, the ex-system designer who has resigned himself to an advisory position in Armonk. His work is at least fairly interesting; he is secure, well-paid and flush with benefits; he can take self-improvement courses, pitch horseshoes on the lawn at lunchtime, sign up for IBM Club charter flights to Europe, and take a vacation day in town with his wife without asking for permission from three levels of management. It is with these amenities in mind that one ex-IBM'er says, "You can talk all you like about paternalism. It's the first company that ever treated people like human beings."

The men who yearn to play a tougher game are concentrated most densely in the Data Processing Division where, recruited from the campus, they start as salesmen, serving their apprenticeship in the field and hoping to move to staff jobs in Armonk or at division headquarters in White Plains by the time they reach their early thirties; there, as one man put it, "never to dirty their hands again." They learn most about IBM through observing their superiors. "It's like standing in a movie line," remarks an alumnus. "You try to read the faces of the people coming out, to see whether you should cash in your tickets."

As the manager moves up in the organization, he tends to tie his fortunes to those of some senior man, emulating the model's political style and praying he has picked a winner. The job of administrative assistant to a well-placed executive is considered a plum, the best-placed executive, of course, being the chairman himself. George B. "Spike" Beitzel, one of the few well-born IBM executives, was assistant to Tom Watson in the early sixties. During his stint in the chairman's office, according to a former colleague, Watson and his own mentor, Al Williams, then president, had a fierce fight about Williams's joining Watson in signing the annual report. "Al insisted that his name be there; Tom said no. So Al threatened to take it up with the Board of Directors, and if the Board refused him, he'd resign. Tom bounced it off Spike, and Spike told him that he was wrong. So the showdown at the Board meeting never took place, and Tom was grateful to Spike later on for saving him from himself. After that Spike became the Renaissance man."

When Beitzel's fourth promotion in four years brought him the post of Data Processing Group General Manager, the executive directly responsible for IBM's entire domestic computer business, many observers thought he was headed for the chairmanship. But in 1972 Spike Beitzel's command was split in two and the commander himself reassigned to head a third, less important group of divisions. When the company chose a president to follow Cary, John Opel got the job, and while Beitzel is only slightly off-side, if he is still the heir to anything it is no longer apparent.

Even Tom Watson's younger brother was not immune to the misfortunes of battle. Dick Watson—who was even more volatile than Tom, and always overshadowed by him—had been given IBM's World Trade Corporation, the international arm of the business, as his personal preserve: the gift, which carried with it considerable autonomy, had been made by his father and was respected and maintained by his elder brother.

The early development of System 360 had been supervised by T. Vincent Learson. In 1964, the year the system was announced, Learson was moved over to supervise selling it, while Dick Watson was placed in charge of the considerable development and manufacturing operations that remained before the product line could be delivered to customers. Each man held the rank of senior vice-president, but it appeared (even to Learson, so the story goes) that if Dick performed well in his new position he would take his rightful place as Tom's successor.

System 360 was a gigantic undertaking which revolutionized IBM: it got the company into manufacturing its own components, and it changed the engineering and manufacturing operations into a truly worldwide effort, with overseas labs and plants helping for the first time to produce one product line for use in both domestic and foreign markets; it introduced the radical notion of compatible software for the entire product line, which put tremendous demands on the programmers; and it committed IBM to produce six central processors and a host of peripherals simultaneously. Moreover, in response to competitive action, IBM decided to announce System 360 early, further increasing the pressure on its technical staff.

Dick Watson had never brought out a major product, let alone an entire line; World Trade, where he had spent most of his career, had until then been a marketing and manufacturing organization without development responsibilities. Learson, on the other hand, while he had been trained in marketing also had experience in managing engineering and production. Critics of Learson suggest he set Dick up for failure first by abandoning production responsibilities at the crucial moment and then, with Cary's assistance, bringing in more orders than Dick's people could possibly produce. Dick's critics claim he was done in not by Learson but by the Peter Principle. The denouement came in 1965 when a series of crises in System 360 hardware and software made IBM unable to meet its full delivery commitments. At the end of the year, Learson was back riding herd on the labs and plants to push through the product line, and Dick Watson's desk looked cleaner every day. In 1966, T. Vincent Learson became president of IBM while Dick—a monkey who had climbed as high as he could go—was laterally promoted to the new post of vice-chairman, again responsible for World Trade.

The final word on the contest between Dick Watson and T. V. Learson is Tom Watson's, in a contemporary account of the 360 crisis made available through the government's antitrust suit. It is a draft memo written in October 1965 at the height of the troubles. The memo was not addressed to anyone; it was Watson's habit to write an occasional "memo to the files."

IBM's product development procedures are based on the fruitful resolution of strife between equals: the marketing side presses vigorously for features that will please the customers, while the engineers resist unworkable commitments; their differences are either resolved or arbitrated at a higher level. The original shift of Learson and Dick Watson, says the memo, was made when IBM began to lose too many orders to its competitors. Learson's strength was needed in the field, and it was thought that the engineering operations could use new blood. But, the chairman wrote, when Learson was forceful Dick caved in. "My guess is that we may have about a 20% overcommitment because we've said yes a few too many times."

Moreover, while Dick was good at giving pep talks, Tom Watson thought "his follow-up, his measurement against orders given, his total analysis of commitment or overcommitment, his expense analysis and the details that one would normally expect from an operation at this level, has fallen substantially below acceptable levels." Perhaps, the memo goes on, Dick was not adept at choosing and managing his aides; although Tom Watson admitted that "all of the criticisms that I address to AKW could well be addressed to me," he himself was surrounded by detail men who knew how to carry out orders. "In all cases, my ranting and raving are modulated by my associates and I have sense enough to, most of the time, not rant and rave in public. . . ."

In this memo, Watson himself bore witness that the tensions of corporate life made victims of many of IBM's best men:

> . . . We somehow have an organization that destroys more men than it produces at the upper end of the scale.
>
> McWhirter was a tremendous performer in the field and could easily have qualified to be President of the DP Division and would have done the job well. Somehow he got ground between the forces of division management and ended up a flop. Orland Scott couldn't be a better fellow, and yet somehow we ground him out of a top position. John Gibson, in retrospect, was an engineer-type fellow but not a complete flop, and yet our system ground him out. Andy Eschenfelder has lost much prestige, and yet when one stands back and views the job he has done starting a division from zero and developing a big manufacturing plant with useful output in a period of three years, one is forced to look at Eschenfelder with awe. Charlie De Carlo from many points of view is an outstanding executive. We have been unable to match a job with Charlie De Carlo in such a way as to make him a useful top executive citizen of the IBM Company. Anyone reading this memorandum can add many names to these.

It was one of Watson's strengths that he could, in dark days, subject himself and his company to the most rigorous, unsentimental and perceptive scrutiny. In the end, however, he could not bring himself to change either his own style or that of the organization. If IBM seems to destroy fewer men today than it did in the sixties, the change came not from above but from outside, and from below.

In almost every large corporation, men who move from the field to headquarters positions are often disheartened to discover that autonomy diminishes as one rises in the organization: a headquarters job is a team job, and every decision requires a list of signatures. "A branch manager in Houston has more control than the president of the Data Processing Division," observed one disillusioned former staffer after leaving IBM in the late sixties. Not only have a surprisingly small number of people held real power in IBM, but to make things worse, few have held it for very long. "The whole company is just twenty-five guys playing musical chairs," said this alumnus, who had been working on executive placement at Data Processing Division headquarters in White Plains.

During those years, the division's segment of the Executive Resource list enumerated seventy key jobs. For each job at least three men were listed in order of preference (in IBM language, "prioritized") should the man currently holding it somehow vanish. And of the seventy jobs, approximately seventeen were worth aspiring to: the division president, half a dozen vp's, ten directors. All of the more than two hundred candidates were competent; and the young personnel man concluded that survival in the upper regions of IBM depended on political skill. He was thirty-five; where would he be when he was forty-five? In the penalty box, like Buck Rodgers? Out completely?

During the late sixties a number of young managers began to ask themselves these questions and to decide the movie wasn't worth seeing. Wall Street, in those boom years, offered compelling inducements to think deeply about one's future, to go out and try to build something enduring—not, of course, another IBM, but perhaps a Control Data, a Scientific Data Systems, a Digital Equipment, erected on the principles one had learned so well in the best of all schools. And should the company one founded not work out, one could still escape. In fact even if one didn't found a company, other computer manufacturers were growing, and users were expanding their data processing facilities. And Wall Street itself needed analysts with a grounding in this mysterious, tantalizing new industry. There were plenty of places to go.

The Management Review Committee minutes for 1968 and 1969 show several discussions of "key people leaving the business." According to one source, attrition among sales and marketing people was running at 7 or 8 percent by 1969, an impressively low figure compared with other corporations but "two or three times what it had been in former years, and IBM was plenty worried."

Then came Bill Woerner's raid. James Ling, the Texas entrepreneur, had picked Woerner, IBM's midwest regional manager, to head Ling's new subsidiary, Computer Technology, specializing in facilities management. Facilities management—taking over a customer's data processing installation and running it as a concession—looked like the wave of the future. There seemed to be enough Ling-Temco-Vought money behind Computer Technology to keep it going forever, and a big deal with the Prudential was in the offing. Woerner collared one bright IBM manager after another, offering long-term employment agreements and other inducements that were almost impossible to resist. "He got some exceptional people," says one of the exceptional people. "It was the biggest attack on the IBM loyalty system that had ever been mounted. Actually, IBM held up pretty well. Less than a third of the men approached by Woerner went with him, but even that made nearly a hundred."

As IBM's men in the field sat waiting to be tapped by Woerner, the company revised its bonus plan and Buck Rodgers sent out a memo instructing any branch manager who learned of an impending defection among his men to sell hard the advantages of IBM, its success and its interest in people, without, of course, making any disparaging remarks about the firm the employee was considering.

Ultimately Computer Technology collapsed with the recession and the ill-grounded Ling empire, but Rodgers's instructions produced a new procedure at IBM: exit interviews at three levels. First, the departing employee's immediate superior and his superior's superior would test his resolve, stressing the problems in starting a small company and the inevitable scarcity of colleagues one could talk with on the intelligent level one was used to. If neither of these arguments proved persuasive, the boss of the defector's boss's boss had a go at him, ostensibly to ask what IBM could do in the future to keep people from leaving.

And finally, there was the ultimate formal interview. "You cleaned out your desk slowly, and thought about all your past gone," one alumnus recalls. "On my last day I went down to this guy in the rabbit-warren in personnel. He's got a checklist: you hand in your IBM identification, travel card, Blue Cross-Blue Shield. Then he asks you once more, for the record, why you're leaving. 'Entrepreneurial opportunity,' I said. 'How do you feel?' he asked. 'Great,' I answered, rather shakily. He just sat there, looking puzzled. 'Everybody loves us,' he said, 'but everyone's leaving.' "

What is most curious is that while all this was going on, IBM's management committees were talking of the need for substantial personnel cuts in order to trim expenses. Not only was System 360 nearing the end of its cycle, but unexpected trends in the leasing and purchase of equipment had brought about an uneven financial picture. Much value was being placed on the "healthy pruning of fat." The truth was that IBM could well afford to do without the number of men it lost, but it did not want the pruning done by Woerner or any other entrepreneur. That touched the vital issues of morale, loyalty and company spirit.

Most of the entrepreneurial opportunities in the computer industry vanished during the 1970 recession, and IBM itself cut its Data Processing Group by some twelve thousand over two years. It managed to cling tenuously to its traditional no-layoff policy, accomplishing the cuts mostly through attrition, keeping the hiring flat, instituting an early retirement plan, and transferring staff and manufacturing people (who accounted for most of the surplus) into sales jobs. But "if someone does quit," said a manager who stayed, "they're damned glad to send him off."

That recession ended, but the industry did not again offer the wealth of prospects for new ventures that it had in the sixties. Moreover, even the surviving companies no longer felt confident that an infusion of new managers enticed away from IBM was the best prescription for corporate doldrums. In 1971, ex-IBM'er L. Edwin Donegan tried to fortify the computer division of RCA with a substantial graft of IBM troops and techniques; the body rejected the graft, and Donegan brought down the division. There have been similar stories over the years; perhaps IBM'ers needed a decompression period before they could operate successfully on the outside.

The result of all this was that a safe berth with the industry's undisputed leader, a $70,000-a-year salary with benefits and the traditional amenities of IBM life began to look rather more attractive than autonomy, adventure and the increasingly outside chance of making one's million. And when external opportunity subsides, so does internal daring. One heard less about fallen heroes, and less about IBM destroying men.

In 1970 the criticism one might have leveled at IBM was that it was too prodigal with its talent: it hired the best young men; it bred and schooled them to win, then it broke them, or offered them too meager rewards. Now, perhaps, corporate life has grown too safe and dull. Certainly the company has changed some in the past decade. In 1968 the average age of IBM managers was just under thirty-nine; in 1980 it was just over forty-one. One can walk into a large urban branch office today and notice two striking things. First, the people gathered in small groups around the computer terminals— the ones whose snapshots posted on the bulletin board depict the full complement of the office—look different. Many of the men have facial hair; there are more women; there are more black and Oriental faces; the names are ethnically varied. And the branch manager— whose faith is unquestionably genuine—describes the IBM esprit de corps as the inevitable product of a world devoted to excellence and service to the customer, in which every employee's skills are "optimized" and matched to his duties while his goals are "prioritized" and his career path individually plotted, a rational world in which the mentor and the novice, sometimes stubbing their toes together, roll up their sleeves and ultimately solve the knotty problems, and no one is penalized for circumstances beyond his control. It is a seductive world, if indeed it exists. Still, one wonders what will happen to these new monkeys as they climb, and whether the time will come when the IBM esprit will seem as quaint to those within the company as it does to outsiders.

5

IBM: The Sixties

—

I

AT THE HEART of almost any discussion of computing is the machine's dual purpose. We have seen how the early development of the computer proceeded along two distinct lines, the scientific and the commercial, and while technological progress has enabled these lines to fuse, computer applications are still characterized as "blue-sky" or "bread-and-butter." Similarly, a company that produces the machines or their software hopes to be regarded as both "innovative" and "hard-nosed." IBM in particular, because of its feverish drive toward leadership, feels the pull in both directions; the corporate ailment is schizophrenia.

At no time did the ailment assert itself more painfully than in the early to middle sixties, when the company began its transition to maturity through the development of System 360, the most ambitious project it has ever undertaken and the one which shaped the future not only of IBM but of the entire computer industry for the next decade. In 1966 *Fortune* reported the total outlay for the system—an entirely new product line with associated peripheral equipment—as $5 billion over four years, $0.5 billion for research and development and $4.5 billion for the actual computers, plant and equipment; there is a chance that *Fortune*'s r & d figure, arrived at before all the work was completed, is too low. IBM emerged from the trauma with five new factories, half again as many employees, a components-manufacturing division which outproduced every firm in the semiconductor industry, a truly international development and manufacturing operation, and a multiplication of bureaucratic procedures designed to ensure that such a trauma, in the course of which careers were made and broken, would never happen again.

Despite all this, and despite the nervy decisions IBM made in circuitry and software for System 360, it was a bread-and-butter project, designed to solidify the company's dominance of the mass computer market. Initially, it was hoped that the system would satisfy the needs of both science and business, and only later did IBM discover that it had neglected to serve its most sophisticated customers, the universities and government laboratories that were hungry for products at the outer reaches of technology. Determined not to lose a single battle and yet indecisive about the commitment this one deserved, it came to grief by hurrying to close the gaps. There are two reasons for getting into highly advanced technology: one is that one hopes to ride the wave of the future, and the other is that one seeks to enhance one's prestige. IBM entered time-sharing for the first reason, and developed a supercomputer for the second.

In 1960 IBM engineers, having successfully launched the second generation of transistorized computers, were beginning to think of the future. The company had two engineering divisions, one with headquarters in Endicott, which made the small workhorse machines that served to introduce many companies to computing, and the other based in Poughkeepsie, which produced larger computers for commercial and scientific use. The two divisions were intensely competitive, and as technological developments enabled them to expand their product lines, each began to invade the other's preserve. At the head of both was the redoubtable Learson, who was beginning to think that IBM made too many incompatible processors, thereby straining the company's ability to produce software and peripherals.

Endicott was quiet during 1960, but Poughkeepsie was proposing a new series which would offer greatly improved transistor technology and might be brought out within the year. A brilliant southerner named Fred Brooks, who headed the division's systems-planning, was an enthusiastic spokesman for the new series, but Learson leaned toward the belief that IBM's next major investment should move the company into a wholly new realm of technology. Faster, cheaper integrated circuits, which packed several different circuit elements on a single chip, were becoming available; new peripheral storage devices allowed the user to summon the piece of information he wanted at will, instead of riffling through an entire data file; software men were devising "languages" not unlike English which enabled the programmer to speak more naturally to the machine.

Learson knew these developments heralded a wealth of new uses for the computer.

The first thing he did—favoring what is known in management jargon as "abrasive interaction"—was to move Bob O. Evans from Endicott to Poughkeepsie and into the slot above Brooks. Evans had come to IBM to work on the 701 and ultimately proved to be their most durable engineer. He was of the same mind as Learson, looking toward integrated circuitry and a simplified product line that would serve both science and business. Evans and Brooks interacted abrasively for several months, and finally top management killed Brooks's project.

In the fall of 1961 Learson organized a committee of technical experts to formulate a policy for IBM's next generation; the committee was called SPREAD, for systems programming, research, engineering and development. Evans and Brooks were part of the group, with Evans ultimately leading it, although the major technical contribution was to be made by Brooks.

The SPREAD report presented a plan for IBM's entire computer line through 1970. It took into account five factors: the new integrated circuitry, which promised more powerful, economical, and reliable machines; demands in the marketplace for "real-time" systems that could supply data instantly to users querying from many remote terminals; the inordinate current pressure, resulting from the large number of dissimilar computer systems, to produce applications programs for customers; the lack of any consistent IBM image in the marketplace; and the need to coordinate the requirements of the domestic divisions and the international subsidiary. The plan had to fit in with IBM's general business goals: a net growth of 20 percent a year in processors installed, and no widespread premature return of currently leased products (which would affect the timing of the introduction of a new product line).

SPREAD proposed a single family of five compatible processors ranging in size from that of the smallest stored-program machine then being produced by IBM to one slightly exceeding the largest. One line of peripherals would work with all the processors. The new family would serve both scientific and business users, as well as those who wanted to communicate directly with the computer from remote terminals. In order to meet the requirements for growth, the line would have to open new markets through the new applications it made possible.

Compatibility offered numerous selling points. The customer might buy a small machine with the knowledge that as his needs grew, he could graduate to a larger model with a minimum of costly reprogramming and retraining. Large customers could write and test programs on the big machine at the home office and then run them on smaller computers in divisions and branches around the country. Customers of varying sizes could share and exchange programs they had developed.

For IBM, a compatible family presented the obvious benefits of economies of scale: peripheral and software development and the training of field personnel would be cheaper and easier. Although the report concluded that "compatibility will not make IBM a materially better target for competition," it did note some competitive disadvantages. The opposition might design its products to be compatible with IBM's line, thus making inroads among IBM customers as a "second supplier" conveniently able to run IBM programs; competing salesmen, having studied one IBM machine, would be well versed in all of them; and the family concept would make it easier for competitors to anticipate IBM's future moves. The SPREAD committee also noted that a new family would be incompatible with current IBM products, a radical change which might anger customers; perhaps some means of transition would have to be provided.

Also, to avoid premature returns of current machines, the company would have to stagger the new ones, starting with the models whose predecessors were oldest. SPREAD suggested that the first machines be announced in early 1964.

Top management accepted most of the SPREAD committee recommendations with enthusiasm and set about organizing the project. Evans was to supervise the entire venture. Below him, Brooks was in charge of the design of the entire family and the building of four mainframes at Poughkeepsie; Endicott would do another mainframe, and the labs at Hursley, England would produce a sixth.

From the beginning, the magnitude of the project had made some people uneasy, and as the work proceeded the grumbles grew louder. The division which made small computers—and brought in two-thirds of the company's profits—felt its products had many more years of life in them and resented what they thought would be premature replacement; also, the need for compatibility with the larger machines was likely to drive up the price of that replacement. Then, just before the 360 project was launched, Tom Watson decided to move the company into manufacturing its own components, in order to protect proprietary circuitry and gain economics of scale. Creating a new components division alienated some of the engineers. Some technical people were unhappy with the choice of circuit technology, and finally, the salesmen feared that the pricing of the new line would result in lower commissions.

In December 1962 John Backus, the chief inventor of FOR-TRAN and a distinguished name in software, wrote a criticism of SPREAD, suggesting that a full line of compatible processors was too ambitious an undertaking, particularly when the architecture of the line was supposed to remain competitive through 1970. A month later, in a memo to Dr. Emanuel Piore, the group executive who headed the research divisions, Backus expressed the "fear that . . . our best designers and measurers may be so debilitated or fearful . . . in the current Gung Ho atmosphere, we may fail to reject deficient designs." He called for a "scientific discipline in which people could be judged by their creative powers rather than by their eloquence." Dr. Gardiner L. Tucker, the Director of Research, also wrote Piore, observing that the SPREAD assumptions about compatibility hadn't been adequately tested; decisions on the biggest venture IBM had ever launched ought to be made more systematically.

Watson knew that programming System 360 would be a difficult, important and expensive job. IBM had been spending about $10 million a year on software. SPREAD had anticipated a $125-million programming expense for the 360 line. System 360 would have an elaborate operating system, that piece of software which is a combination traffic cop, bus dispatcher and executive secretary, scheduling the jobs the computer will work on according to their length and importance and allocating storage space so as to make the best possible use of the machine's resources. Many of these functions had previously been performed manually by the operator at the console in the computer room; and while the notion of an automated operating system did not originate with IBM, OS 360 would be the most advanced software project IBM had ever attempted.

Moreover, the job was complicated by the need for compatibility and the programmers' unfamiliarity with the hardware. Software designers do not have the engineers' opportunity to test their ideas with a breadboard model: primitive versions of the program are either shipped to the customer or scrapped (many of the bugs in any computer program cannot be picked up in the laboratory; they must be found in the field, when the customer loads the machine with work and uses it in ways the designers have not envisioned).

All of these obstacles could have been predicted. What Watson and his executives had to learn from experience was the sheer management difficulties of running a project which at its peak would involve two thousand programmers.

It is worth pausing for a moment to look at these difficulties, since the problem of managing large software projects is widespread in the industry, accounts for many of the computer system failures and delays that one hears about, and is perhaps the greatest impediment to advances in computer technology. Fred Brooks himself— who left IBM after the 360 was finished for the more peaceful milieu of the University of North Carolina—analyzed these difficulties in a book called *The Mythical Man-Month*, which was excerpted in *Datamation*.

The scheduling of most software projects is based on the assumption that if one man takes ten months to write a given number of instructions, ten men can do the job in one month. But men and months are interchangeable only when a task can be partitioned among many workers who don't need to communicate with each other. It works, says Brooks, for reaping wheat and picking cotton, but "the bearing of a child takes nine months, no matter how many women are assigned." Many software jobs are sequential operations: first the specifications are laid out, then the code is written, finally it is tested and debugged. Even though the coding can be apportioned to several programmers, once the parts of the project have been coordinated these programmmers waste as much time talking to each other as the division of labor is supposed to save. And when new programmers are added to the project, some old-timers must stop work to fill them in; training is also sequential. In fact, Brooks says, adding more men can lengthen rather than shorten the schedule.

In many creative activities, Brooks remarks, one must face not only the inadequacy of one's ideas but the limits of the medium: "lumber splits, paints smear, electrical circuits ring." The programmer, however, "builds from pure thought-stuff. . . . Because the medium is tractable, we expect few difficulties in implementation; hence our pervasive optimism. Because our ideas are faulty, we have bugs; hence our optimism is unjustified."

Brooks observes that schedule slippage is due to "termites, not tornadoes. . . . Yesterday a key man was sick, and a meeting couldn't be held. Today the machines are all down, because lightning struck the building's power transformer. Tommorrow the disc routines won't start testing because the first disc is a week late from the factory. Snow, jury duty, family problems, emergency meetings with customers, executive audits—the list goes on and on. Each one only postpones some activity by a half-day or a day. And the schedule slips, one day at a time." When there is a small problem, the manager doesn't want to bother the boss with it; as the problem gets larger, he tends to soften the bad news. Finally, most bugs are discovered when the software is close to delivery, and other activities—hardware shipments, the preparation of the customer's installation—depend on having it ready. When the project is behind schedule anyway, a host of new problems descends.

"An omelette, promised in ten minutes, may appear to be progressing nicely," Brooks says. "But when it has not set in ten minutes, the customer has two choices—wait or eat it raw. . . . The cook has another choice; he can turn up the heat. The result is often an omelette nothing can save—burned in one part, raw in another."

Tom Watson began to turn up the heat in the fall of 1963. He did so because sales of IBM's larger machines had been slipping for the past year—partly because customers may have anticipated a new announcement and partly because they sought better equipment for remote computing. He made significant management changes at the highest level, moving Learson from development to marketing and bringing Dick Watson in to head development. Development and manufacturing were to be speeded up, and a traditional technique for achieving this end is to introduce new blood. Also, as we have seen, the crisis appeared to be in sales; Learson was a strong sales executive; and System 360 was moving into its marketing phase. This major change was accompanied by appropriate shifting of group executives, vice-presidents and general managers.

In December 1963 Honeywell announced a new machine called the H-200 which was a stronger competitor of IBM's then-current small computer, their most popular model, updated to deliver much faster processing for the same price. To compound the injury, Honeywell was offering a program called the Liberator which would adapt the customer's IBM-compatible software to run on the Honeywell machine with minimum fuss. As Learson wrote Watson and Williams, the Honeywell announcement was "even more difficult than we anticipated." He suggested some prompt enhancements of the current line, drastic price cuts, and an effort to move up the announcement of the small 360 model from its target date of March 1964.

The Endicott division was still against the small 360 model: it believed a greatly improved version of the old machine would be more effective against the Honeywell competition. But other IBM engineers devised a way to enable the 360, sacrificing some efficiency, to run the customer's old programs while he rewrote them at leisure. In January 1964, when Learson saw this "emulator," he came out for simultaneous announcement of the entire line which would offer customers a clear motive to wait for the 360. The various departments and divisions in the company were asked for their views. Opposition came chiefly from two departments—product test and finance.

Tom Watson had laid out strict rules for testing new offerings. His policy memo stated that "No new product will be announced for general availability to all customers, entered into regular production, nor delivered until it has been approved by an IBM testing department." Permission to waive this rule could come only from the Corporate Management Committee, then IBM's highest management group. In December 1963, a product test report on the small 360 model stated that announcement of this particular machine in March would be "very risky" for both the hardware and, in particular, the software. The earliest date to introduce this model with normal risk would be November 1964. The report did not specifically appraise the other 360 machines but suggested that their announcement in March would also be "very risky." On March 16, three days before the final management decision was made, the head of Product Testing delivered the department's official position of "nonsupport" for the proposed April 7 announcement, maintaining that a large part of the testing was incomplete and there were "known major problems" with the system.

IBM's lawyers in the government's antitrust suit state that "Product Test historically nonsupported EDP announcements offering significant advances over past offerings, and S/360 was IBM's single most significant announcement. Moreover, S/360's newness made the conventional testing function of the Product Test Department all the more difficult." An IBM software man who lived through the 360 observes, "Product Test hadn't done programs that much in the past, and nobody knew much about testing them. But it is certainly true that in any human organization that's under pressure the first thing that's short-changed is quality control."

Corporate finance also opposed the April 7 announcement: it felt the prices of the new line were too low, and the rush was preventing adequate analysis. Finance suggested various strategies to protect the machines in the field while meeting competition and earning an acceptable profit. Documents suggest the protest fell on deaf ears. One financial staff assessment delivered to Dick Watson in February contained the observation, "Believe it to be financially irresponsible to dive in without knowing the depth of water." According to a postmortem written two years later by Hilary Faw, the controller, "A hand-written note in my files indicated Mr. A. K. Watson allowed us only two minutes to make this presentation."

Learson describes it this way: "If we'd listened to the accountants we'd never have had the 360. Evans, Brooks and Amdahl knew they had a sound principle, compatibility, and bet their future and the company's future on it. They thought if we just did the first model all our resources would be put on that and we'd never get to a second machine. You had to announce all six models."

In the end, the decision to announce six processors and forty peripherals in April was a marketing one. As Tom Watson analyzed it in an October 1965 memo to the files, the company had been overconfident. "By '62 we were beginning to hurt in the field ..." he noted, "and by the spring of '64 our hand was forced and we had to, with our eyes wide open, announce a complete line—some of the machines 24 months early, and the total line an average of 12 months early. I guess all of us who were thinking about the matter realized that we would have problems when we did this, but I don't think any of us anticipated that the problems would reach the serious proportions that they now have."

The first crises occurred in components: there were difficulties with both the technology and the quantity. The minutes of two corporate review meetings held in February and March show discussions of components problems. It was hard to predict circuit reliability in the laboratory; failures showed up only when the machines had been running for a while. The circuits were enclosed in a coating of epoxy to protect them from humidity and corrosion; the epoxy contained a plastic which would swell and then break the connections when it was exposed to high heat. These normal problems of "scaling up" in a new technology would be compounded by the pressure to deliver an unanticipated volume of components in a hurry. The demand for circuit modules would double in 1965, and IBM needed more factory space immediately.

The manufacturing problems did appear during 1965, slowing production and at one point stopping it entirely; in addition, the operation was plagued by a series of materials shortages. It was at this time that Learson resumed authority over the plants and labs, which he operated in crisis style. Production difficulties were conquered by the end of the year, but deliveries of System 360 were behind schedule.

It was also 1965 by the time IBM began to realize the magnitude of the programming problems. The difficulties in managing the project were as Fred Brooks later described them. A post-mortem task force, reporting to Watson in August 1966, cited poor planning as the cause of the setbacks, observing that the programming department had not been brought into the planning of the 360 early enough and was then managed separately: "It started out-of-phase and still is." The promises the company had made for the software were too ambitious, because it had not measured which features were essential to the customer and which he could do without. Thus programming costs were grossly underestimated.

In March 1966 Tom Watson, addressing a meeting of important IBM customers, spoke frankly about the company's software problems and remarked that programming costs would run nearly as high as the tab for hardware development. A Watson memo of this period fixes the engineering cost of System 360 at $270 million, and the total research and development figure given to *Fortune* in 1966 was $500 million, which leaves $230 million for software. But it was 1967 before all the 360 software was delivered, and another two years before the programs were tuned up and running well. One IBM software man estimates that in all the company probably spent some $500 million to develop, maintain, repair and enhance the 360 systems software, including the programs that controlled the computer's operations and those that translated higher-level languages into binary code. Enhancements to that software which enabled it to run on the next product line probably cost another $500 million. Neither of these figures includes the numerous applications programs which IBM prepared to help the customer get out the payroll or keep track of inventory on the 360.

The programming slippages made life more difficult for the salesmen and systems engineers in the field, who needed thorough grounding in the features of the new line; and the customer education programs were widely criticized. Nonetheless, it is significant that in September 1966, at the height of the troubles, *Fortune* reported that IBM had shipped four thousand 360 computers.

This figure is most of all a tribute to IBM's marketing ability, through which it was able to hold on to its customers despite the direst of technological and management crises. *Fortune* observed that "The difficulties have done something to that extraordinary IBM mystique of success. The mystique is probably gone for good— although the successes may just go on becoming greater and greater." But one might quarrel with *Fortune*'s contemporary conclusion: the mystique had not gone; it was simply altered. Yes, IBM made mistakes; but it alone had the money to recover from its blunders and turn them into triumphs, and its salesmen could sell anything.

When all the anguish was over, System 360 proved to be a tremendous boon to IBM, and it is difficult to imagine that anyone in the company on hindsight would undo the decision to launch it. In the computer community at large, the 360 was thought on balance to be a good product. But IBM did not achieve the total compatibility it had dreamed of, and the effort to produce all-purpose software was often cited as the reason for the inefficiency of the 360's operating system.

Considerable soul-searching after the project was completed produced various documents that asked, "What did we do wrong?" Dean Phypers, a Watson aide, summarized discussions he'd had with Watson on the subject, reporting that "Random cries of 'out-of-control,' and 'can't do anymore' were coming from both the operating divisions and corporate staff during this period. They were not effectively communicated to top management. This problem in part must be attributed to the corporate atmosphere of 'it must be done.' " And a memo written by John Opel in 1966 declared, "Henceforth, we will instruct our people to avoid like sin a repetition of such a broad announcement and any announcement before its time."

II

In October 1965, when IBM seemed to be drowning in 360 troubles, Tom Watson wrote out his gloomy thoughts on how the company had come to be so engulfed. One of the failures he deplored was the roster of aborted executive talent we have noted. And he observed:

> I think there is a real question as to how often we can mold technical people into top management positions. My own guess is that this must be the exception rather than the rule. . . . In the first place I don't think they are gaited for the jobs and second, I don't think we really know how to evaluate them. I think we are looking at them more as good personality sales boys and measuring them against that kind of a profile rather than a technological management profile. . . . What concerns me is the prying of a man out of a laboratory directly into a top management position . . . they simply don't have the practice and background to think as sales and general administrative people do.

At the heart of IBM's operation is the tension between the technical men and the marketing men. It is a conflict basic to the computer industry and indeed to other high-technology businesses; it exists in various forms in all industries that merchandise advanced intellectual effort and creative talent, including, for example, films, publishing and even television. There are, of course, technical people in laboratories that produce cosmetics and breakfast cereals, and they also struggle with the businessmen in their companies, but the battle holds little romance for outsiders. When the product at its best has stature, however, it is this fight that helps to give the industry its color.

It is widely believed that IBM is particularly good at turning such conflict to its own advantage. But after reading the documents produced in battle, one hesitates to credit IBM with unusual brilliance in managing the struggles between warring factions. Things seem to go wrong as often as they go right, and if IBM is able to triumph in the end it is partly because individuals are bright, competent, dedicated and hard-working and partly because IBM has more money.

Watson's observation expresses the traditional view of IBM's top management and parallels the programmers' saying that "marketing is king, engineering is prime minister, and software is the court jester." The name of the company's highest management tribunal may change from time to time, but its roster never includes an engineer or a software designer; such men can aspire to be vice-presidents, heading the divisions and occasionally becoming group executives (no paltry honor)—but they will not get to the throne. Theodore E. Climis, who headed software development at IBM for some years, describes his specialty this way: "We are part of the shadow cabinet. Although we are in the mainstream, it is not always the critical path. That's because software is like a shoe on a horse: essential, but not major. Because of the high demand for programming talent, even the marginally competent can stay employed." (As new technology shifts profits from hardware to software, the programmer may come to dominate the engineer but this hasn't happened yet.)

Here is a young corporate staff man essaying pop sociology: "The engineers in the labs look like country guys. They have short socks and scuffy loafers and suits in off-colors, greenish or goldish. They eat lunch without their jackets. The programmers wear corduroy pants and sneakers. The marketing guy never rolls up his sleeves and eats lunch in his jacket. He wears wing-tipped cordovans. The wives of engineers are simple country girls. The wives of marketing men are status-conscious suburban females. Engineers might be right-wing Republicans; marketing men are moderates; programmers are liberal Democrats.

"The engineers are very status-conscious. You start as a junior engineer with four to an office. Then there's two to an office. Then one to an office. Then a door on the office. Then a bigger desk in the office. Then a wooden desk. Then drapes and a rug. The salesmen don't care so much because they're rarely in their offices anyway. The marketing guy wants true power, while the engineer wants outward symbols of it."

As the technical men move up in the company, they acquire more polish, but one could probably still walk into a room full of IBM people, spend a few minutes discussing subjects not designed to reveal a man's background, and separate the marketing men from the technical men. While the political distinctions made by the young staff man are debatable, they do suggest that since engineering is a more disciplined activity than software, its practitioners tend to be more conservative than programmers. But of the latter, Climis says, "They are a liberal-minded group and at the same time conservative. They are out to change the world as long as you don't change them. The community looks on itself as having goals above and beyond the interests of the company. They question their management; the best of them are aggressive and border on the obnoxious. The pecking order is informal, but it's there: it's more a case of peer judgment than credentials."

While technical men who get into the loftier regions of management sometimes end up in Siberia, it generally holds true that marketing men have power while technical men have security and freedom. When things go well for the technical man, he knows the satisfaction of seeing his product popping off the production line; *he* designed the ZILCH system or the x324 terminal, and no one can take that away. The marketing man's victories, particularly once he has left the field, are more ephemeral; feverishly he tries to *quantify*, gathering numbers and preparing graphs to show his alertness. Here, for example, is a 1969 memo from David Allen, then director of commercial analysis, to his staff, which was about to prepare the Quarterly Product Line Assessment, evaluating IBM's products in comparison with the competition: "We want to stress creative and objective analysis . . . every previous report has introduced new techniques of analysis and new measurements of performance. I expect this report to continue the practice of innovation. . . . Anyone can update a previous report; your job is to take a fresh and probing look at your area of responsibility with each successive quarterly assessment." One wonders whether it is possible to measure the performance of the same group of products in a new and still worthwhile way every three months, and one feels for the analysts.

The technical man knows his talents are unique, and he is hard to replace, and he can say what he damn well pleases. The marketing man is cannon fodder, and he must be very careful. When a technical man is angry, he raises his voice. Technical meetings are full of noise and bustle and profanity, but no one takes it very seriously. They may be fighting over whether a machine should be cooled by water or freon; "everyone knew there were water freaks and freon freaks," says an alumnus. Marketing men are building kingdoms out of sand; when they are angry, their voices get softer while they boil inside. A man who has spent time in a laboratory knows that some things just don't work, and the discovery that they won't work is also a valuable contribution. A man who has been a salesman has been trained to feel personally responsible for failures: it did not matter that the customer's son-in-law worked for Honeywell; a more persuasive argument might have saved the account.

At the lowest level, the technical man and the salesman see each other only when the salesman marches an important customer through the lab to give him a sampling of scientific marvels to come; the salesman is the magus, and the lab man is one of the entertainments he has conjured up, and they regard each other warily. Abrasion comes at the middle and upper levels. The technical man's point of view depends on whether he works in routine product development, charged with bringing out a successor to the tape drive, or whether he is in one of the groups responsible for looking into advanced technology. Ordinarily marketing is broadly responsible for revenues and engineering for profits, which means keeping costs down and not sacrificing the current line for the next generation. But engineers and programmers, particularly those concerned with advanced technology, may get their notions of future needs from papers read at professional meetings, and so they worry about what will happen five years from now; marketers study competitive loss statistics, and thus agonize over next Thursday.

The technical man may say the company must get into newspaper terminals, and he happens to have an excellent product on the drawing board; the marketing man has more immediate worries until some competitor brings out a newspaper terminal that looks like a winner, whereupon the marketing man tells the technical man to get the lead out, the technical man says the product isn't quite good enough to be announced, and the marketing man calls the technical man compulsive. In all cases they are fighting over where the dollars and the people ought to go; even at IBM, neither supply is infinite. Since IBM's personnel policy is to avoid layoffs, it cannot take on a swarm of extra employees for a promising venture with the intention of letting them go later.

Two kinds of tensions, then, attended the development of IBM's advanced technology projects during the 360 period: the corporate drive to win at both blue-sky and bread-and-butter applications, with the problem of striking a balance between them; and the personal tensions between technical and marketing men whose rapport with each other was inevitably flawed.

It seems right to begin the story of time-sharing with Andy Kinslow, who was, in Watson's phrase, "pried out of the laboratory" and deposited in a complex and alien business world. Kinslow was far lower in the ranks than the officers whose problems concerned Watson. The chance to design the time-sharing software was his first big promotion, and when the project, called TSS, failed it was Kinslow who took the failure hardest.

In 1961, the year he got into time-sharing, Kinslow was a thirty-four-year-old senior programmer in the Advanced Systems Development Division. ASDD lived on the border between blue-sky and bread-and butter, and IBM could never come up with a useful standard for measuring its accomplishments. It does not exist today.

Its mission was threefold. First, it was to develop and test products which would open new markets to IBM by using the computer in new ways. Often this could involve a joint effort with a particular customer, like a project under way with American Airlines during Kinslow's time to develop one of the first computer-based reservations systems. Second, it was to come up with new ventures in information handling which didn't involve special hardware; for example, the sale of data in particular fields like legal research, which the Division investigated during the sixties. Finally, it was to play the devil's advocate: if upper management felt the regular engineering divisions were not doing justice to some new product or technology, ASDD would be asked to take a different approach, and presumably, out of the competition would come the best solution.

Much of ASDD's job was to think up cures and then persuade marketing or product development that the diseases they remedied were worth curing; as soon as a project looked like a likely venture for IBM, it—and the technical and marketing men who ran it—would be transferred into the regular product divisions.

Because ASDD dealt in innovations, it is estimated that only one in a hundred of its projects ever reached the marketplace. Nonetheless, their developers would be passionately attached to them. Even those men who had entered the division believing themselves to be practitioners of science alone would have to acquire the skills of the salesman and entrepreneur to keep their projects alive, promoting a small amount of money to support their early research and a significant investment in the later development, negotiating for the best people in competition with other innovators, choosing the right patron in Armonk, White Plains or Poughkeepsie, protecting their dowries from erosion and their staffs from attrition. Sometimes their tenacity approached paranoia (when management of the San Jose ASDD labs wanted to kill a project for a computer-driven remote sign-painting gadget, it became necessary to build a brick wall around the equipment to keep away the engineers who had championed the project). Few individuals could endure this tension for long; the division had a high mortality rate.

ASDD's planning was influenced by the same technological advances that governed the development of System 360: faster, cheaper integrated circuits, random-access storage devices, and easy computer languages. What they added up to for ASDD was "on-line, real-time" computing. The airline ticket reservation project, SABRE— through which a ticket agent could query a computer three thousand miles away about space on the three o'clock flight to Chicago, reserve a seat instantly, and instruct the computer to reduce by one its complement of available seats—would be one of the first commercial real-time systems in operation; IBM had been working on it since 1956. SABRE, which wouldn't start operating until 1964, incorporated two notable technological advances: the ability to run several programs at once and the technique of running two or more computers at harness.

Despite the complexity of an airline reservations system, however, its needs varied little from day to day. The next step would be to put a large group of unrelated users on-line to a computer, one doing engineering design, another doing market research, a third processing a payroll and so on; both the roster of users and the requirements of each individual would constantly change, presenting additional design challenges.

Designers of on-line computer systems often envisioned a corporate board of directors meeting at which the chief executive or his secretary would hit a few keys on the terminal and the sales figures as of that instant would flash across a television screen. Kinslow, however, wasn't interested in executives' needs. He missed the satisfactions of earlier days when, as a programmer, he could "stick close to the console of the computer and plot my course by what happened there." By 1961, however, the programmers had to hand over their work, punched on a deck of cards, to the operators in the cool, glass-enclosed computer room. But for on-line, real-time, "conversational" computing, programmers like Kinslow would still have a terminal—the equivalent of a console—right in their own offices.

The most economical way to manage conversational computing was to allow a big machine to work on many users' problems for a fraction of a second each, moving from program to program and then repeating the cycle: thus, time-sharing. People are slow; computers are fast. Since the machine could make its rounds in milliseconds, the user would have the illusion that the computer was his alone. While certain hardware features could facilitate time-sharing, it was carried out mostly through software. In 1961 the technical community outside IBM was just beginning to talk about time-sharing, and within IBM a handful of small projects in ASDD and the Research Division were beginning to explore different aspects of the technology, even though the company didn't consider any of them very important.

Kinslow volunteered to head one of these groups. Like all the other time-sharing projects, this one would use second-generation equipment; the 360 did not yet exist. But, as in all ASDD projects at the start, if the experimental system Kinslow designed came off well and if a real market for the technology materialized, it might be the basis for a project in the next generation.

"I got a headcount of six people," Kinslow says, "and I started to round up a crew, painfully one-by-one. If you've been around you have a circle of acquaintances, and you talk to guys you know; your manager wants prestige, so he spreads the word too. You look for sharp cats with motivation who think the problem is big enough to leave their wives at night. My people had three to five years' experience; three of them didn't even have college degrees. Nowadays, of course, there's a fetish for master's degrees or Ph.D.s.

"You get everybody together and get up at the blackboard and block out how to do it. When you get something that seems logical, you divide the system up into pieces and everybody goes off and writes code. Then after about three months of this somebody says it doesn't feel right, so there are two or three days of arguing and you throw out half the code and start again. We did this about three times before we knew we were on the right track. Finally, after everybody's checked his own code, it's time to try it out on the machine, and you go in on Saturday morning at nine o'clock when you can have the computer all to yourself. Of course the system you designed doesn't work, and you have to find out which piece is wrong or whether it's all of them together. We ran it forty-two times the first Saturday and found a bug every single time—those were the easy bugs.

"During the week we'd get the computer an hour or two at a time. Gradually your system improves, which means the bugs are harder to find. You get five or six guys to play with the terminals using test data, and your people are in the machine room watching. It looks ok to them until one of the guys at the terminals comes in and says fifteen minutes ago it didn't work. The machine does half a million executions in a second, and in a fraction of a second it starts doing the same thing over and over—that's called a loop. You try to find the loop by printing the contents of the computer's memory. In the final stages it's really hard to find the causes of those loops. I would come home, have dinner, and go sit at my desk till 1:30 just staring at five lines of code. Finally you get it running, but it's so slow it's unusable, and you think here you've taken a million bucks and six people's time and thrown it away."

It took three years for Kinslow's group to get their small system—seventy-five thousand lines of code—working well in the lab, and during this period the movement for time-sharing began to gather momentum among technical people outside IBM. In October 1962 the Advanced Research Projects Agency of the Department of Defense set up a department to support research in information processing techniques. The first technique that interested them was time-sharing, and they launched a dozen-odd time-sharing projects across the country at universities, federal contract research centers, and research and development firms. MIT's Project MAC (a double acronym for Multiple-Access Computing and Machine-Aided Cognition) proved to be the leader in time-sharing research; Stanford, Carnegie Tech, the Rand Corporation and its offshoot, System Development Corporation, were also to do significant work. "It was obvious time-sharing would be big," Kinslow remembers. "At the Joint Computer Conferences there would always be a panel discussion on it, which played to standing room."

During the summer of 1963 Project MAC held a conference of leaders in the research community and representatives of the manufacturers. IBM assured MIT of its interest and cooperation, and MIT ordered a large second-generation IBM computer. But by the spring of 1964 it became obvious that MIT needed more sophisticated equipment to continue its research, and it called for proposals from the manufacturers.

IBM engineers made several visits to MAC to try to interest them in System 360; meanwhile, Kinslow was asked to help prepare the company's proposal. But as several memos suggest, there were both philosophical and technical problems. In order to get enough money from the Defense Department, the MIT project had to use equipment developed to serve its own approach to time-sharing; a 360 individually modified for this purpose was unacceptable; the features required would have to be incorporated in a commercially available product. In other words, MIT wanted its manufacturer to make a real commitment.

But time-sharing was a highly controversial subject within IBM. MIT was partial to a particular hardware widget that facilitated shuffling programs in and out of the computer's main memory as they were needed. To superimpose that widget on the 360 now would, many engineers and programmers felt, increase the machine's cost and slow its performance. Kinslow, of course, was among those who wanted the job done: to him, time-sharing offered a convenience for programmers that justified some sacrifice in raw efficiency. But the 360 engineers won: you could time-share a computer without MIT's widget, and IBM was not about to redesign the line to comply with "suggestions that required a great deal of baking." So IBM would not go far enough to satisfy MIT. General Electric, its leading competitor, felt differently and won the MIT contract.

Shattering news in IBM traditionally brings forth a task force and a barrage of memos. The 360 designers held to their previous position: they thought it would be difficult to design a compatible machine with the features the advanced time-sharing customers wanted; they feared the diversion of money and people from the main product line; and they felt there would be no avalanche of customers seeking the new technology. For the few universities who required it, IBM could simply add certain fillips to the regular 360 operating system.

The dissenters were people working on time-sharing projects and some technical men at a higher level in research and advanced technology. They noted that two important customers besides MIT had rejected System 360 and several more big accounts were now in danger, all because of IBM's delay in recognizing the importance of

time-sharing. There was more at stake than these few prestige accounts: IBM was ultimately risking all its computing business except,
as one advocate observed, "accounts where tradition or the superiority of the IBM sales force can overcome the fact that we offer an
obsolete product." The reason for this, he said, was that the real
problem in applying computers was the productivity of the programmers, a factor which time-sharing improved significantly. And once a
programmer worked in a time-shared installation, he wouldn't want
to work anywhere else.

Another dissenter said, "We have earned the reputation of being
hard to talk to. This must change." It was an issue about which A. L.
Williams, IBM's president, felt even more strongly. He set down his
views in notes that he presumably carried into a meeting. Williams
saw in the loss of the MIT contract a failure of IBM to manage the
conflicts between engineering and marketing:

> Because of the long confused chain of command . . . our people
> have not been able to be light on their feet in being responsive to
> customers. Our marketing people cannot make a commitment to a
> customer until they come back and first negotiate with a hardware
> division. . . . Where a hardware division would rather put the money
> and the people elsewhere, marketing has a prolonged negotiation
> while the customer waits and wonders. . . . There is no question that
> [the hardware divisions] being parochially oriented to their own P & L's
> rather than to the marketplace is slowing down our response time, is a
> source of undesirable in-fighting within the house, results in arguing
> and deciding who shall do what, and hampers the assignment of what-
> ever of our technical resources *wherever* they *may be* to the *best* solution
> of a given marketing hardware problem. (The italics are Mr. Williams's.)

But despite the enormous heat generated by the MIT loss, management found the arguments of the 360 designers persuasive and
nothing more was done to get IBM into time-sharing. There was
known to be considerable abrasion between the 360 engineers and
the leaders of Project MAC at MIT; perhaps the loss of the MIT
contract could be attributed to a personality clash.

It was October 1964 when Bell Labs chose GE. There was no
way to rationalize *this* loss: Bell Labs was, as one former IBM executive puts it, "the number one smart commercial user," and its preference for GE could not be attributed to the eccentricities of aca-
deme. Bell received several visits from IBM executives, ending with

a visit from Learson and Dick Watson, who sought to know directly why their company had lost the business. Bell's reasons were very like MIT's.

At last IBM was ready to act. A third big opportunity was coming up: a time-sharing system for Lincoln Laboratories, another MIT research facility, due in December. It offered a chance for IBM to recover some of its sagging prestige in the university community and to save some of the business that was wavering. Certainly IBM could not afford to lose this one too. And so Learson created still another task force, to handle the Lincoln Labs bid and solve the time-sharing problem in general. To head the group he chose Watts Humphrey, who had just won a competition for a Federal Aviation Administration contract in Washington, a tricky situation which had involved choosing which level of advanced technology to offer.

The task force reported directly to Learson and Dick Watson. It included technical men like Kinslow and the leaders of other time-sharing projects, and also the salesmen from the most critical time-sharing accounts. The engineering was fairly straightforward: a piece of gear called a Blaauw box, which performed the hardware functions of the MIT widget, would be hooked up to the 360 model 65 to make what would ultimately be called the 360 model 67. The software was more complex because it would have to serve not only Lincoln Labs but other customers as well. It was supposed to be compatible with the 360's regular operating system, so that the customer could do time-shared computing in the daytime and switch to the ordinary kind at night. However, in the winter of 1964 there was not yet a regular 360 operating system to be compatible with: the height of the software crisis, in fact, still lay ahead.

The strategy, as Humphrey wrote Learson, was to map out the most widely salable system possible within Lincoln Labs' requirements and deadline, and then to work further on the system as a general product; once Lincoln had accepted IBM's proposal, if changes occurred in the system design as TSS (for time-sharing system) became part of the product line, Lincoln would be persuaded to modify its specifications so that IBM wouldn't have to design two systems.

The task force worked late into the night and on weekends, and as one member recalls, "The technical man was king while there was pressure to get the proposal out. But I saw all these marketing types lurking in the background, and I knew that as soon as we got out of the proposal stage they'd bring in a whole infrastructure of marketing managers who would push down the technical men and then start making all kinds of extra commitments. I'm sure Andy Kinslow thought he'd have more control when he agreed to design the system. He's a direct, honest, plain-talking New Englander. But I also think he went into TSS a boy and came out a man."

After the Lincoln Labs proposal went out (IBM eventually won the contract), Humphrey organized the TSS programming effort. The project included some two hundred programmers, twenty of them helping Kinslow design the system and the rest handling coding, testing, documentation and other support jobs. In January 1965, TSS became an engineering division project. Trouble began almost immediately. Humphrey instituted a procedure called customer-aided design, in which members of the TSS team solicited suggestions from leading prospects. The University of Michigan, for example, favored a complex scheme called segmentation to handle the assignment of memory space; the head of computing at Michigan consulted for General Motors, and so GM wanted segmentation, too. Of course, the GE system that Project Mac and Bell Labs had bought had promised segmentation. But not only was it a difficult feature to provide, it might limit compatibility with the planned 360 operating system. Kinslow went out to Michigan to discuss the subject but the university was adamant, and Kinslow caved in. "They seemed so certain," he says, "that I thought it must be me that's nuts. I could see their ideas were good and they all fitted together. The only trouble was you needed the next generation of hardware to carry them out." It is, of course, questionable whether Kinslow's objections would have carried any weight, but he remained silent and the decision was made in March 1965 to add segmentation along with other features that customers were requesting. The additions doubled the original estimated programming costs of just over $8 million.

Documents suggest that as early as February 1965, the engineering division—which had opposed time-sharing and was now obliged to take on its development—was complaining that costs and commitments were out of control. The time-sharing machine and its software had not been formally announced, but IBM was describing it to customers in the hope of selling it as a low-profile response to those who requested it. But without an announcement it was difficult to freeeze the specifications, and pressure to announce the machine was growing. In May the head of 360 software protested strongly against any imminent official announcement. He observed that marketing had not formally specified what it wanted IBM to accomplish in the time-sharing software; that both hardware and software specifications were incomplete and many important customers disapproved of them; that field engineering had not declared itself able to maintain the system; that testing plans were not clear; that technical issues relating to compatibility hadn't been resolved; and funding for the project hadn't been defined. He would not object if IBM announced the hardware without the software, or if all the programming responsibilities were assigned outside his shop. However, he pointed out that even without time-sharing, the branch offices had more 360 orders than they could install, and that "The IBM workload in programming is not only growing at a faster rate than ever in history, but in a more uncontrolled way than ever before. This can only lead to the abrogation of commitments on a large scale in the years 1966 and 1967."

The 360 model 67 was announced in August 1965, for delivery a year later. At that time IBM expected to sell 107 systems (a system might include more than one processor), anticipating an astonishingly small profit of $600,000 on the central processor, or .009 percent (their usual profit goal is 30 percent), because model 67's potential customers were mostly universities, who received a substantial discount on their equipment. It was chiefly the discount which would lower the profit, and the figures show how highly IBM rated the influence of these university customers.

Humphrey says that at first the additional problems created by time-sharing looked reasonably straightforward, but at that time even the regular 360 operating system had looked reasonably straightforward. Besides apportioning processor time and main memory space among the different users, however, the time-sharing system had to prevent the greedy individual user from occupying too much auxiliary storage or monopolizing the printer; it had to protect each user's privacy; it had to know when the system was saturated and prevent additional users from signing on; and it had to do this without itself taking up so much space in the computer that the machine's response time would be slowed (to this day it can be an irritating experience to sit at a time-sharing terminal during peak hours; the widely touted illusion that one is working at one's own personal computer is fragile, indeed).

All these requirements sorely taxed the programmers, and since the rest of the programming staff was tied up with the regular 360 software, IBM had to hire two independent software houses as subcontractors. One firm botched its assignment. Schedules slipped and cost estimates zoomed: $29 million in October 1965; $44½ million in July 1966, the latter due to marketing's request for additional features and accelerated schedules.

In the beginning of 1966, Watts Humphrey had been promoted to head all software at IBM, including both the 360 system and TSS. He directed a review of all the company's commitments to eliminate the more impractical ones, and a new man was brought in to head TSS. In the middle of 1966, IBM announced an indefinite delay in the delivery of TSS; model 67 would be shipped with ordinary 360 software. In January 1967, it announced "a major decommitment of functions": IBM would work on improving the basic TSS software (the first of which would be shipped that fall) but many of the promised features could not be guaranteed for delivery, ever. Before the announcement, IBM's forecast had grown to 170 systems, for $388 million worth of business, enough to yield a small profit. Right after the announcement, nearly a hundred orders were canceled.

Fierce fights continued inside IBM. One report declared that the first software would be unacceptable to the user in both efficiency and stability, and that it was uncertain whether this could be much improved by simple changes or whether a major rewrite would be necessary. A substantially improved system could probably not be ready until the middle of 1968. Still, the company felt it could not kill the program without arousing further anger among customers. In the summer of 1967, it decided to limit the marketing of model 67: current orders would be filled, but new ones would require approval.

That summer Andy Kinslow decided he had done all he could for TSS and sought reassignment. The jobs that were available seemed unexciting, and so he left the company and has been an independent consultant ever since. As the system's designer, he felt—and still feels—that he was the symbol of its failure. A few years ago, he wrote:

Time-sharing was a very controversial subject at the time. As a concept it was strongly opposed by many people both within and outside of IBM. If you are *in* IBM, you are always a natural target for many people on the *outside*. So there were two groups waiting for TSS to fail, and the decommitment gave them a lovely opportunity to crow. . . . To this day I still get snide remarks from the university crowd.

With all its troubles, the time-sharing project did manage to hold some key customers for IBM, and a small group of programmers at the company's Cambridge Scientific Center designed a simple time-sharing system which others found satisfactory. Some customers decided to take the regular 360 software, to which a modest programming feature was added for time-sharing purposes. Still others developed their own software.

The GE-MIT system did fulfill its promise—but at a prohibitive cost, and only a handful were sold. For many years it remained the most sophisticated effort in the field. The time-sharing market is a healthy one, even though it did not grow as quickly as it was expected to, and some of the problems Andy Kinslow encountered were not adequately solved for a decade. Yet many companies selling time-sharing services use later IBM equipment which benefited from the work done on TSS. In all, IBM did not suffer acutely for its blunders, even though a 1969 forecast fixed programming expenses at $57½ million and showed a $49 million loss for the entire model 67 program.

Watts Humphrey, who now holds a staff position at IBM, is easier on Kinslow than Kinslow is on himself. "Andy was a technical designer," he says. "He had a small group; his forte was creative design work and he was good at it. He was not a hard-fisted manager, but he wasn't supposed to be." And in summing up the project, Humphrey observes, "As a technical man I'd say TSS was a success in teaching us a whole series of technical concepts. As a product developer, I'd say it was a very expensive education."

III

At NASA's Goddard Modeling and Simulation Facility in Washington, meteorologists are developing improved techniques for computer-aided weather prediction. Solar energy moves the molecules in the atmosphere; that motion, affected by the topography and rotation of the earth and governed by the basic laws of physics, causes changes in the weather. To prepare a forecast, the meteorologists divide the earth's atmosphere into a three-dimensional matrix grid. Weather stations on land, at sea, and in the air measure the temperature, humidity and wind velocity at each point on the grid and feed the information into the computer, which uses this data to solve equations derived from the physical laws. Since weather changes are the chain reaction of molecules jogging their neighbors, the solution for each grid point influences the forecast for the points adjoining it.

In the past decade there has been much improvement in weather prediction: a wider use of satellites has enabled meteorologists to gather data inexpensively over the oceans and deserts. Another refinement continually being made, however, is directly tied to computer power: the denser the matrix, the more detailed the information for forecasting. For today's grid, Goddard uses an Amdahl 470 v6 computer. This machine, which for Goddard's particular application performs ten million instructions a second, takes four hours to do one day's weather forecast. As this is written, NASA is procuring a new computer which will work ten times faster and complete a day's forecast in less than half an hour. Goddard will then be able to move from three-day to one-week forecasts. Not surprisingly, the appetite of meteorologists for computing power is virtually unappeasable.

There are only a few dozen such trenchermen—the laboratories of the Department of Energy (formerly the Atomic Energy Commission), some aerospace companies, universities and other institutions that do advanced scientific and mathematical research. Many were among the prospects for the Defense Calculator; ever since then, they have sought the most sophisticated and powerful equipment for computation, the machines the industry calls supercomputers—or even more evocatively, number-crunchers. While most of the leading customers for time-sharing were engaged in projects whose prime purpose was to advance computer technology, users like Goddard and the AEC laboratories thought of the machine simply as a tool for research in other fields; computer developments that sped them on their way were just by-products.

Supercomputer users make finicky customers. Their needs are expensive to satisfy, and the prospects of successfully doing so are uncertain. Since the volume of supercomputer sales doesn't justify the financial risk of producing the machines, other arguments must be adduced for entering the market. The two strongest are that supercomputer customers are prestigious institutions whose endorsement produces increased sales of more popular equipment, and that discoveries made in designing the advanced machines ultimately enhance the regular product line. Since the value of these factors is difficult to measure, the supercomputer is, for IBM and other mainframe manufacturers, an irritating problem that won't go away.

Time-sharing presented its greatest challenge to the software designer; the supercomputer is mainly a rigorous exercise in hardware. The goal is to gain speed through both the circuitry and the architecture of the system: one uses the fastest (and therefore the most advanced) components available and then one seeks the cleverest scheme for organizing them toward the peak of performance.

IBM's first supercomputer was STRETCH, a project begun in 1955 under contract to Los Alamos, with the intention of selling additional machines to other customers. The advanced circuitry used in STRETCH was second-generation transistors; the architecture was particularly ingenious. STRETCH incorporated a "look ahead" feature which, while the computer was performing one operation, examined the next instructions and set the switches for them, much as a secretary whose boss is on the telephone might look up the number and fetch the pertinent files for the next call he will make. But the job of looking ahead proved more complicated than it at first appeared: metaphorically speaking, the boss might discover in his initial telephone conversation that he needed to call Joe Zilch and Harry Green before getting to John Doe, whose file the secretary had thoughtfully retrieved. This sort of problem was not insoluble, but the solutions themselves consumed extra space in the machine, and some bottlenecks did persist. So the computer was slower than its designers had hoped it would be.

No one thinks STRETCH was a bad machine; indeed, it is widely praised. Still, the predictions for its performance had been optimistic; therefore, Tom Watson decided it was only fair to whack down the price. The cut he made, however—from $13½ million to $8 million—was sufficiently drastic to suggest that the machine was either overpriced originally or underpriced through panic later on. Whichever was true, Watson decided it was uneconomical to continue building STRETCH computers to sell for only $8 million; therefore IBM would produce these just for Los Alamos and the handful of other customers who had already ordered them. IBM had spent about $50 million on research and development for STRETCH (r & d representing only a portion of the total cost of producing a computer) and in all the program lost about $20 million.

Some years later Watson, talking of those development costs, observed, "A better fifty million we never spent, but it took us seven or eight years to find that out." At the time the program was killed, both the chief designer, Stephen Dunwell, and the executive in charge of it, Charles DeCarlo, had gone into the penalty box. Watson, recalling this, said, "Poor Dunwell had to crawl into a cocoon for three or four years, but I apologized to him publicly later." What caused Watson's change of heart? It was the belated understanding that STRETCH technology influenced the design of subsequent successful computers.

The supercomputer's difficulties flowed as much from the ledger as from the laboratory. IBM's accounting rules decreed that the costs of development and tooling up for a new technology—advanced circuitry, for example—were charged to the first product that used it; in other words, there was a penalty for pioneering. Much later, once the early product and its successors had been on the market for a while and the company was assessing their profitability, there might be a fairer apportionment of costs—but by this time, the first product might already have been withdrawn.

Because IBM's management rated STRETCH a disaster, large scientific computers became a low-priority item for the next two years, and during this period William Norris's Control Data did not sit idle. In August 1963, they announced the 6600, the most powerful computer on the market. The company had already produced some distinguished equipment; and its chief engineer's ambition to design giant machines meshed perfectly with Norris's belief that the only way to succeed in the computer business was to hit IBM where it was weakest.

A faction of technical men in IBM had been deeply disturbed by Watson's analysis of the STRETCH disaster. Many, of course, had worked on STRETCH, and their assessment of the episode as a noble and worthwhile pioneering venture was not entirely unbiased; besides, some of them found a project furthering atomic research a more elegant gig than designing payroll-processors (and the company one worked for was a classier company if it produced supercomputers). While this was not their sole motive for trying to push the company back into super machines, the word "prestige," so frequently used in arguments for the giant computers, did carry these implications.

There were also executives in upper management who silently agreed with the big machine men. And a committed supercomputer advocate was STRETCH-project alumnus Harwood Kolsky of IBM's San Jose lab. At the time of the CDC announcement Kolsky was on leave of absence and serving as a technical consultant to the AEC labs at Los Alamos. Shortly afterward he returned to IBM, and in a heated memo to Evans and Piore reported that his old friends at the AEC were asking whether IBM was coming apart at the seams. System 360 was geared toward the mass market—a strategy which in itself Kolsky did not criticize—but in planning it IBM had overlooked those "gold chip" users whose influence on the computer community greatly exceeded the actual profits they brought in.

Then Kolsky made a suggestion, couched in just the sort of language ("Only a bold stroke will save the day . . .") that would appeal to Tom Watson. He proposed that IBM seek a contract to develop a high-speed computer for the AEC. One version of the memo—which Kolsky, in his deposition in the Government-IBM antitrust case, identified as a first draft—contains the bluntly incriminating phrases "It should be deliberately done as a competition-stopper. . . . It should be deliberately done as a money-loser (or more tactfully, a shared-cost development for the benefit of the Government)." A second version of the memo is more refined: "It should be competitive and designed to get our machines back into our customers' future plans. . . . Profit should not be the sole motive and we should be prepared to enter into a shared-cost development for the benefit of the Government."

A week after Kolsky dispatched his broadside, Tom Watson made his own sentiments clear in the "janitor" memo mentioned earlier, the essence of which was that the ability of a dinky company like CDC to produce a machine more powerful than anything in the IBM line was a direct slur on IBM's virility. Soon after, Watson got hold of Kolsky's memo and routed the second version of it to a number of high-ranking executives.

In early September IBM held its annual meeting for top brass at Jenny Lake, Wyoming. It was an explosive session, as one alumnus remembers. "The salespeople were saying they couldn't hold the line against CDC. The engineers were bitching about our lack of advanced technology and the research people wanted more money. Tom just said 'I want a machine. I refuse to be second best.' When we killed STRETCH, we sank our flagship, but nobody liked to remind Tom of that."

Watson set up a task force to build a machine that would blot out the 6600. The basis for the new machine was Project X, an incipient supercomputer which had been struggling for funds; the head of the task force would be DeCarlo, now retrieved from the penalty box where he had been sent on the death of STRETCH.

The plan was to negotiate with two customers for a machine "rated at approximately 2.5 times 6600," at the same time the marketing division would "announce our plans to all of the other accounts in this market, describing in general terms what our intentions are and yet keeping the conversations regarding specifications on a range basis." It was clearly an effort to hold the line against CDC while the engineers tried to come up with a competitive machine. But the salesmen had a rough time of it: the price quoted by engineering was way too high, and the Gold Chip customers would buy only a machine made generally available as part of the product line. Nobody wanted to be a guinea pig. The 360 announcement was imminent, and the scientific marketing men wanted to include a paragraph on the supermachine, now called the model 90; but the problem, John Opel wrote, was "how to state to the public our plan to build a system whose specifications, price and performance capability is unknown." The statement produced was both vague and enticing:

> IBM is developing an ultra-high performance system Model 90. . . .
> The objective is to produce a system which achieves new levels of
> performance and is capable of operating efficiently on programs written for other models of System/360. . . .

Documents from the summer of '64 show continuing confusion about the specifications and price of the large machine. In June, a few weeks before the product was due for formal review, the president of the engineering division wrote his superior, "At this point in time, it is evident that we have no models of anything running and cannot, in my opinion, commit machine performance, machine size, circuit description or the like." In April the first two machines were slated to sell for $9½ million; by late June, engineering was talking about $4.5 to $5.7 million, with losses ranging from $39 to $56 million for the whole program, depending on how many computers were sold at which price. Finance dissented, because the program would be unprofitable.

In August, the head of Product Test sought confirmation of management's decision to announce without the usual testing, over his department's objection; presumably, he wanted to get off the hook. The answer he received was that testing had gone far enough to assure that the overall goals of the project had a "reasonable" chance of being achieved, and that the machines would be offered as part of a "reach" program significantly beyond the state of the art.

This "reach" program had been described in a White Paper a few days earlier. The paper advanced the standard arguments the big machine men had been making for years: the need to push speculative technologies for the benefit of the entire product line, to work jointly with sophisticated users, to make a delivery commitment in order to focus the development efforts, and to move ahead without determining profit in advance because of the speculative nature of the projects. The only odd thing about this document is its author, who was not one of the technical managers like Kolsky or Piore or DeCarlo, but Henry Trimble, then secretary of the company and its chief legal officer. Trimble's authorship suggests an eye on future antitrust problems, an effort not to make policy but to justify it.

In response to the continuing competitive challenge from Control Data and because of the usual technical difficulties that plague the omelette when the heat is turned up, IBM continued to respecify, redesign, rechristen and reprice the supercomputer, which ended as a series of machines under the general heading of "models 90," some of which were never completed. The company finally built seventeen machines and lost $126 million on the project. By contrast, Control Data sold nearly a hundred of its competing supercomputers—but their effort to match IBM's new announcements caused serious financial problems for the young company, and it sued IBM for antitrust violations.

IBM never solved the problem of the supermachine. A handful of giant-computer projects died in childhood during the late sixties and early seventies. The minutes of management committees show continuing squabbles between divisions over who should fund the projects. Task forces reported. Harwood Kolsky kept on writing memos. But the supercomputer could not be governed by the usual rules of marketing and finance; it was a complex technological challenge that had either to be embraced wholeheartedly or left alone. A long-range supercomputer project in IBM's research laboratories is now tackling the knotty problems of adapting the most futuristic circuitry to mass production. But for the present and near-future, the development divisions have been leaving supercomputers alone.

6

IBM: The Seventies

It is a common public impression, not discouraged by scientists, engineers and industrialists, that modern scientific, engineering and industrial achievements are the work of a new and quite remarkable race of men. This is pure vanity; were it so, there would be few such achievements. The real accomplishment of modern science and technology consists in taking ordinary men, informing them narrowly and deeply and then, through appropriate organization, arranging to have their knowledge combined with that of other specialized but equally ordinary men. This dispenses with the need for genius. The resulting performance, though less inspiring, is far more predictable.

—JOHN KENNETH GALBRAITH, *The New Industrial State*

I

IN DEVELOPING System 360, IBM had struggled to define itself. When that turbulent time was over, the company could direct its efforts toward consolidation, fine-tuning and orderly growth. The shareholders, the customers, and the employees could stomach no more turmoil for some time; there was a new product line to bring out, but the slogan for its development was evolution-not-revolution.

Certainly the company had learned from its 360 troubles: the organization was tighter, the checks and balances more controlled. These factors helped to make the development of System 3—a small computer hatched at the same time as the larger System 370 line—comparatively untroubled. The course was not always free from conflict, risk or setback, but it did invoke the successful, well-managed problem-solving for which IBM is famous. Also, some of System 3's success lay in the nature of the project: that is, it set a reasonable number of people working toward an unambiguous goal. Like any other company, IBM does noticeably better with projects that are small, crisp and manageable.

Mike Joyce was twenty-seven when he left the district office in San Francisco for Data Processing Division Headquarters in White Plains to help market System 3. As an assistant district manager he had been making $25,000 a year in salary and commissions; his new job would pay only $19,500 a year, and Joyce would be a product administrator, the lowest man in the planning hierarchy. Still, it represented a two-jump promotion, and he noted with some satisfaction that the other product administrators were well into their thirties. For five years, ever since joining the company in 1962, Joyce had been reading and executing the orders from White Plains and Armonk; now he would help create those orders.

During the two years he spent on System 3, Joyce developed a well-justified awe for the procedures of bringing a product to market at IBM, procedures which by 1967 had been laid down in loose-leaf notebooks four inches thick and distributed to all managers involved. He watched his superiors being shuffled and reshuffled and concluded that "you need one hell of a product to generate the revenue to pay damn good people to fight till they're bloody over a tenth of a percent, and the fighting over small differences makes the big difference between IBM and everyone else."

Joyce didn't start out wanting to make it big in business. His earliest ambition was to be a pilot, but after flying for a while, he got to thinking it was like driving a bus. Then he got a master's degree in sociology and planned to teach. But after marrying, he joined IBM as a systems engineer and soon moved into sales.

As he discovered a talent for selling, his pace and his values began to change. By the time the System 3 assignment came he had given up his sociologist's interest in the culture of IBM; he was too far into it himself. During his stint in White Plains "the demands built up, and so did the pressure to perform under them. I was very ambitious and running scared. My whole life became making System 3 happen, and other parts of me just died. Toward the end I began to realize that I wasn't having fun any more, that I didn't want to do this forever."

System 3 was already under development when Joyce arrived in White Plains. The impetus to produce it had come straight from Frank Cary, who had been chosen in February 1966 to head the Data Processing Group, the newly created unit which supervised the divisions that developed, manufactured and sold computers. Cary was thus the most powerful line executive in the company. "When I'd been in the job six months," Cary remembers, "I went to a meeting of the top thirty managers in IBM at our lab in the south of France. For a long time the World Trade people had needed a small computer system, and they put out an impassioned plea to the Systems Development Division to provide one. I got a direct assignment from top management to see that this was done. I found we'd had innumerable starts which had all been failures for the same reason— we'd never made our cost objectives."

IBM had emerged from the 360 period with a gap at the low end of its product line. Current customers could be expected to buy larger, more powerful machines, bringing in additional money for the near future, but even the most receptive computer user had an upper limit. IBM's customer list was a pyramid with, at that time, a large slice out of the lower middle. At the bottom were at least fifteen thousand customers who still used accounting machines, which now rented for about $600 a month. Many of these customers were ready for their first computer, but IBM's cheapest full computer system cost about $4,000 a month. The company needed steady infusions of new computer customers who, like skiers, oenophiles and antiquarians, would sink increasing sums into their new habit. Once these customers had taken the plunge with Univac or NCR, it would be much more difficult, even for IBM, to woo them away.

While Cary's interest gave this problem particular urgency, the Systems Development Division, home of IBM's development engineers and software designers, was also aware of it. SDD had its own staff of planners, financial people and marketing specialists. It also had Larry Wilson, an IBM Fellow who had been at the SDD lab in San Jose for the past three years, working on input-output gear. A mechanical engineer who died a few years after the introduction of System 3, he is almost always remembered as "a genius"; he held seventeen patents and had received several awards from the company besides the IBM Fellowship.

Wilson believed the way to produce an economical small computer was to build a machine that processed smaller punched cards. Such a machine would be more compact and thus simpler and cheaper to design and manufacture, and it would not require a $10,000 room-of-its-own with raised floors and special cooling. He and his assistants had come up with some preliminary designs which attracted the interest of Harry Tashjian, an engineering manager who worked for the small systems man in the SDD lab in Rochester, Minnesota. Tashjian got permission to set up a group in Rochester to develop Wilson's ideas, and in January 1966 the group went to work.

It was Tashjian's job to choose and fight for technical features—more advanced circuitry than was customary in small computers, and a dispensation from compatibility with the main product line—which later proved important to the machine's success. Cary backed him. "He came out to Rochester several times, and let it be known he was supporting us," says Tashjian. "When you're getting started on a new project, you have to compete with other projects. Cary stuck up for us so the project couldn't be killed."

By the end of the year Wilson had come up with an input-output machine which could read, punch, collate, print and sort cards in one pass without intervention from the operator. The cards it used were just over one-third the size of the traditional 80-column IBM card (they looked a little bigger than credit cards), but were designed to hold more information. SDD engineers had been working through much of 1966 to get System 3 ready for approval as a product in whose development and marketing several IBM divisions would participate. It would go to Cary in the spring of 1967. At this point, however, the marketing division balked. The familiar 80-column IBM card was an institution customers had cherished since 1928. Some prospective customers weren't novices; they had libraries of programs entered on the old cards which would have to be repunched on this weird round-holed mutant; moreover, the System 3 user, as his installation grew, was supposed to move up to a 370 (wasn't that what the project was *for?*) but the 370 had no device which accepted the small cards, and so the customer would have to repunch all over again.

Mike Joyce was called east in February 1967 to be interviewed for the job of product administrator and to participate in a sampling of field opinion on the prospects for the new machine. At various stages of a product's development it is customary to call in knowledgeable men from the branch offices to ascertain, in marketing lingo, "whether the dogs would eat the dogfood" (if the dogs really *love* the dogfood, sales take a quantum jump).

An SDD man explained that the company was considering a new computer designed for small accounts; what were the chances for success? Incidentally, the machine used "revolutionary new media." "The SDD man was so security-conscious that he refused to tell us what the new media were," says Joyce. "When we finally beat him down he announced the small card as if he were telling us Mary was no virgin. Marketing and SDD were both looking for corroboration of their positions, but neither of them got any real satisfaction."

It was then that Joyce was engaged as one of two product administrators who would draw up the marketing strategy for the new system (later, as System 3 neared completion, the number of administrators grew to six). In White Plains, he considered the amenities and discomforts of his new position: among the former was the personal stationery which is one of IBM's first managerial perquisites (since it has the manager's name, not the company's, outsiders often believe they are corresponding with IBM executives at home); in the discomfort column was a nine-by-nine office with walls so thin that Joyce, working till eleven o'clock several evenings a week, could hear the steady breathing and occasional cursing of his colleague next door.

Every new product, Joyce learned, went through three Phase Reviews before its announcement. The Phase Reviews were long meetings at which representatives of all the divisions that made up Data Processing Group and World Trade, IBM's international subsidiary, reported on their progress and stated their requirements. (Despite several reorganizations, the Phase Reviews continue and the principles underlying them are the same.) SDD delivered the specifications of the machine, the cost of designing it, the number of people involved, the schedule and a suggested price to yield the necessary profit. The Components Division had to agree that SDD's figures jibed with the price of circuits. Systems Manufacturing Division calculated production costs according to a "learning curve" which assumes that as the company gains experience in building the product, manufacturing expenses will decrease; the projected manufacturing figure therefore represents an average cost over the life of the product. Next Field Engineering reviewed the cost and ease of maintenance. Large installations had resident field engineers who kept their oscilloscopes at the site. The small customer would be serviced by traveling maintenance men, and the oscilloscope is a heavy piece of equipment to transport. This maintenance problem suggested a modular design for System 3, which would allow the service engineers to replace parts in the field, bringing broken units back to IBM factories for repair. For a low-revenue product like System 3 the field engineer was an expensive property. "Unless you made the machine very reliable you'd blow your costs and profits," according to Cary. "In the larger systems you don't have to optimize each portion so carefully."

Then came the turn of the marketing division. The marketing men, conceding that with development's specs, at development's price, they could sell fifteen thousand Systems 3's, might have gone on to say that if development would increase the operating speed and the memory capacity and add another language to the machine's repertoire, they could certainly unload twenty thousand. Those extra features, development might have countered, would jack up the price 20 percent, to which marketing would reply that at the higher price they could sell only seventeen thousand. Since small computer customers are particularly sensitive to differences in price, System 3 would have to make its profits on sales volume, economies of scale and long rental life.

IBM'ers rarely disagree: they "nonconcur." If nonconcurrences are adamant, the Phase Review meetings are repeated. Eventually the group executive, with advice from his own staff, adjudicates, and since most decisions are ultimately financial decisions, considerable power at the group level rests with those lofty, mysterious men who put all the figures together and decree prices (and thus profits and quotas). This power is far from absolute: finance's recommendations can be appealed to top management, and are often overruled. But financial data is closely held at IBM; moreover, the skills possessed by financial men seem arcane to the salesman and the engineer. "Pricing is a black art," says one IBM alumnus; another says, "Financial men? Like the Cabots, they speak only to God."

The black art, obviously enough, consists of balancing costs against revenues. Ideally, production costs should account for 25 percent of the price of an IBM computer system. Expenses (research and development, marketing and administrative costs) should take another 45 percent; and the remaining 30 percent should be profit. Executives of IBM's mainframe manufacturing competitors look at these percentages with considerable envy: they themselves must allow roughly 35 percent for production costs and 50 percent for overhead, and they are pleased to make 15 percent profit. They must charge lower prices to compete with IBM; and thanks to relative economies of scale, it can spend nearly twice as much on overhead as it does on manufacturing, which is what enables it to continue overwhelming its competitors.

The financial men's task is to set a price that's not too high and not too low. A machine is priced against the equipment it's replacing: one rule of thumb, for example, is called Grosch's law, which dictates that if you give the customer four times the capacity of his old equipment, you can just about get away with charging double the old price for the new model. (Changes in technology have sometimes altered this ratio.) In a rental business, "self-impact" can edge the minimum figure up: if the new machine is too inexpensive it may compete with IBM products out on lease which haven't yet made their profits, or impinge on other machines now under development. The black art gains complexity because it involves calculating the best mix between purchase and rental for a given product (and setting prices to encourage it) and estimating, with the help of the marketing men, how long a rented machine will stay in the customer's shop.

"IBM's Finance looks at profit as a cost, not a residual," says Paul Vilandre, an alumnus who worked on the pricing of System 3. Still, several factors can lower the profit of a product. Competitive pressure is one; another, which operated in the case of System 3, is the desire to get into a particular market. Finally, as the antitrust documents suggest, IBM's profit goal applies to a full computer system: at different times in its history the company has chosen to take a lower profit on the mainframe and make up the difference on the peripherals or vice versa. Since the recommendations of finance can make life hard or easy for both the cost-conscious engineers and the revenue-conscious salesmen, the aloofness of the financial man is not hard to comprehend.

It fell to Mike Joyce and the other product administrators for System 3 to help put together Data Processing's market strategy, estimate overhead costs and furnish the information for group staff's sales forecast. Joyce was part of what John Kenneth Galbraith called the technostructure—"those who, as participants, contribute information to group decisions." As an individual, he did not make policy—but men like Joyce furnished the ammunition for corporate battles among their superiors. "All I knew," says Joyce, "was everybody hated this computer; Guth, the director of systems marketing, wanted the big card; and everyone was scared of Guth."

But by the time the product reached its first Phase Review in the spring of 1967 Cary and his staff were already leaning toward the SDD small card position. Cary asked marketing to call in another group of field people to see, once more, how the dogs would like the dogfood. "There was a terrible lot of emotion on this issue," Cary remembers. "I opposed the big card because the forecasts for its success were wishful thinking. The marketing resistance to the small card was mostly emotional. I directed them to get the machine out with the small card and the cost savings in the initial design and later, if it was successful, we'd add big-card equipment."

Even after the first phase review and Cary's small card decision, haggling continued within the marketing division. One of Joyce's official duties was to persuade the company to offer an array of software packages designed to help System 3 customers in various industries make the most of their new computer. Applications software was controlled by Archie J. McGill, the division vice-president who headed Industrial Marketing; McGill, who had his own staff of programmers producing packages for a wide variety of computer products, continued to sit on Joyce's requests. This was a fairly typical IBM intracorporate dispute: if McGill claimed he had no money in his budget for the packages Joyce requested, he might use System 3's needs to increase his own allotment or persuade his superiors to charge the packages to SDD. At any rate, "he wouldn't fight us and he wouldn't join us," Joyce remembers. "It went on till the beginning of 1968. The forecasters in Group were pounding the table and we couldn't give them figures till we had applications support. Finally we had to do two forecasts, one with and one without support, to get a commitment from McGill."

The hassle over applications programs was also part of a larger problem peculiar to System 3 which paralleled the engineers' cost-cutting efforts. During the late sixties the price of an IBM computer included not only the raw hardware and operating systems but also applications programs and the company's systems engineers, who acted as programming consultants for the customer; IBM considered both services a marketing expense. The number of systems engineers varied from customer to customer, and IBM's critics claim that extra staff were laid on as an enticement to important and wavering customers to keep them in the fold. IBM supporters say that, on the contrary, a large installation, whose revenues justified the gift of several crack systems engineers, had enough personnel and sophistication not to need them, while the novice customer demanded all the help he could get. "In essence, you had CBS paying for Glitch and Co.," says a former systems engineering manager.

System 3 was expected to strain IBM's systems engineering staff to the limit, with the chaos of thousands of customers installing their first computers. "If you had to go out like a bee from flower to flower putting in System 3's your marketing costs would be exorbitant," Cary says. "Early in the game there was an effort to package the applications."

The first solution was a service called the Application Customizer. The customer filled out a questionnaire on his programming requirements; his answers were punched on cards and fed into one of IBM's computers, which produced documents and other aids that guided the user's own staff in coding. The second solution, Joyce's idea, complemented the customizer service: it was to bring the customers to the systems engineers instead of sending the se's out. The company would open Basic Systems Centers across the country, where users could go to gain working knowledge of the new products before they took delivery.

Much of the product administrators' daily work involved estimating marketing costs and supplying data for sales forecasts. They needed, for example, to gauge the average productivity of a salesman in small account territory. IBM can do this sort of thing with relative skill, but it is, one alumnus observes, "very educated guesswork at best. I would get figures by calling maybe twenty to forty salesmen and branch managers. A really thorough study would take ten years. Also, in a branch office the product you're working on is competing with a slew of other IBM machines for the salesman's attention. You have to pretend that all he's got to sell is your computer." Joyce and his colleagues came to the conclusion that the special problems of selling small computers called for a team of salesmen who would do nothing else; otherwise, a product that yielded such low commissions might get short shrift.

Joyce, Vilandre and their associates also knew that the marketplace would be scrutinized by the sharp eye of IBM's central intelligence organization, the Commercial Analysis department. Commercial analysis, which at the time of System 3's development numbered about forty operatives in the marketing division and their counterparts in other divisions, had headquarters in White Plains; until the government's antitrust suit put figurative klieg lights on the department, it worked not in secrecy but in obscurity. Its task, says David Allen, who ran the department in the days of System 3, was (and still is) "to track and evaluate competitive activity and potential."

Its interests were both domestic and international. Each major IBM competitor had its own shadow in Commercial Analysis: Honeywell clippings were funneled to the Honeywell expert. Teams attended all the major trade shows. "At the Spring Joint Computer Conference," Allen remembers, "you could walk up to the Burroughs booth in your IBM Badge and ask them about some new product, and they'd tell you they have six guys working on this and twelve guys on that and here are the software problems. You'd think how dumb can anyone be and you'd walk back to the IBM booth and see your guys doing the same thing."

The department's favorite source of information, however, was the men in the field. In 1961 it had instituted COMSTAT, a reporting procedure which required the salesmen to notify Commercial Analysis of all competitive wins and losses, and "doubtful situations" in which a competitor had a 20 percent or better chance of winning the business. ("IBM cannot afford to be complacent," ran the script for an audiovisual presentation to salesmen on the basic principles of COMSTAT. "IBM must know what competition is proposing. . . . The importance of each entry cannot be overemphasized. All entries fit together to form a pattern.") COMSTAT furnished the data for Commercial Analysis computations of IBM's market share in various categories of equipment—and thus became a bulwark of the government's antitrust case.

The department produced a number of helpful publications. Whenever a competitive product was announced, Commercial Analysis would send out a flash report explaining its significance, followed by a description manual. In the Quarterly Product Line Assessment, ordered by Cary himself, each of IBM's current and impending machines would be rated in relation to its competition—"superior," "equal" or "deficient"—and the annual best-seller list enumerated the top ten competitors' products. In addition, IBM'ers

could call on the department for special help. When a salesman discovered an account was in "doubtful situation" because of competitive bidding, he could ask Commercial Analysis for a report on what
happened the last time IBM bid against Univac.

While IBM has accused various competitors of industrial espionage, the industry leader itself has not been so charged; its dominant
position and antitrust vulnerability make the rewards not worth the
risks. Allen was enjoined from using a competitor's alumnus in Commercial Analysis until a year after the man had moved to IBM from
the competing company. Once, he remembers, "a friend of mine in
a customer installation got hold of a fat Univac presentation and sent
it along to me. I looked at the first page and realized it was their
five-year plan, and it hadn't even been marked confidential. I closed
it up fast and shipped it over to our lawyers, who returned it to my
friend."

By 1968, Cary had sent down his own executive assistant to head
the System 3 project. Buck Rodgers, president of the Data Processing
Division, dispatched his administrative assistant to be second man.
Guth was promoted to head the midwestern regional office. IBM
was expanding; the group was moved into a temporary rented facility in Mamaroneck. "I left my nine-by-nine office in White Plains
and two guys moved into it," recalls Joyce. "Our new offices consisted of little khaki booths in a building where they shut the heat off at
six o'clock. The whole team had somehow moved up one level, so
my boss's boss was now a director. The workmen barreled into his
office, moved the wall out one foot, put down a carpet, deposited a
chrome water pitcher, and were gone."

Finally, the marketing of System 3 began to move ahead. The
Basic Systems Centers were approved; Joyce's new boss was able to
persuade Buck Rodgers to force the issue of support from Arch
McGill. The product looked ready for announcement in December
1968. Then Joyce's boss announced he was going on a task force
which would meet near group headquarters in Harrison. The purpose of the task force was top secret, but the rumor was that IBM,
under the threat of incipient antitrust charges, was about to revise its
price structure and start charging the customer for systems engineering, applications software and training courses. A week later Joyce
received a call from his superior. "He told me to forget everything

we'd worked on for the past two years. IBM was going to *unbundle*, and we'd have eight weeks to do the whole thing over. I had better get right over."

The two-story building in Harrison now housed some two hundred men. "It was under heavy guard, and you needed a badge to get in," Joyce recalls. "At one time or another I saw every important corporate officer in that building. Sometimes the company would send over a big smorgasbord for lunch. All the normal channels were bypassed—you could walk down the hall and get an immediate decision. Damn near our whole office ended up on that task force, and I was working with people I'd fought since the start of System 3. I'd bet that small group accomplished more in two months than the whole company in two years."

Unbundling was a huge trauma for IBM. The "total systems solution" that the company had for years been offering its customers included hardware, software, education and training, maintenance (for leased systems) and systems engineering services. By selling the total package, IBM gave the illusion that services were "free"; the customer was unable to break out the costs of the individual components. The package dated back to precomputer days, and it had proved an inspired way to introduce customers to the mysterious new machine, calming their fears, furnishing skills they themselves had not yet developed, and giving them a warm feeling toward their supplier. The "free" education, training and systems engineering counsel was a cornerstone of what was called "account control": what the customer knew about data processing was the company line, and he planned his installation and upgraded it according to the suggestions of the IBM systems engineers who were ever vigilant for competitive intrusions.

If these services were a security blanket for the customer, they served the same purpose for the IBM salesman. Without them, account by account, life would be substantially tougher for the man in the branch office. Also, the customer might be exposed to all sorts of unhealthy outside influences: instead of paying for IBM systems engineers, for example, he might prefer to retain an independent consulting firm, and, as a 1965 corporate study which opposed unbundling had observed, "The outside consultant may recommend equally or more suitable competitive equipment." Worst of all, a host of new competitors, no longer faced by the bundle, might enter different segments of the industry: mainframers, for example, could safely produce black boxes, knowing that independent software, consulting and education firms would take on the burden of support services.

IBM had resisted unbundling in the past, but now it knew the government's antitrust suit was impending. Several private lawsuits were also in preparation, leaving the company vulnerable to hundreds of millions of dollars in treble damage payments. The IBM package could be considered a "tie-in sale" on which the courts would not look kindly. "Why do we unbundle?" asks a March 1969 memo written by a member of the planning staff of IBM World Trade. "Because we are forced to!"

Unbundling presented difficult logistic problems. IBM would have to decrease the price of its hardware. If it was going to sell its applications programs, charge for the time of its systems engineers, and set up a new consulting department which would undertake contracts for specific customer projects, what were all these services worth to the customer, bundled and unbundled? What were they worth to IBM? Would the demand for unbundled services justify retaining the entire force of systems engineers?

In the spring of 1969 one financial executive considered the prognosis for IBM's new service business so questionable that the company could not base its future plans on substantial revenues from the enterprise. Thus only a small reduction in the price of the hardware was advisable (IBM settled on 3 percent). Then the company had to decide whether to give rebates to customers who had purchased their machines outright (and had thus presumably paid for services they would no longer be receiving); and whether to cut prices equally for future purchase and rental customers. IBM wanted to price its equipment so as to encourage rental over purchase, but needed to be able to defend itself against the charge of discriminating between customers. In either case—unbundling or not unbundling—the company would risk ill will and lawsuits.

The task force, then, had much hard work to do. Joyce's job was a small part of it, and involved costing and pricing services which had never before been sold separately. Experienced systems engineers, for example, working on exotic military problems or doing sophisticated operations research for large corporations, made $24,000 a year and could command high fees; what could you charge for a novice, right out of college and receiving on-the-job training at a System 3 installation? Joyce spent two months working out a new cost structure for System 3 and other small machines, and was then promoted to corporate headquarters in Armonk. The unbundling effort continued for several months, until the decision to unbundle was announced publicly on June 29, 1969.

While the industry considered unbundling a historic event, it is difficult to assess its effects. The 1970 recession prompted customers with tight budgets to assign to their own staffs jobs once performed by systems engineers; but the systems engineers are still around, working the buffer zone between assistance to the IBM salesman in persuading a customer (without charge to the customer) and assistance to the customer (for a fee). One government antitrust witness testified that unbundling had encouraged users to "consider software as a product"—a psychological reaction which is difficult to translate into dollars. The software industry has grown since unbundling was announced, but there are other factors which may have contributed equally to its expansion. IBM had no trouble peddling its computers in what salesmen mournfully called "the new world," but the company did not take over the software and consulting industry: the same witness observed that the company was not a major competitor in software.

It had looked as if System 3 would be ready for announcement at the same time as unbundling, and some in the company wanted to announce the two together, offering the small computer as a forceful example of the new business practices. But the marketing division thought this would be the end of System 3, and lobbied to postpone the announcement till some of the hubbub had died down. Luck was on the marketers' side, because System 3 wasn't quite ready on June 29, and it made its debut a month later.

Following IBM custom, the computer was announced first in New York and then in branch offices; Vilandre remembers going down to Miami for the introduction there, at which the branch manager, wearing diapers, came up through the audience tossing out small cards. This uncharacteristic frivolity, he says, was meant to show that IBM could adapt to the less-serious small computer environment.

Overruling finance, Cary had chosen the lowest of the three

prices proposed for System 3. As a result, the machine symbolically broke the thousand-dollar mark, coming in at $945 a month for the smallest configuration but running most customers a few hundred dollars more. And it fitted neatly into 150 square feet of floor space. At the start it looked like a winner. Then it suffered in the 1970–71 recession, which hit small businessmen particularly hard, but later, when the economy rebounded, System 3 became IBM's all-time best-seller, with more than twenty-five thousand machines installed.

As for Mike Joyce, he had found the price of System 3 exorbitant for himself. He shared the disenchantment of many young IBM managers in the late sixties and began to think of different goals; first he simply moved to Xerox and then he dropped out of corporate life altogether, moving to Dutch Flat, California and becoming a minister of the Church of the Universal Masters. If his work at IBM had required extreme precision, "honing things to the last quarter-of-a-percent," today he talks of his beliefs with a haziness that seems directly opposite; this work, as far as one can make out, involves physical therapy and psychic healing. Having devoted himself ferociously to one hemisphere of the brain, he is now dedicated with the same intensity to the other. Still, Joyce's admiration for IBM—as a distant organization—has grown over the years. What he respects most about his former employer is its ability to resolve differences and the old Watsonian credo of "respect for the individual." His attitudes are perhaps the most extreme example of the ambivalence that many IBM alumni feel toward the company that nurtured them.

II

In October 1969 Bo Evans, one of the leading architects of the 360, took over the engineering division and with it the responsibility for developing System 370. For the preceding few years Evans had been president of IBM's Federal Systems Division, the unit that handles computer projects for the government, designing "leading edge" systems to meet the needs of NASA, the Federal Aviation Administration and the Defense Department. While some of the advanced features used in government systems would always be uneconomical for the main product line, the work in Washington provided a window on the future, indicating the directions in which computing would go as the technology moved forward to make new applications practical; the division had about a five-year lead on the rest of IBM.

The years in Washington had given Evans strong opinions about IBM's plans for the future. By the early seventies more and more customers would be talking long distance to their computers via terminals hooked up to telephone lines; the customers wanted it and the technology made it feasible. A computer would have to run an increasing number of programs simultaneously. The key to this was faster, cheaper and more copious memories, a goal that could be achieved through a combination of advanced components and sophisticated machine design and software. The newest semiconductors, combining several circuits on a half-inch-square module, offered high speed and twice the density of the old magnetic cores. A design feature called virtual memory could shuffle segments of the user's programs between the computer's fast, expensive main memory and the cheaper, slower disc storage, giving him the illusion that the main memory he had to work with was twice its actual size. This was the widget that MIT had requested in its time-sharing system five years earlier and which IBM had neglected to provide and tried to graft on later with disastrous results. Now advances in circuitry favored the introduction of virtual memory on the newer machines, but to work well it had to be the focus of both hardware and software design.

The night before Evans was to report to his new job, he had dinner with his predecessor, and they discussed IBM's plans for System 370. Evans was shocked to discover that once again IBM had not included virtual memory in the hardware design. They had considered introducing it in the 370, but there seemed no way to make it compatible with the software the customers were already using, and it was unlikely that these customers would accept another major conversion. And further work on the problem had been deferred when a divison budget cut was planned.

Moreover, the two large models that would kick off the 370 series were going to use old-fashioned magnetic cores, although the later small and middle-sized machines would offer semiconductor memories. In fact, the Components Division said it couldn't produce enough of the most desirable type of semiconductors before the mid-seventies, and so the memories on the two middle-sized computers immediately following the large initial models would incorporate a stopgap variety.

Within an hour after Evans arrived at his new office he had organized a task force to work full-time on a plan for getting virtual memory on the 370. He also began to negotiate for semiconductor memories on the whole 370 line. When the Components Division could see no way to speed up their schedule, he set up another task force to review current procedures and find ways to accelerate the production of the new semiconductors.

Both task forces were reasonably successful; it looked as if both virtual memory and the new components could be produced in two years, and Evans and his superiors considered holding up the entire line until these features could be incorporated. But System 360 was nearly six years old. It was reaching that point in the product cycle when orders traditionally slow down in anticipation of a new line, and the sales figures were beginning to reflect the weak economy. Both the customers and the marketing force had the doldrums, and as Tom Watson later told *Fortune,* "You have to keep feeding them new things to keep their morale up."

So IBM decided to introduce the first two 370 models as originally planned, relying on increases in speed to attract the customers. The technological advances that Evans had promoted would begin to appear in the subsequent, progressively smaller 370's. Meanwhile those first two 370's—the "vanilla 370's," as they came to be called inside IBM—would be redesigned with the new technology to produce what were known as the "fudge ripple 370's."

All these plans were further complicated by the appearance of two new classes of competitors. The first group, the independent lessors, had been purchasing significant numbers of IBM computers and leasing them to customers at rates way below IBM's own rental charges. While the lessors' purchases had brought money into IBM's coffers, the money came in all at once, creating a sudden bulge in the financial statement for 1968 which then deflated in 1969 and 1970, upsetting the shareholders, because IBM was no longer showing the orderly growth that comes from having most of one's machines on rental.

The second group of competitors were peripherals houses that made printers, disc drives, tape drives and memories that were compatible with IBM mainframes and rented for considerably lower prices than the IBM equivalents. In 1970 IBM got into a price war with these peripherals companies, and much of its attention was focused on thwarting them.

It was a difficult time. Between 1950 and 1969, the computer industry had grown at a rate of 15 to 20 percent annually, and believed itself recession-proof. But the years 1970 and 1971 were hard for all computer manufacturers. The recession happened to coincide with the end of the product cycle. Throughout the fall of 1970, the trade press frequently carried reports of smaller computer companies reorganizing (a tactic to stave off bankruptcy). Bright young entrepreneurs now sat alone in lavish, quiet offices with empty coat closets and no one at the reception desk, and often computer men calling old friends for lunch found that the number they had dialed was not a working number. In early 1971 the Association for Computing Machinery, the senior professional society in the industry, offered free seminars for out-of-work programmers at which personnel specialists gave advice on job interviews and resume-writing, a branch of expertise the programmers had never before thought of cultivating.

The activities of the computer lessors had forced IBM to plan in 1968 to introduce budget cuts in 1970, but its planners had nevertheless underestimated the seriousness and duration of the recession. System 370 was expected to restore the former rate of growth, but financially troubled customers continued to cancel orders and return equipment, and the introduction of the new line brought fresh problems. Users began taking a canny, consumerist approach to data processing. During the growth years, the newest computers in the showiest computer rooms had been status symbols for chief executives; now the bosses bragged to their peers about clever "downtrading," in which one more powerful 370 replaced two or more 360's. Some of those who didn't trade down returned their 360's to IBM and bought the same models from leasing companies at a sizable discount.

The recession also hastened a significant change in the overall character of IBM. In 1970 domestic earnings had declined, and only a zoom in net income for the international subsidiary enabled the corporation to show increased earnings for the fiscal year. In most years since then, the international subsidiaries have surpassed the domestic branch in net earnings and their requirements have carried increased weight in IBM's planning.

III

The strength of IBM throughout its history has depended on its men in the field; while they are not the whole story, it is they who have created the aura of superior competence, keeping the customers loyal despite unsettling announcements like late software and unbundling, and encouraging the user to follow the "migration patterns" that would please the ornithologists at Armonk (to be sure, the salesmen's information helps Armonk make its plans).

In 1960, when J. H. Pascal, the manager of the company's New York Financial Branch Office, was just an ordinary salesman, he had the best record in the company, and as president of the Hundred Percent Club he got to lead the gathering of six thousand of his peers. Now, in the company's opinion, he exemplifies the virtues it attributes to IBM field personnel as a group.

It is hard to disagree with that view. Pascal's manner is earnest and enthusiastic; he is knowledgeable, open and direct, willing to tackle any question, and he never looks at his watch. It is difficult to imagine anyone spending two hours with Pascal and not feeling disposed to order IBM equipment or sign on as a salesman in the New York Financial Branch Office, which sounds as if it provides the most satisfying work in the world.

What is atypical about Pascal is that despite his obvious ability he has been in the field for twenty years. While some IBM branch managers, particularly in smaller cities, are content to be the satraps of regional units, the usual goal of the crack salesman is to get to corporate or division headquarters as soon as possible, there to promote his ultimate accession to the presidency. Pascal has made it clear that he prefers to work in New York City, within easy commuting distance of his home in Long Island; he refuses both to uproot his family and to add the extra travel time required to get from Long Island to Westchester. He and IBM both accept the fact that he will never be a corporate officer; but there are enough branch offices in New York to ensure that the skills of a veteran will always be in demand, and that the veteran himself will continue to feel challenged.

In big cities IBM tends to assign a different industry specialty to each branch office; the New York Financial Branch, on Forty-second Street and Third Avenue, sells data processing equipment to banks and credit organizations like American Express. The bullpen where most of the salesmen have their desks is as cheerful as a kindergarten, with triangles of bright blue, red and orange on the wall and small groups of men and women gathered around computer terminals. The desks look surprisingly clean, and one might almost think the salesmen and systems engineers have not yet moved in. Branch offices don't bustle, because many of their people are out making calls. Ten years ago, according to Pascal, you'd have seen paper from floor to ceiling, but today all the customer records are kept on the division's computers in White Plains, ready to be summoned on the terminals. The contents of the library—manuals and technical journals—are stored on a few trays of microfiche cards.

"When I started as a salesman," Pascal says, "you'd have a list of prospects in your vest pocket, and you'd call on the prospects in your dead time. You'd cover the whole territory. A young, hungry salesman would walk into, say, the Downtown Athletic Club, and find the guy who ran the punched-card equipment, and tell him that for a certain price he could automate the billing and the food and liquor control. The man would ask you to do a study, and you'd go back to the office thinking, 'I've got a live one.' So you'd spend two or three days a week for a month working on this proposal, and then he'd come up with objections he'd never mentioned before, or he'd say 'I can't get serious now.' Today a good salesman wouldn't allow this to happen. What we do is called 'qualifying.' As I talk to you I say, 'If I wrote a proposal, would you be in a position to sign an order?' If you say you'd have to go to the president of the club, I'd ask if we could go together. I'd say, 'If we invest time in this, would you be willing to come to a demonstration or attend a seminar?' If I don't do this I'm going to go down a lot of paths that don't lead to a useful conclusion. I don't say, 'Will you order?' but 'Will you work along with us?'

"In my territory where the accounts are large, we don't make one cold call any more. We may knock on a hundred and fifty doors in the same company over a six-month period before anybody makes a decision. In 1960 I handled Citibank alone. Now it's too complex, there's too much going on. We have teams of two to five people and sometimes many more working on an account. In this branch office there are five different types of sales positions—an associate marketing rep, a marketing rep, an advisory marketing rep, a senior marketing rep and a consulting marketing rep. Which ones are on a team depends on the account, on the business opportunity. Whether the customer is large or small, the computer operations are important enough for the top executives to get involved. With a multinational bank like the Chase Manhattan, for example, we interface with their offices around the world. With a small company that does a million in sales, three hundred thousand dollars is a big decision.

"At least once every year the sales team on each account takes a few days for planning. We ask what are the objectives of this particular customer, what are the obstacles to his achieving his goals, how can we help overcome them, and what solutions can we offer. How do we support the customer—do we add applications to the present system or sell him a new system? There may be seventy different things we can do, so we prioritize them and develop a plan, assigning responsibilities and time frames to different members of the team. Then six months later the team goes away for a few days to some other IBM location, away from the phones, and we measure our progress. Along the way we try to do some of this with the customer—he should be aware of what we are spending our efforts on, and he may say we're barking up the wrong tree. The 'customer,' of course, is a lot of people in the organization. It may take three months, six months or a year to get an order signed."

Pascal believes that "salesmen are not born. Marketing skills are acquired and honed, developed and improved." But as to whether *anybody* can be a salesman, he says "Absolutely not. If you haven't the desire for skill in dealing with people, you'd better not sell. One of the most important jobs I believe managers have in a branch office is to try to be as certain as they can that each individual is doing the things that give him satisfaction and enjoyment, that the content of his job is such that he's bringing his strengths to it, not playing his weaknesses. Often we have to decide whether an individual has the ability for a particular job, and if we take the chance the man surprises his manager. In IBM we most often take the chance."

As computer technology has grown more complex, so has the training IBM provides for its salesmen and systems engineers. For the first year or year and a half, says Pascal, recruits are "in the *get* state. That is, we don't expect a lot of give or productivity then." New employees spend a week of orientation in the branch office, meeting colleagues, visiting a customer, and taking a computer-aided course as preparation for six weeks of classes in the fundamentals of data processing at the company school in Dallas. Then they come back to the branch and are each assigned to help one of the salesmen on the job for a customer. They spend a month applying what they learned in school and taking some more programmed instruction, and then return to school for a five-week class in virtual memory systems marketing. "The salesmen and the systems engineering trainees are in a class together," says Pascal, "where they develop a nice esprit de corps. They spend a lot of hours in class and then do case studies together at night and make presentations in the morning."

Both systems engineers and salesmen are encouraged to develop specialties—to become particularly knowledgeable about software or telecommunications or electronic funds transfer. "With sophisticated customers you can't command respect without some depth," says Pascal, "so we try to drill some vertical holes." Still, there are differences among individual salesmen: one will enjoy working on a long project while another hates detail and wants to be a generalist. The ideal salesman can talk equally well with data processing managers—who look for mastery of the technology and its lingo—and their bosses, the businessmen, who require layman's language and a feel for corporate goals.

It is clear, then, that IBM salesmen (and their counterparts in other computer companies) are no ordinary peddlers, a fact vouched for proudly by Learson, who did his time in the field during the thirties and forties; Cary, whose branch office experience goes back to the early fifties; countless IBM executives and alumni who sold in the sixties and seventies; and Pascal himself. His work has a high intellectual content and requires a fair understanding of the customer's business. But IBM salesmen are also known for their competitive zeal, and both the pressures of competition and certain ethical standards influence their behavior.

IBM employees are required to read and sign once a year a handbook of business conduct guidelines that deals with ethical competitive behavior, among other matters. The handbook notes that "large firms must bend over backward to avoid even the appearance of illegal or unethical conduct. IBM's policy, now, as in the past, is to comply fully in letter and spirit with the antitrust laws."

A number of practices—some of which are not overtly illegal and are permitted by the company's competitiors—are forbidden to IBM salesmen. They are not supposed to sell by disparaging competitors, either directly or by innuendo, even if the derogatory information happens to be true. They are also not to get business by trading on the company's size, success or position in the industry: they may talk about the quality of IBM's products and services but may not boast about how much it spends on r & d or the number of systems engineers throughout the company. They are particularly forbidden to discuss IBM products which have not yet been formally announced, and to attempt to delay a customer decision to order competitive equipment by hinting that a new IBM product is under development. If the customer is going to be a guinea pig for a development project, there are procedures which must be followed.

One rule which only IBM imposes on its salesmen is the prohibition against "unhooking," the graphic term for selling to a customer who has already signed an order for a competitor's equipment (once the Honeywell machine is installed, of course, it is fair game).

Other IBM strictures concern the different ways in which a salesman can legitimately give a customer preferential treatment. The 1956 Consent Decree requires that IBM do its best to fill orders in the sequence in which it receives them, but a customer can make a formal request for early delivery, which may be granted if some other customer has canceled his prior claim. An early delivery position is highly desirable, and customers often order machines before they are sure they will accept them, just to "get in the queue." During the middle seventies a good place in the queue became so valuable that customers were willing to pay as much as $100,000 to advance their delivery dates; other customers (and even noncustomers) would place early orders for the sole purpose of selling their places for profit, and IBM had to institute rules to forestall this speculation.

Before the Consent Decree, IBM salesmen used a favorable delivery position as a tempting fillip to keep an important customer happy. Today, delivery schedules are governed by headquarters and are out of the individual salesman's control.

In the various antitrust suits against IBM, it has been accused of breaking some of the rules. Both the government and Control Data (whose lawsuit was settled) have cited the marketing of the model 90 supercomputers before the specifications and prices were firm and any equipment had been built. (IBM's pretrial brief in the government's case describes the early announcement of the 90's not as "prematurity" but as "prompt disclosure" for the benefit of customers and competitors making plans.) If the government's claim is upheld, it will be a black mark against the executives who made policy on the model 90 and not against any one salesman. Most lawsuits against IBM have focused on corporate activity.

The trade press, however, has reported instances of questionable practices allegedly used by individual IBM salesmen: competitors have charged that bid specifications were rigged to favor IBM; data processing managers have claimed that after they recommended competitive equipment the IBM salesmen went to their superiors and criticized their competence or came to them and threatened to do so. In some cases IBM has denied the charges; in others, its management has apologized to the official and dismissed the salesmen in question. Charges of intimidation by IBM salesmen are part of the industry lore, but they are difficult to document. A 1973 *Datamation* survey of data processing managers concluded: "We found some questionable tactics that IBM uses to maintain its position, but none that are any worse than those used by its competitors. (However, there is the possibility that *any* questionable practices, when undertaken by a company with most of the clout, are measurably more effective.)"

There are grey areas surrounding the conduct rules. Even customers who have already signed with Honeywell can receive literature on new products; if they are interested, they write IBM requesting a sales call and noting that the Honeywell order is no longer firm. A salesman whose customer is leaning toward Univac might tip off a mutual friend who's dissatisfied with Univac equipment; the friend, if the salesman is lucky, will caution the customer against this error of judgment. Alumni of the branch offices do talk of circumventing the rules, but say that punishment is swift and sure if one gets caught.

Tales of rule-breaking multiply as one digs deeper into the past, when greater financial and emotional pressures were placed on the salesmen. Computer salesmen at IBM—and at all the other major manufacturers except Digital Equipment—work for a base salary plus a commission. The commission depends on the achievement of goals set by the salesman and his branch manager; these goals once consisted entirely of a quota in points, with one point for each dollar of monthly net revenue increase generated by a sale. Commissions would be geared to the percentage of this quota a man brought in. In recent years other objectives have been added to the point quota, such as adding new applications to the user's current system, or persuading certain prospects to attend seminars and demonstrations. As the industry has become more complex IBM has shifted its emphasis to long-range planning which will keep the customer in the fold and ultimately bring in the dollars.

The commission is the carrot, not much different from that extended to men who sell hats, books or lipsticks. But computer salesmen are also threatened by a most unusual stick, a negative commission called the "chargeback." If the customer returns a piece of equipment—whether it's because he's switching to Burroughs or cutting his data processing budget—the salesman must give back his commission on the original deal. In fact, a salesman having a bad year might exceed his commission base in chargebacks; the excess is then deducted from the following year's commission. New salesmen can be charged back or credited with commissions won or lost by their predecessors.

Branch office alumni recall that around October of a bad year, salesmen's maneuverings have grown elaborate. The story is told—perhaps apocryphally—of one marketing rep who, finding himself minus forty thousand points during a recession year, asked his manager for an increase in quota. He reasoned that forty thousand points would be a smaller percentage of a larger quota, and his chargeback would be lower. A salesman could buy some time—and earn half the commission—by obtaining a letter of intent from some sympathetic data processing manager. Things would get tricky, however, when the salesman was transferred: his successor would find "water" or "garbage" on the books (orders on record which he believed were not serious). Should the new man trust to salesmanship and prayer, trying to make the orders firm and get the rest of the commission when the computer was installed, or should he blow the whistle? A salesman of the early seventies, after explaining these gambits, observed, "Most salesmen are straight. When I found out I was getting promoted, I charged back all my garbage." A salesman of the early fifties remembered, "Finding garbage was part of the game. You kept your mouth shut and tried to build on your predecessor's business, and your successor did the same with yours."

Even without the spectre of the chargeback, a million-dollar computer system is a high-ticket item; the commission on its sale can buy a lot of orthodontia and piano lessons. Closing the deal can take months, even years of hard work, and there is a long time between initial order and installation. For this reason, IBM has gradually increased the proportion of the salesmen's income represented by straight salary. In 1971, the straight salary share in the marketing division was raised to 80 percent, where it has remained ever since.

Similarly, the current attitude toward chargebacks, as Pascal explains it, sounds more compassionate than in previous years. "We don't want to penalize a person for being in the wrong place at the wrong time," he says. "Sometimes we can foresee a loss of revenues for legitimate reasons, and we will protect the salesman by taking him off commission for a period of time."

The pressures on IBM salesmen are not purely financial. Especially in an office like the New York Financial Branch, which deals with large customers whose data processing operations are by now closely woven into the business, IBM rarely loses an entire account; rather, the customer may decide to bring in a second supplier, may give a new application or installation to one of the smaller manufacturers, may return some peripheral equipment and substitute a cheaper equivalent, or may decide to put someone else's terminals on a real-time application. The upshot is a loss review, at the branch, district or regional level, which could prove embarrassing for the salesman, even though IBM recognizes that the salesman's delinquency may not be the reason for the loss and the company makes a thorough effort to discover where the weakness lay. But in a company that makes so much of esprit de corps, the approval of one's peers is particularly important.

Salesmen don't usually get fired for losing one important piece of business, but if a man doesn't meet his performance goals for some time, Pascal says, he and the salesman will set narrower targets for a shorter period, and if the salesman continues to struggle, "We may mutually come to the conclusion that the job is a hassle for him, and a change of career is probably appropriate."

This doesn't sound much different from what happens in any

job, and Pascal points out that "a marketing person doesn't have to be right all the time. If they did, people would be too conservative and never take risks. There are a lot of stories about the stick versus the carrot in the old days, but IBM always preferred the carrot to the stick. The best people are motivated by the carrot." Despite Pascal's own benign managerial philosophy, however, many IBM alumni might disagree with his generalization, suggesting that IBM has never lacked managers who endorsed the stick.

Enough IBM salesmen have committed those ethical lapses peculiar to the industry to merit their mention, but not enough have erred to justify a major place in the lawsuits against the company. It may be that the growing sophistication of the customer, as well as changes in technology, the business climate and IBM's own policies, have reduced both the opportunities and the incentives for abuses at the branch office level.

"When I was a salesman," Pascal adds, "there was a tremendous thirst for material reward. The almighty dollar was your motivation, and success was measured by your earnings. Today the marketing people are motivated more by recognition, the personal satisfaction and challenge and rewards. Society in general has become less materialistic. But our people thrive on competition. In the old days the salesman was more entrepreneurial—he was running his own business. Now marketing people are more team players, and the team members motivate each other. The job is different, but I won't say it's more complex; that would be like comparing Jack Dempsey with Muhammad Ali. It seemed pretty complex ten years ago when I was doing everything myself."

PART III

THE DWARFS

7

How the Dwarfs Made Out:
The First Wave

DURING THE SIXTIES, IBM's leading competitors were known in the computer industry as the Seven Dwarfs. The dwarfs were easily identified by the products they sold and the way they did business, in a style which was, to varying degrees, set by IBM: they were the only other companies that marketed full computer systems (the mainframe, the peripherals and the operating software) for general business use, and their products were mostly leased, not purchased. Ranked according to each one's share of the dollar value of computer systems installed worldwide in 1967, the dwarfs were Sperry Rand, Control Data Corporation, Honeywell, RCA, NCR, General Electric and Burroughs. (In 1952, when IBM entered the computer business, its total sales were dwarfed by those of two of the dwarfs: GE had annual revenues eight times as large, and RCA's sales were more than double IBM's.)

From 1970 on, the roster began to change. General Electric and then RCA left the computer business; their places were filled by Xerox, which bought the only large mainframe company outside the group, and Digital Equipment Corporation, the leading manufacturer of minicomputers, which served a different market. In 1975 Xerox bowed out and the "dwarf" sobriquet fell into disuse; there were only six left, and Digital was somewhat different from the others, but "dwarfs" is still a handy and graphic term for these companies, which stand out clearly among others in the industry. DEC and its competitors have since entered each other's markets; in 1979, in fact, Digital Equipment's computer business was bigger than Honeywell's. Each of the dwarfs is a small IBM, with some parts of its body still more developed than others.

The dwarfs—past and present—divide conveniently into two

groups, those that existed before the computer was invented and those that are creatures of the computer era. This chapter will cover the surviving dwarfs in the first group, Sperry, Honeywell, Burroughs and NCR; chapter 8 will show how RCA ran aground; and chapter 9 will deal with the computer-era dwarfs, Control Data, Digital Equipment, and the company that Xerox bought.

For many years the dwarfs had to scramble for survival. IBM was seen as their only significant opponent: to compete with its powerful mystique, they had to offer either equal performance for a lower price or better performance for the same price. They had to spend heavily to provide the IBM-style bundle of peripherals, software, systems engineering support and maintenance, but they earned far lower revenues to pay for the investment; and even that small income was deferred by the obligation to lease the equipment.

The dwarf customer sacrificed lavish support for lower costs or technological superiority. IBM's support was both material—more systems and maintenance engineers and applications programs—and psychological—choosing the dominant company left the data processing manager less vulnerable to his boss's criticism when things went wrong. The harried dwarf salesmen countered this by establishing personal rapport with the customer; some dwarf users found IBM cold and arrogant. An RCA branch manager called his style "belly-to-belly selling," which at best meant a more direct approach to the customer's particular data processing needs; at worst it gave rise to the sort of situation recounted by the RCA man:

> I would go into a high-level call with a seventy-five-thousand-dollar-a-year executive and the first thing he would say would be, 'My tv set broke down, what can you do?' Once the chief financial officer of a big corporation called and said his tube was down. I drove up to Scarsdale at midnight in a rented station wagon with his tube in a big carton. He saved twenty bucks on the tube and it cost us forty bucks to get it to him. I could never afford the luxury of being immune to unreasonable requests.

In this group of four dwarfs, the first to show a profit on its worldwide computer operations was Sperry Rand, in 1966; the last was NCR, in 1973. The goal of each dwarf was to secure a large enough customer base to support its research, development and marketing. Because of their heavy investment in programming, customers tend to stay loyal to their traditional supplier as long as he makes no dreadful mistakes. As the customer's edp spending grows, so does the supplier's income. Competition arises when a user is installing some new application that needn't be tied into his regular data processing operations, or for customers buying their first computers. IBM still sets the industry standard; when it brings out a new line, the dwarfs have to respond because unsatisfied dwarf customers can still fall into IBM's lap. But many industry observers believe that the dwarfs are mostly competing with each other. Customers fall into two groups: the dedicated IBM users who wouldn't dream of buying from another vendor, and those who are inclined to be more adventurous. The dwarfs fight each other for these.

In the middle seventies, however, fresh competitors began to challenge both IBM and the dwarfs. Several new companies offered so-called plug-compatible mainframes, which used IBM software and IBM or independent peripherals, and gave the IBM customer better performance at a lower price. In a limited way these companies fought the dwarfs directly for the seducible IBM users; much worse, IBM itself hurried to market with improved products and cut prices, forcing the dwarfs to keep up with its faster pace. The minicomputer manufacturers were also becoming a challenge.

After following different paths the dwarfs in this chapter have become increasingly alike in recent years, but even in their origins lies a pattern for the growth of the industry which developed under the shade of IBM. The story begins during the period of flowering technology that followed World War II. A small group of bright engineers with entrepreneurial ambitions would start designing computers, mostly under government contracts; the group was either a division of a larger company or an independent venture financed by a few rich benefactors. The contracts expired; either the benefactor died or the parent company lost patience; the engineers sold out to a giant commercial corporation.

The corporation was not quite sure what it had bought. It knew computers would be significant in business somehow; meanwhile, the bright young engineers who understood the machine would develop it, and the corporation would sell it in the traditional way. Later, however, the corporation discovered it was spending enormous sums on the computer division with little to show for it. Thus followed a reappraisal, a change in management, tight financial controls, slashes in the budget, and the departure of some of the young entrepreneurs, now middle-aged but complaining that the game wasn't any fun any more. But the new emphasis on planning and careful spending was good for the company, and in the balmy economic climate of the late sixties, the computer division began to thrive. Then came a recession and an understanding of the investment required to survive and prosper in spite of IBM.

That basic plot took the dwarfs into the early seventies. As for the individual variations, Sperry Rand's Univac division had been launched with the unhappy marriage of the Eckert-Mauchly people in Philadelphia and the St. Paul group which later left to form Control Data. As we have seen, Univac had been the first manufacturer of electronic digital computers, and its employees had watched their superiors, through poor management and infighting, relinquish their lead to IBM; they had seen IBM move so far ahead that Univac could never hope to catch up. There was a time when the general public seemed to believe all computers were named Univacs and the Univacs were made by IBM; all this had sorely demoralized Univac people. The Control Data group had carried off some of the company's most talented engineers. Many of those who stayed behind at Univac in St. Paul bought stock in Control Data (for their wives and children) and sat waiting for an invitation to join it; for years afterward, the St. Paul branch was badly shaken by the Control Data episode.

The fortunes of Sperry Univac only began to change with the ascension of J. Frank Forster, who had joined Sperry Gyroscope in 1939, moved up in its financial ranks, and become president of the Vickers Division, which makes hydraulic systems. By this time, Sperry had merged with Remington Rand and Harry Vickers was president of the merged corporation. Forster watched with interest and concern as three successive division presidents under Vickers failed to shape up Univac. Then, in 1964, after Forster had been firing off memos proposing organizational improvements, Vickers invited him to report on Univac's operations in South America.

Forster's trip yielded so many useful insights that Vickers asked him to undertake a thorough study of Remington's and Univac's problems. Shortly thereafter, word came of Univac's second substantial inventory shortage, the division's president resigned, and Forster was appointed to replace him.

The two previous presidents of Univac had been brought in from outside. Forster had grown up at Sperry, and his friendship with Vickers gave him an authority his predecessors could not claim. "It was the first time Harry Vickers ever put the reins completely in someone else's hands," says a former Univac man. "Frank went off on tour, asking questions and taking notes. He didn't claim to know all the answers and took time to learn from his subordinates, but when he got through questioning you there was no doubt who was boss, and if you weren't sure of yourself he could tear you up."

A small, bespectacled, squinting, grandfatherly man with a face like a toby jug, Forster substituted canniness for magnetism. He would use a day of golf, shooting or fishing or an evening of poker, bridge or gin rummy to take the measure of subordinates several levels down, and to ferret out information not available through the usual corporate channels. The subordinates teed off with trembling hands.

Forster brought Univac just what it needed: the strict disciplines of the financial man. The best way to restore the morale of a debilitated business is, of course, to make it profitable, which Forster did in two years. He stressed planning, reduced the number of competing development projects, streamlined the organization to make it easier to detect good and bad performance, and declared that it was time for marketing men to cease pursuing sales at any cost.

After a year Forster had done so well that he was made president and chief operating officer of the parent company, retaining the leadership of the Univac division as well. He then set out to unite the technical staff. To do this, he chose Robert E. McDonald, an electrical engineer who had moved up through the St. Paul organization to head Univac's Defense Systems Division, which developed the company's military products. McDonald had joined Univac via Engineering Research Associates, the group whose principals later left to form Control Data, but McDonald had stayed on, and even refused to buy Control Data stock.

He had a distinctive, low-key political style. A former associate remembers, "In an era of tremendous turmoil Bob was astute enough to sense when major management changes would be made. Other people would mob the new boss, but Bob would simply wait calmly, and when the visit from headquarters came, he'd show a very efficient and hotshot operation." Although conservative about finances, he could be technologically adventurous and enjoyed spon-

soring "under-the-table" or "bootlegged" projects, in which enterprising engineers were given money to develop a product without
formal endorsement. The result, of course, was that when a commercial need for the product arose, McDonald's people were ready—and
McDonald was skillful in persuading Forster to adopt their technical
suggestions.

Thus the St. Paul faction won technical supremacy over its adversaries in Philadelphia. In 1966, the year Univac moved into the
black, Forster yielded the division presidency to McDonald. New
authority and successful products began to give Univac its technological directions. Its strengths lay in large computers and in machines designed to operate in real time through remote terminals
linked by telephone lines; much of this equipment had originally
been developed by McDonald's former Defense Systems colleagues.
It was a fortunate strategy, in tune with current trends. The division
continued to grow, and by 1969 it was the parent company's greatest
earner.

Univac was still widely considered to be weak at marketing. The
men who led the division tended to have either financial backgrounds (like Forster) or technical backgrounds (like McDonald).
Marketing management was changed frequently, and the top positions tended to be held by ex-controllers, men who had never been
on quota themselves. Univac's critics also complained that the company was dangerously tight with research and development money.

The division did reasonably well in the recession, but the many
corporate failures around them made all the dwarfs think seriously
about whether to remain in the business. While current profits had
legitimately been Forster's main concern when he took over the division, it now seemed that a larger share of the market was essential
to allow Univac to grow. McDonald and some of his colleagues began to look around for ailing businesses which might be candidates
for acquisition, and their eyes fell on RCA. In the fall of 1971, when
RCA announced it was leaving the computer business, Univac executives were already prepared to bid for a large part of their former
competitor's assets. RCA's customer base included about a thousand
computers, worth a billion dollars, installed on the premises of some
five hundred customers. Provided that many of these customers remained loyal, Univac would have a significantly expanded founda-

tion for future growth. Their bid was successful, and they agreed to hire a large number of RCA employees.

While most people in the industry felt that Univac had made a smart buy, its value would depend on how the company treated its new customers. The user needs to feel he can depend on his supplier to improve software and maintain hardware to fulfill the promises of support on which the original alliance was based; when the supplier leaves the industry, the user fears the loss of his investment. He is ripe for defection to IBM, which, whatever its faults, will never go out of business. At the time of the RCA purchase, Univac had just begun to realize the importance of improving its marketing, not only to get customers but to keep them. Its ranking executives visited the important RCA customers to reassure them, and they managed to hold on to most of the RCA accounts. It was Univac's first visible marketing success.

In 1972, a year before Forster's slated retirement, he was killed in a motor accident. Some observers speculated that the new chief, J. Paul Lyet, a noncomputer man, might downgrade the computer operations, but he didn't, and Univac continued to grow stronger throughout the decade.

Honeywell's computer operation began as a division of Raytheon Corporation, the Boston-based electronics concern. During the late forties the company hoped to sweep the federal government market: the National Bureau of Standards had ordered two of the company's large, innovative Hurricane computers. But Hurricane took so long to produce that the NBS decided to build its own machines. Raytheon, perhaps hoping a less imposing name might change its luck, rechristened the machine Raydac. The hope didn't materialize. Raydac, so slow in development, was obsolete at birth, and only one was sold. Not surprisingly, when management learned that its engineers were developing Raycom, a commercial version of Raydac, it told the computer division to find another patron. In 1955 the division joined what was then called Minneapolis Honeywell Corporation, the leading manufacturer of thermostats, which also did a healthy business in aerospace and defense products.

Honeywell appointed one of its more dynamic executives, Walter W. Finke, as president of the division. Finke was a lawyer who had been active in Minnesota politics. While he had no technical background, he was an adventurous man with an affinity for risky undertakings, and he applied his talent and fund-raising experience to the benefit of the division. Even after one false start (with another large, innovative machine that took too long to develop and was outmoded by the time of its delivery), he persuaded his superiors to continue backing the computer efforts. With Finke's hard-driving entrepreneurship, the real talents of the engineers, and the aggressiveness of the sales force that Finke's lieutenants were rapidly building, Honeywell presently became the brashest of IBM's competitors.

The fact that the company had no background in the office equipment industry presented both advantages and disadvantages. The main disadvantage was that it had no customers of its own and had to base its strategy on enticing users away from IBM, a policy with many dangers. The chief advantage was that, unlike Univac, Burroughs and NCR, it did not have to retrain a group of stubborn, habit-ridden salesmen who feared and resisted the new technology.

There were several technical men at Honeywell who understood all this, and in the early sixties a few engineers began to realize that the most successful product in the industry was IBM's 1401, a small computer meant to perform the relatively simply tasks of billing and payroll processing that tabulating machines had done in the past. If Honeywell could design a faster, more powerful successor to the 1401—which IBM, according to reports, was not planning to do—and offer the user easy conversion to the Honeywell machine, the company might just woo away enough IBM customers to make its own operations profitable. A smaller computer could be manufactured efficiently in volume and could be sold faster than the large models. Richard Bloch, who had led the division during its Raytheon days, began petitioning Finke toward this goal in the early sixties. J. Chuan Chu, the engineering chief newly hired from Univac, had tried unsuccessfully to sell his former bosses on the notion, and when he arrived at Honeywell he had good ideas on how to carry it out.

Finke was persuaded, and the project went ahead. In December 1963 Honeywell announced the 200, equipped with a software system called the Liberator which would adapt IBM 1401 programs to the Honeywell machine; the programs would then run faster on the 200 than they did on the IBM computer. Chu had wanted to offer the conversion feature quietly, fearing that too-vigorous promotion would cause IBM to retaliate. But Finke was a swinger, and the Liberator was touted in full-page newspaper advertisements. The strategy was nervy and wildly successful: in the first six weeks enough orders came in to surpass a year's forecasts.

With further audacity, Honeywell had announced the 200 for delivery in seven months, when the usual industry lead time was twelve to eighteen months. Because the company was not prepared to produce all those machines on schedule, it had to rent additional factory space and invest heavily in new equipment. Also, the conversion aids were expensive to produce. The order rate climbed and the deliveries were met, but this success delayed the fulfillment of Finke's promise to break even by 1964, and the unanticipated expenses did not sit well with his superiors. Furthermore, IBM did retaliate: it was so shaken by the 200's acceptance that it advanced the announcement of System 360. The final score was indicative of the relationship between IBM and the dwarfs: IBM failed to stop the drive to the 200; Honeywell thrived beyond its expectations; and what all this meant in the end was that Honeywell replaced some 10 percent of IBM's 1401's.

For a decade Honeywell's computer division had borne the Finke stamp. "Walter operated with a few trusted friends," remembers Claude Smith, who was a marketing vice-president under Finke. "When we were pricing a new product, Cap Smith, vice-president of engineering, the controller, and the production man and Dick Bloch of product planning and I would all go into Finke's office. Cap discussed engineering costs, and the controller went over financial figures, and then Finke'd ask me how many units we could sell. This went on for a few hours. Then Finke would turn to me and ask, 'How much does IBM get for it?' 'Eight hundred,' I would say. 'OK,' Finke would answer, 'Seven ninety for ours.' "

In that decade Finke had taken a company which had placed a million dollars' worth of gear and built it into an operation with a worldwide installed base of $500 million worth of equipment. This growth had a curious but understandable effect on corporate management. As long as Honeywell's computer division was small, the corporation was willing to leave Finke and his team alone, but as the efforts succeeded and revenues began to grow, Minneapolis became increasingly protective of its investment. When James Binger, a lawyer who described himself as "numbers-oriented," moved up from president to chairman of the board, the division was faced with new corporate goals. "The company had decided at upper levels to consolidate its gains, to digest its new-found position in the field and to cease further speculative pursuits," says Richard Bloch. "Finke was opposed to this position. He wanted to push harder." Clarence W. Spangle, an executive with engineering and law degrees and a marketing background, was brought home from managing Honeywell's European subsidiaries to become Finke's assistant. Shortly afterward, Finke accepted the chairmanship of Dictaphone Corporation and Spangle replaced him. Spangle has been characterized as a tough, dollar-conscious professional manager; the Finke men thought him a cold fish, and several of them left the company.

During the Finke days Honeywell had commissioned Arthur D. Little, the management consulting firm, to study the computer marketplace; the Little report had stressed the need for "critical mass," a sufficiently large customer base to finance the expensive research and development that would ensure survival. Although the new management had changed the objective from fast growth to profit, the Little conclusions continued to trouble Honeywell executives: the division was growing with the industry and was beginning to show a profit, but this might not be enough. Sooner or later Honeywell would need a larger share of the market. In March 1970, when the vice-chairman of General Electric called Binger to discuss the future of data processing, Binger was ready.

General Electric had been manufacturing computers since the mid-fifties, and perhaps because the industry had held such high hopes for it—here, after all, was a company with the resources to hit IBM hard—its failures seemed particularly dramatic. GE had always had an abundance of technical talent: in the fifties it had pioneered in computer applications for banking, and in the sixties its willingness to innovate in time-sharing had precipitated an embarrassing failure for IBM. But GE had never really committed itself to computers, and so hadn't defined a strategy or learned how to manage computer projects. It also encountered serious problems in operating its foreign acquisitions, the French Machines Bull and the Italian Olivetti computer division.

Between 1957 and 1970, GE lost more than $160 million on its domestic computer operations, but in 1969 its financial picture was improving, particularly in Europe. Its new chief commissioned a three-month seminar to map an advanced product line for the seventies. Richard Bloch had left Honeywell for GE, and he now directed a task force of sixty men from every branch of the Information Systems Group. The task force drew up a master plan for a product line to push GE into the number two spot; to carry out the plan wholeheartedly would cost $685 million through 1974, the first year the new line could show a profit. The task force convinced GE management that if it didn't accept the master plan it had better give up on computers altogether. But GE had other financial problems, and after four months of exhaustive study, it decided to find a buyer for its computer operation. GE talked to several of the dwarfs and found Honeywell both compatible and receptive. While GE's strengths lay in small and large computers and in European markets, Honeywell excelled in medium-sized machines and in the United States. Like GE, Binger felt that mergers among the dwarfs were inevitable, and the first to consolidate would have the best chance of survival. Honeywell could afford the necessary development expenses only by doubling its 5 percent market share through consolidation.

Honeywell paid $234 million in notes and stock for GE's business computer assets; GE would receive an 18½ percent interest in Honeywell Information Systems which Honeywell would buy out by 1980. The acquisition made Honeywell number two in the computer industry, with a market share of about 10 percent. Honeywell now combined the impressive technical skills of GE with a sales force (its own) rated second only to IBM's. It boasted a comprehensive selection of products and strength in the marketplace both at home and abroad. But it also had a hotchpotch of incompatible product lines. The user couldn't move from one to another, and to maintain and support all of them would be expensive. Moreover, these products used the aging technology of the mid-sixties at a time when IBM was bringing out its 370 line.

At first the omens were good. Spangle was crisp and efficient in unifying the two organizations, and the first new products sold well. Honeywell began developing one new series to serve all its customers with the latest technology, but the project proved more difficult than expected and software problems delayed its announcement by more than a year. The new line cost more than $300 million to develop, and the expense of maintaining the old, disparate lines and consolidating factories after the merger was also greater than anticipated. By 1974, when the new line was ready, the recession was on. Honeywell's earnings in 1974 and early 1975 took such a sharp drop that the company had to state publicly that it planned to remain in the computer business. Honeywell began to recover in late 1975 with improvements in the economy and the first shipments of the new line, and its business has looked particularly lively in the past couple of years. But the other dwarfs are still making more money.

In the days when Honeywell was planting itself directly in IBM's path, Burroughs was traveling a different route. The loyal Burroughs user—and, according to a study done in 1970, Burroughs users were the loyalest of all, surpassing even IBM's—often observed that an IBM computer was like a Buick, but a Burroughs machine was a Porsche. A Burroughs user was a buff, with that air of self-congratulation that buffs always have. He was pleased that he had the perspicacity, sophistication and daring to appreciate a really superior piece of equipment and to find Burroughs, because God knew the Burroughs salesmen, who were scarce as hen's teeth anyway, weren't astute enough to find *him*.

Burroughs had been a well-known manufacturer of adding and accounting machines, but by 1948 its president, John Coleman, realized the company would have to go into electronics to survive. Corporate headquarters were in Detroit, far from the scientific centers on the east and west coasts, and Coleman knew there was not much chance of attracting talented engineers to the home office. He hired Dr. Irven Travis, a former colleague of Eckert and Mauchly at the University of Pennsylvania, to establish a research lab in Paoli, near Philadelphia. Travis's efforts looked promising: the new lab won several important government contracts, and Detroit encouraged it to design a commercial computer. But by the time they came up with the plans for a large machine, Coleman had bought a small California computer company and decided to give the project to the California group. Like Univac, Burroughs began with a fierce rivalry between two engineering groups, but the rivalry was not allowed to debilitate the company.

Burroughs defined its technical strategy rather by accident in 1959; having done so, it pursued its design goals single-mindedly ever after. While the other dwarfs and IBM brought in the systems programmers after the specifications for a machine had been set, the group that designed the B5000, the first Burroughs computer, included software specialists from the start, and the software men were on an equal footing with the engineers. The design team numbered only twenty-five men, and according to William R. Lonergan, who managed the project, "Six of them were outrageous geniuses. One was getting a Ph.D. at Cal Tech at age nineteen, and six years later he was busy writing a sort of *Principia Mathematica* on systems programming. There was a white heat in the air—you could almost touch it." Burroughs management was composed of old-line accounting machine men, but Lonergan and his enthusiastic geniuses were able to talk them into going ahead with an enormously complicated machine whose design depended on an arcane algebraic concept called Polish notation, so christened because nobody could spell Lukasiewicz, the name of its inventor.

The goal of all this intellectualism was to make the Burroughs machine easy to use. Other manufacturers were designing for efficient use of memory space and to save machine time. Burroughs designers wanted to save the user's time, and so came up with a computer which could be programmed best in the new higher-level languages bearing some resemblance to ordinary English (therefore they could be learned quickly, and they eased debugging). As Burroughs brought out future Burroughs computer generations, the user could run his programs on the new machines without rewriting them.

The B5000 was the first computer to offer a sophisticated operating system—a Master Control Program which scheduled the user's programs and allocated space in the computer's memory and peripheral equipment. Even a decade later, no rival operating system came near it. Burroughs was the first manufacturer to succeed at multiprogramming (which allowed the user to run several programs at once on the same machine), multiprocessing (in which several central processors worked on a program in concert), and virtual memory (the device which caused IBM so much trouble later on). For all these advantages the Burroughs user paid a price in raw speed.

If these innovations were so wonderful, prospects often asked the Burroughs men, why didn't IBM think of them first? The Burroughs men answered in euphemisms, but the truth was that IBM designers—even in a series as radical as the 360—had to consider the needs and wishes of their current customers, whereas Burroughs had so few current customers to consider it could afford to be daring.

The Porsche didn't sell. The language that worked best on the B5000 was Algol; IBM, choosing to support other languages, withheld its blessing from Algol, and IBM set the industry standard. ("Sure, Algol is an efficient language," says an IBM software man. "So is Esperanto, but nobody speaks it.") The customers didn't know how to apply the new techniques the machine made available, and the last people capable of showing them were the Burroughs salesmen, a brawny lot accustomed to hefting accounting machines from office to office on their daily rounds but clearly mystified by weighty concepts like Polish notation. And the machine was so damned *slow*.

Burroughs floundered around with this beautifully designed white elephant until 1964 when Ray W. Macdonald, the marketing man in charge of international operations, returned to Detroit as executive vice-president. Macdonald's first decision was to speed up the 5000, and his second was to launch two smaller companion machines. By 1966—when he became president of the corporation—he and his lieutenants had decided Burroughs couldn't succeed without offering a full range of products. To do so it had to earn enough money to pay the development costs.

Macdonald's approach had always been to improve the strongest aspects of the business first, before tackling the toughest problems. Burroughs had a partly electronic accounting machine which seemed to promise wide volume and quick profits; on the computer side, Macdonald discovered that a small number of salesmen were bringing in most of the business. So he cut the computer sales force from 400 to 125, putting the balance to work selling the accounting machine, at which they did better. The accounting machine was enormously successful; its profits helped support the company's computer expansion, and it also smoothed the transition of both factories and sales force to electronics. Later models of Burroughs accounting machines, which were all-electronic, could double as computer terminals and continued to help pay for computer development.

At the same time, Macdonald trimmed budgets and wooed security analysts. All these measures sent Burroughs stock climbing, which enabled the company to raise additional money. In 1968, edp showed its first profits. Preferring slow steady growth to the critical mass theory favored by some competitors, Macdonald made no acquisitions until the mid-seventies; by then Burroughs was either second or third to IBM in data processing revenues, depending on which products were included.

Burroughs' technical strategy, fortuitously arrived at, proved prophetic: the cost of memory went down and the cost of programmers' time went up; and all the mainframe manufacturers got into sophisticated operating systems and virtual memory. This meant, of course, that the technological gap between Burroughs and its competitors had narrowed. Service and support had become increasingly important, and this area of the business had suffered from Macdonald's frugality. At the end of 1977, Macdonald retired. Despite all he'd done for Burroughs, he was blamed for leaving a legacy of problems. A strong-willed leader, he had failed to delegate authority or train successors, and the upper ranks were dangerously sparse of talent; in building a loyal executive corps of lifelong company men, he had fostered too much managerial inbreeding. The result of all this was widespread criticism of Burroughs for not moving aggressively enough into the markets of the eighties. When, in 1980, another chief executive was needed, the interim management, recognizing the problems, chose an outsider, W. Michael Blumenthal, the recent Secretary of the Treasury

The latest bloomer was NCR. Its recovery took place in the middle seventies when computer people thought the time for spectacular reversals had passed. Here was the company that taught Thomas J. Watson, Sr. most of what he knew about inspiring and managing men; Watson had taken NCR techniques, honed them and renewed them and adapted them to each succeeding change in technology and society, and passed them on to his successors who did the same, and all of them had built a corporation of unequaled vigor, with the remnants of early NCR style still visible and working well more than half a century later. Meanwhile NCR itself moved deeper and deeper into stagnation, until everyone thought technology and modern business methods had passed it by, and few would bet on its survival. Then a *deus ex machina* appeared, a mysterious Englishman who came from Japan and swiftly set about making changes that would render the company almost unrecognizable five years later.

NCR's entry into the computer business took place in the late forties, when a group of engineers working on a missile guidance for Northrop Aircraft were given the preposterous task of developing an airborne digital computer. They didn't succeed, but the assignment stimulated their imaginations. "We saw the implications of this business," says Donald Eckdahl, later an NCR vice-president. "We knew the computer would revolutionize industry and we tried to convince Northrop that they had a fantastic opportunity and should do something about it. They allowed us to take our machine to the Institute of Advanced Study to demonstrate it to von Neumann: that was the high point of my life. He wrote a glowing report to Jack Northrop, but we couldn't seem to convince Northrop to go into commercial computing. The group of us had meeting after meeting, and then we decided to quit and form our own company."

The company was called Computer Research Corporation. It was founded in 1950, and for most of its short life it inhabited a complex of small apartments above a bakery in Torrance, California. CRC secured several promising contracts to develop computers for aircraft laboratories in government and industry, but when one of its two financial backers died in 1952 both his widow and the other backer wanted out. The CRC men scrambled about in search of other sponsors—they even tried Bing Crosby Enterprises—and finally sold their company to NCR.

Like many office equipment manufacturers, National Cash had been forced by the advent of the electronic computer to think seriously about the future. As the late Stanley C. Allyn, then NCR's chairman, wrote in his memoirs:

> The vital question that faced NCR in the 1950's was: Should the company enter the electronic data processing field? If the anwer was yes, we knew it meant many millions of research development dollars, plus the retraining of manufacturing, marketing, and service personnel. If the answer was no, we knew full well that future growth would be seriously limited. We would be living from then on with a ceiling on opportunity. So we decided once more to move ahead.

In the opinion of many of the original engineers and the more future-minded marketing men, NCR didn't move fast enough. Some NCR executives point out the differences between IBM's and NCR's business in the precomputer era. IBM sold punch-card equipment,

an aggregation of specialized machines—the card punch, the verifi-
er, the printer and so forth—which sat in the central accounting
department of a large organization; the movement of voluminous
information through them required a primitive form of systems design. The information had to be converted to machine-readable
form; once entered it could be organized and retrieved in different
ways for different purposes, and the equipment was manned by specialists. This, then, was a rudimentary data processing department,
and the engineers, salesmen and executives of the company that
made the equipment had already mastered many of the fundamentals of the computer business. NCR, on the other hand, sold ledger
card machines, which were self-contained, operated by clerks with
little special training, distributed through large organizations or used
by small ones, and relatively inexpensive; requiring no coding and
only limited systems design, they were essentially a combination of a
typewriter and an adding machine. It thus required a far greater
mental leap for NCR people to understand computers.

Throughout the fifties and even into the sixties, the company
spent a lot of time considering how to fit the computer group into its
regular organization. Corporate management, headquartered in
Dayton, Ohio, began to discover the complexities of manufacturing
and marketing computers and when a small one was unsuccessful,
Dayton became disenchanted. The computer division, management
decided, would be restricted to research and development. The company did take one gamble. As Allyn reports in his memoirs:

> One of our first important decisions was whether to make our first
> computer . . . a vacuum-tube machine or to jump directly into the on-
> rushing solid-state technology of the mid-fifties. At that time transis-
> tors were still quite expensive and their potential was not entirely un-
> derstood. But we took the risk, and skipped completely the first-
> generation vacuum-tube era.

NCR also decided to have the machine manufactured by General Electric—a move Allyn credits to impatience and others chalk up
to faint-heartedness. Either way, the company lost valuable learning
experience, and the next product line ran into reliability problems.

Like Burroughs and Univac, NCR faced the problem of fitting
computers into its sales operation. Should the company hire computer salesmen or train its own salesmen in computers? Who should sell

what—are the computer men kept aside, as a chaste intellectual elite, or do they mingle with the accounting machine people, and does the customer see only one NCR salesman or several pushing different product lines? And how on earth do you pay everybody?

For NCR, with its corps of aggressive, individualistic, well-paid old-time drummers, these issues seemed particularly difficult to resolve, and the company was revising its methods of assignment and compensation—which were probably the most complicated in the industry—well into the seventies. At first, all computers were sold from the home office. Later, the computer salesmen were distributed among the larger branch offices, but by this time they had lost the knowledge and inclination to cover the territory; they would sit in their offices waiting for the telephone to ring. Their accounting machine colleagues turned into hard-driving competitors: why buy a computer, said the man-on-the-beat to the customer, when three accounting machines will do? No accounting machine salesman in his right mind would give up a commission to the computer salesman: he called his colleague only when the customer seemed deadset on IBM, and then the computer salesman would spend six months trying vainly to rescue the account.

When NCR saw the hopelessness of this arrangement, it assigned commission salesmen to peddle both accounting machines *and* computers; computer specialists were brought in as support when technological problems arose. This didn't work too well either, because NCR hadn't set up sufficient incentive for the salesmen. "Computers took up 75 percent of your time, and because of the commission structure they would bring in 25 percent of your income," says one alumnus. The NCR senior sales rep was careful of how he spent his time, since he worked exclusively on commission and had to share it with his subordinates, and since he paid all his own expenses from client entertainment right down to business cards. A branch manager's percentage of the profits in a plum territory could amount to $100,000 a year, while his superior, the district manager—whose goal in life was a lucrative demotion—brought in $40,000 through a modest bonus plan. The reward for executive talent—an opportunity to move to Dayton, Ohio at a starting salary of $10,000 a year—was ample reason to conceal one's managerial ability. It was not until 1969 that NCR began to adjust its branch office structure to the computer era.

While Burroughs had used its accounting machines as leverage to propel itself into the computer business, NCR invested in small and medium-sized computers for its banking and retail customers. But by the time its third-generation line came out, IBM's System 360 was solidly entrenched and the NCR machines made slow progress. Meanwhile, the company let its cash register and accounting machines moulder in obsolete mechanical technology. The banks bought Burroughs terminals; retailers like Sears and Penney bought Singer point-of-sale machines, the new electronic cash registers designed to talk to a central computer system (Singer had developed these terminals for its own retail business because it couldn't persuade NCR to produce them). When at last NCR came out with electronic terminals for banking and retailing, it had a crowd of competitors. Neither side of the business was doing well, and the factories were hampered by the inefficiencies and high labor costs of mechanical technology. NCR's Dayton-bred management, sheltered by the clublike atmosphere of the company's Horseshoe Dining Room, talked mostly to each other.

The company's earnings declined substantially in 1970, as the recession began, and in 1971, when the effects of a lengthy strike at the Dayton plant were added to NCR's other troubles, it earned a disastrous $.04 a share. The strike continued well into 1972, when the board of directors finally decided to appoint a new president. The man they chose, William Anderson, was not a corporate officer; some thirty men outranked him, and he had never even worked in Dayton. An Englishman born in China, he had always lived in the Far East, and had headed NCR's Japanese subsidiary, where he compiled an impressive record of increased sales, earnings and productivity. With a clear sense of what was ailing the company, the board had reached outside the Dayton establishment—but as Anderson himself observes, "I was new and not new. They didn't have to teach me about the business and the company."

As chief operating officer, Anderson was given a free hand. Unlike his predecessors, he made a firm decision to move the company as rapidly as possible out of mechanical technology and into electronics, and to enter the computer business wholeheartedly, which meant that NCR would have to offer its customers the broad product line and trendy communications features necessary to keep them loyal. Anderson overhauled every department in the company. In manufacturing, he closed and consolidated plants, decentralized the organization, updated the inventory systems and changed policies on which items would be made by the company and which bought from outside suppliers. He realigned the sales force toward IBM-style industrial specialization, which required retraining seven thousand employees. He also reorganized research and development, and within five years the company had doubled its investment in r & d; in 1976 NCR introduced its first new computer line in eight years, and the announcement was followed by a barrage of additional ones over the next year, all incorporating the latest technology. NCR customers now had larger and larger computers to move up to. By 1977, the company had cut its work force by twenty-five thousand employees, and of the thirty-four corporate officers in power at Anderson's appointment, only eleven remained. Anderson himself had become chief executive on the chairman's retirement, and in 1976 he made news by persuading one of Burroughs' stars to join NCR as its president; the appointment had symbolic significance, too, serving notice that Burroughs had a tough opponent.

Most surprisingly, although NCR was still number six in computer revenues, if you figured in its terminal sales the company was actually second to IBM. Both technology and market trends were running in its favor. Banks and other large customers were more willing to mix their systems with equipment from several vendors. As technological improvements lowered hardware costs—a change which also enabled the dwarfs to produce equipment more economically—ever smaller customers were ready for their first computers, and this was a market NCR had traditionally served well. The current movement toward distributed processing, in which terminals and minicomputers are dispersed in offices, stores and branch banks to be run by nonprofessionals, reflects, ironically, a return to the very approach that had kept NCR from succeeding with computers in the past. This time, of course, the local machines are tied to a central processing system, and NCR can handle that, too.

They have survived the difficult years, and they are all in reasonable health, and the strongest impression one now gets is that these four dwarfs grow more similar with each passing year. The language, of course, is the same: if Mr. Arbuthnot, the late Frank Sullivan's cliché expert, worked for a dwarf he would speak about "major competitive thrusts." Their strategies, too, are based on an inevitable Master Survival Plan.

In the early seventies, Mr. Arbuthnot would have maintained that "you can't compete with IBM across the board." Today, Neil Gorchow, Univac's vice-president for product strategy and requirements, says "We compete with IBM across the board." All four companies are beginning to manufacture their own semiconductors. Each takes pride in the "breadth" or "scope" of its product line. They cannot safely ignore the small user, because that's where growth comes from; and once the user is hooked, he needs bigger machines to migrate to, or else he will find another supplier. The dwarfs also can't safely ignore the dominant trend toward distributed processing.

Each company believes it has special qualifications to serve that trend: Univac has excelled in the large machines that can manage great volumes of data for multinational corporations with worldwide computer networks; Honeywell has made minicomputers for a long time, and has linked them with bigger processors; both Univac and Honeywell are pushing hard in minicomputers now. NCR started with terminals and small machines that could speak to other vendors' large computers and has now added large machines to its own line. While Burroughs has moved more slowly than its competitors, terminals and large machines have always been its specialty. All four have developed systems software for distributed networks.

In applications software, aimed at particular industries, the dwarfs must be selective. "We look at the size of IBM and the number of dollars they spend on research and development," says NCR's Anderson, "and the way they have multiple programs going while we pick and choose. Often we decide an application is not worth it because IBM is there and the market isn't big enough for us, too. When we talk about r & d it's no longer nuts and bolts—it's applications packages and operating systems. Some customers have such big and complicated applications that you give them the tools and they do their own programs, and other customers have such simple applications that you do the same thing, but in the middle are the ones that want packages. They pick the vendor who knows their industry best."

All four are spending more than they used to on applications software and have organized their sales people according to customer industries, choosing those where they will make their major competitive thrusts. Burroughs and NCR, for example, are thrusting after the banks, which seem to be least in thrall to IBM. Univac is having at the airlines all alone, or rather *mano a mano* with IBM, but it joins Honeywell in thrusting at federal, state and local government customers. All four dwarfs thrust at manufacturing companies.

The result of the Master Survival Plan is that no ranking of the dwarfs has much significance any more. The complexity of the industry affords innumerable ways to apportion market share, and each of these companies can claim particular strength by some measure. In 1980 each of them brought in between just under $2½ billion and just under $3 billion in computer-related revenues, although Honeywell's income was down, at a billion-six, if you ruled out the income from its French affiliate, Cii Honeywell Bull, of which the American company owns 47 percent.

Another factor further complicates the problem of ranking the dwarfs. Since 1976, IBM has been introducing new computers that have drastically altered the traditional price structure of the industry. For the past twenty years, *Computerworld* noted in January 1978, IBM's prices "generally grew at about 45% for each 100% gain in performance." With the new products, however, IBM has introduced better performance for a *lower* price than that of the comparable previous models, and despite the dwarfs' responses, *Computerworld* observed, "IBM's machines went from being the industry's high price alternatives in March to the point where they ended the year on the lower end of the mainframe pricing totem pole." In the industry argot, IBM has folded its umbrella; this and the rapid technological changes brought on by integrated circuitry are making the business more volatile than ever, and it is difficult to predict how each dwarf will fare.

8

Programmed for Disaster:
The End of RCA

A young dilettante of the arts
Once gathered the finest of parts
But failed to check whether
They fitted together
He now has a flute that shoots darts.
—Limerick composed by employee,
RCA Computer System Division,
as part of a company-sponsored
quality-improvement campaign

WHEN Robert W. Sarnoff, chairman of the board and chief executive officer of RCA, announced on September 15, 1970 that "it is our intention to make RCA a major multinational enterprise doing business principally in computer-based information systems," the statement was greeted in the trade and business press with what the late A. J. Liebling used to call "*ademonai, kodemonai*" (the two words, Liebling noted, were Japanese for "on-the-one-hand-this" and "on-the-other-hand-that," a technique characteristic of interpretive reporting).

The scene of the announcement was RCA Computer Systems' new $22 million manufacturing plant at Marlboro, Massachusetts, where the company was holding a press conference to introduce its latest series of computers. In stating that the computer division, which had been in business since the mid-fifties, was "determined to attain an industry rank second only to IBM in this country. In order to accomplish this goal, RCA is prepared to commit whatever resources are necessary," Sarnoff appeared to be risking his personal prestige on the division's success. He had picked a new general manager, L. Edwin Donegan, Jr., a marketing executive with eighteen years of IBM experience; and Donegan, in turn, was busy importing an army of former IBM colleagues to serve as his lieutenants. The headquarters building of RCA Computer Systems, in Cherry Hill, New Jersey, was decked out with posters showing Donegan and his management team, captioned "The New Direction Is Up."

Ademonai, wrote the trade and business reporters, RCA was employing a gutsy well-planned strategy, and the IBM-trained managers were a plus factor. *Kodemonai,* the corporation was embarking on a rocky road, and Sarnoff's promises were the same as those made time and again by IBM's other competitors. Of course, the reporters knew that nothing in the computer industry was sure (*ademonai*), but the idea of RCA playing Avis to IBM's Hertz was (*kodemonai*) certainly appealing. In the following months the press regularly reported that RCA Computer Systems was having trouble meeting its objectives—was, in fact, making some serious blunders—but it is fair to say that both the computer industry and the journalists who cover it were caught short by Sarnoff's second announcement, delivered just a year and two days after the first, that RCA was quitting the computer business and would try to sell the division.

As we have seen, the recession of 1970 and 1971 proved traumatic for the entire industry, and even before Sarnoff announced his commitment to success in computers, there were signs of rough weather ahead. But despite the heavy losses RCA Computer Systems had suffered during the following year, even Ed Donegan was astonished when he reported for a meeting at 30 Rockefeller Plaza on a muggy Friday afternoon and was told immediately that The Newer Direction Was Out. At 3:30, managers in the division were put on standby alert; at 5:00, well after the close of trading on the New York Stock Exchange, they received Sarnoff's carefully drafted statement. In the Northeastern Regional Office, the district managers, gathered for a budget review, heard the statement, called their wives, ordered a case of champagne, consumed it and adjourned for more news on the radio or read it in Saturday's newspaper.

At the Marlboro press conference Sarnoff had talked much of IBM. His farewell statement, however, simply alluded to "the severe pressures generated by a uniquely entrenched competition," and so pointed up the peculiar characteristic of the computer industry—not only the dominance of IBM but the massive capital requirements, the hardships of leasing, and the complexities of designing, manufacturing and marketing the equipment and its software. He noted that to remain viable, the division would require a $500 million investment during the next five years.

Robert Sarnoff's willingness to stake his reputation on success in this brutal business seems quixotic, but RCA had flourished under the leadership of Sarnoff's father, the late Brigadier General David Sarnoff, whose career spanned half a century of technological pioneering. At IBM, Thomas J. Watson, Jr. felt compelled to justify his right of succession; Robert Sarnoff sometimes compared his situation with Watson's. The younger Sarnoff, who served his apprenticeship at NBC, took over the presidency of RCA in 1966 and the chairmanship in 1970. Like Watson, he set about streamlining his father's organization. He improved communications among the different divisions and instituted a corporate staff to coordinate them. He placed a new emphasis on marketing and brought in a former Ford executive to direct it. He gave the company a new look, revamping the corporate offices and introducing a modish logotype to replace the old lightning-in-a-circle and dog-listening-to-Victrola.

Bob Sarnoff decided to give priority to computers: industry growth figures were certainly dramatic, and until mid-1970 there were no signs that the growth would slow down. He hoped to capture 10 percent of the computer market by 1975. To bring this about, he chose L. Edwin Donegan, Jr., the personable, enthusiastic ex-IBM'er who had come to RCA to head its computer division's field sales organization in early 1969.

RCA men fumbled for words to describe Donegan's extraordinary effect on people (*charisma* was the term they used most often). When he talked at a meeting, they told you, Ed Donegan took up the whole room. When he called you in for a chat, sat on the sofa in his office (never behind the desk) to get your inputs, you were the only other person in the world. When he leaned forward and talked about *total dedication* and *commitment* (who ever heard those words around RCA before?) you knew that Ed Donegan believed, believed in the division and believed in you, and you believed too. It was a spell to which friends, enemies and acquaintances (not to mention Donegan's superiors) were susceptible, even though it embarrassed them.

Donegan was shortish and stocky, with wavy brown hair and open blue eyes, and looked as if he might toss you a Frisbee any minute (at the time of his debut, Donegan was forty-two and could pass for thirty; a year later, trouble had aged him, and he looked all of thirty-eight). While his delivery was breezy, he was no orator, and his private conversation was laced with words like "quantum jump," "iteration," and "prioritize."

Donegan's colleagues—wittingly or unwittingly—painted a picture of a lonely, driven man. "I've never heard Donegan tell a joke, or anyone tell a joke in his presence," remarked one. "Ed is never off-line," added another. Ed, one was told, attacked his diet with the same dedication he brought to everything else. He didn't look fat, but his weight sometimes went up to 200 pounds, and then he would live on water and hard-boiled eggs until he got down to 170. He took tennis seriously, and wanted to win ("Mostly he plays doubles," noted an associate, "with the strongest partner he can find").

It was the winning spirit, the IBM spirit, that Ed Donegan tried—and failed—to bring to RCA. He hoped that IBM techniques, IBM philosophies and IBM alumni would give the company the vigor it needed to achieve Sarnoff's goals. But IBM is so large that only the highest levels of management get to see how the complex factors of technology, marketing, manufacturing and finance are put together; below the level of division president or corporate vice-president, a man learns only his part and must extrapolate the rest. The history of the industry is dotted with stories of IBM'ers schooled in, say, marketing, who went out to manage other companies and fell down on production or finance. "At IBM," says one of its alumni who moved to RCA, "you hear young men speaking in numbers with big strings of zeros after them, but they don't really control that much money, and the organization moves itself."

Ed Donegan's last assignment at IBM had been to develop a new venture in information marketing services; its most important project was a time-sharing service through which a customer who didn't need his own computer could rent a terminal connected by telephone with an IBM data center. From both a marketing and a technical standpoint the venture never met its forecasts, but this in itself was not considered a reflection on Donegan: entrepreneurial efforts like this one, which took IBM into fields it had never entered before, often didn't work out. There was, though, a feeling that Donegan had oversold the project originally.

Two things are important about this adventure. First, when Information Marketing was started, its entire staff consisted of Ed Donegan and a few technical people who had conceived the projects. At its peak the department was, according to estimates of several of its alumni, a $30 million operation with a staff of 400, and ex-IBM'ers credit its rapid growth to Donegan's ability to sell his superiors, who were among the toughest, most exacting managers in the industry. Second, this assignment, the most responsible Donegan held for any time at IBM, gave him little of the experience called for in running a computer company. He had never supervised the planning and development of a major hardware product; had never bought mainframe components or managed manufacturing; had not controlled the programming systems development of a complete computer family; had not been responsible for cost estimates or pricing of a hardware product line; and because of its experimental nature, his project did not carry the high risks involved in an important computer operation. All these factors proved significant to Donegan's performance, but it is interesting that most of the statements above could also have been applied to Frank Forster of Univac and William Anderson of NCR.

Since RCA had been preeminent in the manufacture of electronic components, computers seemed a reasonable extension of this technological know-how. It began developing its first computer in 1953, but like all the other dwarfs, it discovered that it knew less about computer design than it should have, and it knew even less than the other dwarfs about computer marketing; although the company made a variety of consumer products and had engaged in many military projects, it was unfamiliar with the niceties of selling capital goods directly to the commercial user. Moreover, several of the dwarfs entered computers from a base in the office equipment industry and had their own rosters of customers. Like Honeywell, RCA had never had a customer list and had to base its strategy on weaning users away from IBM.

The division's early history included a few successes, many more failures and some retrenchments. By 1964, however, it managed to show a profit of a few hundred thousand dollars. That year, RCA decided to bring out a cheaper copy of IBM's ambitious new System 360. The RCA line would be compatible with the 360: that is, programs designed for the IBM system could be used with RCA products as well. Compatibility, the division's executives reasoned, would make it easier for dissatisfied IBM customers to switch to RCA (IBM, however, could just as easily steal RCA customers, and, as one RCA man put it, "They're better thieves than we are"). RCA might also pick up some business with IBM customers who wanted a supplier in the house to keep IBM on its toes, and RCA customers could take advantage of the extensive library of software produced throughout the industry for IBM machines. Honeywell had once used a similar strategy; but since the Honeywell machine ran software for the old IBM line, not the new, it offered current IBM customers an extra incentive to change suppliers. Honeywell recognized that this approach owed its success to a windfall in timing, and did not use the strategy again.

When IBM announced System 360, RCA's new line was well along in its development, and the engineers discovered their product had much in common with IBM's line. Why not, then, go even further? RCA had no industrial espionage effort going; its designers simply took the rather detailed customer manuals IBM issues for its products and started to copy the machine from the skin in. As far as the user was concerned, the RCA Spectra 70 behaved like a 360, although its internal architecture was different. It was, all in all, a rather impressive achievement, considering the makeshift method of its design, and the fact that it was produced for delivery within two years on a total annual development budget of $15 million. System 360's research and development, as we know, had cost at least half a billion.

At the time Donegan joined RCA in 1969, the division was under the aegis of the late James R. Bradburn, executive vice-president and general manager, and Edwin S. McCollister, vice-president for marketing. McCollister had arrived in 1961, and over eight years had given the division much of its particular flavor. He was a burly man, with rosy cheeks and straight black hair. Dressed in a checked suit and puffing on one of the eight cigars he consumed during the workday, he cuts a Runyonesque figure. Like Donegan, McCollister, who was fourteen years older, had been trained at IBM, but it was a different IBM when McCollister knew it. Between 1956, the year of Thomas J. Watson, Sr.'s death, and 1970 the company's revenues increased tenfold and its employees tripled; McCollister had left in 1954. He got his field experience in the late forties, when IBM was selling punched-card accounting machines. He loved helping the customer use the equipment, and he loved the machinery itself. Later on, when McCollister was working in the home office, Mr. Watson went around on December 24 and wished each employee on the New York staff an individual Merry Christmas.

McCollister, as anyone who talked with him for a while began to suspect, is not a garden-variety corporate executive: he thought there was more to life than his job, would rather cut the grass than play golf, and had a penchant for introspection. He was in line for the general manager's position at RCA until 1965 when, as a friend melodramatically put it, "he signed his own death warrant." RCA was encountering production and maintenance problems on its new Spectra line, and McCollister suggested that the company bring in Bradburn, a specialist in the field; he did so knowing full well that Bradburn would come only with the general managership as an enticement. "I thought we'd have a better chance of making it with Bradburn aboard, and so I said I'd be willing to work for him," McCollister remembered.

McCollister had run a lean and informal operation, and the family-store atmosphere continued after Bradburn's arrival. McCollister had little use for reports or managerial channels: if he wanted to know what was going on in the field, he went into the field and found out for himself. Moreover, whenever a district manager had a problem, he called McCollister. "Ed McCollister was approachable night and day," said an RCA alumnus, "and that was his Achilles' heel. He just wasn't son-of-a-bitch enough to discipline the salesmen. Problems that should have been settled at a lower level would bubble up to the top."

The corporation began to recognize computers as a major area for future growth and to pour money into the division. Bradburn managed to triple revenues during his tenure, and to cut the division's heavy losses during the last two years of his administration. He set about correcting the division's manufacturing and maintenance problems. Maintenance was a considerable expense for all the dwarfs: because their customers were spread out, they had to employ an uneconomical number of field engineers to cover the territory. RCA's maintenance effort was particularly inefficient since the work was handled by a separate division that had nothing to do with computers. "You can't maintain reliability in a computer which hasn't had reliability designed into it," says a former RCA man; at IBM, no products are built without the concurrence of field engineering. A major Bradburn accomplishment was to have computer maintenance transferred to the computer division; it took him two years to persuade the corporation to do this.

Many of the technical problems that plagued Donegan later, however, could be traced to the Bradburn era. Bradburn, a laconic engineer, proved just the opposite of McCollister: though he projected a certain Gary Cooper charm in relaxed conversation, he was said to be an austere and thorny manager. The engineers, the programmers and the product planners were squabbling over future products, and Bradburn was not the man to inspire or unite them. There was friction between Bradburn and the chief engineer; the old Spectra team fell apart, and Bradburn had no strong group to replace it. The development budget had tripled during the Bradburn years, and at the time Donegan took over, said an RCA man, there was "damn little in the way of new product to show for it."

In the late sixties RCA made some questionable software decisions. The chief of systems programming felt, not unreasonably at the time, that IBM's software was far too ambitious for the equipment and produced a modest operating system for the Spectra. In 1967 RCA brought out two additional Spectras designed for timesharing, which many technical men thought required the use of virtual memory. At that time only Burroughs had been able to carry out this concept both effectively and at a reasonable price. RCA decided to concentrate its energies on developing its own virtual memory system. The best programming talent was shifted to this project, while the leftovers maintained the Spectra software. But only a few of RCA's customers and prospects were ready for virtual memory, and when IBM's 360 software was finally completed, RCA was left with a noncompetitive Spectra system to cover most of its business. Many people in the sales organization and some programmers felt the company was "mortgaging the present for the future."

The year 1968 was a bad one for RCA. The computer division achieved only 75 percent of its sales quota, and Bradburn and McCollister decided to hire a new sales manager. At Bradburn's request, McCollister put the headhunters to work. In the fall of 1968 they came up with Donegan's name.

Donegan had graduated third in his class at the University of Nebraska, a fact which particularly impressed McCollister. He had joined IBM as a salesman in 1951, embarking on a career which looked highly creditable: his background showed an interesting diversity of experience for a sales manager. He had been a special representative in the chain and wholesale industries market and later became national industry manager in this field. He had managed a small branch office in Reading, Pennsylvania, and a large one in Philadelphia, and in 1964 was chosen to head the sizable district office in New England (shortly after Donegan arrived in New England, former colleagues report, there was a conspicuous shuffling of the branch managers under him; a new district manager is supposed to get rid of the deadwood, but as one ex-IBM'er put it, "this was a bloodbath"). Moreover, Donegan was obviously hard-driving and likable. Now, having once signed his own death warrant in recommending Bradburn, McCollister put his head in the noose.

"I told Donegan he was being hired as a sales manager," McCollister recalls, "but also made it clear that he was getting interviewed for my job. I said that within two years I would get either a promotion or a lateral, probably a lateral. I'd been in the rat race long enough, and I had battle fatigue."

Donegan proved to be an absolutely first-class sales manager. He was also a tough disciplinarian. A former RCA man remembers: "I was sitting in Donegan's office when a district manager called with some hard-luck story. Donegan told the man it was his problem, and perhaps they ought to have a chat about whether the man should continue as district manager."

The salesmen were making quota again. McCollister was pleased. "Donegan was bright, hard-working, and knowledgeable," he says. "He gave the field organization a feeling of central purpose, and as a new player he did it better than I could. I had no difficulty with him as a subordinate."

Bradburn was pleased, too. The engineer was then operating as both group vice-president and general manager, and he knew that the division would eventually need a new gm. "Sarnoff regularly asked us to identify our future managers," recalled Bradburn. "I gave him a plan which suggested Donegan as one of the options. I thought we shouldn't make any changes for the next two years, though, since Donegan was a good sales manager but not experienced in other ways, and I'd heard he wasn't cost-conscious at IBM."

In January 1970, however, Donegan became general manager of

the division. Bradburn was now group executive, nominally Donegan's superior but obliged to confine his efforts to three minidivisions which made computer-related products. McCollister became a marketing vice-president on Bradburn's staff ("Nowheresville," said an associate). Joseph W. Rooney, an old IBM colleague of Donegan's who had joined the company in the summer, had McCollister's old job. A year later, Bradburn left the company "for personal reasons" (his termination agreement called for severance payments totaling $231,400) and McCollister was afforded plenty of time for introspection in his large, silent office.

When Donegan took over, the Spectra was beginning to run out of steam, and RCA's new product line had been stalemated in development by long debates among the technical people. The customary action in such situations is to hold on by offering customers discounts on long-term leases for the old product line until the new one is ready. IBM, however, was due to announce its System 370 that summer, and according to a study done for RCA by Arthur D. Little, Inc., it was important to make an announcement within twelve months of IBM's.

RCA studies projected that System 370 would be a gentle but expensive enhancement of IBM's earlier line, so Donegan felt confident that he could put new covers on the Spectra, improve the prices and trot it out as RCA models 2, 3, 6 and 7. What customers really needed, he said at the Marlboro press conference, was not so much more computing power as extra memory space. RCA would give them a bit more power and a lot more memory at a price only slightly higher than what they were now paying for a 360. Moreover, for a fee to be arranged with the customer, RCA would guarantee that it could get his IBM programs running on RCA equipment by a specified date. This (with various other contractual bonuses) was what Donegan called "the strategy of interception." At the time of the press conference, IBM had introduced the first two vanilla 370's, which seemed to bear out his assumptions. Donegan noted that "the computer technology of the seventies is highly forecastable."

But IBM's technology, alas, was not forecastable. It subsequently brought out the two transitional 370's, innovative machines whose prices competed all too well with RCA equipment. And RCA customers discovered they could indeed get more for their money with the new series—by turning in their Spectras. RCA strategy was doing a fine job of intercepting its own machines: the manufacturing plants were busy producing new equipment, which was essentially the same as the old equipment, while customers returned old machines that hadn't yet recouped their costs. Then IBM, responding to other competitive pressures, offered drastic price cuts on its peripherals, which considerably lowered the overall cost of an IBM system. For RCA it was the *coup de grace,* or as Joe Rooney, Donegan's majordomo, observed a month before the division fell, "it impacted us."

Meanwhile, Donegan was busy remaking the division, using the same techniques that had made such a big splash in IBM's New England district six years earlier. By early 1971 he had installed ex-IBM'ers to head nearly every major function. Moreover, RCA people were being replaced by younger men who had been much lower down in IBM. Donegan's changes seem more a matter of politics than youth worship. If you bring in your people, they will be loyal; if you offer young men important promotions, they will be beholden to you; and anyway, IBM'ers are the best people in the world. It was bruited about that men without IBM backgrounds had little chance of advancement. Donegan also believed that you get better loyalty by growing your own salesmen, recruited from college campuses, instead of hiring Hessians from Burroughs and Honeywell. He brought in nine hundred trainees in two years. The hurry was demoralizing. RCA was staffed mainly by ex-IBM'ers at the top, new recruits at the bottom and confused, insecure old-timers in the middle.

Donegan believed in communications, a commendable concept, but the quantity of paper issuing from the home office reached ecologically disturbing proportions. "I write more memos than my whole staff put together," Donegan once told a visitor. Donegan, in the IBM style, liked to bring in promising young men, one at a time, to serve as his administrative assistant. Besides the administrative assistant, his staff consisted of four secretaries and varying numbers of young men assigned to the general manager's office on a task-force basis. The young men spent a lot of time drafting Donegan's memos, and the secretaries typing them; all the memos had a due date for reply, and one secretary kept a log of which responses were due when. "At first," remembers one of Donegan's task-force assistants, "people were flabbergasted to receive all those personal memos from the general manager, asking pointed, intelligent questions on every subject. After a while, though, he saturated the market."

Donegan believed that "the amount of equipment you sell is directly associated with the number of people you put in the street"—an oversimplification of IBM tenets—and so he nearly doubled the sales force. In 1971, however, when new systems were being sold at the expense of Spectras, the extra salesmen were an extravagance. (Thomas J. Watson, Sr. had increased IBM's sales force during the Depression, with considerable success. When criticized for doing it, he said, "When a man gets about my age, he always does something foolish. Now some men run to playing poker and others to horse races, some to ladies and one thing and another. My hobby is hiring salesmen.")

There were other extravagances. The management team, encouraged by Sarnoff's promise of heavy financing, thought RCA was a class company and ought to start behaving like one. The new factory in Marlboro had been built by Bradburn in better days, and he had also planned a $16 million headquarters building. Donegan might have delayed plans for the new building but didn't. He also decided to move the home office and much of its staff from the old headquarters in Cherry Hill, New Jersey to the Marlboro plant in 1971. Travel expenses between Marlboro and Cherry Hill mounted. As one former Cherry Hill man reports, "It took three days and four thousand dollars' worth of airline tickets to schedule a meeting. I was riding the Boston shuttle four times a week." The division rented a small jet, which made the Marlboro–Cherry Hill junket twice a day, and was, according to a Marlboro alumnus, "full of secretaries flown up from Cherry Hill to help with the filing." The spending sometimes surpassed IBM's, says one of the IBM'ers: "In my old job, if I had three or four West Coast things going I tried to do them all together. At RCA they'd fly a guy to and from California for a one-hour meeting. One man was hired from Denver. The company paid for his apartment in Cherry Hill, flew him home every weekend, and then had to start transporting him to Marlboro. On the shuttle you'd see twenty guys from RCA get off and each one rented his own car to drive to Marlboro."

Donegan inherited a weak technical organization and made it moribund. First he reorganized the Computer Systems Group along IBM lines. At that time, as we have seen, IBM's Data Processing Group consisted of a marketing division which was responsible for revenue, an engineering division with profit responsibility, and other divisions for components, manufacturing and field engineering. A product went through a series of phase reviews during which the various divisions fought it out, honing their arguments, until the group staff, guided by its financial men, stepped in to arbitrate. Even in an organization of IBM's size, resources and discipline, the process was not perfect. Donegan set out to duplicate the IBM procedures he knew, but RCA staffers found the structure unwieldy and the phase reviews confusing. Organizational chaos prevented the engineers from recognizing and solving important problems.

The future product line (called NTS, for New Technology Series) proved to be both ambitious and expensive. It was difficult to achieve compatibility with IBM's 370 and earlier RCA models. Engineers were designing unique, complicated circuit packages instead of buying cheaper off-the-shelf components which would have been satisfactory, and the circuits they designed didn't work. The equipment was, according to one engineer, "a bitch to maintain. We were in over our heads and nobody called for help." Costs skyrocketed and development of two out of three of the machines underway in Marlboro had to be curtailed.

At the Marlboro press conference, Joe Rooney reported that an RCA equivalent of IBM's impressive new 3330 disc storage unit was in the works, and that meanwhile "we are announcing our intention to support the 3330 . . . at no profit to us . . . for use with our new RCA series." RCA never kept this promise, nor did it decide how to produce a similar disc file (which is an essential piece of equipment). The engineers ordered the IBM product to copy. It arrived in the summer of 1971, "beautifully packed, with all its elaborate documentation, and the sight of it just demoralized people," says the engineer. "If marketing problems hadn't killed the division in 1971," he observes, "engineering would have brought us down sooner or later."

The chain of events that did bring the division down, however, began with the battle of the business plan, in which Ed Donegan tangled with one of his own men, a young ex-IBM'er named Larry Reeder. The business plan is a thick document presented by the general manager of each division to the chairman of the board. It contains the gm's forecast for the coming year: how many orders will be booked, how many machines will be delivered, the revenues, the expenses and the manpower requirements. It was prepared by the division's financial staff in the fall and went through reviews at various levels until it was delivered to Sarnoff in December.

In the fall of 1970, the financial men were preparing the business plan. To do so they had to get figures from the heads of each function—engineering, software, marketing and so on—and then present the completed plan to each chief for approval. When they came to Reeder, who had financial responsibility for the marketing organization, they met trouble. As a Reeder associate tells it, "The business plan called for $323 million in worldwide revenues for 1971, and we'd done only $259 million in 1970. It specifically projected a 40 percent growth in revenues from Reeder's own organization, which didn't mesh with what Larry knew about the business in the past, and he was disturbed. He asked for a breakdown of where the revenues would come from. It turned out the financial people were looking for $80 million in sales volume from purchased and long-term-leased computers—which was an enormous increase over the 1970 figure—and at the same time a major jump in rental revenue. We had a certain order backlog, which would flow into sales or rental, but was inadequate to support both projections." Reeder's colleagues, under pressure from Donegan, were eager to believe projections that supported an optimistic forecast. That forecast, Reeder felt, was based on inadequate data.

Larry Reeder went to his boss, Joe Rooney, the second man in the division, to tell him that the business plan was $80 million off, which meant an $80 million loss for the division since the business plan called for breakeven. According to the Reeder associate, Rooney told his young subordinate that guys in finance don't make $80 million mistakes. After Reeder had developed a presentation for Rooney, Rooney told him to go to Bill Acker, the division's vice-president for finance. "Acker erupted," says the Reeder associate, and again Reeder worked up an eight-page draft of calculations. "Ten days went by, with no response from Acker, and it's December 22, time to go to Sarnoff. Sarnoff already had a copy of the plan, and all that was left was the formal presentation."

Reeder went back to Rooney and said, "Tell Ed not to present the plan; we'll get killed." Rooney told Donegan and Donegan talked to Acker over the weekend. A few days later, Acker's new controller, Carmen Ferraioli, "came in with three of his troops to make Larry understand. Larry is sitting there with his obstinate business manager, and neither of them is buying; it goes on from three-thirty to seven, and then Larry and Carmen go out for a drink. At some point Larry was told that Ed wants a breakeven plan, and Larry wasn't playing on the team."

The following week Donegan told Rooney and Reeder that there had been an audit over the weekend, and Carmen discovered sizable revenue problems, with $10 million of arithmetic mistakes and another $30 million in errors in judgment, all of which were made before Ferraioli arrived. Donegan then called Sarnoff and told him that the business plan would be six weeks late.

The financial staff then began to build a new plan from the ground up. "BP II was a more realistic job," says the observer, "although Ed was still pressuring to keep it high, and there were some bad decisions. Donegan presented a plan calling for $261 million in revenue, with losses of $37 million. The corporation accepted it, although from private memos they really suspected we would lose $44 million." The pattern of profit and loss, however, was rather bizarre: the division was to lose $8 million in the first quarter, $20 million in the second, $14 million in the third and then make a whopping $5 million in the last quarter.

It was now early April 1971, and 30 Rockefeller Plaza was silent. Then suddenly corporate management began to ask what had gone wrong with the first business plan, and to say that maybe BP II wasn't so hot, either. The division spent sixty days responding to lengthy memos from Sarnoff, his staff and accountants. The blame for errors in BP I, a division report, was somehow shifted to corporate finance. The corporate controller resigned abruptly during the spring, and the executive vice-president for finance, a veteran RCA man, took early retirement.

By June, Sarnoff had been getting some flak from shareholders and investment bankers. Perhaps to allay their worries, he appointed a new president of the corporation (Sarnoff had been both chairman of the board and president). Anthony L. Conrad, an RCA man for twenty-five years, had been executive vice-president, services, governing the corporation's most profitable divisions and subsidiaries. Conrad, who would take office August 1, was known as the best operational executive in the company. RCA-watchers noted a rather Byzantine arrangement by which Sarnoff himself kept control of the corporate staff and of NBC, his first love, while the other operating divisions and subsidiaries would report to Conrad.

Toward the end of the month, a rumor spread that RCA was planning to sell off its computer division to Xerox at a large loss; the rumor caused suspension of trading in RCA on the New York Stock Exchange. On July 1, Sarnoff sent a statement to the SEC, avowing that "RCA has no intention of selling its Computer Division. It has had no discussions with anyone in the past concerning such a sale. There are no discussions currently under way." Of course RCA and computer industry people talked bitterly about the statement when the division went out of business. At the Government-IBM antitrust trial, Conrad testified that at the time of his election in June, "to the best of my knowledge and belief there was no thought of exiting the business," and that he first learned of such thoughts in "approximately the second week of August." Ed McCollister does say that "during the second quarter" he had set up a meeting between Conrad and officials of NCR to discuss the possibility of a merger, but that nothing came of it. As for Xerox, as far back as 1970, when Donegan had just taken over and the division's future looked bright, Xerox is known to have had informal internal discussions about merging the two computer efforts, and to have dismissed the subject without consulting RCA. In early July Sarnoff was still defending the division's prospects to several importunate members of the board.

The division tried to boost morale by holding a two-day managers' meeting in Marlboro, but it only made things worse. There was a videotape message from Conrad, expressing confidence in the management team. Rooney and Donegan spoke, "saying we were doing terrifically in the marketplace," recalls one manager. "They glossed over the serious problems in hardware and software, and said our equipment was competitive, which it wasn't. Then they called in the button men—the director of industrial marketing, for one—who stood up and proved the world was flat."

Even before the meeting, Larry Reeder was still beleaguered. Reeder was in charge of production schedules. His associate remembers, "Our order backlog was lower in July than it had been in January. We'd been having more cancellations than new orders, but the order books didn't show it. You're supposed to report gross orders minus cancellations and discontinuances. The division was reporting gross as if it were net. Reeder felt we should at least take the cancellations out of the factory schedules. So Larry is keeping two sets of

books, one for Donegan's sales record and the other for the plant, so
we wouldn't build up huge inventories."

On July 16, Carmen Ferraioli quit. Before leaving, he audited
the books and found that unreported cancellations and discontinuances represented one million dollars' worth of monthly revenue.
Acker was relieved of his financial responsibilities and the division's
new vice-president for finance was a gift from Conrad, the new
president: an old-line, green-eyeshade financial man named Julius
Koppelman who nominally reported to Donegan but had strong loy-
alties to 30 Rockefeller Plaza. Koppelman appeared with Ferraioli's
audit in hand, and a corporate vp questioned marketing about the
water on the books. Two of the latter's lieutenants sat in on phase
review meetings. Conrad paid a call on the division in late July,
asking for a worst-case estimate of the division's losses. Acker said
maybe $45 million, he wasn't sure. Koppelman listened. Conrad
promised to return on August 10 for a final report, and Koppelman
went to work.

Several documents prepared for Conrad by members of the corporate staff during the summer of 1971 have been exhibited during
the IBM-Government antitrust trial. One, written by Richard Sonnenfeldt, who worked for the corporate financial vice-president, was
sharply critical of RCA's market strategy: it noted that "to attack
IBM head on amounts to attacking a well-led army with a comman-
do company in an open field," and added, "any idea that within this
strategy we can achieve profitability is nonsense." The report recommended retrenchment and expense-cutting, and a shifting of RCA's
computer efforts toward specialization by industry and application—a strategy similar to that ultimately followed by the dwarfs
who survived. It said that unlike many of its competitors, RCA was
rich enough to play a waiting game, and that in three to five years
some of the other dwarfs might be ripe for acquisition. It promoted
the idea that the company could "work out an approach that can
win for RCA, other than divesture" [*sic*].

Another staff report, however, was less sanguine. This report predicted an operating loss of $63 million for the Computer Systems
Division in 1971. It also suggested that the division's accounting
methods were not as conservative as they should be and led to an
overoptimistic assessment of the unit's performance. Were RCA to
adopt the methods used by Univac, for example, it would show an

additional $15 million loss. Moreover, were RCA to discard an unrealistic procedure for recording income from long-term leases, the adjustment for the current year would add another $23 million to the division's losses, raising the total to $104 million; it would also lower the revenues projected for future years. (There was some dispute later about the accuracy of this particular statement.) Finally, the report called attention to several other inadequacies in financial controls, for which the division shared responsibility with corporate finance. The report then observed that

> None of these specific operating problems taken alone would lead to a major re-evaluation of the future potential of the computer business for RCA. In combination, however, these problems reduce the credibility of any projections which indicate profitability is near at hand.

The result of all this was that RCA could not expect to break even on computers before 1975, and that through 1976 the division would need an additional $700 million in cash. The extra demands of the computer division would raise the corporation's requirement for outside financing during this period to $1 billion. If all went well, the company could raise the money, but the slightest downturn in the economy or in RCA's other operations would hamper its prospects, and reports of continued computer losses would not sit well with the financial community. Finally, as the company's investment in the computer division grew, so would the book value of its assets, and it would be that much more difficult to sell out in the future; RCA would be riding a tiger it could not dismount. It was time to plan divestiture.

In early September, corporate officials spoke informally with several possible buyers, but none expressed interest, and chances for selling the division looked gloomy. According to an article in *Fortune* which ran a year later, "Sometime during this period, Sarnoff came to the conclusion that RCA had to abandon the business, even if no buyers materialized."

Whatever Sarnoff's personal feelings, such a conclusion would have been inevitable. In those days, battles in the boardroom were not the style at RCA. "Once convened, the board acted with seeming unanimity or purpose," reports a high-level RCA alumnus. "All the maneuvering had gone on before. It was like the two Macedonian generals who met in the middle of the battlefield and gave each other a headcount—I've got so many horse-soldiers, so many spear-chuckers, how many have you? The guy with the biggest head-count won, and nobody needed to fight."

In recent years, RCA had become something of a conglomerate, numbering among its subsidiaries Random House, Hertz, Banquet Foods and Coronet Industries, a home-furnishings manufacturer. All were among the more profitable operations in the company, and presumably resented the drain of corporate resources into Computer Systems. The change in the division's forecast from breakeven a year earlier to a loss of $62 million or more must have been quite a blow. Two of the new subsidiaries had their chief executives on the board of directors. Coronet's president, Martin B. Seretean, as the corporation's largest stockholder (he owned 1,477,703 shares of common stock, far outdoing Sarnoff), had considerable clout. He is said to have remarked that there were lots of better ways to spend $700 million. Donald A. Petrie of Lazard Freres and Stephen M. DuBrul, Jr., of Lehman Brothers, the corporation's investment bankers, were also eager to unload the albatross, and so was Robert L. Werner, executive vice-president and general counsel. Moreover, there were three RCA old-timers on the board, as well as a vice-president of Metropolitan Life (from whom the corporation had often borrowed money) who would have supported the move to get out of computers. Add Conrad and Banquet Foods, and you had ten spear-chuckers right there.

On September 16 Sarnoff met in his office with Conrad, Werner and two other RCA executives. One of the two was Chase Morsey, the Ford alumnus Sarnoff had brought in several years earlier to head marketing. Morsey had been a leading participant in Sarnoff's original decision to emphasize computers; now he was the financial vice-president. When he delivered the latest report on the division's status and prospects, everyone at the meeting supported the decision to leave the computer business. Sarnoff called a special board meeting for the next day, keeping the purpose of the meeting secret for security reasons.

The report Morsey delivered to the board followed the reasoning of the second corporate study. The board agreed to exit the business immediately. Once you'd shopped around for a buyer, Werner noted, the word would get out, and RCA might have the SEC on its back. Werner is also reported to have been worried that the company might be subject to charges of fraud if it signed long-term contracts with customers after having made a policy decision to get out.

Nearly a month after the division went out of business, RCA reported an extraordinary loss of $490 million. The loss represented a revaluation of the division's assets on the assumption that since RCA Computer Systems was no longer a going concern, these assets had a substantially different value to the corporation. In addition, the total writeoff figure included an estimate of additional onetime costs to be incurred as a result of discontinuing the division, such as severance pay, disposal of plant facilities and so forth.

The amount of the actual loss was probably overstated. It is common practice that when a corporation decides to take an extraordinary or onetime loss, an attempt will be made to treat other operating losses incurred during the period as part of the "onetime" loss, thus making the remaining operations look more profitable. As long as the corporation has enough capital to run its other operations it can absorb the onetime loss. On the Monday after the farewell announcement, RCA stock went up 2⅝ and continued to climb while the rest of the market was behaving rather badly. The stock went up because the computer division had been a continual drain on corporate finances, and now the drain was stopped; in the eyes of the financial community, RCA was, as one analyst put it, "cutting off the gangrenous arm." Andy Conrad was now running the company, they said, and things would be different. As for the $490 million figure (reduced by an estimated tax recovery to $250 million), it might have to be changed on later statements to reflect income derived from the subsequent sale of part of the division (this did happen; the amount of loss was reduced by $78 million).

In the weeks immediately following it was difficult for an outsider to make a fair evaluation of RCA's action in dissolving a division which had so drastically sapped its resources. Perhaps, as corporate apologists would undoubtedly observe, going out of business is like breaking an engagement: there is simply no kind way to do it, and clean-and-quick may be the best. But in RCA's subsequent behavior there was much to criticize. The company's policies appeared to have been guided by three considerations: to keep the division salable, to avoid legal complications and to save face. These are all quite natural motives for the men who guide a corporation with 339,000 shareholders, but RCA was evasive in clarifying its commitments to customers and tardy in defining layoff policies. This equivocation created confusion and ill will. Finally, on November 19, after rumors of marriage with almost every major company in the industry, RCA announced it was selling its customer base to Univac.

Despite all the evidence of questionable management at the division level, there was surprisingly little bitterness toward Donegan among RCA Computer Systems employees (except, of course, for some of the men he displaced); this is evidence of Donegan's remarkable personal appeal. While few associates, if any, were close to him, he could inspire affection: a former administrative assistant, who had worked in Donegan's office for nine months, spoke at length over the telephone with a devotion that could not be counterfeited. "That time with Donegan was almost like going to business school. He took time out of his busy schedule to train people. I'd say he was the most brilliant man I've ever worked for."

A large share of the blame belongs to the corporation. One of the few RCA old-timers on the Donegan team reflects, "In retrospect, I think we tried to do too much too fast. But where was 30 Rockefeller Plaza during all this? Shouldn't they have blown the whistle and said, 'Hey, what's the rush?' "

It is a question that should be asked. The corporation was expert in electronic technology but never made the effort to learn the other aspects of the complex computer business. Sarnoff chose an insufficiently experienced man to lead the division and gave him his head. Throughout the Donegan era, there was no computer expert on the board of directors. "We were," says one former RCA computer man, "like a child who is given plenty of spending money but no wisdom and understanding."

9

How the Dwarfs Made Out: The Second Wave

———

IN THE EARLY to middle fifties, Sperry, Burroughs and NCR entered the computer business by absorbing small companies founded by young engineers who had pioneered in computer development and then encountered financial difficulties. A decade later, however, three similar small companies were able to attract investors, survive and prosper, enriching the founders, the venture capitalists and the early shareholders. In the sixties, companies with some reference to computers in their names began to acquire an aura of magic, and the most palpable aura surrounded Control Data Corporation, Digital Equipment Corporation and Scientific Data Systems.

The first wave of computer companies, the ones that sold out, had been ahead of their time, using a primitive, costly technology to serve an undeveloped market. Then, in the fifties, the computer industry began to find itself. Transistor circuitry and the tiny magnetic cores devised for memory made the machines cheaper and more compact and reliable. IBM developed the commercial computer market. A second wave of dwarfs came along, and in an odd way they benefited from IBM's definition. They could find their own market among scientific customers who were secure enough not to lean on the giant, a market whose requirements the giant didn't fill.

In the early sixties, when Control Data, Digital Equipment and Scientific Data Systems began to attract attention, the Wall Street bubble was beginning to swell. The financial community started to acquire a little learning about computers, and the three new companies began to thrive beyond their expectations.

Each flourished under the direction of one man, a man whose

style, dreams and quirks became the company's; a stubborn, moody, complex founder whose subordinates regarded him with reverence and a touch of fear and called him "visionary" whatever the criticisms of the world outside (the employee stayed on in awe; or the employee left in disgust; there was rarely a middle ground).

The most commanding of the three was Control Data's William C. Norris, a spare, laconic man given to salty language and terse parables derived from his boyhood on a farm near Red Cloud, Nebraska. Control Data men loved to talk of his thirst for work and detail, of Norris carrying home a thick technical manual at five o'clock and delivering a careful analysis of it at eight the next morning; of his expecting the same performance from his executives and his countering complaints with the reminder that he used to load grain from his father's silo into a truck, and "the harder you shovel, the faster it falls." They note his tirades over such frills as carpeting in the executive offices. If he tended to pay a premium for the seventy-odd small companies he bought over the years, they were necessary, part of the grand design.

Control Data achieved success by building supercomputers, the most powerful and sophisticated machines of their day. The company's history shows its chairman's penchant for growth and his eagerness to gamble during hard times that the supercomputer will be debugged and the acquisitions prove profitable, an almost religious belief that Someone is watching over Bill Norris.

There were roots for this style in Norris's youth. The farm life was idyllic enough when he was a boy, when he trapped skunk and possum and sold the pelts for pocket money, and when the three Norris children rode one pony to a one-room schoolhouse. But as he grew older, in the dust-bowl years of the thirties, Norris saw the Nebraska farmlands fall victim to the whims of nature. He resolved to find a career that would give him more control over his destiny; this notion of control has driven him ever since.

Later, after he had founded Control Data, he came up against IBM, a giant force of money and men that seemed as inexorable as a drought or a hurricane. "We are now living at IBM's sufferance," he told a *Fortune* reporter. To his own executives and to security analysts he drew an image from the sea. IBM was a shark, and most smaller companies were pilot fish, swimming under the shark's jaws, taking its leavings, always worrying about getting eaten. To survive, to have control, you had to *become* a shark yourself; hence the acquisitions. The club for outstanding salesmen at Control Data is called the Shark Club, the sort of name that CDC men, a rugged lot whose offices are cluttered with stuffed ducks, wall-eyed pike and other trophies, find inspiring.

In one of Norris's most often repeated parables he recalls that in order to find a métier more secure than farming, he had studied electrical engineering at the University of Nebraska; he graduated during the Depression and couldn't find a job, and so he went home to run the farm. During 1934 there was a drought; there was no grain, and the corn was burning, and the only green thing in sight was the Russian thistle, which seemed to be growing everywhere. Other farmers were selling their cattle, convinced there would not be food enough to get the animals through the winter. But Norris didn't want a farm without livestock. As a boy he had noticed cattle nibbling Russian thistles, a sight surprising enough to stick in his mind. Perhaps by mixing the thistles with cottonseed cake, he could get his cattle cheaply through the winter; he would gamble on the rains coming in the spring. "We moved and stacked more than a hundred acres of green Russian thistles," Norris remembered many years later. "I had difficulty finding people to help because no one wanted the onus of being involved in such a foolhardy enterprise." He even bought other farmers' cows. The gamble worked; the cattle survived, and there was rain the next spring. You always had to count on a certain amount of luck, he said, but if you didn't take that initial gamble all the luck in the world would do you no good. In periods of financial drought, Norris refused to sell his companies—his cattle—and in the spring the rains always came.

Before the war Norris was a sales engineer at Westinghouse, and in 1941 he joined the Navy, to be assigned eventually to a special communications section doing highly classified cryptography. When the war ended, the Defense Department realized it might be useful to preserve this assemblage of technical talent accustomed to working under top-secret conditions. It was suggested that if Norris and his colleagues could find private financing to set up a computer research and development company, they might find the goverment generous in awarding contracts. The group found the financing, and the Defense Department proved as good as its word.

Engineering Research Associates, as the new company was

called, dealt almost exclusively in special-purpose data processing equipment produced to the Navy's order; to show the size of the computer industry at that time, Control Data now estimates that by the end of 1952 ERA had built and delivered more than 80 percent of the value of all electronic computers then in existence in the United States. Drew Pearson had written an explosive column, revealing that this small, inexperienced St. Paul company had obtained secret Navy contracts without competitive bidding and had later hired some naval officers. According to Univac's Arthur Draper, the Navy wanted Pearson to lay off, and hoping that the sponsorship of a substantial corporation like Remington Rand might lend ERA a more respectable aura, proposed to James Rand that he buy the firm. Control Data's own version says that ERA needed capital to expand into the commercial market and its chief financial backer thought a sale to Remington Rand was the best way to get it. Probably for both reasons, Norris and his associates reluctantly consented to the acquisition. "The Christmas of 1952," notes a Control Data company history, "was a somber affair. . . . At a sad meeting in Norris's office, Norris distributed electric shavers to his management personnel in lieu of the usual Christmas turkey."

We have seen Remington Rand become Sperry Rand, merging its two computer operations—ERA and the former Eckert-Mauchly Computer Corporation—into the Univac division. The ERA people lasted barely five years: rivalry with the Eckert-Mauchly group and the frustrations of dealing with a weak management wore them down. In 1957, when a management consultant came to Norris with a proposal for a new company, he found the engineer thoroughly receptive.

Norris and his associates decided to finance Control Data by selling shares directly to the public, without the backing of an underwriter. This method was considered so unusual and risky for a new company that the Minnesota State Securities Commission, to protect investors, required the firm to furnish a presubscription list of people who had read the prospectus and would buy the stock if it became available. Within ten days Control Data provided a list of three hundred names (mostly friends and former colleagues from Univac). They had, in effect, sold out the entire offering before it was officially made. Norris himself took 75,000 shares at a dollar a share, an investment which, in the boom year of 1967, after the stock had split twice and was selling at $165, was worth some $55½ million.

The prospectus of Control Data stated that the company's principal initial business would be research and development for the military, and that the company would also get into components and computer accessories; it did not intend to compete head-on with IBM and the other giants of the industry. But among the former ERA men whom Norris wooed away from Univac was a talented engineer named Seymour Cray, who convinced Norris that a powerful, relatively inexpensive solid-state computer built from printed circuit modules would prove highly profitable. You could sell it to sophisticated customers—the Department of Defense, the aircraft companies, the universities—who did not require a heavy investment in marketing and support; they knew quality when they saw it, and preferred to do their own programming. Developing Cray's 1604 computer was a costly program for a small company to undertake, and Norris had just spent half a million dollars on his first acquisition, a production engineering firm. Still, he took the gamble, and the salaries of CDC employees were cut in half while the 1604 was in progress.

The 1604 computer's success in the scientific community—CDC reported its first profits after less than two years of operating, an extraordinary record for a mainframe company—gave Cray a reputation for genius, a fame nourished not only by further design successes but by the man's peculiar, reclusive personality. As the company grew Cray began to complain that it wasn't any fun any more: administrative and ceremonial duties were getting him down. He had a single-minded ambition to design the largest computers in the world, and about these machines he could talk eloquently; on any other subject he was silent. What Cray wanted was to work in some quiet woodsy place like his hometown, Chippewa Falls, Wisconsin, where he owned some land. As for Norris, he was betting on Cray, who was clearly a man worth coddling. He built a lab on Cray's land, and Cray became known as the Hermit of Chippewa Falls. Norris visited the lab twice a year by appointment and Cray came to headquarters every six weeks or so. The rest of the time he worked far into the night with his soldering iron. When one of Norris's aides brought some professors, prestige customers, out to the lab to see The Hermit, Cray gave an illuminating talk on his current project and then, in honor of the occasion, took the visitors out to the local diner—an almost unheard-of mark of favor since Cray usually brought his lunch in a metal pail. But after finishing his hot dog—with dispatch—Cray arose, said he'd better be getting back to work, wished the professors a pleasant trip and walked out. There was, perhaps, a certain showmanship in such a performance, but if so, it didn't hurt the company.

In 1963 Control Data announced the 6600, which was to be the greatest achievement of Cray's career, an aristocrat of a machine designed to enthrall that small, elite group of customers like the Atomic Energy Commission and the United States Weather Bureau whose thirst for computing power was nearly insatiable. The 6600 would be twenty times more powerful than Cray's first machine and three times more powerful than STRETCH, the supercomputer that IBM had killed a few years earlier. The first model was slated for delivery to the AEC's Livermore Laboratory in February 1964. But the 6600, with 350,000 transistors, proved more difficult to debug than had been expected, and it was not ready for installation until six months later. Meanwhile, IBM had set its formidable organization to work on producing and marketing a supercomputer that would eradicate the 6600.

System 360 was announced before Control Data could install the 6600, and at the top of the IBM line was the model 90, a faster machine than its competitor. While no prototype of the machine existed in IBM's laboratories, the company's most persuasive technical salesmen went out among the gold-chip customers to tout the 90.

The year 1965 saw ferment throughout the computer industry. As the 6600 went into volume production it developed manufacturing difficulties, and now Control Data was selling against IBM. In order to close deals with two additional AEC laboratories, Norris agreed to accept heavy penalty payments for late delivery. When RCA and IBM announced price cuts on smaller computers, he followed suit and also, in panic, lopped $2 million off the price of the 6600. At the same time many of Control Data's customers who had purchased their machines in the past were now choosing to lease them, thus postponing the income CDC needed, and several of the small companies that Norris had acquired in 1963 were still losing money.

Norris held on. He was gambling that the rains would come—that the 6600 would live up to its promises, that the acquisitions would flourish and that the Lord might visit some small plague on IBM's model 90. In all respects, he proved right. By the end of 1967, sixty-three nicely debugged 6600's had gone out to gold-chip customers, and, off in the Wisconsin woods, Seymour Cray was at work on a new machine, to be nearly five times as powerful as the current model. IBM's model 90 became the series 90; four different versions were announced; but by 1967 none had been delivered. That year Armonk abandoned the series, announcing that the company would produce only those machines that were currently on order.

The experiences of 1965 had left Norris bitter. He felt he had been fighting a mythical enemy. The models 90 existed on paper, not in the lab; IBM salesmen would talk to the customers, and then they would enhance the specifications of their machines, forcing Norris to promise more for the 6600. Then IBM would escalate, and CDC would have to make more promises—thereby putting an increasing strain on its engineers and programmers. The mere suggestion that IBM was working on a superior new machine—even if there was nothing to look at—made customers hold off from ordering 6600's; and then model after model in the IBM series never went into production. The episode of the models 90 was the third such skirmish CDC had had with IBM.

Norris began to feel that IBM's competitors could find redress only in the courts. In 1965 he had asked Control Data's lawyers to gather evidence of possible antitrust violations by IBM. A year later, CDC began to submit memos describing alleged violations to the antitrust division of the Justice Department, in hopes that the government would sue IBM. The CDC lawyers continued to collect data, but the government made no move. Finally, CDC lawyers visited the Justice Department to find out if the government intended to sue IBM; they were told it didn't. In December 1968, therefore, Control Data filed suit against IBM, charging thirty-seven instances of monopolistic practices, some of them in direct violation of IBM's own code of ethics. The most important charge concerned IBM's alleged marketing of "paper machines and phantom computers"— products "which were not yet in production, and as to which it had no reasonable basis for believing that production or delivery could be accomplished within the time periods specified." A month later, on the last working day of the Johnson administration, the government separately sued IBM.

At the same time, Norris was developing strategies for combating IBM in the marketplace. Early on, he had realized that Seymour Cray's genius alone was not proof against so formidable an opponent. He built up a lucrative sideline in peripheral equipment; through internal development and the acquisition of small suppliers, CDC became the largest purveyor of wholesale peripherals in the industry, selling to mainframe companies reluctant to invest in developing their own peripheral gear.

Norris's acquisition policy was part of his effort to survive by diversification. Since the 1956 consent decree, IBM had been obliged to sell computer services through an arm's-length subsidiary, the Service Bureau Corporation, and this had weakened the giant's dominance in the services industry. During the mid-sixties, Norris began to buy service bureaus, which handled computer work for customers whose machines were overloaded or who were too small to set up their own installations. As CDC grew, it became apparent that customers needed more technical support than Norris had anticipated; since Control Data had to train large numbers of technicians anyway, he set up computer schools to accomplish the training program at a profit. In 1968 Control Data, its stock zooming again, could afford to swallow a corporation nearly ten times its size: Commercial Credit, a finance company with gross assets of more than $3½ billion. Thus farmer Norris could irrigate his crops in time of drought, and fisherman Norris had his shark at last. As more of Control Data's customers began to lease their machines, Commercial Credit could assume the financial risks; it could lend money to students at Control Data computer schools; the other possibilities for synergy were numerous. And it turned out that Commercial Credit fulfilled its promise. The 1970–71 recession hit supercomputers hardest of all; when Control Data's computer operations lost $46 million, it was Credit that allowed Norris to hold on.

In particular, Norris held on to the IBM lawsuit, while other plaintiffs in the throes of the recession chose out-of-court settlements. In 1971, in the midst of lengthy discovery proceedings, IBM filed a counterclaim against Control Data that was every bit as gamy as Norris's complaint. CDC had accused IBM of reciprocal marketing practices; now IBM leveled the same accusation against CDC. If certain brokerage houses installed Control Data computers, CDC would give them underwriting business; more ominously, if underwriting firms currently dealing with Control Data refused to get the sales message, CDC would take its trade elsewhere. The Control Data internal memos unearthed by IBM lawyers during discovery proceedings were notably indiscreet.

There had been an undercurrent of dissension about the lawsuit within Control Data, but after IBM's countersuit even the doubters seemed to support Norris enthusiastically, and the lawyers went ahead gathering and organizing information for the suit with vigorous cooperation from Control Data executives. CDC surpassed the Justice Department in money and people and understanding of the industry; it knew where the bodies were buried, and it pointed out the graves to Justice. IBM had cause for nervousness as long as Control Data's suit remained active, and good reason to seek a settlement. In January 1972, according to a CDC executive, IBM's lawyers began to suggest obliquely that there might be a way to settle the suit. By the spring of '72, two IBM vice-presidents and two Control Data vice-presidents began holding informal discussions.

Negotiations sputtered along until the fall, when T. V. Learson announced his impending retirement as chairman of IBM. The IBM lawyers began to make oblique suggestions again. Mr. Learson would like to leave his successor with a clean slate. There was no sense talking through ambassadors; the chief executives should get together. Around Thanksgiving, Learson and Norris began to discuss settlement.

It was January 15, 1973 when IBM and Control Data at last announced settlement of the lawsuit. The cornerstone of the agreement was CDC's purchase of the Service Bureau Corporation from IBM for its book value of $16 million. For some time IBM, hamstrung by the restrictions of the 1956 consent decree, had despaired of making SBC a lucrative business: while the subsidiary was narrowly profitable in 1971, it had lost money for the two preceding years, and management had often discussed whether to sell it off or phase it out. Norris, on the other hand, believed that the services side of CDC's business would eventually outperform the hardware side; he had consolidated his small service bureaus and data centers into a sizable network, Cybernet, which specialized in remote computing services, in which a terminal in the customer's office was hooked up to a large computer on CDC premises. Cybernet was geared to scientific customers; SBC provided similar services for the business market; and their union would make CDC the largest supplier worldwide in data processing services. Most industry experts felt that IBM's conservative accounting practices had undervalued SBC; on the open market, it would be worth $45 to $50 million.

CDC also got a package of subsidies totaling $101 million. IBM would underwrite benefits for SBC employees for ten years; SBC's own computers would operate rent-free for six months; IBM would buy $25 million worth of SBC services and award CDC another $30 million in research contracts; and IBM would pay CDC's legal fees. IBM itself would stay out of the services business for the next six years.

The benefits of the settlement for IBM became apparent a week after it was announced. During the discovery proceedings Control Data had received some forty million documents from IBM, many of which were also available to the Justice Department. With the aid of CDC staffers, the lawyers had skillfully separated the wheat from the chaff and produced a computerized index to 75,000 pages of IBM internal memoranda. The Justice Department depended on the index in preparing its case. But on Saturday before the settlement was announced, CDC and IBM employees had worked until four in the morning destroying their lawyers' "work-product." While such destruction is customary following out-of-court settlements, the definition of "work-product"—which usually means lawyers' notes—was broadened to embrace the computerized index, a decision which the Jusitice Department and many people in the computer industry thought highly improper. IBM and Control Data claimed that no actual evidence had been destroyed, that the index was theirs to dispose of and its destruction was part of laying down the cudgels. The issue became another skirmish in the government's battle with IBM, but there were no repercussions to Control Data. Still, to many observers Norris-the-crusader became a slightly tarnished idol.

The recession with its layoffs and other austerity policies, the uncertain outcome of the lawsuit, and delays in the design of the newest supercomputers had damaged morale at Control Data; now, after the settlement, the company began to move forward again. Despite a continued seesawing of crises between the credit and computer sides of the business, Norris and his company proved surprisingly resilient. In 1973 Seymour Cray resigned to form his own company, and his departure reinforced the company's resolve to shift its emphasis to other products. CDC dropped out of supercomputers for several years, but the success of Cray's company and the interest of a new set of corporate customers in number-crunchers has brought the company back, racing to catch up with Cray.

CDC is the largest purveyor of computer services, a market which International Data Corporation predicts will reach $12½ billion by 1984. CDC's services include the sale of raw computer power available through a terminal in the customer's office, with or without applications packages; special industry services such as Ticketron and various offerings to the financial community; the sale of actual information accessible through the customer's terminal; and consulting.

The largest part of the business—$725 million in 1979—is in peripherals. Services, consulting and education brought in $600 million and mainframes $500 million; CDC now tends to characterize the mainframes as support for the services. In recent years Norris has talked increasingly about social responsibility. The company is bigger and richer, and Norris is seventy, an age when a man thinks about what he will leave behind; a corporation, he says, has to do something for society as well as for its stockholders. The company's social responsibility projects began with the traditional plant-in-the-ghetto ventures espoused also by IBM and Xerox; then, however, Norris began to direct some of the company's business efforts into areas of social need.

He is a passionate believer in the use of computer technology to help solve social problems. More efficient methods of sharing technology, he feels, would lead to faster progress in developing alternate energy sources, conservation and environmental protection, and would also produce new jobs; accordingly, CDC sells TECHNO-TEC, an information service which lists prospective buyers and sellers of various technological innovations, and when Norris gives speeches all over the world promoting technological cooperation, he also sells TECHNOTEC, doing well by doing good. CDC has organized a program to develop computer-aided health care services among the Rosebud Sioux; the sizable donation the company has made to the program will, it hopes, yield a service which can be marketed in developing countries.

Like the late economist, E. F. Schumacher, Norris the farmer believes that the solution to many agricultural and food problems lies in a return to small farms, aided by computer and communications technology; CDC has organized Rural Ventures, Inc., a consortium to push development of small-scale agricultural enterprise. The company is deeply involved with computer-aided education and has invested heavily in PLATO, an impressive but costly hardware and software system. It is marketing PLATO not only to schools, colleges and corporations, but to social agencies that train dropouts. There are differing opinions on the worth of all these projects, both to society and to Control Data, but the company's commitment to them seems more solid and sincere because Norris has made them business ventures, not sheer charity.

Past criticism of CDC held that it was a one-man company, ruled by an autocrat surrounded by yes-men. In 1980 Norris announced plans for an orderly succession. He also said he might very well stick around for another five years, and among CDC's young tigers, the odds were running heavily that Norris would outlast them all.

II

In 1957, the year that Norris started Control Data, another company, Digital Equipment Corporation, was founded by a man whose style and ideas were almost directly opposite to Norris's. Kenneth H. Olsen—who is tall, pudgy and soft-spoken, where Norris is slight, wiry and sharp-tongued—wanted to build small, fast computers that were cheap, simple and fun to design and use, machines to be approached without reverence and without the intermediaries in the computer room. He has never acquired a company; he has always believed that growth is not a goal but something that comes automatically if you do a good job, and something you must manage carefully for fear of losing control. Olsen didn't take Digital public for nine years. He founded the company with $70,000 from American Research and Development, a venture capital firm headed by General Georges Doriot, a Harvard Business School professor. In 1972, when the aging Doriot sold ARD, its interest in DEC was worth $350 million. If Olsen was content to remain a pilot fish, as Norris might put it, he was as nimble and healthy a pilot fish as any in the ocean, and among the most widely respected chief executives in the industry.

Olsen spent his boyhood in Stratford, Connecticut, which was a center for the manufacture of machine tools. Believing that electronics was "the machine tool of the future," he studied electrical engineering at MIT. In 1950, when he was twenty-four and pursuing a master's degree, he went to work as a research assistant at MIT's Digital Computer Laboratory, the ancestor of Lincoln Labs. The laboratory's main project, which had been under way for three years, was the design of the Whirlwind Computer, commissioned by the Office of Naval Research and the Air Force for aircraft simulation and, by extension, for any applications in which the computer directs a process, from air traffic control to guided missile warfare. This was what the experts called "real-time" computing, in which the machine had to receive information—often fed to it by a layman—and react to it immediately. The uses planned for Whirlwind imposed special requirements for speed and reliability. As its chief designer wrote:

> In a system where much valuable property and perhaps many human lives are dependent on the proper operation of the computing equipment, failures must be very rare. Furthermore, checking alone, however complete, is inadequate. It is very unlikely that a man, presumably not too well suited to the work during normal conditions, can handle the situation in an emergency.

This pressing need for speed and reliability led the laboratory's chief, Dr. Jay Forrester, to devise the magnetic core memory, in which tiny doughnut-shaped cores, strung together in a grid, were magnetized either to the left or the right to represent a 1 or a 0 in the computer's binary code. Once Forrester had designed the core memory, however, it took sixty-five engineers (among them Ken Olsen) four years to make it work well enough to be produced in volume. Whirlwind's success had brought MIT an assignment to design the Air Defense Command's SAGE system, a massive computer-and-radar network for the detection of enemy aircraft. The laboratory had decided to put core memory into the SAGE computers. Olsen's boss, Norman Taylor, who worked for Forrester, wanted to design a small machine to test the memory before using it in SAGE; Forrester thought the project a waste of time. So Taylor gave Olsen, who appeared to be a bright, hard-driving young man, the job of designing the memory-test computer "under the table," with a ten-month deadline. Shortly afterward, Olsen told Taylor the machine couldn't be produced in ten months. "Do it in nine months," said Taylor, "and I'll buy you a case of Scotch." Olsen didn't drink, but he couldn't ignore the challenge: he and his staff worked nights and weekends to get the computer built in nine months, and Forrester was so delighted he forgot he'd been unenthusiastic to begin with.

Whirlwind and the early work on SAGE had given Olsen definite ideas on how computers ought to be designed and used, but he was a research engineer without commercial experience until he got his next assignment. IBM had won the contract to build the SAGE computers under MIT's direction. Taylor remembers, "When IBM started to build this monster I told Olsen to keep control over it; we were concerned about the reliability of their circuitry. Ken lived in Poughkeepsie for two and a half years, in the bowels of IBM. There was this whole new world called production that he didn't know anything about, but he was a bona fide engineer; if something didn't work he'd take his coat off and redo it himself. He could do anything. The inefficiencies of a large operation like IBM's were appalling to Olsen. One piece of equipment had to be done over more than once. We wondered why they didn't use their own computer to keep track of parts. One day Olsen said to me, 'Norm, I can beat these guys at their own game.' The next job I gave him was a transistorized research computer. He was the manager, not the designer, and he built a strong team spirit. He'd learned a lot from IBM, from watching the way large companies operate."

By 1957 the thirty-one-year-old Olsen had a solid background in real-time computing, transistors and production. He was, according to Taylor, "a standout in his group. He had achieved at that age what most people took ten years longer to do, but his experience at IBM had whetted his appetite for bigger things." A group of businessmen had approached Olsen to start a company; Olsen didn't like their proposal, but he was attracted by the idea of going into business for himself. He began to lose patience with academic life: "I thought it really wasn't fun unless you influenced the outside world," he says.

Olsen and Harlan Anderson, an associate, began to look into the mechanics of entrepreneurship. They read the financial statements of many different companies and sounded out General Doriot, the venture capitalist. "When we made our first proposal to ARD," Olsen remembers, "Doriot told us our profit projection of 5 percent wasn't enough, that we'd better raise it to 10 percent, and he said to promise quick results, because most of the men on his board of directors were over 80."

Doriot says, "We told Ken not to emphasize computers. Here were IBM, Burroughs, RCA in that business. To have two young men come to older men and talk of competing with them didn't sound quite modest. A lot of companies needed circuit modules for testing their equipment and didn't want to make their own, so we settled on that for the first product, and the proposal mentioned that the company eventually planned to make computers. Ken had managed people in the lab, he was extremely perceptive, he realized the relationships between production and distribution. He has a full understanding of the market two or three years out, he knows how to take the available techniques and use them imaginatively, and his ideas are not so advanced that they're dangerous. In its first full year DEC made 50 percent more sales than it planned and three times the profit. And I think DEC needed less counseling from us than most of the companies we've been connected with."

Olsen and Anderson found inexpensive space in a Civil War-vintage woolen mill in Maynard, Massachusetts. Today, DEC occupies the whole mill; the company has put up other new buildings, but the mill itself—a labyrinth of stairways and doorless offices with a network of pipes and rafters overhead—makes the industry's most distinctive corporate headquarters. It is a reminder of the early bootstrapping days when, Olsen says, "We did most of the work ourselves, painting, cleaning the johns, moving machines. I was the toolmaker. I did photography in my basement and etching in aquarium tanks."

When Olsen and Anderson weren't cleaning the johns and making tools they sold, calling on people they knew in the scientific and engineering community, many of whom were MIT alumni who knew Olsen's reputation. It was nine months before they hired a full-time salesman, and DEC's sales force grew slowly—too slowly, some said—in the early years. A former sales manager for a competing firm remembers, "DEC had a super machine, but you had to find them, go up to Maynard and beat on the mill door. They could have given us real trouble if they were aggressive marketeers."

The salesmen DEC did hire were a different breed, not programmers or business school types but engineers. They were—and still are—the only salesmen in the industry not on commission. Commissions, Olsen said, were all right for Pepsi-Cola or Portland Cement. "It's demeaning," he adds, "to pay for something you imply a man won't do any other way. We hire qualified technical people. They haven't that tremendous drive for a sale, but there's more stability."

For three years, DEC sold circuit modules, which were used for testing but later became the building blocks for the company's first computer. Olsen wanted to get his machines out of the computer room and into the laboratory or on the factory floor; the first model was not called a computer but a Programmed Data Processor, shortened to PDP-1, and sold for $120,000 when competing machines were going for $1 million. By 1965, the arrival of integrated circuits allowed DEC to charge $18,000 for the PDP-8, which was an instant success. During the mid-sixties, miniskirts were fashionable, and someone—not Olsen or anyone at DEC—dubbed the PDP-8 a minicomputer. While miniskirts bloomed so did minicomputers—between 1965 and 1970 DEC's sales increased ninefold and its net earnings multiplied by nearly twenty—but when the miniskirt died, the minicomputer flourished even further. Faster, cheaper, more compact circuitry and new manufacturing techniques were bringing prices down by as much as 20 percent a year. The success of the minicomputer was leading the experts to change their ideas of the way computer technology would develop in the coming years.

In the past, computer specialists had believed that the most economical way to process data was by sharing the power of a large machine among a variety of jobs. This was the "computer utility" theory, on which Bill Norris had built his company. The advent of the minicomputer made it practical to give over a small machine to one particular job. Minis were first used to gather data and do experiments in laboratories. Next they moved into factory automation, to keep track of parts, control the operation of machine tools and monitor the flow of ingredients in processes like cookie-baking. In business data processing, the mini could play an important role in large networks in which a central computer communicated with many remote terminals over telephone lines; the mini would take over some of the complex tasks of managing the networks, freeing the central machine to compute.

Every time an advance in technology lowered the price of the machines, a new class of users would automate; publishers, for example, began to use minis in 1965 with the PDP-8. But when the price came down a notch the publishers, instead of choosing to buy a cheaper machine with the same power, sought a more powerful computer at the same or even a higher price, while other industries would buy the cheaper machine. Getting into minis was like trying to eat one potato chip. The minicomputer introduced a new element of playfulness into data processing, as DEC and its competitors tried to top each other with announcements of colorful applications. Some minis were especially built for rugged wear, but even the ordinary machines could take a beating. Minis appeared on submarines and in coal mines; they operated machines that sorted trash and picked potatoes; they educated students in elementary schools and prisons. "We gave one of our first computers to MIT," says Olsen. "Students could sign up to use the computer free. It was booked way in advance, and there were kids so wrapped up in the machine that they stopped washing and eating, not to mention going to classes."

As advances in circuitry drove hardware prices down, a new theory called "distributed" computing grew up. In a manufacturing company it worked this way: the minis controlled the machines in the factory, and at the same time fed data on their operations to larger machines which logged local output and inventory and sent this material to the home office computer, which monitored company-wide operations. If the bigger computers broke down, the mini kept plugging away, and if one mini was down, the disaster was contained. The same principle applied in offices, where the mini could do local processing by day and forward data to regional and central computers at night; it could also serve as a terminal. In banks and department stores, the chain included a terminal on the selling floor, a mini for the whole branch, and a central computer in the home office. Instead of the monster management information systems that had to be laid out entirely in advance and took five years to program, one could automate in small doses.

In the past few years it has become virtually impossible to define the term "minicomputer"—or at least to find a definition on which vendors, consultants and market analysts would agree. Price, for example, is no longer a useful criterion. In 1980 the user could pay from $2,000 to $250,000 for something called a minicomputer system, and even this scope is conservative: a high-priced mini, loaded down with peripherals and extra memory, can run up to $500,000.

Five years ago, minis could be crisply defined in terms of function, primarily in the operating system: a mini could not run time-sharing and ordinary batch-processing applications concurrently nor, in fact, could it handle more than one program at the same time. While this is still a useful guideline, it is by no means infallible: the fancier minis can now do all these things.

Another distinction largely—but not universally—true today is a matter of marketing: minicomputers are sold, not rented. DEC could produce inexpensive computers because its scientific customers— who were sophisticated about computing and had a limited budget—didn't want systems engineers and software packages and training programs; these accoutrements of a continuing relationship with the user marked the leasing business. During the mid-seventies IBM produced several machines which were low-priced and limited in function, but they were called "small business systems," not "minicomputers," because they did offer this hand-holding and were mostly rented. IBM didn't announce a true minicomputer until 1976, so christened because the user had to purchase it and it came with very little programming support. IBM, in 1980 fifth in minicomputer sales, is moving up fast but is not expected to surpass DEC in the near future.

Traditional computer systems require data processing employees in their operation; both minis and small business systems can be run entirely by civilians. The types of civilians, however, differ: an official of Data General, the third-ranking minicomputer manufacturer, says his company sells to "smart users," while small business systems are sold to "dumb users," small companies acquiring their first computer. Some of the smart users are engineers and scientists, but an increasing number are large corporations practicing a phenomenon called "off-loading": when the large mainframe has more work than it can handle, instead of ordering a bigger machine they put the extra applications on minis, one reason why IBM had to start making minicomputers. Even before IBM got into minis, however, DEC and some of its competitors began to get maxier, to allow their customers to upgrade.

A minicomputer can be turned into a small business system, and the companies that do this are a new class of supplier: they buy quantities of stripped-down DEC or Hewlett-Packard or Data General minis at the wholesale discount, add peripherals, develop applications packages, and sell them to retail customers; most of these systems houses find it economical to specialize in serving customers in some particular industry.

The wholesale market is a bulwark of the minicomputer business, but since it requires deep discounting (and possible price-wars) and is especially vulnerable to recessions, mini manufacturers need to increase their sales to end users. Competition from IBM and the dwarfs in this market has pressed them to offer more support, and thus to hire more programmers, sales people, technical writers and maintenance men, which requires not only more money but new skills.

The mini manufacturers are also pressed at the low end of the price spectrum. This pressure comes from the microprocessor, an integrated circuit chip the size of the "o" on this page, which performs, in primitive fashion, all the arithmetic and logic functions of a central processor. The simplest microprocessors, which can be purchased in quantity for about a dollar a chip, go into consumer products; they are now almost exclusively the domain of the semiconductor manufacturers. More sophisticated microprocessors, sometimes assembled in boards, might be used in peripheral equipment or communications gear for telephone switching; these, which mini manufacturers do sell, are elaborately programmed and often compatible with the vendor's minicomputer line. Finally, microprocessors assembled on boards with memory chips go into "desktop" or "personal" computers. A question for the future is to what extent the mini and semiconductor manufacturers will invade each other's preserves.

III

Both Norris and Olsen, dominating as they were, were able to think of the corporation as something that would outlive them; they were strong, strict parents who raised a child carefully, controlled it while it was young, taught it their own values, but recognized that some day it would become a mature, independent being. While Norris's efforts to achieve critical mass and Olsen's desire to keep control of an organization that was growing 40 percent a year reflected two opposite styles, they were aimed at ensuring the survival of the corporation, not just of Norris or Olsen. Four years after DEC and Control Data were founded, there appeared another computer company,

Scientific Data Systems, which achieved the same rapid success and remarkable growth as its two predecessors, and which helped bring the computer industry glamour on Wall Street and a sense of pride that computer people, technical men, young men could compete in that tough industrial world whose leaders had regarded them as just a bit eccentric. But the president of Scientific Data Systems—the only one of the three companies which did not survive—was a different sort of man.

"We didn't work for SDS, we worked for Max Palevsky," says a Palevsky alumnus. "SDS was the personification of Max Palevsky. We were his amplification and fulfillment."

Palevsky, the son of an immigrant housepainter, grew up in Chicago and went to the University of Chicago, where he earned two bachelor's degrees, in philosophy and mathematics, and continued to do graduate work in both fields. He expected to make a career as a university professor and eventually went out to the West Coast to study at the University of California. But he came to believe that philosophy was a field which did not accommodate small contributions (either one was a Wittgenstein or one was nothing) and the scholarly life made him restive. Bendix Corporation had just bought the computer division of Northrop Aviation, and in 1951 Palevsky found a job there as a staff mathematician. He had some success in designing one of the primitive machines current in those days and then proposed a new computer whose radical design would take advantage of the latest advances in circuitry. Bendix turned down the machine—rightly so, Palevsky now thinks, considering how little was known about the future directions of computing. Still, the defeat was difficult for the young designer to swallow, and in 1957 he left the company, hoping to find a backer for his machine.

Palevsky canvassed every electronics company in the Los Angeles phone book until he found some interested listeners at Packard-Bell. He helped found a computer division there and secured the first contract to build the machine for Wernher von Braun's group at Redstone Arsenal. The computer sold reasonably well to other customers, too, and Palevsky's next idea was to build a small cheap machine to serve the growing scientific community. Packard-Bell marketed that computer with even greater success, but by this time the parent company had gotten into financial difficulties. Palevsky felt the company's present management would never solve its problems and asked to have the computer division set up as a separate financial entity, issuing its own stock. Packard-Bell responded by firing Palevsky. At loose ends again, he began to look for someone who would back a new company geared toward building small computers for the scientific market.

Wall Street was unexcited. To most of the financial community, computers still meant IBM alone, and the idea of a small company trying to compete with IBM was ridiculous. "They didn't realize there was a new market that IBM didn't serve," Palevsky remembers. At last he was able to make a deal with two wealthy brothers and with Arthur Rock, a young California venture capitalist who had just left Hayden, Stone to start his own firm. Palevsky and Bob Beck, a colleague from Packard-Bell who would head the technical side of the business, put up $100,000; the other investors added $900,000, and Scientific Data Systems was on its way.

The company's early record was remarkable. Within ten months of its founding, SDS shipped its first computer, and it showed a $2 million profit at the end of its third year of operation. By that time SDS had 200 computers installed around the world; it had nearly twice the sales of DEC, which had been founded four years earlier; its number of employees had more than tripled over the previous year. Behind this success was real serendipity: flawless timing in the fields of finance, technology and marketing and the brains, imagination and drive to make the most of it. Palevsky sought venture capital in the summer of '61; less than a year later there was a recession and the markets dried up. "Then," an SDS alumnus remembers, "God gave us the silicon transistor. It became available just at the time we were founded, and brought a big improvement in reliability and speed. We delivered the first computer with all silicon transistors."

"The market was just right for a premium grade scientific machine," the alumnus continues. "The space program was getting under way—without Apollo there would have been no SDS. There was, of course, heavy spending on scientific research throughout the sixties, and researchers weren't like the businessmen getting out the payroll. They wanted a computer, they were enchanted with what we had, they loved it like a Ferrari or a woman. They were very forgiving. If the computer was temperamental you'd forgive it, the way you forgive a beautiful woman." NASA and its contractors used

SDS machines in the design and testing of spacecraft; the AEC had an SDS 920 at Brookhaven Labs controlling nuclear reactor experiments; oil companies used the machines to analyze seismic data; and the Brain Research Institute at UCLA Medical Center had an SDS computer monitoring the brain patterns of monkeys and men.

Then there was Palevsky himself. At Packard-Bell he had traveled widely, selling the company's equipment, and whenever he met able people their names went into his recruitment file; by the time he founded SDS he had long lists of talented prospects all over the country, and convinced many of them to join him. He was unsentimental about firing employees who didn't perform, but that came later; during the first three years, he noted with some pride, hardly any professionals departed SDS. He was generous with stock options—there are several multimillionaires among SDS alumni—and with commissions. If a salesman made $70,000 a year, much more than Palevsky's own salary, Palevsky would let him have it.

He knew when and how to praise, but he could also be tough. A marketing man remembers, "Max could always find the one thing you hadn't prepared. He was a complete bastard to work for; he demanded total performance or he'd make your life miserable. I was on the rack many times. But he was usually right and I respected him. He could bring a lot of bright, strong-willed people together and get them working in the same direction."

"Strong-willed" was an accurate description of Palevsky's vice-presidents. Bob Beck, his cofounder, was responsible for the excellence of the company's hardware and the efficiency of its design for manufacturing purposes. In 1964, the year SDS experienced an enormous spurt of growth (and the year it went public), Palevsky began to realize that he himself was more entrepreneur than administrator and to look around for someone to run the daily operations of the business. Beck, in the words of a former colleague, "discovered the wonderful world of management. He began to understand esoteric big-company things like budgeting and profit planning." He did these jobs with a fair amount of skill, but according to his critics, he had the technical man's feel for things, not people.

One of Beck's critics was Dan McGurk, the new marketing vice-president. McGurk, a West Pointer and Rhodes scholar who had worked for TRW and Scantlin Electronics, was a personable, irreverent and flamboyant man; his clothes were California-modish, and he was driven to work in a London taxi. He had a quick mind and a salesman's temperament: the inclination to lead by uplift and reward, a distaste for inflicting punishment, and relentless optimism. Beck and McGurk were destined to clash and often did. Finally Beck decided he'd had enough of SDS and retired to a ranch in Montana.

Political infighting reached its peak in 1966, when SDS was bringing out its third-generation Sigma computers; it was expanding rapidly and increasing production, with all the attendant problems of growth. "We could get the first computer out the door in the early days because all the senior people in the company were hammering the last nail in," suggests one of the former SDS men. "It was a job shop operation, with the machines almost hand-built by senior men. As time goes on you get less and less qualified people with less and less interest. Now it's just another manufacturing company, turning out cookies." As McGurk remembers, "The company reorganized again—if we didn't reorganize every six months we were getting sloppy. I was in charge of everything but finance and personnel. Programming was six months behind, the new plant was a shambles, we had new heads of engineering and programming and our third manufacturing manager in a year. I had never run manufacturing before, and there was a new man under me in charge of it. But somehow we got through, and in 1968, our best year, we broke $100 million in revenue."

About then Max Palevsky—who is usually described as a man with a short attention span—seemed to lose interest in SDS. He had proved he could start a company and bring it up to $100 million. He had amassed a sizable personal fortune. There was something sad, even obscene, he said, about people who achieved success early in life and never tried anything new afterward, people who took refuge in their first triumphs and kept on doing the same thing. He was not an engineer, and he felt himself an outsider in the world of technology. He became active in the peace movement and in Robert Kennedy's presidential campaign. He got into producing movies. By 1969 he was only coming into the office a few days a week; he remained interested in product planning ("Product planning was Max's department," says an old SDS man. "The product planners were all impersonations of Max; they dressed like him and talked like him.") but left the rest to vice-presidents. And so Palevsky was glad to hear from the president of Xerox.

In 1969 the Xerox Corporation had a new chief executive officer, C. Peter McColough, a Canadian lawyer and Harvard Business School graduate who had come up through the marketing organization and was responsible for the pricing strategies that had much to do with the success of Xerox copiers. McColough had long felt it was essential to Xerox's future strength that the company get into the computer business. Some day the world would be criss-crossed by huge information networks: a secretary would enter a document in some sort of futuristic terminal and it would be sent all over the world by satellite, while the information the document held would be stored in a computer to be recalled and reproduced on demand. For Xerox machines to be part of this network you had to make all the hardware, sell the customer the whole system. It meant competing with IBM, which obviously felt the same as McColough did: IBM was bringing out an office copier. McColough later insisted he never planned to be Number Two in the computer industry, but there were many magazine and newspaper articles in the early seventies which showed the Xerox chief squaring off against Tom Watson, and the McColough quotes in the articles did not suggest a modest goal.

McColough and Joseph Wilson, the first Xerox chief, had discussed merger briefly with Palevsky in 1965, but the timing was wrong for both sides, and Xerox continued to study other ways of getting into the computer business. Starting one's own division was too difficult; it made more sense to acquire. There was some talk with General Doriot about buying DEC, but clearly Ken Olsen wouldn't budge. Xerox's acquisition people talked to many companies. Xerox wanted a pure computer company, not some division of a larger corporation, and when you ruled out DEC and the unavailable Control Data, it came down to SDS. McColough called Palevsky and shortly afterward paid a quiet visit to Max's house. He went back east with a load of papers to study, and a couple of weeks later he visited Palevsky at home again. McColough, his acquisition man, Palevsky and Arthur Rock, the original backer whose stake in SDS was now worth $60 million and immeasurable prestige, closed the deal over lunch.

SDS stockholders received one Xerox share for two SDS shares, which fixed the price Xerox paid for the computer company at $918 million—nearly four times the sum paid a year later by Honeywell for GE's computer division, an operation which offered a much broader line of products and services and was already selling to the commercial customers Xerox wanted to reach, which SDS was not. Moreover, SDS followed the liberal accounting methods favored by many small companies in the computer industry, deferring certain marketing expenses and reporting long-term leases as sales, practices which made the year's earnings picture look more attractive than it was. McGurk, who was called back from a trip to participate in internal discussions about the merger, remembers that "In all these negotiations you have a high figure and a low figure, a price you ask for and a price you'll take. It turned out that our range was exactly the same as Xerox's. What we asked for was what they'd settle for, but we spoke first. Peter said in a few years the price would not be as important as establishing a sound foundation for our relationship."

By the time Xerox bought SDS, there was trouble on the horizon; observers have questioned ever since what Palevsky and his lieutenants knew about impending problems at the time of the sale and how much McColough could or should have figured out for himself. Some 40 percent of SDS's business came from government contracts, largely tied in with the space program; many nongovernment customers, too, were involved in space research. The summer after the merger NASA walked a man on the moon. "You had all the computers you needed in place for the first moon walk," says a former SDS marketing man. "The main body of capital investment in the space program was complete. We acknowledged the problem was coming; we put it in euphemistic terms, saying that 'Business data processing is too big for us to ignore any longer,' but what we meant was that we hadn't any choice."

Ken Olsen and his competitors were beginning to eat into SDS's market. SDS had developed an excellent machine for time-sharing, which it leased to a flock of new small time-sharing service companies that were springing up during the boom years; there were too many such companies, and an economic slowdown could bankrupt them, leaving SDS with a large inventory of unpaid-for computers. Soon IBM would be bringing out a new computer line, which meant SDS would have to do the same, and SDS was still having problems with its software.

Palevsky, McGurk, Sanford Kaplan, the financial vice-president, and Arthur Rock were made directors of Xerox following the merger. Palevsky, nominally chairman of the executive committee of the board, gave the reins to McGurk; Kaplan moved to Xerox corporate headquarters as a senior vice-president. In the fall of 1969, McGurk and his sales managers reenacted a scene that has gone on between salesmen and their bosses since what passes for time immemorial in the computer industry. The salesman, looking to cover himself, describes in vivid detail the softnesses in the marketplace that will make it difficult if not impossible to achieve quota; the boss disregards the salesman's weeping and exhorts him to valor. "We made a presentation to McGurk," says one of the sales managers, "telling him about the problems. We said space was drying up, the minis were nipping at our heels, the software wasn't out of the woods, we couldn't meet the plan. McGurk said 'You guys are prophets of doom. Now get out there and get orders.' And sure enough, we did it. We finished '69 spectacularly. This, of course, completely destroyed our credibility; McGurk raised our quota the next year. And in the first quarter of '70 the whole marketplace collapsed."

The recession hit Xerox Data Systems, as the subsidiary was now called, at just the time when the small company and its big new parent were adjusting to each other. The differences in style ranged from superficial to profound. Even the lingo was different; as McGurk once described it, "when a guy at corporate headquarters in Stamford says 'Your idea is an interesting one and well thought out, but perhaps you might consider some adjustments,' what he really means in Palevsky language is 'you're full of shit.'"

McGurk—who had to fight to get to see McColough one hour a month—objected to the large corporation's expansiveness. "Xerox wanted cross-fertilization," he remembers. "We thought we'd train their field service men in computers, but none of their guys would transfer—they were already making more than our best people. Xerox had a rule that every Xerox employee is a first-class employee and travels first class. We had just loosened up to where corporate officers could fly first class. So Peter puts out a memo saying everyone travels first class, and then I put out another memo saying 'Not us, boys.' I think it bothered Peter, and the XDS people asked me, 'How come we got all this money and you're still so mean?'"

McColough, on the other hand, took issue with some SDS practices. "SDS had been a hardware house and a discount house, and Xerox was neither," says one of the marketing men. "We sold a lot of equipment wholesale, which was heavily discounted. Xerox was distressed about this policy—they didn't approve of the wheeling and dealing that goes on in a small company. Without discounts we lost a lot of business." Xerox also changed the subsidiary's liberal accounting policies; the adjustment made business look as bad as in truth it was.

McGurk continued to be easy-going about the seriousness of the recession, and due to upheavals in XDS's financial management, its figures were too sanguine by some $15 million. This was revealed when many of the time-sharing customers began defaulting on their bills and the corporation had to undertake a full audit, with an embarrassing writeoff as the result. Also, operating losses for the year exceeded $20 million. "When this happened I said to Max that if I were Peter, I'd replace me," McGurk says. And McColough, whose own credibility with investors had been seriously damaged, did just that.

With an ex-IBM'er in charge, XDS lost as much from operations as it had under McGurk. By this time, in order to succeed in business data processing, Xerox had to win over IBM customers—and it clearly had not the support skills to compete with the giant. Its product line was obsolescent, and the minicomputer manufacturers were denting its historic markets. A task force concluded the subsidiary would never make significant gains and recommended a retrenchment into its traditional scientific market. The computer operation was dispersed and absorbed by other corporate divisions.

Finally, in July 1975 Xerox announced that it was leaving the mainframe business, taking an after-tax writeoff of more than $84 million. Its computer losses between 1970 and the end of 1975 would total $264 million; at a news conference, McColough admitted that the acquisition of Scientific Data Systems had been "a mistake." Since McColough still hopes to be a leading supplier of the "office of the future," Xerox is active in peripherals, some of which combine computer and copier technologies, is getting into communications, and still sells computer services. Honeywell has taken over the maintenance and support of Xerox's old customers.

Palevsky achieved some fame in the outside world as a heavy contributor to the McGovern presidential campaign and as a producer of some interesting films, including Costa-Gavras's "State of Siege." McGurk founded the Computer Industry Association, an organization of small companies dedicated to lobbying for the restructuring of the computer industry (that is, the breakup of IBM), and did a highly effective job of bringing the IBM antitrust case to public attention. Both are very rich men.

Two and a half years after Xerox had left the business, a survey by Datapro Research Corporation ranked Xerox highest of all the major manufacturers in customer satisfaction; that is, the users who had held on to their Xerox equipment were the happiest of all. Even the rather low rating they awarded to the Honeywell maintenance and technical support did not counteract the strong lead achieved by the quality of the Xerox mainframes.

PART IV

THE ENTREPRENEURS

10

The Perils of Trespass: Telex and Its Fellows

As COMPUTERS have become more complex, the variety of peripheral equipment necessary to help them work efficiently has increased. For input there are machines that punch and read cards, devices that enter data on magnetic tape or discs, optical scanners and remote entry devices such as electronic cash registers, supermarket scanners and keyboard terminals. For output there are high-speed printers, microfilm devices, plotters and more punched-card machines. For extra storage of data, an installation may use tape drives, disc drives and semiconductor additions to the computer's main memory; the newest devices store data in the form of tiny "bubbles" on magnetic film, and other memory innovations are in the works.

Computer mainframes are entirely electronic; peripheral equipment is mostly electromechanical. Each specialty requires different talents from its engineers, and while the needs of the marketplace are complementary, technological advancements in the two fields have kept a somewhat separate pace. The mainframe designer works with circuits which are readily available and often standardized; his job is to organize these circuits to perform sophisticated functions with economy and style, and once the computer design is down on paper, a good part of the battle is won. He has the architect's gift of seeing a total system and orchestrating the work of subcontractors— the circuit designers and the systems programmers, for example—to bring it into being. The peripherals designer, on the other hand, lives in a world of belts and pulleys and hammers. He must align and calibrate innumerable small parts that move at ferocious speed. To do this, he needs to find materials that withstand heat and dust and dampness and rough wear; without the necessary developments in synthetics and metallurgy, all his ingenuity may be useless.

It was this sort of cleverness that enabled a small group of engineers at IBM's newly built San Jose laboratory in 1953 to devise the RAMAC 350 disc file, a machine which, along with its descendants, significantly expanded the application of computers. In those days the most popular device for auxiliary storage was the tape drive, which stored data in magnetized spots on a reel of oxide-coated tape; electrical current sent through a read-write head (like the head on a cassette recorder) would induce a small magnetic field on the tape, with the presence or absence of this field signifying a 1 or a 0 in binary code. The tape drive was (and still is) an economical means of processing a batch of transactions in sequence, but if you wanted to pull out any one piece of data you would have to run the whole reel of tape past the head until you came to what you were looking for; the tape reel was 2,400 feet long. Even in today's tape drives, it takes nearly two and a half minutes to unwind an entire reel of tape, while the computer's main memory retrieves data in millionths of a second. Because of the difference in tape and central processor speeds, the notion of using tape for direct access in an installation which processes thousands of inquiries a day is impractical.

Imagine what it would be like, the engineers thought, if the customer could get at that information right away; he could find out, as of that very minute, the amount of money in a bank balance, the number of parts in a warehouse, or whether a seat was available on the eight o'clock flight to Chicago. When the part was used or the seat was sold, the inventory file would be changed immediately. IBM's systems design had been built on the principle of sequential batch-processing—the monthly totaling of a company's accounts—and to many people in the corporation it seemed heretical to build equipment for direct access: that smacked of old-fashioned manual accounting methods. A few marketing executives, however, understood that customers' needs were changing, and they encouraged the engineers to go ahead. The engineers considered designing a direct-access device to work something like a jukebox, with the data stored on discs—a wild idea, perhaps, but worth looking at.

The project presented formidable problems of precision. To hold the necessary amount of information, fifty discs each 24 inches in diameter had to be divided into tracks, like the bands on a long-playing record, with twenty tracks to an inch. So that the customer could always find the piece of information he was looking for, the head must be able to arrive at a given spot predictably and repeatedly, regardless of the climate or altitude of the computer room.

In a tape drive the magnetic tape was stretched over the read-write head; on the RAMAC file the head could never touch the disc, but it had to maintain a constant level above the disc close enough to register a magnetic field. And the disc was whirling like a dervish all the while. Even at 50/1000ths of an inch thick, the discs were too bumpy; finally the engineers found a special aluminum which could be inserted in a crushing machine that took the wrinkles out. This helped, but some waviness persisted because the discs had to be stacked vertically to get the machine through a doorway, and vertical stacking causes discs to droop.

Eventually they solved the problem, but it took three years and $10 million to develop the RAMAC file, which was a primitive machine and difficult to maintain. When it was done IBM's engineers continued to work on improvements in disc storage—and so, gradually, did engineers from competing companies. They aimed first to make the discs smaller, and removable, and then to make the machine faster and more precise; and to produce flatter and thinner discs and lighter heads positioned even closer, and to find a better quality of coating, all improvements which would enable the discs to record information at greater density. All these goals were eventually achieved. Today's 3380 model disc system retrieves data at thirty times the speed of the first RAMAC, and can store more than two hundred times the information. IBM points out that the smoothness with which the 3380 head must fly over the disc surface, if extrapolated to much larger proportions, would be equivalent to that required of a 747 jet flying 0.1 inch above the ground over a distance of several miles without bumping its wheels.

In 1979, independent peripherals manufacturers—that is, companies producing the equipment to operate with other vendors' mainframes or minicomputers—earned revenues of more than $8 billion. This sizable income, however, was fragmented among two hundred companies, which ranged from Control Data to the likes of Adage, a graphic terminal company with revenues of about $7½ million. Control Data, of course, is both an independent and a dwarf, but the other independents each concentrate on a few products. A peripherals manufacturer need not make the massive investment in engineering, software, manufacturing, marketing, education and maintenance required to sustain a full computer line; neither does he benefit from the protection offered by such a diversified business, nor from the special ties that exist between mainframe supplier and customer.

The peripherals business is a milieu of small entrepreneurs which began, not surprisingly, as a wholesale industry selling to mainframe companies who found it cheaper and easier to let someone else develop the gear. End-users were hesitant enough to do business with corporations as large as Sperry Rand, Honeywell and Burroughs; to trust a young company seemed unthinkable. The question of whether a new product will work is only half the data processing manager's worry; the other half is what happens when it doesn't. The product's failure may bring down the whole system. A small supplier may not have enough competent maintenance men to service its machines; perhaps the company will not be in business when the product breaks down next year. Then there is the nightmarish prospect of the small company's maintenance men confronting IBM's blue-suited field engineers in a midnight shootout over *whose* product caused the system failure.

Accordingly, the first independent manufacturer to get a foot in the door was Mohawk Data Sciences, which had invented an input device that didn't plug right into the computer but sat outside the computer room. It was a machine that entered data from a keyboard directly onto magnetic tape for mounting on a tape drive, thus eliminating the familiar but inefficient keypunch. The Mohawk Data Recorder was fast and cheap, it saved the operator's time and reduced the number of operators, and one reel of tape could store data that would require 36,000 IBM cards. At first, few users were willing to pioneer, and the Data Recorder sold slowly. But by 1966, when other independent peripherals manufacturers were beginning to attach their equipment directly to IBM computers, two-year-old Mohawk had planted some 1,500 machines in installations across the country, and with them the revolutionary idea that a small company might develop, sell and maintain an exciting product.

By the mid-sixties the dwarfs were becoming strong enough to make their own peripherals, and the wholesale manufacturers were watching their market evaporate. One small company, Telex, made a tape drive with a distinctive feature that could be exploited: its circuit design was similar to that of IBM's tape drive. With a few adjustments, you could plug the Telex machine right into an IBM mainframe, mark it up to more than twice the manufacturing cost and still undercut the steep prices of the IBM drive. Telex sold its first IBM-compatible machines in early 1966. During the next two years several other small firms also began competing with IBM in peripherals. They soon invaded the market for disc drives; some hired engineers away from IBM.

The data processing manager who bought "plug-compatible" peripherals was still considered somewhat avant-garde—until the economy turned down in 1969 and all computer customers started looking for ways to trim their budgets. They discovered you could save 20 percent by installing independent disc or tape drives, and that many independent products actually offered better performance than the IBM models which had, after all, been developed several years earlier. The "pcm's" (for plug-compatible manufacturers) offered free trial periods and other enticements in hopes of gaining an advantage over IBM. By the end of 1969, Memorex stock was up to 173, and in fiscal 1970, Telex's net profits increased by an astounding 285 percent. In 1970, pcm's began poaching on a new and dangerous area of IBM territory: they were actually replacing the main memory of the computer.

"Reports Show that I/P's Offer from 20 to 60% Savings," ran a headline in *Computerworld* in February 1970. Neither IBM nor the pcm's would give out sales figures, and so reports on the actual inroads made into IBM's market were conjectural. The prevalent opinion held that the pcm's were taking nearly 10 percent of IBM's customers; that 10 percent was IBM's "threshold of pain," and when the small firms reached it, IBM would take action.

In February 1970, IBM designated peripherals a "key corporate strategic issue"—that is, one of a handful of problems requiring the special attention of top management. Six months later a senior vice-president on the corporate staff wrote a memo calling peripherals "the number one problem in our business today." Beneath the jargon of many of IBM's internal documents lay a panic which seemed to transcend the actual gains of the pcm's; their success bore emotional and philosophical implications which were deeply disturbing to IBM salesmen, engineers, planners and executives.

By the end of 1970 an IBM study was reporting that the pcm's had displaced 14 percent of IBM's tape systems and 5 percent of the discs. To an outsider, this share seems hardly sufficient to produce a number one business problem. The dwarfs, after all, had 31 percent of *all* the tape systems installed in the U.S. and 16 percent of the disc systems, a share which IBM conceded to them without alarm; certainly IBM strove to make its tape drives better than Univac's, but only because the quality of the attached peripherals affected the customer's choice of mainframe. The computer business had always been a *systems* business, and IBM believed it was entitled to a 100 percent share of the tape and disc systems attached to IBM mainframes. Now this new kind of competitor had come along, and some 13 percent of IBM installations were, as the report put it, "contaminated" with pcm tapes or discs.

"Contaminated" is an emotional word: it suggests the first corrupting whiff of airplane glue, the loss of virginity, the bite of the apple. Since unbundling, customers had become more receptive to the idea of dealing with several suppliers. Losses to the pcm's during 1970 were nearly three times the figure for 1969. IBM expected much of its future revenue growth to come from peripherals, which then represented 63 percent of the hardware dollar; by 1975 that percentage would go up to 70. By the time of this study some action had been taken, but the forecast still looked gloomy.

The peripherals companies were a particularly galling type of competitor. IBM, after all, invested huge sums of money in producing computer systems—for basic research, for development of hardware and software for a complete computer system in which all the elements were planned to work in harmony, for training salesmen and systems engineers. The salesmen sold the system to the customer, spending months and sometimes years helping him to configure that system to suit his needs. Then, when the system was all in place and working nicely, the pcm came in and offered to replace one of the IBM boxes with another absolutely interchangeable box that offered better performance for the dollar. Unlike the dwarfs, who competed fair and square, shouldering the same burdens that IBM incurred, the peripherals vendor seemed to the IBM'er a parasite. And once the pcm had proved its competence with a list of satisfied customers and the financial figures that suggested it would stay in business, there was very little the IBM salesman could do to fight back.

The battle had to be joined at a higher level, and in September 1970, it was. During the summer, IBM had announced an advanced disc drive for use with System 370, but the drive would not be ready for shipment for another year. To hold the fort, the company introduced another drive which bore the internal code name of Mallard.

IBM disc systems had been sold in groups of four or five jukeboxes, called spindles, which were bolted together and attached to the central processor via a controller, a free-standing box which handled the shifting of data between the spindles and the mainframe. Now engineers had found a way to eliminate the controller, which accounted for a healthy chunk of the price of a disc system and whose absence would cause the independents some difficulty in attaching their units. Some of the controller's work could be built into the central processor; the rest of it would fit right into the disc system if you cut out one spindle. Otherwise Mallard was just like the old system (it was, in fact, built from old disc systems which, nudged out by the independents, were coming off rental in great numbers) only much cheaper.

But Mallard fit only the 370, and most of the vulnerable IBM disc drives were hooked up to 360 computers. To attach Mallard to a 360, you needed to put back the controller, which made Mallard almost exactly like the old product, but priced right below what Memorex and Telex were getting for their similar machines. When IBM adjusted its price structure to match the pcm's' other practices, Mallard offered even greater savings.

Why didn't IBM simply cut the prices on all its old drives instead of bothering with Mallard? When Bo Evans, president of the engineering division, was asked that question in court, he answered, "We would be out of business." Evans was exaggerating, of course, but an all-inclusive price cut would have yielded a huge drop in revenue. If, on the other hand, the cuts required customers to have the old product carted out and the new one wheeled in, a good number of users wouldn't take the trouble, and IBM would go on receiving the higher price on many of its units. Gerald Brock, an economist at the University of Arizona who studied the computer industry, wrote:

> The freight charges and disruption involved, as well as lack of information or lethargy on the part of some computer managers, allowed IBM to have a competitive low price product while still receiving the higher rent from many customers for some time after the price cut.

Before the second Mallard announcement IBM had, with its customary thoroughness, studied the financial status of Telex and Memorex; it knew that the pcm's would have to respond by cutting their own prices, and this would seriously reduce their income, their profits and their ability to finance future marketing and development. Wall Street was aware of this too, and the stock of the pcm's plummeted after Mallard. But with the independents' response, their sales began to increase again, particularly since many customers found the Mallard configuration unsuitable; while the product hurt the small companies financially, it failed to protect IBM's equipment base.

IBM now saw the need for more drastic action; instead of entering an outright price war, it aimed to make the most of the lead time that existed before the pcm's could copy its new products. The way to do this was to offer long-term leases at substantial discounts from the old month-to-month rental price; the financial penalty for cancellation would be sizable. The benefits of such a measure were clear. PCM announcements always followed IBM's by several months; when the IBM equipment was on month-to-month rental, the pcm salesman could simply walk in and ask the customer to replace the IBM gear with his own lower-priced machines. Now when the pcm salesmen made their rounds they would find the customer bound to IBM for up to two years. After the IBM lease had expired, the pcm might sell his gear to the customer, but IBM would soon be out with a newer product, and the customer would switch back to IBM before the pcm had recovered his costs. To remarket his displaced equipment to another customer, the pcm would have to slash the price, but this would postpone profits for so long that the pcm couldn't afford to develop new products. As one IBM analysis of the effects of a long-term lease plan on competitors described it, "corporate revenues lower—no funds for mfg., eng.—dying company!"

At best, IBM closed its eyes to the probability that a long-term lease plan would put competitors out of business; at worst, it set out to do just that. The company announced the Fixed Term Plan on May 27, 1971. It was an immediate success: within two months, 40 percent of IBM's installed base in discs, tapes and printers was signed up for the plan, and the percentage continued to grow substantially.

Watson himself had spelled out the need to sacrifice current revenues to protect the company's market share, its base for future growth: as the Management Review Committee minutes reported, "TJW wants clear understanding that company swallow whatever financial pills required now and get ready for the future. We can't have ourselves mesmerized by the balance sheet . . . must return this business to a growth posture and operate accordingly."

The plan was to cause a loss of revenues exceeding $75 million during 1971 and 1972—the financial pills IBM would swallow to ensure far greater profits once the pcm competition had subsided and more IBM gear was staying in the field for longer periods. But at the end of July IBM, citing the "increasing cost of doing business," raised the prices of its mainframes. Shortly afterward, an IBM analyst wrote that "the net effects . . . will probably be a wash insofar as business volumes are concerned." A few financial pills, apparently, had been spit out.

While it was protecting its discs, tapes and printers, IBM also had to worry about pcm's replacing the main memory of its computers. In the fall of 1969, a task force studied the seriousness of the threat in plug-compatible memories. The group started by estimating the rewards for an independent company that might enter the memory market in 1970. Two types of concerns might do this: a new, three-men-in-a-garage sort of firm set up for the purpose, and an established semiconductor company like Texas Instruments or Motorola. The new company would take four to six years to break even, depending on what IBM was charging; after that it would begin to do nicely. Heavy startup costs and a long deferral of profits would limit the number of new companies entering, but the semiconductor manufacturers, selling memories at as little as half the IBM price, could realize substantial profits within three years. Still, the group concluded that less than a quarter of IBM's forecasted 1976 base would be vulnerable to this competition. Thus IBM took the middle road, pricing 370 memories below their 360 predecessors but still avoiding the most drastic cuts.

Task forces continued to study the problem, but by early 1971 the pcm's had made greater inroads than IBM had expected. Their success was particularly alarming because unlike the plug-compatible progress in other peripherals, it affected mainframe sales. IBM had always placed not only a minimum but also a maximum limit to the amount of main memory a customer could buy with a given machine; if he wanted more, he would have to take a larger model, whether or not he needed the extra computing power. Now, a penny-pinching customer could hold on to his smaller machine and buy all the extra memory he wanted cheap from the pcm's. One possible solution was to raise the minimum compulsory memory attached to each model, so that by the time the pcm salesman appeared the customer would be up to his ears in memory; if, however, you raised it too high you might encourage downtrading.

The solution to the problem came with the fudge-ripple 370, which, during the later stages of its development, had been given the unfortunate code name of SMASH (this name weighed against IBM in subsequent antitrust suits, not only because it implied the smashing of competitors but because some people thought it sounded like SMERSH, the Russian spy organization in the James Bond novels. Evans testified weakly that the code name had come from his suggestion to "put this whole smash, all these products, out at one time").

The moderate technological advances offered by the fudge-ripple machines allowed IBM to shift substantial profits from the vulnerable main memory to the safe central processor. The fudge-ripple memory was actually 57 percent cheaper than its vanilla predecessor, a cut chalked up to the low cost of semiconductors; the mainframe cost 54 percent more, a rise which could be credited to better performance via virtual storage. The fudge-ripple's memory, instead of residing in a separate box like its predecessors, was built right into the mainframe, a development IBM said offered improvements in cost, performance and reliability, but which also thwarted independent efforts to replace the memory.

These were the chief (but not the only) actions IBM took against its peripherals competitors. Most of the pcm's suffered financial difficulties during the early seventies. In 1969 and 1970, for example, Telex had been able to sell nearly $120 million worth of tapes and discs to the leasing companies, who were important customers of the pcm's. Between January 1971 and March 1973, however, Telex's leasing company sales dropped to $30 million. The price of the Telex equipment had eroded by 35 percent. In January 1972, Telex sued IBM for violation of the antitrust laws. According to the judge's findings in the lawsuit,

> Marketing expenses increased. Backlog and order rates were reduced. Recruitment of adequate personnel became more difficult as uncertainty as to Telex' future viability increased. "Front end" ex-

pense has been increased by inadequate concentration of products and services. Competition among Telex and other plug compatible manufacturers for remaining business has intensified. Telex' ability to secure financing has been impaired, and Telex has had to pay more for financing.

The case went to trial in 1973. The plaintiff's exhibits put on the public record more than fourteen thousand pages of IBM internal documents, including the minutes of top management committee meetings, task force reports, pricing studies, and internal memoranda. IBM had always been notoriously secretive to press and public. Now, in what *Business Week* called "one of the largest breaches of corporate security and privacy in history," anyone could read how Tom Watson was fretting over tiny competitors and just what some IBM analyst thought it would take to put Telex and Memorex out of business. The contents of the documents were reported widely. The Computer Industry Association, a new group composed largely of peripherals manufacturers, was selling the entire package of documents for $3,000; an organization which felt a little less flush could buy just the minutes for $695, and if you were flat broke you could visit the CIA's reading room in New York.

There was a dark side to Telex as well. One of IBM's counterclaims was "theft of trade secrets." Telex had to bring out its equipment soon enough to have a long rental life before IBM announced a newer product. When Telex began to sell plug-compatible peripherals, the targets of its attack were already on the market and could be copied by reverse engineering; now IBM, no longer complacent, was introducing new machines at a faster rate, and reverse engineering was a luxury Telex couldn't afford. The smaller company could afford, however, to recruit IBM employees who knew in detail what IBM was bringing out. It enticed these people through generous salaries and bonuses to transfer their knowledge to their new employer.

The information the ex-IBM'ers brought with them to Telex was not simply the general intelligence, skill and industry experience that makes any candidate attractive to a prospective employer; it included proprietary data copied from IBM confidential documents describing forecasts and product plans. One Telex document flatly stated that "what we are after is not skill per se but information." The IBM employees Telex hired were those who had worked on the specific products Telex wanted to copy; one disc man was offered a $500,000 bonus contingent on delivery of a copy of the new IBM drive by a given date, a schedule which was unrealistic for anyone not working with proprietary information.

Judge A. Sherman Christensen, who had come out of semiretirement to hear the case, was praised in the trade press for his grasp of the niceties of the industry; a man of decent sensibilities, he recognized no heroes and ordered for IBM and Telex a plague on both their houses. Because IBM had violated the antitrust laws, Telex won $352 million in treble damages; because Telex had misappropriated IBM's trade secrets, it owed nearly $22 million to IBM.

It required no special knowledge of the industry to see that Telex's behavior, while less financially injurious than IBM's, was illegal and immoral. But the antitrust laws which, according to Judge Christensen, IBM violated, are complex and liable to much subjective interpretation. The judge noted that many of IBM's practices did not conform to common yardsticks for anticompetitive behavior: it did not, for example, cut prices below its costs and stood to make a profit, eventually, from the marked-down equipment (even though the profit was partly based on the assumption that IBM would clip the independents' wings). Long-term leasing plans were a common practice in the industry: IBM was the last company to institute one.

The judge did say, however, that despite some cost and performance justifications, IBM lowered the price of its memories and raised prices on the mainframes "with the primary purpose of creating barriers to entry for potential plug compatible memory competitors." As for the long-term lease, it was directed specifically at plug-compatible markets, instituted neither across the board nor as a random experiment, and was thus "directed not at competition in an appropriate competitive sense but at competitors and their viability as such." The offenses of which IBM was guilty were monopolization and attempt to monopolize, and its pricing actions reflected its predatory intent.

Two months later, however, on the basis of posttrial evidence from IBM, Judge Christensen decided his calculation of damages due Telex had been in error, and knocked off nearly $100 million. He also modified one of his injunctions against IBM. The amended decision did not change his conclusion that IBM had violated the antitrust laws but may have weighed psychologically against Telex in the subsequent appeal.

The appeals court was presented with a tarnished David opposing the Goliath of IBM; it was difficult to feel much sympathy for Telex, and on the other hand there was the morass of antitrust issues, the complexity of defining the market that IBM allegedly monopolized and the fact that IBM's behavior did not conform to some traditional measurements for antitrust violation. In January 1975 the court, finding Judge Christensen's market definition too narrow and IBM's actions routinely competitive, reversed the decision against IBM; it sustained the decision against Telex but took $3 million off the damages Telex was to pay.

Telex, which couldn't afford to lose, eventually set aside an appeal to the Supreme Court and settled with IBM. Two other peripherals companies had launched antitrust suits against IBM, but neither of these was successful; a directed verdict in one case and a hung jury in the other ended the story well short of true vindication for IBM.

The first entrepreneurs in the peripherals business were engineers. They were technically clever; also they had the imagination to dream and the grit to go hungry until their dreams came true. Building the company often became a family affair: while the entrepreneurs soldered the product together their wives painted the office and kept the books. Later entrepreneurs, whether their backgrounds lay in engineering, marketing or finance, were smarter about money and had timed their entry so they didn't need to starve: they knew something about the venture capital markets, could discuss their plans articulately, and found the money men—equally susceptible to visions of a glorious future—gratifyingly open-handed. Most of the entrepreneurs in both generations had worked for corporations and had demonstrated enough competence to rise to the upper levels of middle management, whereupon they left to found that universal paragon, the company with no procedure manuals or organization charts. It took brains and stamina to go out and build a business— but it was a different sort of brains and stamina from that required when the company got big and began to be noticed by larger corporations run by men in their fifties who had stuck around to see how the pieces fit together and had learned when to sit tight and when to come down hard.

As soon as the peripherals companies began to retail their products, they encountered some of the problems that faced the dwarfs:

heavy expenses for research and development, manufacturing and maintenance, and a stretched-out period of return on their investment because the products were leased. Their difficulties were compounded by the need to produce products both superior to IBM's and compatible with them. While Telex's outright industrial espionage may not have been a standard practice, the pcm's often did hire IBM personnel to speed their development efforts. These men could be persuaded to give up their secure positions only by the offering of bountiful equity packages. The pcm's needed rising stock values not just to attract financiers but to entice talent.

The pcm's were able to get started because they and their backers assumed that IBM, for fear of rendering its own equipment obsolete, would be slow to introduce new machines, and that it would keep up its price umbrella. And the inventiveness which characterized the pcm's engineering success was paralleled by equal creativity in their accounting departments.

The small companies had to borrow money in order to grow, but to get the money they had to show they were already growing. The best way to do this was to put the accounting rules to work. Under certain circumstances, for example, it was permissible to account for a lease as if it were a sale, reporting the full revenues expected over the life of the equipment during the first year that the machines were installed. This practice, widespread in the computer industry, was justified by the assumption that the customer would not return the machines, even if the lease were cancellable for all or part of its duration. The recession and IBM's actions against the pcm's often proved that assumption to be extravagant, producing a financial picture that was far too rosy, and in 1972 the Accounting Principles Board tightened the criteria for reporting leases as sales.

Another gambit was to defer reporting such routine costs as research and development and marketing until the product had begun to earn revenues: you could charge these costs to capital investment and then amortize them over the life of the product. The investment community accepted this strategy until IBM's price cuts decreased the pcm's sales and compelled the small companies to cut their own prices. It then became apparent that the products were not going to bring in the predicted revenues, and the money spent in developing and marketing them was—well, spent. Several pcm's had to take writeoffs during fiscal 1972 and thus showed big losses.

After IBM's retaliation, security analysts issued reports on pcm's which ranged from damning with faint praise to just damning; investors grew increasingly skittish and stocks plunged. The pcm's could not raise the capital they needed, and attempts to diversify ran aground. In 1973 Memorex, defeated in an effort to enter the mainframe business, lost $119 million; Bank of America, its largest creditor, in effect took over the management of the company and replaced the chief executive. Similar if less expensive disasters were widespread: some companies later recovered, while others died a painful death.

Today the peripherals industry is a vigorous one. The developing technology requires new devices for input, output and storage. Minicomputers need their own peripherals; the wholesale business has picked up. As for IBM plug-compatible peripherals, the independents have between a quarter and a third of the market, a share not much lower than the direst predictions IBM made back in 1970. Still, there are only three companies left making this equipment; the others either died or merged or got into other products. Nobody enters this part of the business any more.

Control Data is still in it; Memorex is troubled, but hangs on; and so does a company called Storage Technology Corporation, one of the industry's popular success stories. STC was founded in 1969 by four former IBM engineers with $300,000; it began by making tape drives, and as a late arrival didn't suffer from IBM cuts on 360-vintage products. Its equipment was advanced, its sales aggressive, its service good, its expansion and diversification fairly cautious, and to some extent it benefited from the attrition of its competitors. Its considerable achievement in tape drives financed another in discs. With all this, by 1979 Storage Technology felt sufficiently insecure to seek a merger partner. It was a year when a pcm could look around and see history repeating itself.

The notion of 370 plug-compatible mainframes had originated with Gene Amdahl, the former director of IBM's Advanced Computing Systems Laboratory in Menlo Park, who had played a leading role in designing IBM computers from 1952 to 1970. Amdahl's lab had designed a large computer with advanced circuitry and architecture. The pricing of the machine, however, had to fit in with the rest of IBM's computer line, and there was no way to do this and make an adequate profit. So IBM killed the machine. Amdahl didn't walk out immediately; but in 1970 there arose a personal incentive to resign and his frustration tipped the balance toward leaving.

Amdahl felt that IBM's need to short-shrift the large computers offered a good entrepreneurial opportunity; provided one gave the customers a machine compatible with their previous heavy software investment, and provided the reliability and maintenance were good, you had an easily identified market of sophisticated customers willing to purchase their machines, and a high-revenue product that could carry the maintenance. It took some time for Amdahl to raise enough money to get started, but he was able to ship his first computer in 1975; it was installed and running well in a couple of days, and the best marketing Amdahl got in its early years was by word-of-mouth from satisfied customers. By adopting a purchase-only policy, the company made a profit in the first quarter after it started shipping. In 1976, when Amdahl had installed fifteen machines to customers including AT&T and NASA, it made a successful public offering of more than a million shares of stock. Some observers noted that the company, like the peripherals pcm's of a few years earlier, was vulnerable to the whims of IBM; still, Wall Street was in the mood to believe in Amdahl, and it believed.

In four years Amdahl built a business of more than $300 million and attracted a slew of other companies into the market; by 1979 the pcm mainframe industry amounted to nearly a billion. IBM had begun responding in 1977, with an updated version of its earlier strategy. It brought out machines which surpassed the pcm models in performance for the dollar—the improvement of IBM's 3033 computer over its predecessor was so drastic that a leading computer consultant testified in court that it was directly aimed at Amdahl—and the pcm's had to cut their prices in return. IBM slashed purchase prices on old machines to make them competitive and raise cash, while keeping rentals constant to reap long-term profits from the more conservative customers. Once it had shifted profits from vulnerable peripherals to unchallenged mainframes; now, when mainframes were vulnerable too, it moved profits from hardware into software by charging separately—and steeply—for more and more of its operating system programs (some of this shift, to be fair, came inevitably from declining hardware costs, but the style and timing were directly pegged to the pcm's). The pcm's had to react to IBM's moves—but they didn't have software to shift their profits into.

As for bundling, its modern equivalent is a development called microcode, in which features that used to reside in hardware or software are placed on an integrated circuit chip which is expensive and difficult to copy; without it, the competitors' machines are less compatible.

IBM's moves didn't catch the pcm's until 1979, when it brought out a particularly aggressive new line of middle-sized computers. The weakest pcm, Itel, left the business; the strongest, Amdahl, saw its revenues, earnings and stock plummet, and along with its counterparts in peripherals, Storage Technology and Memorex, it realized that only critical mass and diversification would protect it from the whims of IBM. In the summer of 1979 Amdahl talked merger with Memorex, unsuccessfully; in the fall of 1979 Storage Technology talked merger with Memorex, also unsuccessfully; in the spring of 1980, Amdahl and Storage Technology agreed to merge, but the deal was squelched because STC and Fujitsu, Amdahl's chief backer, couldn't agree. By the fall of 1980, the pcm mainframe industry had rebounded somewhat, but owed some of its good fortune to a stretchout in IBM delivery schedules. Its future will be murky for some time.

11

IBM Giveth and IBM Taketh Away:
The Leasing Companies

———

HARVEY GOODMAN is no longer a New Yorker. When he comes up from Miami he drinks gin-and-tonic in November and wears the collar of his sport shirt spread-eagled over the lapels of his jacket. He is a big barrel-chested man who carries himself as if he were about to sing tenor. His luxuriant white sideburns seem bleached by the sun, not the years, and certainly not by the misfortune of having been ousted in a boardroom coup from the chairmanship of the company he founded.

Goodman's company, known as Data Processing Financial and General when he ruled it (later the "General" part was dropped, to signify more modest ambitions), is a computer lessor: that is, it buys computers from IBM and leases them to customers at a discount from the IBM rental fee. The lessor is able to do this because it depreciates the equipment over a longer period than the conservative four-to-five-year span favored by IBM. In their heyday, the lessors took a ten-year depreciation, and because of the correspondingly lower deductions, they could lease a machine at 10 to 20 percent below the IBM rate and still show nearly 30 percent annual pretax profit on the rentals they received. Overhead expenses were low, since the lessors didn't design, develop, manufacture or maintain anything, and since they had very little marketing to do. IBM, after all, had announced the product, prepared the field manuals and touted the machine's virtues. Many of the machines the lessors bought were already on rental in the customer's shop anyway, so all the lessor had to do was persuade the customer to buy his computer, sell it to DPF&G and lease it back cheap.

That, at least, was the theory on which companies like DPF&G were able to borrow enormous amounts of money from banks and insurance companies to buy more machines which would bring in additional revenues to impress the investment community. Wall Street, in turn, would reward the company, in the bull market of the late sixties, with higher stock values which again increased its borrowing power. If your stock was going up you could also do very nicely selling convertible debentures, a security that is highly attractive to investors. When the stock was $18 a share you would issue a $1,000 bond convertible into 50 shares. Then, five months later, just before the interest fell due—and when the stock had gone up to $25 a share—you would call the bond. So the bondholder could choose between getting his $1,000 back or converting it to 50 shares of stock which were now worth $1,250. The bondholder would make the obvious choice, and you would have saved the interest, converted the debt into equity on your balance sheet, and so increased the apparent value of your company once again.

All this was possible because investors had faith in the leasing company theory. Later, when the holes in the theory began to show, when the companies were left with huge debts they couldn't pay and machines they had trouble unloading, when they had made other investments which turned out to be less than prudent, there was considerable bloodshed.

The story of the leasing companies makes a neat morality play that illustrates the consequences of greed and pride. But it is also true that IBM owned the theater and sat in the wings working the lights and raising and lowering the curtain. The play began with the consent decree Tom Watson signed in 1956. Among the provisions of the decree was the requirement that IBM, for the first time in its history, offer its machines for sale as well as for rent. The company had one year to comply with the decree, which specified that IBM must give its customers the opportunity to buy the machines they were now using at a discount of 10 percent for each full year of age; once a machine was more than eight years old it could be purchased for a quarter of the original sale price. The pricing structure set up in the consent decree expired in 1958, but afterward IBM introduced a purchase plan for its customers which essentially continued the conditions of the decree.

The first entrepreneurs to recognize the opportunities the decree offered were Walter Oreamuno and Jorge Gonzales, two IBM-trained Costa Ricans then in the consulting business in New York.

Oreamuno had been a schoolteacher and Gonzales an army officer in Costa Rica in 1943 when IBM held a competition to select likely candidates for training in the U.S. It would, of course, be a decade before IBM got into computers; the young men were to learn how the company's accounting machines worked and then return to their countries to sell and install them. Oreamuno and Gonzales won the contest, and when their IBM training was completed they went home and got jobs in the Costa Rican Census Bureau. After the war they returned to the United States and worked successively for Columbia University, a brokerage house and a bank. In a few years they had become crackerjack engineers who could get into a machine with a soldering iron and stretch its capabilities by just altering the circuitry. By 1954 they had also cultivated enough prospective clients in the financial community to justify starting their own consulting business.

After the consent decree they advised their clients to take advantage of the new low purchase prices, but the banks and brokerage houses had been thoroughly sold by IBM on the virtues of renting equipment, which could be traded back immediately when new models came out. So Oreamuno and Gonzales began to think of buying the equipment themselves and signing the customers up for a discount lease that was longer than IBM's one-year contract but short enough to be marketable. They would buy partly depreciated equipment that customers were now renting and also machines that had been returned to IBM, which the manufacturer was now obligated to sell to second-hand dealers.

IBM was difficult to deal with, Oreamuno says. "For three and a half years they sent us from office to office in search of the man in charge of complying with the consent decree. They said it was a complicated thing to set up, a matter of diverting an ocean, not a stream."

It was also hard work persuading customers to save money by leasing equipment from their firm, Management Assistance, Inc., instead of IBM. While the consent decree compelled IBM to offer the same support to purchase and rental customers, the users knew the salesmen would be gone and suspected the systems engineers might be a little less eager, the maintenance men a bit slow to respond at odd hours. In all, it took MAI until 1961 to get its leasing business under way.

Oreamuno and Gonzales didn't want just to provide a financial service. They dreamed of creating a mini-IBM, with its own fleet of salesmen, systems engineers and maintenance men in branch offices across the country, a company that would do the whole job not only cheaper but better than the organization it was modeled after. In the early days MAI made no effort to lease computers, and the bulk of its business continued to be in accounting machines, the founders' specialty. The banks that financed MAI felt the two men should stick to what they knew. Moreover, the use of computers was not yet widespread, and it was difficult to tell how fast the technology would change. Whatever the advances of the computer, MAI felt, there would always be a place for the accounting machine: it would go on as indomitably as the old Underwood typewriter. Oreamuno and Gonzales made a point of not buying or leasing all the equipment in a given installation: if the customer decided to return a few accounting machines, he would be likely to choose the more expensive equipment on rent from IBM.

Oreamuno and Gonzales did a formidable job of salesmanship all around. Most equipment leases outside the data processing industry, whether they cover planes or railroad cars, are signed on a full-payout basis: that is, the contract lasts long enough for the lessor to recover all his expenses by the time it expires. MAI's customers, however, were used to the IBM one-year lease and would not commit themselves to sit with the equipment for five years, which was the average time remaining for MAI's middle-aged machines to pay for themselves. So the entrepreneurs persuaded the banks to lend them money for five years on a two-year lease which would not recoup the cost of the machines. On the one hand Oreamuno and Gonzales were telling the banks that customers feared the equipment might become obsolete; on the other hand they were convincing them that the customers would keep the machines for another three years, or if they didn't, new prospects would come along.

"At first, the customers were hard to convince," says Oreamuno. "Then we sold two or three important names and the idea began to catch fire. We were helped by a mild recession: that always makes the customers want to sharpen their pencils to the last inch." So MAI began to grow, slowly in the beginning and then like wildfire, the revenues more than doubling in '64 and nearly tripling in '65. Although IBM had announced System 360 in 1964, MAI continued to buy accounting machines—those good old Underwood typewriters—up through the summer of 1966, often paying the customer a premium to close the deal: the customer had an old machine now available from IBM at 50 percent off the list price; if you split the discount with him you'd still get the hardware cheap.

In 1966, the year the guillotine fell, little MAI had more than $170 million worth of equipment, including some computers and an estimated 8 percent of the IBM punched-card accounting machines in the country. As a mark of status, it owed the banks nearly $100 million. Still, its management felt secure: a solid IBM customer like the Prudential Insurance Company, for example, also did substantial business with MAI. The leasing company, in accordance with its founders' dreams, was building and training a corps of maintenance men, but had to continue using IBM field engineers in the hinterlands. That summer, the company received the alarming information that IBM was nearly six months behind in its billing. When the chits finally came in, MAI found it owed $1 million in back maintenance costs. At the same time, deliveries of System 360 were increasing, and Oreamuno and Gonzales began to doubt the validity of the Underwood typewriter theory. They looked to diversification—into 360 leasing and plug-compatible peripherals, an idea they helped originate.

As MAI worked to trim its operating costs, customers began to return punched-card machines in quantity. By 1968, MAI was forced to take a writeoff of $17 million for off-rent equipment in addition to its $3 million operating loss. During the next two years the company approached the brink of bankruptcy. (It finally went through a big recapitalization and successfully entered other parts of the computer business; its founders are long gone.)

At the same time, other lessors had set up shop, and they learned absolutely nothing from their predecessor's difficulties. By the early sixties risk leasing—that is, signing contracts that gambled on the customer's keeping the equipment past the term of the lease—had become an extremely attractive investment opportunity. If you bought a new computer, you could take advantage of the newly passed investment tax credit, which amounted to a 14 percent pretax discount on the cost of the equipment; on an older machine, there was the progressive discount that IBM had begun to offer its customers after the consent decree. Moreover, as D. P. Boothe, one of the

early lessors, points out, IBM charged the customer an extra 30 percent for each additional shift of use beyond the first eight hours.
Boothe, therefore, could also charge for the extra shifts, keeping his
rates, of course, below IBM's. If he was careful to deal with customers who used their computers twenty-four hours a day, Boothe could
recover his expenses in thirty months.

In 1962 Boothe Leasing was acquired by Greyhound. Pod Boothe
looked toward expansion. He had hired John Randolph, a former
Textron executive, to head the New York office. Randolph, a former
customer who had displayed an impressive toughness in negotiations,
was a well-tailored Englishman who exuded the sort of polish that
would inspire confidence in board chairmen and money-lenders.
Boothe and Randolph were, however, financial men, and they felt it
was important to have someone aboard with the technical skill to
evaluate computer equipment. Randolph recommended two old
friends, Howard Levin, a former university mathematics teacher,
and Jim Townsend, an engineer, who had done operations research
for several corporations and were now partners in a consulting business. Boothe and Randolph retained Levin and Townsend to "find"
equipment on commission.

Levin and Townsend, who dealt with the customers, found the
same trepidations that had plagued MAI: what would happen if you
needed an IBM field engineer at midnight on Sunday? Townsend
remembers, "Even when we demonstrated the savings—in a little
computer analysis program we'd worked out—they thought we were
against motherhood. We were trying to hand out $10 bills on a
streetcorner and finding no takers." While the business was small,
however, it was profitable and looked promising to Boothe, Randolph, Levin and Townsend. Because of the favorable pricing of
second-generation computers they were able to recover their investments promptly, and since they had calculated quite accurately the
announcement and delivery schedule of System 360, they were not
overloaded with inventory.

The announcement of System 360 made Greyhound's board of
directors notably skittish. As Boothe later testified in Greyhound's
antitrust suit against IBM, "there was great and odious comparison
between the value of a bus, 'by God,' which would always bring a
price in the market someplace at such and such a figure; but these
mysterious black boxes were unknown quantity, and they didn't

have the faintest idea whether they would ever be worth anything or not."

Greyhound decided to put its computer leasing operation on the market. Boothe, Randolph, Levin and Townsend put together a new corporation to buy out Greyhound. But when Greyhound management saw how quickly the four men were able to secure financial backing and how eager Boothe was to put his own money on the line, it decided that maybe it had something after all, and reneged on the sale. A series of internecine squabbles developed, which ended with Randolph leaving Greyhound in 1965 to found his own company; Levin and Townsend beginning to buy and lease equipment for their own account and breaking all ties with Greyhound in 1966; and Boothe clashing with Greyhound management and going off to found *his* own company in 1967. In two years, one computer lessor had undergone cellular division and become four.

Leasing company stocks were beginning to climb. Wall Street's interest had already been piqued by the success of two other enterprises in the field. In 1959 Saul Steinberg, a senior at Wharton, began to prepare a thesis on the decline and fall of IBM. With the support of a professor who was skeptical about growth stocks, Steinberg set out to prove that IBM had sown the seeds of its own destruction, which would occur sometime in the sixties. After a couple of months of research, however, he revised his prediction. "I began spending thirty or forty hours a week just on IBM," he remembers. "I thought the company was a money machine." Steinberg pleaded with the professor to allow him to change the theory of the paper, but the professor threatened him with a failing grade and no graduation. Steinberg picked a new topic, but the potential of the computer business continued to haunt him.

By 1961 the young man, now working for his father, had figured out the economics of leasing. Steinberg started Ideal Leasing Corporation as a partnership with his father, who contributed $25,000, and his uncle. The partnership had one lease contract financed by a bank loan. By 1966 Ideal Leasing had already become a public company called Leasco, and had assets of $21 million.

While Boothe and his group were scrambling to establish themselves in the leasing business, while Steinberg was acting on his bright idea, Harvey Goodman was having greatness thrust upon him.

Goodman, the son of a Brooklyn cop, had always done well in his studies without much boning up: while attending City College in the daytime to get an accounting degree he found time to study law at Brooklyn College by night, and even made the law review. In 1953, working for an accounting firm, he had dealings with IBM and learned that the company gave a test for job applicants. "Tests meant challenge," says Goodman. "I was good at tests. I wanted to see if they would hire me." When Goodman passed the test, he thought he'd take a crack at the interview, and came out with an offer. He went to work as a systems engineer, ostensibly as preparation for a sales job but still expecting to use a short stint with IBM to enhance his skills as a tax lawyer. "I loved the machine, and I was impressed by all the people with advanced degrees," he remembers. "One day I saw a salesman with a $10,000 commission check. I asked him if it was annual commission. When he said it was just the result of a very good month, I decided to stay at IBM and become a salesman."

Goodman moved fast in IBM's sales organization. Soon he was making more than $30,000 a year, and one year he led the country in new accounts. Then he was promoted to a forecasting job in White Plains. It was an exciting place to be. IBM's plans for future products, products that would perhaps change the nature of the computer industry, depended on the sales forecasts that Harvey Goodman and other young men like him produced. Sometimes he would be asked to follow through on requests that came straight from Learson—one might even say that Harvey Goodman was the man, or at least one of the men, who gave T. V. Learson his numbers, and all this was a heady feeling for Goodman. He discovered there was a knack to forecasting, and once you picked it up you could give out figures practically off the top of your head.

There were headier feelings to come. One day—it was now 1958—Goodman's friend Fred, an over-the-counter broker, suggested that Goodman think of some creative way to make money in the computer business. It was just the sort of puzzle Goodman enjoyed, and he sat up late that night thinking about it. The next day he called Fred. "People think computers will be obsolete in a short time," he said. "They're wrong. The machines don't wear out so fast. If you could get people to use them longer. . . ." Goodman didn't want to do anything himself, but Fred was welcome to the idea—the same idea that occurred to Oreamuno and Gonzales, Steinberg and the Boothe group, although Goodman didn't know it.

During the next few years Fred, who had persuaded Goodman to write a proposal, introduced him to a series of investment bankers. Goodman went along just for laughs, and was always relieved when the bankers showed no interest. Finally Fred gave up, but another friend of Goodman's showed the proposal to William Frost, the son of a rich industrialist. After meeting Goodman a couple of times— Goodman pleaded reluctance, but kept going along—Frost began to warm up to the idea, and persuaded Allen & Company, the investment bankers, to join him in financing a leasing company and guaranteeing its debts.

"Frost and the man from Allen drove out to my house in Roslyn in a chauffeured limousine," Goodman remembers. "I was terribly naïve, sitting there in my tee shirt. They pushed and I was into it. I felt I was advancing within IBM but I didn't like the environment. So I wrote a heartfelt letter of resignation and moved into Frost's tiny office." Frost, Allen and Goodman himself had each put up $50,000 to cement the deal.

Like all computer lessors, Goodman needed ready cash at favorable interest rates. His job at IBM hadn't given him experience in the complexities of borrowing money and he had to depend on his backers to arrange loans; he found Frost and Allen & Company neither knowledgeable nor helpful. "We were borrowing at 12 percent when the prime rate was 4 per cent." he says. "You couldn't do a deal at those rates." After six months he finally negotiated a three-year lease on a million-dollar computer for Texas Instruments. The deal broke the ice and Goodman then found several other promising possibilities. Without help from Frost or Allen he arranged a loan at half a point above prime, and at last the company began to move. "By May 1962, the end of the first year, I had a gross income of $120,000 from six months of leasing one computer to Texas Instruments," he says. "If I did nothing I'd have doubled my revenues the next year, but I made five or six major deals. The numbers started to look exciting: each transaction was large. And the whole company was me—I answered the phone and swept the floor."

In 1965, just as Goodman was needing more cash, the Texas Instruments lease expired and TI decided to buy its machine. Goodman showed a sizable profit, and he and Allen decided that Data

Processing Financial & General—which still consisted of only one full-time employee—should go public. Goodman remembers, "We came out at $11 and the stock zoomed to $17 the next day. It was hot as a firecracker. The prospectus was accurate but I couldn't believe there was that much value there. It was a dream—it was insanity. Then Wall Street starts calling, saying 'What will you earn next year?' I said, 'More. Every year is a base for the next. Maybe we'll double our revenues next year.' "

"I was working on extremely attractive deals," Goodman continues. "Get your money out in 41 or 42 months. In March of '67 we went for $12 million worth of convertible debentures, and they sold like hot cakes. As money became easily available I was willing to take greater risks instead of going for the longer three- or four-year leases. My hypothesis was I could look at an installation and see how long the computer would stay in it. In those days I was the only leasing company president with an IBM background."

By the mid-sixties, Goodman and his colleagues were involved in leasing System 360, which created a new set of economic conditions and assumptions.

The depreciation period on second-generation computers, while it was always longer than IBM's, varied among the lessors, but the profit depended heavily on IBM's substantial charge for extra-shift use. This dependence was unofficial: on paper, Pod Boothe would calculate a 6½-year payout period for a computer running eight hours a day, with the profit accruing afterward. But in fact he would never make a deal unless he knew the customer kept the machine going sixteen or twenty-four hours a day, and so he expected—quite correctly—to recover expenses in less than three years.

When System 360 came out IBM geared its prices to the longevity of integrated circuits. The company knocked down the extra shift charge to 10 percent, and in order to stay competitive the lessors had to give customers the extra shift free. The question of whether the computer could still earn money over the lengthy depreciation period was no longer academic: the leasing companies were betting that after ten years the machine would still have a salvage value of 10 to 15 percent of its original cost. Moreover, IBM's rental credit had given the lessors an advantageously low purchase price. But as the entrepreneurs began to win customers, IBM became increasingly wary of losing account control and cut this credit severely, thus shut ting off another avenue of fast recovery for the lessors.

To be fair to the leasing companies, there was some technical justification for the gamble they took. System 360 represented an advance so great that few customers were ready for it. IBM had to devise an emulator to make the 360 behave like a second-generation machine until the user was able to do the reprogramming necessary to exploit its special features. Harvey Goodman, Howard Levin and other lessors who were technically knowledgeable could see the customers running one job at a time on a machine that could handle three. They also knew the investment IBM had made in developing System 360—the operating system alone had cost a quarter of a billion dollars to develop. Programming was a bloodbath for manufacturer and user alike; IBM would not obsolesce System 360 so fast, nor would customers be receptive to newer models.

It would be nice to believe that the leasing companies operated on a set of technical assumptions which had been worked out and documented with the kind of thoroughness that usually accompanies IBM's own planning. Certainly the entrepreneurs dutifully trotted out these arguments on the rare occasions when they were forced to defend themselves. But since several important factors were left out of this theory, it is probable that Goodman and his colleagues didn't think things through. First of all, the theory supposes that having produced the ultimate computer system IBM's engineers, programmers, planners and salesmen would sit back and relax, that its worldwide complex of manufacturing plants would lie idle while the supply of fully depreciated 360's brought in handsome profits but did little to enhance the company's growth. It assumes that even if IBM did decide to keep its employees busy developing and marketing a new line, customers would have enough self-control to resist buying it until they had squeezed every drop of usefulness out of their old machines. It suggests that IBM would be benevolent enough to allow the leasing companies to seduce its rental customers without taking any action, and it disregards the consequences of competition between the lessors.

The climate of the middle to late sixties was not conducive to long-range planning. "When you have people going from $10,000 net worth to $10 million net worth in three years there isn't much time to think about the future," says John Puttre, a DPF executive who has survived several changes in management. "Respectable

Wall Street firms were raising over a billion dollars to finance computer acquisition and they weren't asking any questions, so why should Harvey and the other lessors? And you must think of this: How many men do a million-dollar deal in their lifetime? I've done many. How many men get to negotiate a $25 million bond placement? Harvey did three. How many men get to call on the controller of General Motors? I have. When a man does these things, it affects him."

In October 1966 IBM made a hasty but historic decision which it regretted later. The decision was known in the industry as the three-by-three, because IBM raised its rental prices by 3 percent and lowered purchase prices by another 3 percent. The leasing companies could now buy machines that much cheaper and follow IBM's rental increase by raising their rates accordingly. They would show a small jump in annual income for each invested dollar; if you multiplied that increase by the ten-year life of the machine, it meant that any given computer could earn substantially more than it did before. This piece of news was well received by investment bankers who arranged the financing of a billion-and-a-half-dollar buying spree during 1967 and 1968, vastly increasing the amount of inventory the lessors would have to unload when the original leases expired—but of course, nobody worried about that.

At the same time, the leasing companies were becoming more aware of each other. As competition among them grew fiercer, they began to grant more concessions to customers in order to get the business—not because they felt the business was scarce but because they were supposed to be exciting growth companies. They signed shorter leases, or wrote five-year contracts with options to cancel after two, which was the same thing. A large customer offering a multimillion-dollar deal might expect a heavier discount than was normal. Or the customer would be given the option to add extra memory and peripherals at the same reduced rate over the term of the lease, thus obliging the entrepreneur to increase his inventory of equipment without regard for whether the add-ons were remarketable when the first lease expired.

Now suppose that IBM did come out with a new computer system before some of the leased 360's recovered their expenses and before others, which had been bought earlier, could earn a profit. Obviously the market value of 360's would plummet, but other problems would also develop, and the leasing companies barely considered them. A number of customers would return their 360's as soon as the lease expired in order to rent the new models from IBM. Should the leasing company be unable to find another home for the computer immediately, even with a sizable price cut, the machine would be sitting in the warehouse earning nothing at all for several months—and in the lessors' ten-year schedule, every month of revenue was important.

To place the computer with another customer the leasing company would incur additional marketing expenses, and the bill would be steeper than it was when the machine was in its prime—"releasing is unromantic, foot-slogging work," says Boothe. Then, the computer that comes off rent has to be shipped from the old customer's installation to the lessor's warehouse, refurbished, reconfigured with different peripherals to suit the new customer's specifications, and shipped out again. This takes time and costs money, and not the least of the expense is administrative. Today, Harvey Goodman's company, DPF, has a large staff that does nothing but "asset management"—moving and reconfiguring the computers and keeping track of expenses like personal property taxes that vary from state to state. No reserves were set up for this in the company's palmier days.

Most of these contingencies were foreseen by Abraham J. Briloff, an accounting professor at City University of New York, who suggested in an article in *Barrons* that the leasing companies' assumptions were overoptimistic. The main purpose of the article, however, was to point out that "generally accepted accounting principles" approved by the American Institute of Certified Public Accountants permitted lessors to report inflated earnings. It was all a "fandangle," a "fantastic ornament" or "tomfoolery," said Briloff. The fandangle depended on the method the lessor used to amortize revenues and costs, calculate depreciation and report tax benefits: different bookkeeping styles could produce dramatically disparate results. Hardly anybody listened to Briloff until 1970, when the leasing empires collapsed and his warnings were reverently remembered by all the suddenly hard-nosed securities analysts.

From the mid-sixties on, IBM watched the rise of the leasing companies with increasing alarm. At first the company worried about obvious problems like the loss of profits. A purchased machine will recover expenses and bring in a relatively high profit immediately; if a similar machine goes on rental, it will pay its costs and earn a slightly lower profit over the allotted four-to-five-year span. Once the rented machine stays out beyond this period it starts to pull ahead of the purchased machine, adding some 2 percent profit every month. The large "rental deck" of machines that had already paid their costs was the basis of the wealth in IBM's coffers.

In all its deliberations about the leasing companies, IBM had to remember that a number of good customers—especially banks, aerospace companies and insurance firms—were also buying machines, simply because they preferred to own their own equipment. The company couldn't afford to alienate these "hard-core" purchasers. Still, the Management Review Committee had set a goal of discouraging purchases until the fall of 1966, when IBM suddenly did an about-face and instituted the three-by-three decision. One reason for the three-by-three—which seems so incomprehensible in light of the company's avowed objectives—can be found in documents and court testimony. In 1966 the problems of designing software for System 360 were most serious. Perhaps the operating system would never achieve the sophistication that IBM had planned for it. If so, the 360 would be highly vulnerable to competition, and might not even live out its allotted span. It would earn lower revenues, while the programming delays brought higher costs. The expansion and development expenses for System 360 had left IBM's cash position dangerously low. The company had been obliged to make one of its rare stock offerings, and the next year it would borrow heavily. The three-by-three was a *carpe diem* decision: better get as much money out of the 360 as we can, and get it now. While we're putting the software in shape, let's take another look at prices.

Within a year IBM began to see the consequences of its new policy. By 1967 one vice-president told the Management Review Committee that "leasing companies in total were now bigger than any single competitor." Then there appeared another problem, which might become even more serious than the loss of plain profits or account control. A purchasing binge by the lessors produced horrible distortions on IBM's growth chart. In the years when the lessors were laying on supplies of equipment, there would be a nasty bloating of corporate revenues; then, when the gluttons had satisfied themselves, the swelling would deflate, leaving Thomas J. Watson, Jr. to explain to the shareholders why revenues were suddenly flat— or even down.

The "control" that IBM maintained by renting its own equipment extended further than the simple advantage gained by having one's salesman continually on the customer's premises. It meant financial control, the ability to adjust prices on machines in the field in order to correct previous pricing errors, respond to economic conditions and bring revenues into line with goals. It meant technological control, the ability to introduce new features (like virtual memory) at the most convenient time, to gain wider acceptance from customers who might be reluctant to commit to purchase and to rectify inadequacies. And it gave IBM the financial stability required to pursue its no-layoff policy, the policy that protected the company from unionism.

Later, during the recession, it became clear that the lessors threatened IBM in other ways. They were natural allies of the pcm's; in particular, as more and more of the lessors' original 360 contracts expired, they would have to remarket the equipment, and the existence of inexpensive plug-compatible peripherals to attach to the mainframes proved a boon. Finally, it had always been IBM's policy to maintain a constant price for a product throughout its life: that is, when System 370 came out, the company did not reduce its 360 prices, even though the new line offered better performance. It could do this because many customers preferred to postpone the headaches of upgrading; in effect, these users were paying a premium to retain obsolete equipment. The lessors, on the other hand, offered cheap second-hand 360's just like the ones in the customer's shop; they cut into the revenues of both 360 and 370.

Between 1968 and 1970, IBM had many new products to bring out, including the last models of System 360 and the first of System 370. The action it took to combat the leasing companies—whose financial problems it analyzed with the same thoroughness it had applied to those of the pcm's—would be tied to the pricing of this equipment. The principal tactic was a move in the opposite direction of the three-by-three, a move that would raise the price the lessors would have to pay for their computers without a corresponding increase in rental rates to allow the leasing companies to charge more.

IBM prices are calculated in terms of a figure called the multiplier, which is simply the number of months' rent required to meet the purchase price. A machine that rents for $10,000 a month and sells for $420,000 has a multiplier of 42. A leasing company, however, will require more than 42 months to get its money back because it charges a lower rent than IBM's and must figure in interest and administrative expenses peculiar to third-party leasing. Greyhound, in its antitrust suit, claimed that if IBM needs 42 months the lessor will not break even for 79 months. When IBM raises the multiplier the effects on the leasing company are most serious: extra costs go up with the passage of time, and as the machine gets older the lessor is forced to slash his rates.

That wasn't all IBM could do. Maintenance charges are extra on purchased computers; should IBM raise these charges, it would further lengthen the payout period for the leasing companies. In 1968 IBM brought out two models of System 360 with multipliers of 48 and an increase in maintenance. While these particular models were not in the size that comprised the bulk of the lessors' business, they might have seen which way the wind was blowing.

System 370, however, was supposed to deliver the *coup de grace.* The first two machines had multipliers of 56 and more than double the maintenance charges. When IBM unbundled, it cut prices on both the rented machines then in the field and on future purchases; it didn't give a rebate to former purchasers like the leasing companies, who had paid for services no longer available and had passed these costs on to their customers. Finally, the Fixed Term Plan, while aimed at the pcm's, established IBM as a competitor in the long-term discount lease business. It was an uncongenial world the lessors faced in the early seventies.

As their companies grew, the lessors began to realize how dependent they were on borrowing money to finance their purchases; perhaps, too, they suspected that computer leasing wouldn't last forever. To raise additional cash and to hedge their bets, they thought it wise to diversify. But the zeal with which several leasing companies pursued their acquisitions—and their choice of candidates—suggests that greed and gall were motives as strong as prudence. "There was lots of pressure from Wall Street in '67 and '68," remembers Townsend. "We used to have people lined up in the hall with deals. 'You guys have the Midas touch,' they would say." But the lessors' Midas touch had come from one clever idea made disproportionately successful by creative bookkeeping and the bull market. An acquired company needed management skill to make it go, and few of the leasing entrepreneurs had ever managed anything.

Howard Levin, Townsend's partner, got the show business bug in 1968, when the company expanded its quarters to the floor above and he met the previous tenants, a theatrical producing firm. They worked out a deal whereby Levin-Townsend and the producing firm would each invest $1 million in a package of four shows. Levin thought the venture would be a good way to make Levin-Townsend better known to the general public. The first show was "Maggie Flynn," which lasted a few months, and the second was "The Fig Leaves Are Falling," which ran a few days. Then Levin had the sense to quit.

The Broadway fling, which cost $500,000, was a relatively minor folly, but Levin made other moves Townsend and the board of directors considered serious mistakes. He poured $3½ million into Cobbs Company, a failing franchiser of restaurants and gift shops. He bought the inappropriately named Bonanza Hotel and Casino in Las Vegas for more than $10 million and instantly got into a payment squabble with Kirk Kerkorian, the former owner, and a contract dispute with the former operator who happened to hold the gaming and liquor licenses. The ensuing litigation cost $400,000 and the delay brought Levin-Townsend an immediate million-dollar operating loss. An expansion into computer services was less flamboyant and more logical but it, too, lost money in the recession.

While these diversifications were going sour, Levin was behaving more than ever like an industrial magnate. In the Greyhound days he had been afraid to fly, and always took the train to the west coast. Now he was renting a jet costing $60,000 a month, redecorating it and, in a gesture that some described as Napoleonic, neglecting to have the floor recessed so that anyone taller than Levin (and almost anyone *was* taller than Levin) would bump his head on entering. Personal friends of Levin were added to the company payroll—including a restaurant consultant, an art advisor and a corporate physician (an obstetrician, Townsend noted at the time; Levin counters, "he performed a number of nonobstetrical chores and only got $100 a month"). At company expense Levin ordered a $28,000 Mercedes

("Leased. A trade-in on an old Cadillac," he says). He presented Mrs. Parks, the treasurer, with a $900 attache case ("On her fifth anniversary with the company," Levin explains. "New briefcases encourage people to take work home") and an ostrich handbag ("to replace one that was stolen on a company trip").

Whatever Levin's justifications, his showy style left him vulnerable in January 1970, when his partner decided things had gone too far. Townsend rose at a board of directors' meeting and, his voice cracking, moved to oust Levin. The motion was carried. Later Levin sued Townsend and the other directors to get his job back, and the affair received wide publicity, certainly making Levin-Townsend better known to the general public, but not in the way that Levin had planned.

Shortly afterward, Levin-Townsend announced it owed $11 million to IBM, which it was not immediately able to pay. During the spring Townsend kept IBM at bay while the debt mounted and a series of merger talks with four companies aborted. Townsend and Levin finally resolved their differences out of court; the debt was rescheduled; and Townsend devoted himself to cleaning house. He changed the company's name to Rockwood Computer Corporation.

Meanwhile Harvey Goodman, in his happy-go-lucky fashion, was traveling the same road as Howard Levin. In 1967 he had raised $12 million through convertible debentures; a second offering brought in $50 million. "We had all this money," Goodman says. "So what were we going to do with it? There was a very profitable hot stock called XTRA, a company that leased railroad cars. Its only competitor was a subsidiary of Railway Express named Realco. We made an approach to the management of Railway Express to buy Realco, and they told us they were negotiating for the sale of the whole company. I felt that Realco alone was worth $100 million, but I wanted a bargain, so I offered to buy all of Railway Express for $30 million.

"Lo and behold, it turned out they were considering my suggestion. They said all 67 railroads that own Railway Express would have to approve the sale and turn in their stock, so I asked for 100 percent of the stock within seven days or no deal. I thought there was no way all those railroads could agree within a week, especially over the Christmas holidays. Meantime the news leaks out and the price of my stock skyrockets. All of a sudden the Railway Express stock starts flying in, and I start biting my nails, because I know there's something rotten. By the seventh day all the stock is in except one plane is delayed in the fog. I'm getting nervous, praying for a further delay. Then we found the one railroad's acceptance was subject to approval by its board of directors, so we had an out. And as I reviewed their reports it looked to me that Railway Express was going rapidly downhill. Our stock lost ground because the deal fell through—it should have gone up."

After the Railway Express caper there was the A & P adventure, in which Goodman's bid to take over the supermarket chain was blocked. While neither episode enhanced Goodman's stature on Wall Street, their abortion was a stroke of luck in light of other diversification moves that DPF & G completed. Goodman invested in a short-takeoff-and-landing airline that never got off the ground, in data centers, a software company and a company founded by some Berkeley professors aiming to build a monster time-sharing machine ("the King Kong of computers," a DPF executive describes it). All of these fizzled. Then when the Justice Department and Control Data launched their antitrust suits against IBM, Goodman instituted a similar suit of his own. The giant corporation would really be afraid of DPF & G, Goodman thought, because he had worked for IBM and knew the company secrets. "I was prepared to invest a million a year in legal expenses for the next five years—we could afford it," he says.

The board of directors disagreed with Goodman, especially since DPF & G was showing a net loss. He was stunned when he entered the board meeting in May and sat through the same scene Howard Levin had endured a few months earlier.

All of the leasing companies attempted diversifications large and small; some of these moves failed while others helped the lessors to survive. The adventures of Leasco's Saul Steinberg were widely reported. After learning that many insurance companies held enormous treasuries of "surplus surplus," or cash and securities beyond the reserves they are required to set aside, Steinberg bought Reliance Insurance Company, whose surplus surplus came to $100 million; a year later he struck out with the Chemical Bank after sister commercial banks, investment bankers, institutional investors and important corporate customers made it clear that Steinberg's hostile takeover would not sit well with the financial community. Then Leasco's investment in Pergamon Press, Ltd., a British publisher, ended in litigation and a big write-down.

The lessors haven't been much more successful than the pcm's at suing IBM. As soon as Harvey Goodman was ousted from DPF & G, the new management settled his IBM suit. A Greyhound Computer Corporation antitrust suit was finally settled for $17.7 million some eleven years after its initiation. Other lessors have either lost or settled their suits.

When IBM began acting against the pcm's, several entrepreneurs in leasing and peripherals saw their common interest and began to offer heavily discounted long-term leases on IBM 360's with the cheaper independent peripherals attached. The need to cut costs during the recession made these arrangements attractive to many customers, and IBM found itself selling 370's against the cheaper, enhanced 360's. For the lessors they offered a means of stemming losses, not a road to growth: the majority hoped to sell off what they could, stretch out the lives of the rest and concentrate on other interests from offshore oil drilling to real estate. Enormous writeoffs were common in the early to middle seventies, and most computer people thought the leasing industry was moribund. But in the next recession System 360, at its low rate, began to look attractive again: fully depreciated machines continued to chug away throughout the seventies.

While the old risk lease is no longer feasible, the stronger lessors—and some newer entrants into the business—have thought of new deals like the tax leverage lease, in which a bank, an institutional investor, a leasing company and a lessee share the risks and benefits of leasing the equipment. In 1980 third-party leasing accounted for more than a quarter of the dollar value of installed general purpose computers. An International Data Corporation study of several years ago noted that as users became more sophisticated, they were willing to put up with the inflexibility of long-term leasing in return for considerable financial savings. As Bertram Cohn, the current chairman of DPF, observes, "Just because the leasing companies were set up for poor economic reasons doesn't mean they have no function at all."

Still, Cohn also recognizes that the lessors' importance in the computer industry will always be limited, that because of technological change he must be conservative about buying new equipment, and that "a computer doesn't grow in value like a piece of timberland"; his own leasing efforts are dwarfed by the volumes of the commercial bakery DPF bought in 1977. Pod Boothe, who is getting some income from the computers he owns but will write new leases only on other kinds of capital equipment, observes, "It is of no importance to a load of coal whether the railroad car it's in was built in 1968 or 1978. But old computers don't perform as well as new ones." IBM's 1979 actions against the pcm's underlined the insecurity of the independent leasing business: the company's new line was an exceptional bargain, and the value of the lessors' 370's immediately plummeted. IBM gave the lessors another twist of the knife by offering an attractive trade-in deal on its own 370's.

Of the early lessors, only Boothe and Steinberg are still in command of the companies they founded.

12

The Music Men:
Software and Services

When I was preparing my speech in New York, I looked up the word "entrepreneur" in the Oxford Irish Dictionary, a leading reference work. . . . The definition I found was that an entrepreneur was "a director or manager of a public musical institution and/or one who gets up entertainments." I find that definition pretty true of many entrepreneurial activities *outside* of musical institutions, sometimes truer than the currently fashionable definition, that of business risk-taker.
—Consultant Dick H. Brandon,
"The Successful Entrepreneur in the Private Sector,"
Speech to the Irish Management Institute, 1970

COMPANIES in the hardware business supply a product that can be hauled into the customer's offices, uncrated and unwrapped, gazed at and patted. Entrepreneurs who supply services based on the computer, on the other hand, provide an invisible, untouchable commodity about which it is most difficult to be objective. In selling the music, not the piano, they face an entirely different set of challenges.

This segment of the computer industry is highly amorphous. What International Data Corporation (IDC) calls the market for independent software, facilities management, and processing services amounted to just over $11 billion in 1980. The software houses produce programs, either tailored to the individual customer's specifications or in standard packages that serve a mass market. Facilities management companies are concessionaires who take over the customer's data processing installation and run it like a company cafeteria. Processing services companies either do the customer's computing on their own equipment or sell time on that-equipment, usually accompanied by software packages or access to some special fund of data. There are innumerable variations on these basic types; and while each company is characterized in terms of its principal line of business, most companies in the field offer a mixture of these services.

The industry IDC describes embraces some 3,200 companies, of which nearly 2,500 recorded 1979 sales of less than $1 million. The largest in the field is Control Data; the second largest is a software house called Computer Sciences, which brought in $411 million in the various service categories during 1979; two dollars behind it was Automatic Data Processing, the services company covered in the second part of this chapter.

IDC's figures do not include the sizable consulting business in information systems done by general management consultants and accounting firms, nor the work of innumerable single practitioners, mostly moonlighting professors and dethroned executives in between jobs (above a certain level there is no unemployment in the computer industry, just a lot of consultants).

The best way to learn about a field so diffuse is to focus on a couple of companies and see where they are typical and where unique. Advanced Computer Techniques is a middle-sized software house; Automatic Data Processing is a giant processing services company; together they represent the two principal segments of this industry.

I

After his high school graduation in 1950, Charles Lecht left his home in Providence, Rhode Island to find a job in New York. He had four ten-dollar bills in his pocket, and he broke the first ten at the Providence railroad station to buy a novel about business. The trip itself was something of a luxury for Lecht, who was used to journeying to New York in the family truck. He settled himself in the train and began to read of a mysterious world in which people wore suits and neckties to work, a world scarcely more real than those described in the science fiction stories he was used to.

One doesn't often see Charley Lecht in a suit and tie today, but the custom-tailored suits he does wear come from Milan. He prefers to work in French jeans with vivid suspenders and collarless silk shirts. Lecht decorated his own office with futuristic steel-and-pigskin furniture, some of which he designed himself. The walls are papered with silver foil, and when Lecht completes his design plan by rounding all the corners in the room, it will look like the inside of a space capsule. Many people who do business with Lecht also get invited to his glass-roofed apartment near the United Nations, which is filled with the objects he fancies: a barber chair; a neon sign; a collection of costume hats (a pith helmet, a bobby's hat and so forth) which also occasionally decorate Lecht himself; the assortment of walking sticks he carries when he is not riding on his skateboard or his motorcycle or in his BMW; and, of course, the family computer.

Lecht's clothes, his office and his apartment all suggest—and are intended to suggest—that he makes a nice living as chief executive of Advanced Computer Techniques, the software company he founded in 1962. But he is a man who seeks admiration more for the taste than the price of his possessions; "tasteful," a word that usually implies conservative tailoring, subdued colors and antique furniture, is the last adjective one would apply to Lecht and his environs, but still the taste is good, not gaudy but flamboyant, original and playful, like Lecht himself. A few years ago, when his hair began to get thinner, Lecht trimmed his Mexican-style mustache, raised a goatee and commenced shaving his head; combined with tinted glasses, all this gives the effect of a modish Leon Trotsky.

Charley Lecht's colleagues, clients, employees, friends and competitors often use the word "showman" to describe him. While Lecht is surely a unique figure in the computer industry, showmanship is not unique, and thus he is part of a tradition which goes back to Thomas J. Watson, Sr., and today embraces not only Charley Lecht but the blue-suited, white-shirted IBM maintenance men whose attaché cases contain rags to clean the customer's typewriter. Lecht himself spent a year working for IBM, and the emphasis on image and spirit is what seems to have impressed him the most: many years later, he hired a chorus from the Association of British Secretaries in America to record favorites from the IBM Songbook, and gave out the record at ACT's booth at the Spring Joint Computer Conference. It is the last living memorial to the IBM spirit of the thirties, rendered in, so to speak, the birdsong of the sixties.

While showmanship in the computer industry originated with IBM, it thrives particularly among the consultants and software entrepreneurs. Some, like Lecht, back up their showmanship with substance; others don't; telling the real from the sham is the customer's problem. Lecht's showmanship is apparent in the way he meets and sells a prospective client.

One morning, Lecht's secretary comes in to tell him there are seven Yugoslavs waiting in the reception room. The Yugoslavs, whose visit is unexpected, are executives of an oil and gas company, with their interpreter. Lecht has them ushered in. He is wearing his current uniform of jeans, leather sneakers, maroon galluses and wine-colored silk shirt, and apologizes for his casual attire: "We are," he says, "a very proletarian organization in our manner of dress." He asks his secretary to make some espresso, to bring in a bottle of "the best Napoleon brandy so we can toast before you go," and to prepare packages of literature on ACT, each with a small robot which is the company's mascot, to go into ACT flight bags for the Yugoslavs. Another secretary comes in and scatters packs of Gauloises on the conference table.

Through their interpreter, the Yugoslavs say they have just bought a Control Data Cyber 171, and want to know ACT's experience with this machine. "Our experience with the Cyber 171," says Lecht, "is zero. There are people in the company who know the technology in depth, and one of the machine's designers, who now works for us, is in Yugoslavia today. But our company hasn't done a project on this machine. I don't want to mislead you by saying we are either too good or too bad. Tell me about your problem."

The Yugoslavs ask Lecht about ACT's experience with oil and gas companies; Lecht speaks slowly, and his sentences take on the stilted quality of the interpreter's. "In oil and gas we are working a lot," he says. "We have worked for Mobil, Shell and Exxon." He talks about the company's services to the oil industry in Edmonton, where ACT has a subsidiary, but says, "We are not the best in the world to deal with in oil and gas production. I say this so you understand that I am accurate when I tell you the things in which we are the best."

The Yugoslavs have been using an IBM System 3; now they have acquired a large and small Cyber. They want first to move programs from the System 3 to the small Cyber, then to put the programs on the large Cyber, using the small one as a terminal. Finally, they will add new programs to the big system. "Our experience is only five years, and these tasks are rather big," they say. "We don't want to start at the beginning but to use the know-how of people who have it. So what are our areas of cooperation?"

"In this area, the transfer of programs," Lecht says firmly, "no one is better than we are." Now he is at the blackboard, and as he delivers a rundown of the steps required for the conversion he illustrates his major points, as computer people invariably do, by drawing a chart. Lecht's talk is more a summary than a revelation, but it is tricky to deliver because he is unsure of both the interpreter's skill and the Yugoslavs' technical knowledge, and he must be clear but not patronizing. "First," he says, "you make a work plan, write the specifications and do an estimate of cost, piece-by-piece. You must go slowly: there are obvious problems. One is the conversion from the 3 to the Cyber—there are data format problems, and the hardware architecture is incompatible. There are changes in the higher-level languages—they always say they are a hundred percent compatible, but they are not. You must try to use the peripherals from the small system with the big system to maintain the integrity of the data base. It may not all be worthwhile. The technology is changing so rapidly that a prudent man keeps one eye on compatibility and the other on what's coming along. Then you have to transfer the programs so they are no longer best for the small but for the big machine. You have to connect the machines so you can move data and possibly programs from one to another. There are problems of documentation and procedure: part of every system is manual and part computer, but how much will differ from system to system."

Lecht sends out for data to answer some of the Yugoslavs' questions, explaining, "as president of this company I have the least knowledge. There are four hundred people here, and they get smarter as you go lower." Lecht proposes to send the Yugoslavs one of the smartest people who knows the Cyber; they will discuss the problem further to see if the two companies can work together. He sends the Yugoslavs on a tour of ACT's offices, and when they return, the brandy is poured. They chat about the concerts in Dubrovnik, and he invites them to his house for drinks that evening; they demur. "I am most sincere," he says. "I live in a glass bubble with a computer. It is the most unusual apartment in New York." After a few more toasts the Yugoslavs say that this has been more than business, it has been "something human," and everyone says goodbye until cocktail time.

The task the Yugoslavs presented was a fairly typical consulting job. They might also have hired a consultant to tell them what equipment to buy. Consultants may review a client's computer operations to determine their efficiency: has the company too much or too little equipment, are the projects too ambitious for the capabilities of the staff, is it the right time to introduce a new application, and how should it be carried out? Users most often seek out consultants during the transition from one generation to the next, and as new technologies like distributed processing come into fashion. They sometimes hire a consultant to explain computer technology to corporate groups: either the data processing manager wants to persuade his superiors to take action or top management hopes to get noncomputer executives solidly behind a new project. This sort of job is a specialty of Lecht's and one he particularly enjoys. As one client observes, "You need show-and-tell, someone who can talk to executives in a language they understand, and someone who won't put them to sleep."

Vendors ask consultants to help with long-range planning. After the GE merger, for example, Honeywell enlisted Lecht to help consolidate the two companies' organizations and product lines. The work done for vendors and users is complementary, illuminating market needs for the manufacturer and informing the user about what new hardware is being developed.

Computer consulting and custom software are two different businesses joined at the hip and impossible to separate. Pure consulting firms like Arthur D. Little, John Diebold and Booz, Allen & Hamilton vary in the amount of actual software they are willing to produce; unlike the software houses, they don't do "body-shopping," the sale of programming services simply to augment the client's regular staff during hectic times. ACT, on the other hand, is a software house which does consulting partly because of Lecht's skills and interests and partly because software houses inevitably consult; one cannot readily separate systems design from advising on the sort of system that should be introduced. The rates for consultants of Lecht's renown can reach $2,000 a day. Lecht charges top dollar (which may be part showmanship), but on a software project, he says, senior staff are actually offered at favorable rates to attract business, while the real profit is made on selling the services of lower-paid junior personnel, who do the actual programming, at a good markup. In hard times, however, clients have used senior consultants to recommend and design the system and let their own people do the programming.

The first software houses were founded in the middle to late fifties, when manufacturers were developing sophisticated product lines. There was, however, a shortage of programming talent, and much innovative work was being done not by vendors but by large users such as the aircraft companies on the west coast. Computer Sciences, now the industry giant, got its start in 1959 when Roy Nutt, a young programmer at United Aircraft who had already built a brilliant reputation, and Fletcher Jones, a resourceful middle manager at North American Aviation, learned of Honeywell's need for a program to translate one of the new languages into binary code. The two men, who had been talking about starting a company for some time, hustled to win the contract, left their jobs and founded CSC. Some of the work for vendors began to fall off as the dwarfs built their own programming staffs, but when IBM encountered difficulties meeting its programming schedule for System 360, it farmed out a lot of software to independent contractors.

The first users to hire the software companies were military and space agencies, which needed large, complex, advanced computer systems; several NASA installations were entirely manned by software houses. Corporations began hiring consultants—university professors and the first alumni of the hardware companies—to tell them whether or not to install a computer. A new phase began in the early sixties, when advances in hardware seemed to promise that the on-line, real-time management information systems predicted by John Diebold, the industry's most famous visionary, and other gurus were at last possible. These systems, said Diebold, would be "the arteries through which will flow the life stream of the business." If you were going to put your whole business on the computer, you needed a man who understood management's point of view, who talked management's language. And so the Booz, Allens, the McKinseys, and the Arthur Andersens began to build edp consulting departments. They staffed them with former IBM systems engineers, ex-corporate data processing managers and new business school graduates, now steeped in the disciplines of management science. At the same time, the software houses—which claimed their deep technical knowledge was essential to carrying out advanced computer applications—also entered consulting. The businessmen consultants and the software consultants disparaged each other—and each had a point. "Information systems designers were often not such good technicians," remembers Frederic Withington of Arthur D. Little, the Boston consulting firm. "But those with the talent to do sophisticated software didn't have the client skills. They smelled bad and spoke Greek."

Just as there were patterns for the development of mainframe manufacturers, peripherals vendors and leasing companies, so is there a historical pattern for software houses, which helps to explain the troubles that have befallen them. It takes only one bright programmer to start a software company, although most began with two or three, and since there is no equipment to buy, it requires very little money; ACT, which originally consisted of Charley Lecht, had an initial capitalization of $800. To grow even a little, the software house needs a good salesman, who might be either the bright programmer himself (if he has the temperament) or an extroverted partner. If the salesman and programmer are good at their (or his) jobs, they will have to hire more people, generally other bright technical men who felt stifled by bureaucracy in their old jobs.

Any service business, of course, depends heavily on personal rapport between the buyer and the seller, buttressed by the seller's reputation in the community. When Booz, Allen, Arthur D. Little and McKinsey got into information systems, they had already established reputations in general management consulting. Charley Lecht and his peers had no such advantage; they were creatures of a new technology which made customers uneasy. Sales calls alone were not enough; to be noticed and trusted, some entrepreneurs wrote books and articles and traveled around the country giving speeches and sitting on panels.

The entrepreneur couldn't stop promoting, and now he had a growing staff to manage; he devoted less and less time to actual consulting and systems design projects, which were done mostly by the staff. The customer was buying the image of a guru who probably wouldn't himself be working on the project at hand; the guru became less and less familiar with details and everyday problems, and painted with an ever broader brush. Moreover, he had to attract, inspire and retain the talented people who would carry out the projects he had sold; people, that is, who had shunned the corporate disciplines which would somehow have to be introduced as the company grew, went public and began to deal more and more with the financial community. With growth and sophisticated financial structure came the need for long-range planning, an activity for which the entrepreneurs had had little time in the past. All the while, they had to adjust to changes in technology, the marketplace and the economy. The varying abilities with which the consulting and software entrepreneurs solved these problems affected the success of their companies. Charley Lecht has encountered all the software entrepreneur's difficulties and managed to survive.

Lecht had made his way through the Providence educational system with considerable distinction: that is, he was nearly thrown out of school twelve times. He hoped to find work as a commercial artist but lacked the training, so he got a job with Arma Corporation as a mathematics technician, computing data on a desk calculator to help the engineers evaluate gunfire control equipment. Suddenly Lecht found it exciting to have his own desk and letter file and to work with sines and cosines; his superiors had to tell him to go home. He did his first piece of innovative thinking for Arma after volunteering for hazardous duty on a submarine and a destroyer which were doing field tests off Key West. Whenever a rocket was launched from the destroyer to a submarine target, Lecht would strap himself to the destroyer's radar shack and photograph the splash with a polaroid camera. Then he would cover the picture with a transparent overlay he had designed to measure how far the rocket was off target. Later the company sent Lecht to Seattle, taught him to fly and put him on an airborne test project.

After two years of collecting hazardous duty pay, overtime, generous union wages and a liberal expense allotment he didn't know how to spend, Lecht had saved up $20,000 and decided to quit Arma and go to college. While studying math at Seattle University he worked for IBM, where he was assigned to design a model for predicting the 1956 presidential election. He wrote the program, ran the computer on a local television broadcast on election night, and received a commendation from the company. After graduation, he worked at MIT's Lincoln Laboratories and taught a course in theory of probability sponsored by IBM at the university; next he got a Master's degree at Purdue while holding a teaching assistantship there and consulting at MIT. Then he joined the army, completing several ambitious assignments in programming and management. By the time of his discharge in 1962, Lecht had accumulated impressive credentials. He described them in a long, engaging resume and mailed it to thirty-five companies, each of which offered him a job.

The job he took, with a consulting engineer he'd known at MIT, carried the lowest salary of all, but the engineer was willing to help Lecht start his own business. This time, however, when Lecht mailed letters offering his consulting services to a host of companies, he got no answers. Then a perfect opportunity presented itself.

Lecht was working on a Navy project for the engineer, which involved extensive use of the LARC computer, that enormous machine developed by Univac and sold only to the AEC and the Navy. A program he had written would not run on the LARC, but worked beautifully on the IBM machine across the hall. The trouble lay in the LARC's compiler, the program which translated higher-level languages into binary code. Univac was obligated to maintain the machine for the Navy, and Lecht had heard that the faulty software was becoming a source of contention between the vendor and this important customer. When Lecht offered to fix the compiler, Univac was receptive; after several preliminary studies it awarded him a $100,000 contract to do the job.

Lecht hired a small staff and moved to the seventeenth floor of the Plaza Hotel, where space was cheap because it had once been servants' quarters. There were pipes on the ceiling, garret windows and secret passages. It was an unusual office, but the Plaza was a fine hotel, and you could order martinis and lunch for the clients, who were beginning to proliferate. Despite its charm, however, the new office eventually proved unacceptable. "Our clients needed facilities clearance for government projects," Lecht says. "An inspector came up and he couldn't believe it—all those corridors, and you couldn't lock the place, and there were the Russians living downstairs. The Beatles were at the Plaza, and hordes of teenagers were screaming outside. Of course, we had to move."

During the mid-sixties ACT, while still a small company, acquired a prestigious customer list and a reputation for delivering good work on time. Still, Lecht was becoming aware of the problems endemic to the custom software business. Droves of small companies—started, like ACT, with the founder's pocket money and one good contract—had moved in to fill the demand for programmers. Many of them hadn't the mettle to survive, but the intense competition was driving prices down.

Custom software was a business without leverage: since the work you did for one customer was useless to the next, your ability to grow was tied to the number of first-rate programmers you could attract and keep. Thus, as a few astute observers pointed out, a software house was more like a law firm or an advertising agency than a manufacturing company. But software houses also faced difficulties unknown to firms that sold professional services outside the computer industry. Law and advertising are mature professions in which the nature of the work and the time required to do it are well defined; clients have had some experience in using these services. Software houses, on the other hand, had customers who knew little about computer technology. For a company trying to make money by doing pioneering work for customers with unrealistic expectations, the odds favor disasters, large or small.

Lecht and many of his peers understood the insecurity of the business. The way to survive was to make software more like hardware, to develop a standard product that could be mass-produced, or to add some better-leveraged venture like the sale of computer time. This would require capital. Fortunately, Wall Street had not thought out the limitations of the software business—all it saw was a rapidly growing number of computer installations (each of which would need software) and the speed with which each single installation was expanding (and needing even more software). In the late sixties, software houses were selling at up to seventy times earnings. ACT went public in 1968; so, in the few years before and after that, did many of its competitors.

This imposed new pressures on the entrepreneurs: growth was not just desirable but imperative. The larger software companies made substantial investments in new ventures. Computer Applications poured some $16 million into the development of a computerized service to report on the movement of products out of grocery warehouses; Computer Sciences invested in a ticket reservation service; other firms undertook similar ventures. The results were at best dismal and at worst—in the case of Computer Applications, for example—fatal. The software houses underestimated development costs and schedules, overestimated market acceptance, and ran headlong into the recession. At the same time, users were beginning to realize that software technology was not sufficiently advanced to deliver the management information systems they had heard so much about; this was the period of trying to squeeze the most value out of the systems you had, of abandoning futuristic frills that would never work out anyway. Some software houses also suffered from cutbacks in the space program and the slackening of IBM contracts that followed unbundling. In all, business was rotten and many companies had overextended themselves.

For all his flamboyant personal style, Lecht was fiscally conservative. ACT's bank debt was minimal and Lecht moved cautiously into diversification. While this restricted the company's growth, it also kept ACT from major disasters. In 1971 and 1972 revenues declined and the company showed its first losses. Lecht was forced to close several offices and lay off half his employees. This layoff and another following the loss of a large contract in Iran were particularly difficult for Lecht, who has always been especially proud of his ability to build a loyal and competent staff; his critics, in fact, say he is too soft about firing people. Lecht has built loyalty by understanding the sort of example you must set for the type of people who work for ACT, and then setting it in the most conspicuous way—yes, you can be different and still be successful; yes, a technical man can be a good salesman; yes, you can go without sleep for days and still do high-quality work—by endorsing sensible management policies; and finally, by having a good sense of humor. If you do these things, you can get away with being demanding and difficult, as Lecht often is.

"An industrial manufacturing company is a hierarchy," Lecht says. "You can manage by giving orders because people are replaceable. You can't give orders in a software house, because you need your staff as much as they need you. You'd better not patronize these people; they can quit too easily." During Lecht's stint on the submarine, he noticed that as soon as the ship went out on maneuvers, the traditional Navy rules of deference to rank were suspended; a seaman could give orders to an officer, who knew that the man in the engine room held the key to his life. When an ACT team works on a consulting project, it behaves like the submarine crew under sea. "Officers don't always act as executives," says Oscar Schachter, the executive vice-president who is second man at ACT. "A technical man may have a vp working for him on a project. Charley or I will run the Xerox if no secretary is around and someone else has a deadline."

Technical staffers who are between projects will find ACT informal about working hours, and most ACT people dress as casually as Lecht; the most conspicuous figure in the company is the grey-suited, white-shirted Schachter, a Yeshiva University and Harvard Law School graduate whose eccentric wardrobe has not hampered his career. Critics suggest that Schachter is needed to bring Lecht down to earth; Lecht himself recognizes the need for such a counterbalance, and pays tribute to Schachter. "Oscar is my caution," he says. While some of Lecht's gestures to create an ambiance seem extravagant— the corporate psychologist who lends a high-priced ear to workers' troubles, for example, and the Dartmouth professor who briefed ACT employees about Chinese history and customs before the company received a delegation from the People's Republic—Lecht has achieved both a palpable company spirit and a low turnover.

In fiscal 1979 ACT had revenues of nearly $16½ million. About 55 companies in the software, services and facilities management business were as large or larger; more than 3,100 were smaller; but ACT's resources are too scattered to make it a significant factor in any one branch of this marketplace. Since the company began to diversify in the late sixties it has done a little bit of everything a software house can do. One way that software houses achieve economies of scale, for example, is by opening service bureaus that use their own equipment to handle the customer's data processing. Lately, service bureaus are bringing ACT 40 percent of its revenues, more than the income earned by the consulting and software side of the business. The company has bureaus in New York, Phoenix, Tucson, Edmonton and Milan. Like those operated by many other companies in the business, they tend to specialize in serving particular industries: the Phoenix bureau, for example, handles billing and office management for doctors, hospitals and clinics, and the Edmonton bureau maintains spare parts inventory and does financial reporting for heavy equipment shipments to northern fuel fields and construction sites.

Lecht hopes the service bureaus and the custom software will soon be on an equal footing with a third part of the business that's still small but beginning to grow. The evolution of this operation follows industry trends. During the late sixties the software houses' desire to mass-produce their products, combined with unbundling, encouraged the rise of the package, a standard set of programs designed to enhance the computer's operating system or to perform routine applications, often specific to one industry. In the past, users had made do with bundled software supplied by the mainframe manufacturers, supplementing it with custom-made programs. But the bundled software was often inefficient, and the cost of custom programming was rising. Once users were free of the bundle, they could choose from an assortment of economical packages. It took time for the software industry to develop good packages that served a wide market, and it was hard work to wean customers from the notion that their own needs were unique: aborted efforts to enter the packaged software market drove many companies under in the early seventies. Now, however, the market is booming: in 1979 software packages brought in $920 million, and International Data Corporation expects them to quadruple their revenues by 1985. ACT has developed several types of utility packages that augment the operating system. It also does some business as a systems house, buying minicomputers wholesale and selling them with its own packaged software added.

In 1977 *Computerworld,* a widely read trade newspaper, serialized Lecht's book, *The Waves of Change,* a statistic-laden speculation on the future of computer technology; as the first serialization in the trade press it attracted considerable attention in the industry and sold enough copies in the $39.95 hardcover version published by ACT and a McGraw-Hill paperback to repay Lecht pleasantly for his labors. Its greatest value, however, was as a marketing tool for Lecht's consulting business. His speaking engagements multiplied dramatically, not only in the U.S. but in far-flung places like Japan and Australia, and ACT is on the map as it never was before. A market research group begun for this project and Lecht's subsequent writing endeavors now sells its work and accounts for about 10 percent of ACT's income. Lecht and ACT are both survivors, and essential to each other. He is a more credible pundit with a solid, flourishing company beneath him; without Lecht's glamour, on the other hand, ACT would be doing good work but have nothing to set it apart from other companies, and it might not grow nearly as fast.

I I

Every Monday afternoon between the hours of noon and three, a small Honda sedan stops at the offices of Don Lucas Cadillac in San

Francisco and collects sheets of data relating to that week's payroll for the sixty-five Lucas employees—the salaried office workers, the unionized salesmen who work on commission, and the repairmen who, among them, represent four different unions, each with its own hourly rate. Twenty-four hours later, the same car returns bearing a red plastic envelope containing the Lucas paychecks, which have been prepared at a computer center thirty-seven miles away.

Users of computing power don't come much smaller or much greener than Don Lucas Cadillac, which has enjoyed this oldest and rinky-dinkiest of commercial computer applications only since 1975, before which time its payroll was processed manually. Don Lucas buys computing services from a company called Automatic Data Processing, whose reputation in the computer industry is fairly remarkable. Throughout the past turbulent decade, ADP's record of growth and success has remained unblemished; while computer people don't hesitate to find fault, one seldom hears a discouraging word about ADP.

A $400 million company with headquarters in Clifton, New Jersey, Automatic Data Processing owes its prosperity to generations of customers like Don Lucas Cadillac, small companies which, on the average, spend less than $200 a month for payroll processing. Their loyalty—and their abundance—gave ADP the income and the stock multiple to acquire time-sharing networks which serve illustrious customers like TRW, Dean Witter Reynolds and Holiday Inns. Thus, ADP has become a company well positioned for the future.

The story of ADP illustrates how an industry evolves and how a company absorbs change. It is also an appealing American success story: when Frank Lautenberg, the company's present chief executive, was ten years old his father, a laborer in a silk mill in Paterson, New Jersey, took him to the factory to hear the frightening din and clatter of the machines, breathe the characteristic overpowering silk smell and run his fingers over the dirty fabric, and said, "Get an education so you never have to work like this." Today, Lautenberg—who got an education—has an air of homeyness mixed with authority: he is what your uncle or cousin would be like if your uncle or cousin happened to be the head of a $400 million company.

The company's founder, Henry Taub, also came from Paterson. When Taub was nineteen and going to college at night, he went to work for an accounting firm, and two years later—in 1949—he had an idea for a new company. Taub had noticed the time, effort and expense his clients were putting into the simple operation of processing the payroll. While the actual accounting work required very little skill, payroll was the one operation which could never be delayed; moreover, absolute accuracy was essential since, as Lautenberg has observed, "each employee was an expert auditor when it came to his own paycheck," and the employers considered payroll information top secret. The result was that a job which could have been done by a $40-a-week clerk was being assigned to senior bookkeepers who made up to $100 a week, that sometimes even office managers and executives got into the act, and that it took two days to prepare a weekly payroll for a company of a hundred employees, diverting valuable management time. Taub thought he could set up a company to collect the raw payroll data, process it and return the checks for the customer's signature at a charge of $25 for a hundred-employee payroll.

He and his brother got a couple of clients to make the small investment necessary to set up Automatic Payrolls, Inc., in Paterson. The equipment the company used was old-fashioned even for 1949: an Underwood mechanical bookkeeping machine, an addressograph machine for printing names, and some aged calculators. Some of the clerks were housewives working part-time. The attitude and style with which the Taubs carried on their business was a product of necessity, not choice, but it has influenced the company ever since. As Lautenberg later remembered in a speech,

> Computers at the time . . . were found only in university think tanks and ballistics laboratories. . . . Our customers were not concerned with the means we used to provide a solution to their payroll problems. We were never asked whether we were using the newest accounting machine or a dated version, whether delivery would be made by bus, truck or car—or whether our staff was full-time or part-time, where we saw the future or how fancy our offices were. We rarely, if ever, had a visitor. . . . The customers' only care, as it is today, was about our ability to deliver the promised service. The methods we chose . . . were selected based on the *minimum* needed to get the job done properly.

Since Taub was an accountant he thought like a professional and did business by referral. Lautenberg, who is four years older than Taub, had an office in the same building; a salesman for Prudential

Insurance, he thought the idea needed only better marketing to succeed. "By the end of 1952," Lautenberg says, "I persuaded Henry to let me print cards at my own expense and try to sell. In short order I was responsible for 10 percent of revenues, which was three accounts, each a thousand dollars a year. So I negotiated with Henry to get a commission. The first year I continued with the Prudential, working for Henry part-time; by January 1954, the company had enough business for me to join full-time."

The notion of farming out an operation as vital and sensitive as payroll, despite the favorable economics, made many businessmen nervous, and the company grew slowly. There were no contracts between the entrepreneurs and their customers, who could dispense with Automatic Payrolls' services on a few days' notice (there are still no contracts for payroll customers). Six days a week, sometimes seven, the Taubs and Lautenberg and their employees worked from eight in the morning till eleven at night, getting out the payrolls they had sold. It took twelve years to reach annual sales of $400,000. That was a milestone year—the year the company went public, bought its first computer and changed its name to Automatic Data Processing.

"We wanted to 'make a living,'" says Lautenberg, bracketing the phrase in vocal quotation marks. "Build the business, take a Saturday off. We still regarded ourselves more as professionals and thought about personal achievement, not corporate. Once you go public, of course, there are different obligations." One benefit of the company's original slow growth was that by the time its management felt the pressures peculiar to public corporations, they had a clear picture of what business ADP was in and the forces that drove it; unlike many of their peers, they were experienced and mature enough to reject new ventures that were not germane.

ADP—or API, as it was originally called—had not been the only service bureau in existence. IBM had a similar venture, launched with the hope that customers would graduate to machines of their own. Through the 1956 consent decree, IBM's service bureau became an arm's-length subsidiary with no special advantages. This permitted the rise of a highly competitive industry, which received further impetus in 1960 from the introduction of an easy-to-use, inexpensive transistorized IBM computer called the 1401, the same machine that ADP bought a year later. Now a Ma-and-Pa service bureau could offer a wide array of services at lower prices, and the number of such ventures continued to multiply. Business was good: customers were becoming increasingly computer-conscious. Those too small to acquire their own machines were happy to have processing done by independent operators, and even larger companies used the bureaus to help out in busy periods. After a few years ADP, looking toward expansion, began to acquire small service bureaus in other cities. The purpose of the acquisitions was, as company executives often put it, "to plant the flag." The acquired company had computers, operations people and enough of a local customer list to get ADP efficiently started, and then ADP would introduce its own sales management and mass-production techniques; if the proprietor of the local bureau could operate in the ADP style he often stayed on and prospered. Other service bureaus would ask the user what sort of payroll procedures he preferred and then custom-tailor them. ADP's management—perhaps because they were businessmen, not computer men—strove to keep programming expenses down. Early on the company had begun to design systems for a wide range of customers and to package services; this lowered costs and enabled the salesmen to cover a broader territory. With the advent of the first computer, ADP added modules to the payroll package that fit the requirements of various industries.

The result was that while in 1963 ADP had sales of $1 million and negligible earnings, in 1973 it had sales of $90 million and pretax earnings of $16.7 million. It had planted the flag in twenty-two cities. While acquisitions had provided the basis for this growth, the act was accomplished by the company itself, with its policy of supporting enterprising local management with sophisticated marketing methods; as Josh Weston, ADP's president, points out, "When we bought the Miami service bureau it had revenues of less than $20,000. The principal stayed on, and now sits on a business three times the size of the whole company at the time we bought him out. There are others like that; their own moxie helped them." ADP has a reputation for conservatism which is in many ways justified, but no company could achieve such growth without also being highly aggressive.

During the sixties the most dangerous temptation for a company with a high stock multiple was to start thinking of itself as a miniconglomerate and acquiring companies in unrelated fields. Lautenberg admits he felt the urge but managed to control it. "Once," he says, "I went to look at a printing company in Texas. We were going to give up a valuable part of our equity to save two percent on purchases and get a company with a five percent margin when our margin was eighteen percent, and once we had it what would we do with it? I came back sobered."

Even within its field, ADP was slow to diversify; once it moved, however, it moved forcefully. In most segments of the computer industry, for example, vendors have found that industrial specialization combines some custom-tailoring with the benefits of mass-production: a good package of accounting services and management reports especially designed for banks or hospitals tends to be successful. Back in 1962 ADP opened an office on Wall Street to provide back-office services for brokerage firms. Perhaps because its experience lay in mass-producing services rather than products, it succeeded where larger competitors (including IBM and RCA) failed. Brokerage services have so expanded that ADP is now the leading supplier to the securities industry, processing, for example, 15 percent of the trades on the New York Stock Exchange. For other industries, ADP stuck to the payroll until 1967, when it began to offer additional accounting tasks. A few years later it started to diversify in exactly the same way it had expanded geographically: it would find a promising industry market, buy a smaller company with a foothold in that market and add its own muscle.

Among the industry markets that ADP has entered since 1971 are those for banks, wine and spirits dealers, hospitals, nursing homes and motor vehicle dealers. One common characteristic makes all these businesses receptive to packaged services. "Where there's an external force that disciplines the information practices of an industry it's easier for us to sell," says Weston. "The automobile dealers, for example, are licensees of the manufacturers, who have imposed accounting and inventory practices on them. We have systems experts on General Motors requirements to help the dealers. The liquor stores, banking and brokerage industries are all government-regulated. The hospitals report to Blue Cross and Blue Shield. If you become expert in the common denominator you can do better for the individual than he could do for himself. Retailing, on the other hand, has made slow progress because nothing disciplines individual retailers to conform to anything."

ADP's peculiar blend of aggressiveness and conservatism also af-fects its attitude toward technology. Batch processing—in which the user hands over his data to the computer center and receives the output a day later—is a second-generation method of delivering computer services, a method real-time computing was supposed to eliminate years ago. ADP now employs a fleet of more than a hun-dred Datsuns, Hondas and Ford vans in thirty-eight cities to carry out this obsolete delivery method, which accounted for nearly half its fiscal 1980 revenues; what is more, the customer base grew by nearly a third. These facts add some perspective to considerations of rapid technological change in the computer business.

Time-sharing was the third-generation method of delivery; new companies dispensing this service were dear to Wall Street during the late sixties, when one young entrepreneur told *Business Week*, "All you have to do is get a few good guys, go down to lower Broad-way, and yell 'Time sharing!' and they bury you up to your neck in money. Then you rent a computer, and you're in business." An over-supply of casually founded, poorly managed time-sharing companies with grandiose aspirations was decimated by the 1971 recession.

The time-sharing company differed somewhat from the old ser-vice bureau in its approach to selling-the-music-not-the-piano: while the service bureau customer had his data processing done for him, the time-sharing user rented a terminal, access to the vendor's com-puter and perhaps a few software packages, and did his own process-ing. Part of the glamour of time-sharing came from the notion of the user having a continuing dialogue with the computer. But one of the discoveries made in the postrecession era of cost-conscious sophistica-tion was that for some applications, interactive processing was over-kill; the user could wait a few hours, perhaps even overnight, for his information. Out of this grew a kind of service called "remote batch" which combined some of the convenience of time-sharing with the lower costs of deferred processing: the user entered his own programs and data at a terminal in his office, and when he had signed off the distant computer went to work. Remote batch has grown fast in recent years; it allowed service bureaus to move into new cities at lower cost and gave the time-sharing companies a chance to broaden their appeal.

ADP never worried much about where to place its technological bets. Weston says, "We are market-driven, not technology-driven," which means that instead of just deciding to get into time-sharing ADP looks at a group of customers and decides what combination of technologies they are likely to need. ADP did go on-line first for the brokerage houses, with an interactive service called cage management which processes trades and directs the flow of securities; remote batch services were added a little later. The company took its biggest leap into interactive computing in 1975 by acquiring The Cyphernetics Corporation, a substantial time-sharing company based in Ann Arbor, Michigan, with telephone lines linking twenty-six American cities and satellite transmission to six countries in Europe. Cyphernetics offered both general time-sharing and access to a number of data bases, including Chase econometric models, demographic information from the U.S. census, and chemical data. Subsequent time-sharing acquisitions were folded into this operation which then became ADP's Network Services Division. Thus the Hondas and Datsuns were balanced by the latest communications technology, and the customer could put together whatever combination of batch, remote batch, and interactive services best suited his needs. ADP is now in a position to follow the pace of the market; as Weston observes, "we can't say any one form of technology is dead."

There are two major threats to the processing services companies, and the way they are meeting them suggests trends that will affect the whole computer industry. The declining cost of hardware and the rise of the mini- and microcomputers seem to cut right into the service companies' market, making it ever more practical for small customers to own their own machines. ADP and several other large service companies are now supplying hardware. ADP has a package called Onsite, in which the customer receives a DEC minicomputer hooked up to the company's time-sharing network. With ADP's software packages, he can save telephone costs by doing most of his own processing locally, but he also has access, through the network, to large computers and data bases. The Onsite computer is maintained remotely by an ADP center in Ann Arbor, reducing the need for local service engineers. A larger customer might buy several Onsite systems and let them talk to each other via the network. What ADP is selling is known as "value added": the premise that the customer would spend more time and money assembling the package himself, and the result would be less satisfactory. The "value added" is the retailer's know-how.

While software and services companies are not, for the most part, developing their own computers, they have been forced into the business of selling hardware. At the same time, as hardware costs come down and the business of assembling chips into a computer becomes more and more a job that almost anyone can do, the mainframe companies must derive increasing profit and competitive advantage from the software and services side of their business. What lies ahead is an increasingly homogeneous industry, with a variety of large and small "computer utilities" selling the customer "computing" in whatever form he wants it. There will be a new set of competitive rules and perhaps a different balance of power. A more immediate spectre on the services scene is IBM, free of its Control Data antitrust agreement not to enter this market. IBM's return to some sort of processing services business has been expected for several years, but as this book is completed, has not yet been announced.

However the technology may change, the idea that drives ADP is the same one that moved Henry Taub to found the company thirty years ago. As Weston observes, "Most of the customers we deal with have more important things on their mind than to muck around with what we can do better." And Lautenberg says, "We've built the company to this size without a product. When you do it in the services business, that's different. Sometimes I look at it as a spectator; I hear ads for ADP on the radio in Colorado or California, and I think, 'Was I here when all this was happening?' Does it feed on itself? If there's a difficult time, does it come down like a house of cards? I don't accept the notion of limitations. We think one day we can be three or four times the size we are now."

PART V

THE TECHNOLOGY

13

The Eighties: A Stronger Rival, A Different Battleground

————

BACK in the early sixties, when transistorized circuitry first made widespread use of the computer, many experts began to make glamorous predictions for the future of the machine; they are, of course, still doing so today. Some of these visions—airline reservations and stock quotation systems, for example—are with us now, already indispensable; others, such as cashless checkless banking, the electronic classroom, remote medical diagnosis and shopping at home via cable television, are still embryonic. Nearly all applications, however, that take the computer far beyond the payroll-processing or number-crunching stage share one characteristic: the consumer is sitting at a terminal in one place querying a machine in another. Someone has to transport the information between the terminal and the computer, and until recently that someone was not a computer expert. It was frustrating indeed for the computer man to know that even when he designed excellent hardware and mastered the difficult logistics of laying out and programming a system that would blanket the continent, the functioning of that system would depend on the beneficence of a group of people whose technology, priorities, motives, rewards, temperaments and jargon were utterly different from his own: the telephone men.

The difficulties computer people encountered in sending data over the telephone lines were technological, financial and legal. The characteristics of the telephone network had been ordained decades earlier according to carefully developed rules which admirably suited the needs of the voice subscriber but were meaningless for computer users; some of the rules originated, for example, in the way sounds are formed in the mouth.

The rate at which information could be transmitted depended

mostly on the width of telephone channels, the highways that carry electrical signals; a secretary pecking out a message on a teletypewriter required a narrower road than the avenue built for voice, while the computer sending back its answer, or the high-speed display terminal, or the concentrator which gathered the pecked-out teletypewriter messages and transmitted them together in one great burst needed a broad expressway. Computers and human beings had a different tolerance of error: a listener could piece together the meaning of a conversation even when several words are distorted, but the machine had no independent intelligence and one dropped digit might be disastrous. There was a wide variety in the quality of telephone transmission equipment across the country, and since the computer customer dialing into the network never knew what path his call would take, he had no guarantee of uniform accuracy. Even the traditional billing time was arbitrary: three minutes, a comfortable duration for a salesman setting up appointments or a child calling his grandmother, had no significance at all for a scientist working out a difficult problem at an interactive terminal or a home office computer collecting daily sales figures from the branches, which could transfer volumes of information in a second. If your requirements for speed and accuracy were greater than the public telephone network could offer, you had to lease a private line, an expense that was hard to justify unless you planned to use the line all day.

Computers were getting much cheaper; long-distance telephone transmission was getting a little cheaper but accounted for an ever larger chunk of the cost of a remote system. The devices required to hook up computer equipment to the telephone network were expensive, too, and they had to be leased from the telephone company. In sum, the computer community wanted more efficient and economical products and services for data transmission, and the telephone men said, "Trust in Bell, Bell will provide." But the computer people had their doubts. You could look at a depreciation schedule for telephone equipment, some of which was pegged for a service life of forty years, and see that Bell reckoned time geologically.

The struggle began, then, with the computer people thinking of the telephone people as an obstacle that had to be bypassed or overcome. As they directed their efforts toward achieving this goal, the telephone people began to regard them as poachers, the type of miscreant a monopolist finds most threatening. And so the computer and telephone people began to fight more seriously, both sides thinking they were simply protecting their own interests; as for getting into each other's businesses, nothing could be further from their minds. That these reluctant adversaries finally became vigorous, unabashed competitors was due to a rush of technology which was inexorable and will continue to be so.

Among computer and telephone people this story is usually titled "The Battle of the Giants" for its leading antagonists, IBM and AT&T. It is not, however, a zero-sum confrontation like the ratings battle that engages the television networks. Rather it is the story of two powerful companies, each of which has dominated its field and thus enjoyed a good measure of control over its destiny. The decisions each company made were yes-no, slow-fast, now-later decisions, the kind where you weighed the risks and either went ahead or didn't. Now technology had brought the two fields together and so created a new one which was growing beyond the control of either company. Instead of yes-no, the decisions were A-B-C-D-E or F; there were too many choices and combinations, and no orderly way to plan and forecast. And the minor characters—large corporations and small entrepreneurs, American and foreign—were more influential than ever before. The battle of the giants was not a fight for limited revenues. It was a struggle to regain the security that comes from knowing one calls the shots.

To the million men and women who work for the Bell System—for its twenty-three operating companies; for Western Electric, its manufacturing arm; for Bell Laboratories, its distinguished research and development facility; and for American Telephone & Telegraph, the holding company which manages the system and furnishes staff counseling—the stewardship of the public telephone network is a sacred trust. The foundation of that trust is an amalgam of economic and legal doctrines known as the "common carrier principle." Economists prescribe government regulation for an industry with the characteristics of a "natural monopoly." Lawyers tell us, based upon precedents rooted in English common law, that a business "affected with a public interest" must be regulated by the government, as the spokesman for the people. The union of economics and law is codified in the legislation establishing the various regulatory agencies in transportation, power and communications.

A common carrier provides a service that is essential to all of us. To furnish that service requires a heavy capital investment; the efficient operation of the service is governed by economies of scale. Even if we live in Magnolia, Arkansas, we are entitled to telephone service at reasonable rates, and so while it may be unprofitable to furnish long-distance lines to Magnolia, AT&T cannot refuse to do so. In return for its willingness to serve the hinterlands, the telephone company was shielded from competitive pressure along more lucrative routes. Telephone people feel it is their highest duty to protect the network: from the linemen climbing poles in Minnesota through the legions of home-grown executives who carry out policy to the chairman of the board and the handful of vice-presidents who make it, they have been raised to believe in the ideal of service under difficult conditions—of, as one executive puts it, "the operator manning the switchboard while the flood-waters rise."

"They are protective and we are innovative," said the brash young computer men who began in the fifties to lock horns with the communications industry. In the past there had been clear-cut lines between telephony, telegraphy and data processing. Now the computer was blurring those lines; the telephone and telegraph people were using computers to streamline their services and the business equipment people were transmitting data between customers. Satellites were on the horizon, and they too would change the technology and economics of communications. How far did the common carrier principle extend? To the computer people, the sacred trust seemed more like the White Man's Burden. "Protecting the network" was just a convenient excuse to guard the monopoly. There was something irritatingly Kiplingesque about the telephone people's attitude—a sort of "we'll tell the little wogs what's good for them"— that suggested the British Empire in its last stages of rigor mortis.

The conflict between computer and telephone men was ironic, because Bell Laboratories had pioneered in computer development. As far back as 1940, Bell had demonstrated a remotely operated electromechanical computing device, and had worked on computing machines for the military all through World War II. Probably the greatest spur to the advancement of computer technology was the transistor, a Nobel Prize–winning Bell Laboratories invention. Since the automated switching systems in telephone central offices were really giant special-purpose computers with logic, memory and in-put-output, telephone people were familiar with some of the niceties of computer design; the company had even flirted with designing a machine to handle its own data processing, a project that was killed in 1958 when IBM came out with a model that Bell found adequate. Many of the systems engineers who worked on that project now con-sidered themselves confirmed computerniks, and promptly left Bell.

When AT&T was cast in the role of communications supplier to computer people outside the company, however, it found that the interests of the Bell System and the computer community were sharply at odds. The conflicts began in the fifties, with the first so-phisticated real-time defense projects, when systems engineers from the computer manufacturers and representatives of Bell haggled over the quality of data transmission. Isaac Auerbach, a consultant, who as a Burroughs engineer worked on the Air Defense Com-mand's SAGE system, remembers, "The relations between the com-puter and telephone people were horrendous. The telephone people thought we were all very demanding. They didn't understand what we were trying to do."

The difficulties in the military projects and the beginnings of commercial interest in remote computing obliged Bell engineers to look at their network from a new vantage point, that of the data customer. Data transmission, for example, was particularly sensitive to distortion from something called impulse noise, a phenomenon whose causes range from thunderstorms to faulty soldering. The voice subscriber hears impulse noise as a stray click or crackle; for the data customer, it causes a serious clustering of errors. The best answer to the problem of impulse noise would have been the re-placement of all the equipment used for transmission and switching of calls on the telephone network. While the computer people real-ized that this was hardly a practical solution for Bell, they did feel that AT&T's efforts to upgrade its service were unduly slow: they noted that ESS, the computerized switching system designed to in-crease the speed and possibly improve the accuracy of telephone service, was not to be installed everywhere until the year 2000. The computer men spoke with the impatience and irreverence of a mer-curial, competitive new industry, while the telephone men reflected the natural conservatism of an established monopoly. "Computerniks are a devoted, fanatical crew," notes one Bell executive. "They thought that when the first data bit got generated Bell should have thrown away forty billion dollars' worth of plant to suit their needs."

Computers and telephones were basically incompatible. The telephone translates the sound waves from a voice conversation into a continuous electrical current which varies as the voice changes pitch and volume. Computers, on the other hand, send out a series of electrical pulses like the marks and spaces of telegraphy; you had to alter these signals before the voice network could transmit them. Translation provides a useful metaphor: people speak English, computers speak Greek and telephones speak Swedish. To hook up the computers to the telephone system you needed a box called a *modem* (for modulator-demodulator) at either end; a modem is, essentially, a piece of Greek-to-Swedish translation equipment (while this comparison will not stand the careful scrutiny of an electrical engineer, it is still the only one which comes close to illuminating what a modem does). The better your modem, the faster and more accurate your translation.

In 1961 Bell began leasing the DataPhone, which consisted of a modem and a network control signaling unit, the gadget which handles the mechanics of making a phone call—dialing, charging, busy signals and the like. The computer people felt they could design better modems and naturally were eager to get into manufacturing a lucrative new product; they also wanted to produce other equipment which facilitated the hookup of computer gear to telephone lines. Bell, however, had a policy that "No equipment, apparatus, circuit or device not furnished by the Telephone Company shall be attached to or connected with the facilities furnished by the Telephone Company." Computer entrepreneurs also wanted transmission facilities that met their needs, and got to thinking that what Bell would not provide for them they would have to provide for themselves. The double-barreled challenge to AT&T in both equipment and services fell into the lap of the FCC.

The Federal Communications Commission had been regulating interstate telephone service since 1934. The regulatory system in the telephone industry evolved haphazardly. Bell achieved dominance in the late nineteenth century through its solid patent position; later, by refusing to connect its long-distance lines to competitors' systems, it was able to buy or drive out many of the local independent companies (while some 1,600 independents remain, Bell controls about

82 percent of the nation's telephones). Regulation of local services began with municipal franchises and fell little by little under the jurisdiction of state Public Utility Commissions. The Interstate Commerce Commission began regulating long-distance rates in 1910. No consistent regulatory policy was ever developed; the ICC, its successor the FCC, and the state commissions went about their job lackadaisically. While the setting of rates does involve financial auditing, there was no regulatory control over such internal policy matters as how research dollars were spent. Indeed, the FCC didn't initiate changes in rates and services; it merely reacted to densely worded tariffs filed by Bell. Since the same equipment is used for both interstate and intrastate calls, the FCC and the state commissions often got into jurisdictional disputes, and Bell's critics accused the company of playing both ends against the middle.

The staff expertise that guides the FCC in decisions on telecommunications policy resides in its Common Carrier Bureau, which had been something of a stepchild since the agency's establishment. Historically, the commission had been more preoccupied with broadcasting; common carrier problems were thought to be more routine, and the bureau always had to make do with a pathetically small staff and budget. While its resources have not increased much over the past couple of decades, it has become notably more vigorous in challenging the boundaries of Bell's monopoly; accordingly, it has been willing to see Bell compete harder.

The commission itself had become more interested in telecommunications during the early sixties, when it was embroiled in legislative hearings for the Communications Satellite Act. The satellites themselves were a sexy, futuristic development that engaged the public imagination—and the debates over who should launch them exposed the FCC to conflicting ideas from a variety of companies. "Life is simple when you're regulating a monopoly," says Bernard Strassburg, who served as Chief of the Common Carrier Bureau from 1963 to 1973. "You get to identify with the entity you're regulating. Most of your input is coming from Bell unless you go out and search for other viewpoints."

By 1965 Strassburg and his aides were beginning to hear increasing complaints about telephone service from computer manufacturers, service bureaus and users. IBM was not a leader in the controversy for several reasons. Except for military projects and the rather special needs of the airline industry, IBM still thought its bread and butter lay in traditional computer-room applications, such as payroll and accounting, which had built its customer base in the punch-card days. Moreover, the company had a fear of regulation, which seemed to threaten anyone involved too deeply with communications: "There was a feeling that if you got in bed with Bell you'd end up with the same disease," says a former IBM executive. Finally, AT&T was IBM's largest nongovernment customer, a fact which caused a certain chariness in the marketing division. The companies large and small who wanted to find a niche for themselves were more interested in remote computing, since it was an area in which IBM was vulnerable.

Half of the questions perplexing the Common Carrier Bureau had to do with the quality of telephone service: whether Bell's recalcitrance was holding back the growth of a new technology. The other half concerned the problems of overlap between communications and data processing. One computer services company, Bunker-Ramo Corporation, wanted to expand its stock quotation service to include such administrative tasks as matching buy-and-sell orders. Bell and Western Union objected strenuously: the routing of messages involved in matching orders was communications, not data processing. If Bunker-Ramo were allowed to offer the expanded service at all, it ought to be regulated by the FCC.

Here, then, were Bunker-Ramo and the new time-sharing services seeking to transmit messages through computer technology. There, on the other hand, were Bell, Western Union and the other common carriers updating their operations with computers and possessing enough excess capacity to enter data processing. A 1956 consent decree forbade AT&T to enter unregulated territory, but perhaps the company might propose bending or changing the conditions of the decree. The common carriers could be competitors of the computer service companies—and at the same time suppliers of their vital communications lines. This situation raised serious conflict-of-interest questions. And how would the diversification affect regular telephone rates: would that imaginary housewife in Magnolia, who just wanted to call her mother or telegraph her sister, be subsidizing the carriers' forays into a competitive field?

In 1966 the bureau issued a notice of inquiry, observing the explosion of computer technology and the tendency of computer and communications companies to poach on each other's preserves. If the old guidelines were blurring, what should be regulated, how and by whom? Were the carriers' rates, services and other policies holding back the computer industry? Just how did companies use (or plan to use) computers, and how would they marry the new technologies?

Response to the inquiry was so heavy that the Common Carrier Bureau had to hire the Stanford Research Institute to analyze it; the SRI study was published in February 1969, and was used as market research in the two industries for a long time afterward. The process of defining FCC policy on the questions raised in the inquiry—issuing a tentative decision, inviting more comments, delivering a final decision and affirming it—continued through March 1972. Then the common carriers filed petitions for judicial review, and it took another year for the Court of Appeals to uphold most of the FCC's decision.

The policy decision that emerged from the computer inquiry dealt directly with only one of the issues raised in the docket, that of overlap between communications and data processing. It supplied rules for telling one from the other and held that data processing should not be regulated. AT&T could not offer data processing services, but Western Union and the other common carriers might do so provided they offered the services through subsidiaries with separate management and bookkeeping. The two remaining questions—whether telephone customers could buy equipment from independent suppliers and whether new companies could furnish communications services the carriers didn't provide—had been answered in separate rulings. But the information received in the inquiry began to affect FCC decisions on these issues as early as 1968.

The telephone companies had always insisted on owning, leasing and maintaining all the equipment directly attached to their network; in most cases they manufactured it, too. Bell's manufacturing arm, Western Electric, is itself one of the leading industrial corporations in the United States; in 1979 for example, despite inroads made by the competition Bell had fought so long to prevent, it sold nearly $11 billion worth of equipment. As for Bell's situation in the precompetitive days, no other regulated utilities were so fortunate: critics of the telephone industry have suggested that it was roughly equivalent to that of Consolidated Edison holding a monopoly of toasters, irons and electric shavers.

Telephone rates are calculated to cover the companies' operating costs plus a reasonable return on their assets, a percentage fixed by the regulatory commissions. More than a fifth of these assets were tied up in plant on the customer's premises—including communications terminals, switchboards, Touch-tone telephones and modems. Should competitors displace the Bell equipment before it was fully depreciated (indeed, should Bell itself, under competitive pressure, have to replace the old gear with new models prematurely) the resulting write-offs would increase the company's operating expenses. If these additional expenses were figured into prices of the new equipment, competitors would make further inroads, but if Bell chose instead to boost the rates for basic telephone service, residential customers would complain, particularly if they felt they were subsidizing Bell's competitive activities. It is not surprising, then, that Bell fought the equipment battle like a mother lion guarding her young.

The issue erupted in a case which came to the FCC's attention just as it was filing the computer inquiry, a case which in itself had nothing to do with computers but became a rallying point for computer interests. A Texas inventor named Thomas Carter had devised a gadget which allowed the customer to couple a telephone handset to a mobile radio transmitter. The Carterfone was a useful device, especially popular with oil companies, whose employees used it to talk with engineers drilling in remote fields; it sold well until AT&T advised its subscribers that if the customer connected a Carterfone, Bell would disconnect the customer. Carter brought an antitrust suit against AT&T, Southwest Bell and a local subsidiary of GT & E, but the court simply referred the case to the FCC. In 1968, when the commission had also heard an earful from computer people who wanted to manufacture their own modems, it ruled unanimously in favor of Carter, striking down all tariff restrictions against connecting customer-provided equipment with the telephone system.

AT&T had argued that since it had responsibility for operating the telephone system, it should have absolute control over the equipment used on that system. Shortly before Carterfone, some nontechnical executives in AT&T management had considered easing company policies on interconnection. Bell engineers, however, charged with the actual protection of the network, took a more conservative view. They were personally responsible for the integrity of our communications system, a duty one didn't take lightly. Moreover, like all of us, they wanted to make their own job easier, and thus resisted the complications of policing a plethora of exotic gadgets. Without the proper precautions, anyone could take his own equipment and solder it to the telephone line and shoot all sorts of harmful signals into the system, and the company would have no recourse but to disconnect the offender after the harm had been done. The engineers would stand up in meetings and enumerate to the nontechnical men—most of whom, they discovered, hadn't the foggiest idea what happens technically when you make a phone call—the catastrophes that might befall the network if Bell allowed the promiscuous hookup of customer gear. Horrible snarls could tie up both the long-distance lines and the central office equipment that handled switching and routing of calls; there could be an epidemic of wrong numbers and billing errors; administrative and maintenance expenses could skyrocket.

Bell management found the engineers' arguments compelling; also, they supplied a legitimate technical (and therefore noble) reason to put some brakes on interconnection. The company's position could be pleaded in the outside world by engineers, who would not deal with economic factors; this would lend a certain purity to their presentation. When the FCC ruled against the telephone companies in the Carterfone case, it did acknowledge their right to protect the system against poorly designed equipment and left it up to the carriers to suggest an acceptable means of protection. Bell filed a tariff requiring that customers who wanted to install their own switchboards, modems and the like must lease from Bell a device called a "connecting arrangement" which handled signaling and would safeguard the network.

The FCC allowed the Bell tariff to go into effect pending further study and set up various advisory committees of computer and telephone people to review the regulations. As the hearings dragged on, the interconnect industry grew. A slew of companies began manufacturing switchboards with all sorts of extra features that staid old Ma Bell didn't supply; IBM had developed a model for sale in Europe, where customers did buy their own equipment, and was now thinking about peddling the apparatus in the United States. Most of the major computer manufacturers and a number of small entrepreneurs got into modems and other devices used in teleprocessing.

There grew up a vocal lobby of users and manufacturers who thought the Bell connecting arrangements were, as one executive put it, "garbage." While the couplers were not in themselves big money-makers for Bell, they cost the user enough to make independent modems considerably less attractive. When the FCC asked AT&T to provide proof that customer-supplied gear harmed the network, Bell's response was inconclusive. After several years Bell began to buttress its technical position with economic arguments. The revenue lost to competitors in equipment would have to be made up by higher rates for you and me.

At the same time AT&T was encountering an even more serious challenge from companies that sought to compete in basic communications services. These companies questioned the application and even the fundamental soundness of the common carrier principle. Back in 1963, a new enterprise called Microwave Communications, Inc. had applied to the FCC for permission to furnish private line service in competition with Bell. The customer could lease MCI lines and use them as he pleased to transmit voice or data. MCI would custom-tailor the lines to meet the user's requirements, and while it used analog transmission techniques just like Bell's, it would go much further than Bell in offering the flexible services customers were requesting. There were no tight restrictions on hooking up one's own modems. MCI's prices were considerably lower than Bell's; it used cheaper methods of building its towers and was not obligated to carry equipment of varying age and efficiency. In August 1969, strongly influenced by the responses it received in the computer inquiry, the FCC finally granted MCI its first construction permits.

Shortly afterward the commission received an application that looked even more exciting. Sam Wyly, a Texas entrepreneur whose computer services company was one of the legends of the go-go sixties, was planning to build a network especially designed to transmit data. Wyly's network would offer all-digital transmission; that is, it would speak Greek, like the computers it served, instead of Swedish, like Bell's network. The analog transmission method—what we've called Swedish—amplified not only the original signal but also the noise accumulated along the route. Digital transmission, on the other hand, used "repeaters" that simply determined whether the signal was 1 or 0, produced a clean new replica and sent it along its way.

Wyly had surveyed the needs of computer customers at a time when many of his prospects had just finished compiling shopping lists for the FCC. In addition to improvements in accuracy, Wyly's Datran would offer desirable speed and pricing. It was an ambitious undertaking, slated to cost Wyly and his investors more than $350 million.

Some thirty other companies petitioned the FCC to compete with Bell, Western Union and the other common carriers in offering specialized services to businessmen. In 1971 the commission ruled in favor of the specialized carriers.

The common carriers had fought fiercely against the decision. AT&T argued that the specialized carriers were "cream-skimming": they would steal Bell's business along the more profitable routes without Bell's obligation to service the hinterlands. The loss of revenue to the new carriers would raise the price and jeopardize the quality of all Bell's services. The data customer could be served quite well by the common carriers.

The FCC, on the other hand, felt that Bell could no longer be all things to all people: the needs of the business community, particularly with its growing dependence on computer technology, were too diverse and too different from the residential subscriber's. Competition would spread the risks and the initiatives: in itself it was a "useful regulatory tool" to keep Bell progressive and responsive. Economies of scale were sometimes offset by those of focusing one's attention on a particular group of customers; Bell's size often prevented it from moving fast enough. The FCC was skeptical of AT&T's claims of financial harm. Most of Bell's interstate revenues came from switched-voice telephone service, which was not to be opened to direct competition, and this market itself was growing more than enough to offset the specialized carriers' gains. The data market itself was booming, and Bell would still dominate it.

Bell was (and still is, of course) the richest corporation in the world, with the largest number of employees and probably the most distinguished reputation for brillance in industrial research. But it had never competed in the marketplace before, and even the FCC was pushing it into a world in which success and even survival depended on skills the company had not yet acquired. Bell was powerful; and both as an organization and as a group of individuals, it was powerfully afraid. It fought back with the skill it possessed in great measure, the ability to navigate and manipulate the regulatory scene. At least it could buy the time to acquire a basic education. That was the strategy used by John De Butts, AT&T's new chairman, who began taking a much harder line toward competition than had his predecessor. In September 1973, De Butts gave a speech calling for a "moratorium on further experiments in economics"—a reconsideration of the FCC's decisions on independent gear and specialized carriers. He seemed to be declaring war.

Each of Bell's new competitors presented a different type of threat. MCI was perhaps the most disturbing: it competed in price, not technology, and ultimately challenged the very essence of Bell's monopoly. At first Bell refused the necessary local hookup between MCI's private lines and the switched public network. After a long court battle, AT&T was ordered to furnish the connections; then MCI came out with a new service through which a subscriber could call anybody without paying Bell's long-distance charges. When AT&T complained that now MCI was no longer offering pure private-line communications but encroaching on the switched services which had not been opened to competition, even the FCC was sympathetic; the Supreme Court, however, was not, and another long legal struggle ended in 1978 in favor of Bell's competitor.

Datran and the independent hardware companies presented a different sort of challenge. In the past Bell alone had controlled the rate at which new technology would be introduced. Down in Murray Hill, New Jersey the talent—numerous Ph.D.'s, a few of them Nobel Prize winners, in every field remotely related to communications—lived in the future, making discoveries, publishing papers, securing patents. Time moved in a more leisurely manner for Bell management in its Edwardian fortress in lower Manhattan. Much of this reluctance to change had been forced on AT&T executives: when rates are based on operating expenses plus a percentage return on assets, one is encouraged to capitalize everything in sight and depreciate it very slowly indeed. This method of ratemaking assumed that there would be no competitive pressure. Without some adjustment, it put Bell in a terrible bind, and the necessary revisions would be drastic and complex.

Bell hoped to squelch the independent hardware competition completely; the couplers required for foreign gear were merely hampering it. While Bell tried to get each state commission to ban all independent equipment for intrastate use, the FCC came to believe that couplers should be eliminated altogether. AT&T lost this contretemps at the Supreme Court level in 1976.

Bell could compete more directly with Datran. While Wyly's application was pending, Bell announced that it too was building a digital data network. By piggybacking on facilities it was installing anyway, Bell could offer the service at prices substantially lower than Wyly's. Because of regulatory delay, the AT&T network never achieved the wild success predicted for it; but it did succeed in preventing Wyly from raising the money he needed to build a coast-to-coast network. Datran went bankrupt in August 1976, just after Wyly filed a $285 million treble damage suit against AT&T for violation of the antitrust laws.

Wyly's was not the only antitrust claim pending against AT&T. In November 1974, the Justice Department had brought suit against the company; in size, complexity and duration this case might well surpass the IBM antitrust suit. In addition, the controversies of the past half-decade had spawned a number of smaller suits by competitors.

Many months before the death of Datran, then, Bell had begun feeling beleaguered. The world it knew was dying; only one chance remained for reaffirmation of the common carrier principle, and it called for a mustering of forces that only AT&T could accomplish.

Bell thought Congress would be friendlier than the FCC or the courts. Lawyers from AT&T and the independent telephone companies spent many months during 1975 and early 1976 drafting the cleverly named Consumer Communications Reform Act. In effect the bill would undo the FCC's pro-competitive rulings and restore the industry's previous monopoly status. Specialized carriers would be licensed only if they supplied a service traditional common carriers couldn't provide. This ruled out not only all existing specialized carriers but every type one might conceive of, since these companies based their existence not on what Bell with its staggering resources *could* provide but what it actually *did* or *would* provide. The bill disposed of the interconnect industry by transferring authority from the FCC to the state regulatory agencies. Not only were many of these likely to rule in favor of Bell and against "foreign attachments," but the necessity to conform to fifty different sets of regulations would make it difficult, if not impossible, for the interconnect manufacturers to plan their product lines.

The words "consumer" and "reform" derived from Bell's claim that residential customers would have to compensate for revenues lost to FCC-sponsored competition, and that these rate hikes might reach 70 percent. Bell's opponents—in the FCC and the White House Office of Telecommunications Policy as well as in competing firms—called this nonsense, and some suggested that, on the contrary, residential customers were now subsidizing unprofitable business equipment. It seemed shocking that neither side could produce conclusive evidence to support its case, but the real costs of providing individual Bell services were not known. Like all utilities, AT&T was obliged to keep its books according to something called the Uniform System of Accounts, designed in 1913, which lumped together costs and revenues for products and services that shared the same plant; in essence, Bell didn't know its winners from its losers. And, while toll revenue did subsidize rural telephone service—the reason the smaller telephone companies were eager to back the bill—the method of calculating the subsidies was arbitrary. If, as Bell claimed, the business customer subsidized the residential, this might still not be in the public interest: the business customer, for example, might as easily be the Heller Candy Company of Paterson, New Jersey as Exxon, and the residential customer might as well be David Rockefeller as old Aunt Sally, and there were numerous other intricate questions of public policy to consider. All of them, however, were academic when you couldn't be sure where the subsidies lay.

The Act—dubbed the Bell Bill by its opponents—was introduced in the House of Representatives in March 1976. Throughout the year, the sophisticated lobbying skills of AT&T were focused on securing congressional sponsors for the bill. Bell employees are encouraged to become active in community affairs, the better to look out for company interests; congressmen were deluged with calls and visits from important constituents who happened to work for Bell. Presidents of the various operating companies visited every member of Congress. Educational literature flowed from AT&T to its stockholders; letters flowed from AT&T stockholders to their congressmen. The independent telephone companies, the state regulators, the Communications Workers of America and the American Farm Bureau also joined the campaign.

The lobbying effort succeeded in persuading some two hundred members of Congress to sponsor the bill. Support for Bell, however, turned out to be broad but not very deep. The bill was killed in subcommittees of both the Senate and the House. Accounts in the business and trade press suggest that the intensive lobbying campaign stirred up backlash. But the discussion of the bill did show many legislators that our telecommunications policy needed reviewing and updating; soon afterward, Congress began studying ways to rewrite the Communications Act.

Still, AT&T management was as pragmatic as it was conservative. Hard as it fought to cling to the past, it knew the effort might not succeed. And so, cautiously at first, and finally with a commitment that deserved respect, the company began to transform itself.

In 1970, the Bell system gave American businessmen a product it believed they were dying to have, a product whose attractiveness seemed so obvious that the company had spent nearly two decades and several hundred million dollars to develop it, a product which, while priced decidedly in the luxury bracket, would soon become as familiar to corporate executives as first-class jet travel to Europe. That product was called Picturephone. Bell's forecasts, dating from the booming sixties, predicted that a million Picturephones would be operating by 1980.

Local Picturephone service, launched in Chicago, Washington and Pittsburgh, cost $100 a month; long distance was extra. In the corporate idiom, Picturephone was "optimized for face-to-face communication," which meant that documents held up to the camera came out looking fuzzy. The only advantage the product held over an ordinary telephone was eye contact, and how much of this you'd get depended on how many people you knew with sets of their own. At the height of the recession, executives found the price too steep. In all of Chicago and one of its suburbs AT&T sold only four hundred sets.

In 1973 the company, recognizing that it had blundered somewhere but not understanding the nature of its error, ordered some five years of additional technical and market research experiments to discover what kind of Picturephones, if any, people would buy at what price and how they would use them; at the end of the testing period, AT&T would either have an improved, salable offering or would throw up its hands and stop trying.

The studies AT&T performed during the middle seventies would have been made by IBM or any other company used to operating in a competitive marketplace *before* introducing the product. There was no staff department at AT&T or its operating companies that did market research; the engineering department and Bell Laboratories, in originating products and services, made only a superficial effort to determine whether a product would sell, and no organization existed to challenge them. There was a marketing department in the Bell System: it was simply the name for the people who sold to businesses having more than three telephone lines, as opposed to the commercial department, which dealt with businesses that had fewer.

When the FCC opened the equipment, private-line and data communications markets to competition, AT&T management became concerned about holding on to customers. The interconnect industry had already made progress in several products when De Butts hired McKinsey & Company to find Bell's weaknesses and suggest how to correct them. The most glaring deficiencies McKinsey discovered were the lack of an organization to find out what customers wanted and to translate those requirements into products, and an insufficiently aggressive and knowledgeable sales force. The consultants suggested that Bell set up a marketing department with sufficient clout to change the old habits of the bureaucracy. De Butts brought Kenneth J. Whalen, president of Michigan Bell, to corporate headquarters as vice-president of marketing, a post which hadn't even been filled for some years.

Whalen himself, as a typical up-from-the-ranks Bell executive, had no experience in the sort of marketing McKinsey had recommended, nor was there anyone else in the Bell system with the required skills. Clearly it would be necessary to bring in an outsider to guide the market studies. As director of market management the new man would have the rank of assistant vice-president, the top level of middle management; AT&T was so inbred that it had never hired an outsider for so important a position, and Whalen had to get special permission from De Butts. In the tradition of high-technology companies seeking to improve their marketing performance, AT&T, in the person of Whalen, chose an ex-IBM'er. Archie J. McGill had been a star at IBM, achieving vice-presidency of the marketing division while still in his early thirties; with his quick mind and feisty temperament he figured prominently in company lore of the late sixties. He had left IBM just before the recession, when a young man who had encountered his first setback—McGill was said to get on poorly with the division's president, Buck Rodgers—might still choose the opportunities of the outside world over the frustrations of the penalty box. After a short episode as president of one of the leasing companies—which ended in a clash of wills between the peppery McGill and an equally strong-willed chairman of the board—McGill was consulting when Whalen hired him. The company recognized that McGill needed assistants with marketing experience: he was allowed to bring in about seventy-five people— half his staff—from outside. Many of them had IBM on their resumes.

McGill had headed industrial marketing at IBM. The first thing he and his staff did was to organize AT&T's customers into industry groups just like IBM's and, working with the operating companies, embark on detailed studies of how each industry used communications now and would in the future; he also got the operating companies to organize their sales people along industry lines. At the same time McGill's group analyzed the data communications marketplace, past and future, to determine Bell's role and share in it.

The market that concerned McGill had three segments: the actual networks that transmitted the data; the terminals which fed it to a remote computer; and the various boxes that stood between the terminal and the network to ensure reliability and accuracy of transmission and economical use of communications lines. Bell and Western Union had once shared almost all of this market; now, a combination of circumstances had lowered the telephone company's share to scarcely more than a third. Computer companies had come out with ever more elaborate electronic terminals, while AT&T's Teletype subsidiary, partly out of nervousness about the limits of the consent decree, had proved a sluggish competitor, sticking to obsolete electromechanical equipment. Now a lively interconnect industry was challenging Bell. The specialized carriers were beginning to operate, and the first satellites for business use would soon be launched. Bell's data revenues had grown fast, faster in fact than its voice revenues, but the data market as a whole had grown faster still, and so Bell's share had diminished.

There were, McGill said, two reasons why this trend would accelerate unless Bell took some action. The companies who made hardware were also cutting into Bell's transmission revenues, because the hardware was designed to help customers use communications more efficiently. The equipment-makers—often computer people—were perceived by customers as "problem-solvers," while the telephone company was perceived as part of the problem. So the customer called in IBM or Burroughs to design a distributed computing network laid out to minimize his phone bills. Then, with the blueprint in hand, he told Bell what he wanted. The communications manager in a customer company had always made points by keeping costs down, while the data processing manager was especially skilled in persuading management to invest two pennies to save five. As computers and communications began to merge, the data processing manager, with his hostility toward the telephone company, tended to take over the whole operation.

Assuming Bell didn't want to continue being just the passive provider of a pipeline, there were several choices open to it. It could supply networks specially designed for various data needs, like the digital service it had just proposed to the FCC; this was better, but not much better, since the phone company would still be losing transmission revenues to the equipment makers. The next position would be to set itself up as a "communications problem-solver"; that is, instead of having IBM tell the customer how to lay out his communications facilities, AT&T would do so. Technology had now so evolved that almost any data communications feature—correcting transmission errors, for example, or arranging data in the proper format—could be built into either the network itself or some box that hung on the network. If Bell supplied both the boxes and the networks, then whichever solution proved best for the customer, the revenues would accrue to Bell. A final option was that the company try to change the consent decree, offer complete computer-and-communications systems, and present itself as a "total problem-solver" à la IBM; the consensus was that the legal difficulties would be insurmountable, and the "communications problem-solver" alternative was the best. It is important, however, that nobody at Bell felt that the company could prosper or ultimately survive by just sticking to plain-old-telephone service. Computers and communications were now too thoroughly enmeshed.

As AT&T was assessing the importance of data to its future, IBM was concluding that *its* future was inevitably tied to communications. LSI—large-scale integration, the compression of increasing numbers of circuits on a single silicon chip—was propelling the company in new directions. By the mid-seventies you could buy a hand-held calculator with the power of the ENIAC. Besides dramatic improvements in performance, there were other important by-products of miniaturization: fewer cables, less energy consumption, simpler cooling requirements. More powerful machines could operate outside the computer room.

While LSI was driving down mainframe and memory prices, IBM had to maintain its historic growth rate. You sold a customer more equipment by getting him to put on new applications, and these now required remote computing. Here LSI was a catalyst: you could combine sophistication and custom tailoring with economies of scale by designing a basic terminal and adding various chip modules to fit it out for different industries. Terminals for credit verification and after-hours banking, electronic cash registers tied to a branch store's computer and then linked with the home office, terminals to monitor factory operations and feed the data to headquarters, would make the old dreams practical at last. Chips would go into ordinary office typewriters, turning them into terminals that could store text and incorporate editing changes at the press of a button. The touch-tone telephone was itself a rudimentary terminal, subject to LSI embellishment, and once you got into using telephones as terminals, as IBM's French laboratory had discovered, you put the chips into the switchboards to make *them* more versatile in the ways they sent and collected messages. All of these developments fed each other; and, as the Management Committee learned in 1968, "systems grow rapidly as terminals are added, particularly in memory."

IBM, the total problem solver, was perfectly equipped to supply the automated office, factory, supermarket and bank; the technology and economics were here, and it was time to move the product line in that direction. You could not, however, move it as far as you'd like when a crucial part of the system belonged to someone else. How could you plan a farflung data network without controlling (or even knowing) the extent, the price and the technology of the communications that would be available seven years down the road? The risks of getting into a new and regulated business, of antagonizing AT&T, its best corporate customer, and of matching the installation and maintenance skills of "firmly entrenched competition" had delayed the introduction of IBM's French-designed switchboard in the U.S. But in the case of data communications, there were more risks in *not* getting in. So the task forces set to work.

IBM announced its plans in 1974. The most dramatic was a joint venture with Comsat General Corporation to provide satellite transmission for private-line service via small antennas right on the customer's roof. The announcement brought mixed reactions: some thought the entry would speed the growth of technology and others thought IBM and AT&T would divide up the communications market and put their competitors out of business, and that IBM would offer bundled computer-and-communications systems to lock out independent suppliers. In 1975 the FCC ruled that IBM could go into the satellite business only under specified conditions. It would have to take in a third partner; it would have to place its satellite operations in a separate subsidiary; the subsidiary and IBM couldn't promote each other's equipment or services; and the subsidiary would have to give out the information necessary to allow non-IBM equipment to hook up to the system.

In December the two partners announced they had found a third, Aetna Life and Casualty. They had formed a new company, Satellite Business Systems, which now sought FCC authorization to build an all-digital domestic satellite system serving large industrial, government and other users. SBS would offer customers a broad highway for voice, data and image communications.

SBS's market studies of leading American corporations from the *Fortune* listings did not suggest a heavy volume of current applications which would profitably be shifted to satellites. SBS was betting that its existence would stimulate new applications. It supported this belief with forecasts that by 1985 data communications revenues would surpass data processing revenues, that the data terminal market would exceed $2 billion and the total business communications market would pass $100 billion. Figures for the growth of large computer systems looked equally hopeful.

Regulatory delays postponed the start of service until early 1981; by July 1980 SBS had only six customers (besides IBM and Aetna) for its luxury service. The *Fortune* 500 had not moved forward fast enough to need the broad highway. SBS announced it was changing its focus: it would now sell a lower-priced service to a larger number of smaller companies, who could share earth stations, and it would stress inexpensive long-distance voice transmission, the sort of service MCI was offering. With the shift, SBS hoped to break even by 1983.

How large a risk was IBM actually taking on its satellite system? By 1980 costs had exceeded the original estimates, and SBS's president was reckoning the enterprise might need a total investment of $567 million—that's $189 million from each partner, without outside financing—by 1984. Rounded out to $200 million, that equals twenty-four days' earnings in 1979, and the investment was actually spread out over eight years. At the very least, it bought a highly effective sword of Damocles to suspend over AT&T's head: AT&T could not assume that SBS would fail, and worked hard to provide facilities competitive with IBM's. IBM's entrance conferred respectability on other satellite ventures and on all enterprises tied to advanced communications. Whoever led the field, the company could be sure of adequate pipelines to complete the new computer applications it needed in order to grow.

IBM also had to tailor its product line to remote use. In the early seventies, the hardware and software for data communications recalled the hardware and software for computing in general during the late fifties; a jumble of incompatible products. It is a complex business to get computers and terminals to talk to each other. There are, for example, various codes that dictate how electrical signals will be made to represent letters or numbers. There are protocols, the "Roger-over-and-out" procedures that govern the exchange of data. There are rules for detecting errors of transmission and for choosing the path data will travel. Some terminals can send and receive information at the same time; others can't. Some of these properties are built into the hardware, others designed in the software, but the result was that a single user would often require separate networks for different applications.

In 1974 IBM announced its Systems Network Architecture, a regime that would govern all IBM teleprocessing hardware and software; in giving direction to a highly disparate product line it was analogous to System 360 ten years earlier. Once a customer had set up a network using the compatible terminals, computers and operating software that comprised SNA, he could add, subtract and shift the boxes without writing new applications programs. One terminal could run several different applications, and several types of terminals could share a communications line. The terminals could perform many administrative and computing tasks, increasing the speed and economy of the system (when you process locally your telephone bill goes down).

Since IBM is not an eleemosynary institution, SNA did not lower the user's data processing expenses; it merely shifted them around in IBM's favor. While he saved on communications and possibly on applications programming, the new software required more memory; and, as IBM had hoped, users began to lay on many new applications, thus requiring still more memory and a larger mainframe. Since the new software was complex, they had to hire systems programmers who were knowledgeable in teleprocessing, finance their attendance at IBM's SNA training course, and pay them well enough to be sure they'd stay on afterward. Thus customers were slow to accept SNA. Those who had been willing to make the investment were pleased with it; many who had not invested seemed to feel, grudgingly, that ultimate predominance of IBM's teleprocessing scheme was inevitable.

IBM's technical men had long been aware of the limits communications can place on computing; remote computing, pro and con, had been an issue at IBM since the time-sharing days. The need to start planning a product line some seven years in advance brought discipline and focus to management's thinking, forcing executives to weigh the role of communications in future systems as early as the late sixties. For AT&T, on the other hand, computing crept up like a thief in the night. Certainly the telephone company made excellent use of the machines in every phase of its own operations; and computer technology was being phased into the telephone network, to improve service, at the rate AT&T considered practical. But in strategic planning Bell was about five years behind IBM: only in the mid-seventies did AT&T management deem serving the data processing community crucial to the company's future and perceive the opportunities that lay ahead. The "product line" is a marketing concept; since AT&T was not a marketing company but a regulated monopoly, it didn't think of itself as having a product line to plan. Rather, it had an eternal network which was always being improved, and on that network it hung various products and services, each designed separately as the need arose.

During the middle seventies Bell introduced several products that suggested it was mounting an offensive across the border into data processing; oddly enough, none of these began as part of a strategy more coherent than "responding to market needs" or "bringing out more modern products." Most were conceived by engineers before the marketing department was set up; the detail work, according to one Bell marketing executive, was often poorly done, and the products were not a raging success. Bell's real offensive was laid out by Arch McGill, and it was as brassy as the man himself.

McGill's studies had revealed the same data communications problems—incompatibility resulting in wasteful duplication and high startup costs—that IBM had noted. IBM was selling the user a system of boxes and programs to solve these problems, but this tied the user to one vendor's hardware and was too expensive for medium-sized and small customers. Also, IBM's system was aimed at intracompany traffic. Suppose Bell were to offer most of the advantages of IBM's architecture scheme, and to enable, for example, Univac, Burroughs and Honeywell equipment to be linked? The customer could buy almost any terminal to go with any computer. If Bell were to build the communications processing features into its network, the user would not have to hire all those systems programmers; the ability to go online in small steps would bring in a whole new set of customers. Different companies could send data to each other: a manufacturer could order from its suppliers, travel agents could talk to hotels and airlines, hospitals could talk to insurance companies. And Bell would then be the foe of computer monopolists, the friend of competition in the data processing industry, the protector of the small user.

These wonders could be accomplished through a technology called packet-switching, which several of the specialized common carriers were then offering. One used ordinary telephone lines to link a network of minicomputers, which would divide the customer's data into little packets of information and send each packet over the fastest available route to its destination, thus economizing on transmission. Each mini would correct errors in the packets before sending them to the next station. Bell Laboratories was already working on its own version of a packet network.

Nobody disagreed with the notion of getting into packet-switching. But Bell Labs wanted to enhance the system it had, duplicating the fairly modest efforts of the specialized carriers, while McGill was looking for something considerably splashier to accomplish his goals.

A packet network could edit and arrange data for transmission, tasks now performed by the most advanced computer terminals; and it might store messages, forms and data, acting as an electronic mailbox. Edward Goldstein, McGill's opposite number in product management, sided with the labs. He worried about regulatory problems and whether the revenues would justify the investment, and, playing the engineer's traditional conservative role, he believed it was better to use a familiar approach that would proceed without slipups. When Goldstein finally gave in to McGill, a year later, he hadn't changed his mind about the risks; he simply agreed that a conservative network wouldn't dent the market, and there was no point working on a problem whose solution wouldn't get you very far.

Bell's Advanced Communications Service was announced in July 1978, with enough special features to alarm every segment of the computer industry. Some of the operations ACS performed were now available from time-sharing services companies, who were not of a mind to welcome their mighty new competitor. IBM, of course, was hoping its network architecture would tie customers to IBM equipment, and now ACS was giving them independence; the Dwarfs, also, had developed architectures of their own in hopes of protecting their customer bases. For IBM there was an additional concern. If Bell's network won a substantial portion of the market, IBM would no longer set the industry standard. To enable its customers to talk to the outside world, it would have to offer compatibility with other codes and protocols. Finally, since Bell's promised compatibility was still somewhat selective, not universal, the independent terminal manufacturers were afraid of being either dictated to or left out; and, of course, if ACS usurped some of the tasks that terminals and other boxes now performed, it could change the nature of the hardware business. Most reports thought ACS was a boon for the user.

Everyone assumed there would be delays in winning regulatory approval for ACS, but in the spring of 1979 the FCC showed it was receptive to the service. The commission, trying to keep abreast of racing technology, had initiated a second computer inquiry in hopes of clarifying the difference between communications and data processing. It concluded that such distinction was now meaningless; voice and data communications were either "basic" or "enhanced," and common carriers should be allowed to offer enhanced services like ACS through separate subsidiaries. This decision was "tentative," and it took another year for the FCC to issue its final edict that all services except basic voice, and all equipment on customers' premises—telephones, terminals and switchboards—would be deregulated and offered through "arm's-length" subsidiaries of the common carriers. The carriers had until March 1982 to comply with the decision. Since the new subsidiaries would be strictly marketing organizations, the commission laid down rules for their dealings with Bell Laboratories, which would carry on the research and development, and Western Electric, which would continue to manufacture the equipment. AT&T, not surprisingly, felt the rules would hamstring the subsidiary; its competitors thought the commission hadn't done enough to remove the subsidiary's unfair advantages. Also, the ruling nullified the consent decree and undercut the Justice Department's antitrust suit against AT&T. From all these sources the industry expected challenges, long litigation and thus continued uncertainty.

As for ACS, it appeared that the engineers had been right. First Bell announced software delays and then it withdrew the application for the service, stating it didn't know when the project would be completed; the hardware would have to be changed and the whole concept modified. There was some talk in the industry that rules for sharing facilities between Bell and the new subsidiary would also affect the design of ACS.

Whatever ACS's fate, the Bell system was changing itself pervasively; the effort started slowly and accelerated during 1978. Twenty thousand marketing employees at every level took company-sponsored courses ranging from three-day seminars to six-week stints at Wharton. The criteria by which managers were measured became more entrepreneurial than bureaucratic, and the company began testing sales commissions. Branch offices were organized for IBM-like industrial specialization; field representatives, installers and maintenance people were aligned in teams headed by "account executives" who sounded remarkably like IBM salesmen.

The task of training employees to work in a competitive business is far more difficult than product development; it requires a change of ingrained attitudes and habits. This training went on in the midst of a massive reorganization at headquarters and within the operating companies. To make the chart look more like the marketplace and to separate monopoly from competitive services, the new grouping dispersed the old functional operating departments under executive vice-presidents for business, residential and network services. A quarter of a million people were slightly shuffled so that everyone's bailiwick was a little bit different, and many people had new bosses who had new bosses who had new bosses. Morale problems grew serious, and the company had to institute programs to help employees deal with stress.

The Bell System itself had a new boss. While John De Butts had done much to groom the company to face competition, he was a symbol of the old intransigence. Perhaps recognizing this, he stepped down in November 1978, a year before reaching mandatory retirement age. His successor, Charles Brown, gave speeches talking about "the new realism," noting that competition was "a fact of life in our business and has been for some time." Brown was, in fact, so realistic that four months after deregulation he announced another reorganization to set up the new competitive subsidiary. Despite the uncertain outcome of the FCC's ruling, Congress's effort to rewrite the Communications Act, and the Justice Department's antitrust suit, Brown had decided the company must do something to shape its own destiny. One of Bell's vice-chairmen was charged with drawing the plans for Baby Bell, as the industry soon nicknamed it; while the shape of the new company and its opening date were still undecided, Baby Bell would start life with $12 billion in assets.

The first part of the battle of the giants was over. IBM had won, because it had—with the help of several small entrepreneurs—moved AT&T into the computer era. AT&T had won because it had moved into the computer era. The battle for control remains. The only thing certain about the outcome is its uncertainty: despite the wealth of forecasts, it is difficult to know what the marketplace will look like in five, ten or twenty years.

That market will include networks, hardware and applications services. There are many new types of pipelines, some mutually beneficial, others competitive. In addition to satellites and cable TV—which help each other—there are promising terrestrial technologies, such as the glass fibers AT&T is now installing, which offer exponential growth in transmission capacity. Now that there is no distinction between communications and data processing, what sort of androgynous equipment can we expect from IBM and AT&T? Each of the cashless-checkless-society applications that might use the new transmission capacity has its own set of problems. Since all these developments affect each other, it is hard to be sure what the territory will be, let alone who will control it.

Many companies are rushing in, and each may enter several parts of the market. General Telephone & Electronics and Xerox are active in telecommunications networks and equipment. While the biggest new name in information systems, including word-processing equipment and terminals to hang on the new networks, is Exxon, with its Vydec, Qwip and Qyx machines, its microprocessors and other computer and communications gear, management changes have led some observers to question its staying power. Other oil companies are also getting into the field. And low-cost telephone service from the specialized carriers is catching on with residential as well as business customers. While the users wait for AT&T's dust to settle, will other suppliers come up with better solutions?

Lately, Americans have looked to the vigorous computer, communications and semiconductor industries—which feed on each other—to rescue us from our industrial decline. At the same time, foreign competition in these markets—from government-subsidized enterprises in Europe, Canada and, in particular, Japan—is becoming more aggressive. Japan, which won 40 percent of the world market in one kind of advanced memory chip, has caught up with, and in some areas surpassed, our semiconductor technology, and its manufacturers are building plants in the United States. The Japanese have been supplying computer system components wholesale to American vendors for some years; now they are moving to remedy weaknesses in software and foreign distribution and beginning to sell their own computers in the US. These developments are certainly cause for alarm—and IBM, AT&T, and the smaller companies all claim that public policies favoring them are essential to meeting the foreign competition.

The industry has entered a period of extraordinary excitement, opportunity and upheaval. Do computer people feel wonderful about it? Yes and no. The comment that follows, from a book called

Technology and Change by Donald A. Schon, was published in 1967. Those who have heard it agree that it has an eerie cogency today:

> Unexpected success is no less destructive of the rational view of corporate activity than is unexpected failure. When the addition of carbon black turns out to increase the strength of rubber; when the book-mending tape turns out to have a multiplicity of unexpected consumer uses; when the new plastic, designed for a cheaper molding process, turns out to perform well in a completely different application—the corporate manager can only react with a wry smile. In ways he did not understand, and was unable to state before the fact, things have gone well; but what has he learned that will prepare him to cope with the *next time?*

14

Where Are We Going?

THE LABORATORIES and offices of computer vendors offer only a
limited view of developing technology. While no vendor plans products without reports from the field, the reports are quickly converted
into estimates of the demand for chips, discs and satellite channels;
in Armonk and places like it the emphasis is more on millions-of-
instructions-per-second than on what the instructions contain. To understand what the future holds, it is necessary to meet some people
who are busy exploiting the technology. If their dreams come true,
they will help to change our lives.

HOME INFORMATION SYSTEMS

The first experimental efforts to bring electronic information systems into the home have begun; a long list of applications that
seemed wildly futuristic three or four years ago are operating somewhere now. For some time, computer and communications people
have known that new technologies would permit the transmission of
enormous volumes of data into every home, school and office in the
country and could, in fact, turn every home into a school and office.
The computer power to manage and store this data is becoming so
inexpensive that by the middle to late eighties it will be possible to
buy a system with the capacity and versatility of a large IBM 360 for
about the price of a color television set. We may want a video disc
player to see Woody Allen pictures at our own convenience, but a
twelve-inch disc that carries *Annie Hall* can also accommodate the
entire *Encyclopaedia Britannica*. When a market research firm
mentioned these possibilities to a panel of ordinary citizens, there
was considerable enthusiasm for "instant education." But suppliers
still wonder whether that enthusiasm will last as long as it takes to
sign a check.

Computer companies are used to serving commercial customers and fear they don't know what makes consumers happy; the telephone companies, while they deal with the consumer every day, are novices at competing for his money. Those in the information business—newspaper publishers, for example—are used to serving consumer needs but worry about their ability to marry these needs to advanced technology. And it is not clear whether and how all these innovations will complement, coexist or compete with one another. And so the fashionable attitude for corporate executives discussing the home market these days is skepticism, which is the take-charge version of insecurity. "Anyone who says he knows this market is lying," insists one of the men who study the field for AT&T.

The earliest proponent of information in the home was the British Post Office, which operates the telephone system in England. The BPO has spent tens of millions of pounds to launch Prestel, a service now active in London and several other cities. The Prestel user presses buttons on a small keypad, rather like a calculator, to summon information stored in the post office's computers, which travels over telephone lines to the user's television screen. The BPO doesn't itself supply the information; it makes money by selling computer storage space to organizations that do, and as a traditional common carrier, charging the consumer a few pence a minute for access to the computer and normal local telephone rates for connection time. Information Providers—IP's, as the Post Office calls them—fall into two categories: those whose data has sufficient intrinsic value to be sold, and those who supply free information—what amounts to an advertisement—about products they sell.

What can you learn on Prestel? Subscribers interested in business are well served. The *Financial Times* offers a daily news summary and abstracts of its recent articles, comment and analysis written especially for Prestel viewers by *Financial Times* journalists and security analysts. There is in-depth coverage of 122 public companies and 8 nationalized industries in the UK, as well as brief reports on 500 more companies. UK economic indicators, exchange rates, interest rates and stock market indices (foreign as well as UK) are also available. All this material comes from Fintel, a joint venture of the *Financial Times* and Extel, but there are several other providers of different types of financial information.

If viewers' needs are practical but less weighty, there is material for travelers on weather, accommodations and cultural events at various destinations; the system carries British Airways' worldwide schedules and daily flight information. A superefficient traveler who hates to leave anything to chance might retrieve *The New York Times'* restaurant guide via Prestel, choose some prestigious or obscure eatery, and cable New York to reserve a table. A compatriot with equal foresight but more prosaic itinerary might learn what's playing at the cinema in Birmingham.

Selections from the *New Caxton Encyclopedia* and *Guinness Book of Records* are on tap to settle postprandial disputes and help children with their homework. There are real estate and employment listings, games, racing odds and children's stories. Prestel offers shopping information on a variety of products and services, and will eventually permit a subscriber to place an order.

This technology can produce inexpensive access to a computer data base because the computer doesn't actually process for the viewer; one can't ask it a question or tap more than one IP store simultaneously. The method of access is the "menu" or "tree search" widely used in applications that bring computer power to laymen who don't want to bother learning even a simple programming language. The screen displays a menu of three items; you hit a button choosing one, which brings you another three-item menu; you keep refining your choices till you get what you want. It takes five menus to find out what's playing at the cinema in London. A cheaper way to get to the right page is by consulting Prestel's printed directory.

Most of Prestel's information is available elsewhere through traditional media; Prestel offers a convenience which varies with the type of material. To summon flight schedules via Prestel would be slightly more expensive than calling British Airways directly; whether pressing all those buttons is less irritating than waiting for an available clerk is subjective. The average Londoner won't have a Birmingham newspaper lying around the house; are masses of London residents dying to know what's playing in Birmingham this minute? On the other hand, while it's cheaper to hike out to the library to look at *Caxton's Encyclopedia,* it would be nice to summon the information at home; what is this worth to Mummy and Daddy? The market for all that marvelous financial data, according to an article in the Prestel directory, is almost exclusively professional.

The earliest television sets fitted out to receive Prestel cost a thousand pounds, but BPO officials say the equipment is subject to considerable economies of scale. In England TV sets are rented anyway, so the subscriber now pays a stiff increment on the regular rate. Radio Shack has begun selling a $400 converter to hook up American TV sets to similar services recently launched in the U.S. It's logical to assume that a viewer wouldn't want to pay for the gear unless he plans to give it plenty of use. Then, however, the phone bills would soar—which is just what the BPO has in mind. A consultant for Quantum Sciences, an American firm which has studied the home information market, thinks this technology "may make swift penetration until people get their phone bills. Then it will come to a dead halt. They'll say, 'How can I get the information cheaper?' "

"Prestel" is the trademark for the system now operating in England; generically, the technology, which is being tried in France, Canada and the United States, is called "viewdata" or "videotex." Although American businessmen exhibit a strong (though usually unfocused) conviction that viewdata will win some place in the U.S. market, few say kind words about Prestel. The BPO's original market research was not sufficient to satisfy Dennis Sullivan, AT&T's assistant vice-president for residential marketing, who says, "They went forward without anything but an inner feeling of market needs." One difficulty was the BPO's decision to delegate editorial responsibility and control to the IP's themselves. The post office simply sold space on the system at very attractive rates to all comers. A hundred and fifty IP's heeded the call; no central intelligence monitors what goes on the system, which thus amounts to a giant electronic vanity press. Moreover, according to John Rothman, Director of Information and Research Technology at *The New York Times*, one of the Prestel IP's, the market trial was so poorly set up that it told little about who would buy what information at what price. Results of more recent American experiments with the technology are not yet known.

The logical carriers of viewdata service in the United States would be the telephone companies. AT&T has moved slowly because of regulatory uncertainty and because the company still hurts from the Picturephone disaster, in which scientists led a venture into technology the public wasn't ready for. Partly through making a virtue out of necessity and partly as converts, then, AT&T executives preach the gospel of rigorous market research. Besides innumerable surveys, the research has included various experimental projects. In Albany, a hundred homes and offices were given video terminals that allowed their telephones to tap a data base for directory assistance; a broader-based trial was then designed for Austin, Texas. Sullivan says, "We want to see if yellow-pages advertisers will spend more to add current information to their listings—if they're having a sale, for instance." While Sullivan won't commit himself to specific features, the display telephone (which need not be prohibitively priced, like Picturephone) could be made to offer enough convenience that business customers, at least, would be willing to pay for it: it could supply listings from different parts of the country and screen incoming calls by flashing the caller's phone number. Once the system is set up and customers have the hardware, such "extended telephone service" might easily become full-fledged viewdata. AT&T has also supplied telephone lines and technical assistance in a viewdata market trial operated by Knight-Ridder Newspapers in Florida. "Our self-interest in this technology is high because our network is ubiquitous for sending voice, data and text," says Sullivan, who adds, in the sporting lingo favored by corporate executives, "We don't have to build the stadium, just get the game."

General Telephone and Electronics, on the other hand, took out an exclusive American license on the British system, then renegotiated it because of a probable preference for the Canadian technology; its caution is of a different sort. "It's not easy to design a sensible market test for a new product," says Dr. Lee Davenport, vice-president and chief scientist emeritus. "One interest we had in Prestel was that we could learn to avoid the mistakes the British are making. Home viewdata appears to be a different service from viewdata for business use—the British treated the two identically. The system allows limited graphics and color. If you're going to compress information to fit on a TV screen it must be pretty attractive. We won't read books or long articles this way. The copy has to be very crisp and lively, like advertising copy. Writing it will be a special skill; you certainly don't want scientists writing the copy. If it doesn't read well you'll kill a good technology."

Davenport makes an able salesman for viewdata. "I think people want and enjoy educational material and can be challenged to do more," he says. "It will be a very interesting medium, because it's capable of branching. I think it could give you multiple-choice interactive educational programs for children as well as adults. The school system could give homework assignments on viewdata.

"I can see information on hobbies, travel timetables and entertainment. People in the suburbs like to go to the movies in nearby towns, but they aren't always listed in the local paper. How about emergency services, like what to do in case of accidents, and poison control? And the household hints you didn't cut out of the newspaper—how to get the wine stain out of the tablecloth. Computer games are selling, but then you get tired of the one you bought and throw it out. Viewdata can change the games, and give you interactive chess.

"Suppose I come home at night and discover I need a new tire. First I punch a button for *Consumer Reports*, then I get the manufacturers' ads for the tires I want to see, and then the different dealers' ads for who's having a special. It's much easier than looking it up in several different places. You can learn all about the new cars before you walk into the showroom. Stores can change their ads hourly according to what's in stock. All this supplements the newspaper ads, which have photographs. And since the information is accessed only by people who want it, it's a powerful advertising medium."

While full-fledged home information systems are still experimental, current ventures in electronic publishing offer some clues about their future. Computer service companies have made a lucrative business of selling access to financial and economic information and data required by particular industries: in 1980, this brought American suppliers $565 million. Such publishers as Dun & Bradstreet, Dow-Jones and McGraw-Hill have also entered this rapidly growing field. But the sale of more general, nontechnical information, even to corporate customers who can well afford it and put it to good use, has been a struggle. The New York Times Information Bank, which has been doing business since February 1973, showed its first monthly operating profits during 1979. It is the most sophisticated general research tool available, and at up to $110 an hour it is priced accordingly.

The Bank contains abstracts of most of the news and editorial material that ran in *The New York Times* between January 1, 1969 and four days before the current date, with some types of news available daily; also, there are abstracts of articles from sixty other publications, including every general-interest magazine one can think of and special-interest periodicals from the *Bulletin of Atomic Scientists* to *Women's Wear Daily*. The corporate subscribers have or can buy a variety of compatible terminals; most are already hooked up to one of the data communications networks, which save on transmission costs. An occasional user can simply call and buy one search by a staff librarian, who will put the abstracts in the mail the same day.

Hunting for abstracts involves a tree search similar to viewdata's but far more refined and interactive. The subscriber types in a subject heading, and the screen displays a list of pertinent files ("housing" might yield the files for "architecture and architects," "taxation" and "zoning" and suggestions for related subjects, such as "interior decoration"). The user can skip several branches by typing requests in a specified format ("zoning *and* Westchester" or "architects *not* Pei") and can limit his selection in other ways. A fair amount of button-pressing may prove irritating to the novice; still, it's faster than going to the library.

The Times Information Bank is an institutional service, and for the foreseeable future will remain one. Rothman doesn't envision selling the bank's data as a package, for example. A video-disc player won't be sophisticated enough to run the search software, and a personal computer would require too much peripheral gear to be practical; then there is the problem of updating. What keeps the service expensive is labor costs: the Times adds twenty thousand abstracts a month, a task which requires twenty-five full-time indexers and freelance help.

It will take many years before computer programs are sophisticated enough to replace the human indexers at the *Times*. A number of abstract services now operating in industry, government and professional societies handle material in technical or other specialized fields. While they, like the *Times*, have automated much of the subsequent production process, they still use people to compose abstracts and choose index headings (unlike the *Times*, they can also save money by having authors write their own abstracts).

As a pioneering venture, the Times Information Bank took some time getting to market. While some 1,100 organizations subscribe to the service and Rothman says the Bank's future is now secure, he also adds, "Selling an information service is terribly difficult because most people can't define the cost/benefit of having an information resource directly available. They still say, 'I'll send Susie to the library.' "

The *Times* reaches one special audience; a service called The Source, which opened during the summer of 1979, reaches another. To tap The Source you need either a terminal or a personal computer. The terminal people tend to be corporate customers, who make up a minority of The Source's clientele. The rest are the small businessmen and professionals who have turned out to be the prime market for personal computers. Since many of these people live above the store, the machines perform light housekeeping duties on the side. Thus The Source is tailored for a mixture of personal and professional uses.

The service offers time-sharing, electronic mail and a variety of data at extremely low rates ($4.25 for an hour of connect time) during off-peak hours; during the normal business day The Source costs $15 an hour. There is a rather steep hookup fee of $100. The Source, unlike Prestel, doesn't sell advertising space; it invites information providers to participate in exchange for a percentage of their data revenues. Since it holds only current material and hasn't the cross-indexing of the Times Bank, The Source is better suited for quick information than serious research.

The Times Bank is one of The Source's providers, with a daily news summary and a consumer data base. The most elaborate news feature, however, is the entire UPI wire—national news, international news, business, sports, weather and syndicated columns. (This is useful to those of us who lie awake all night worrying about the Middle East, and to Washingtonians who want more detailed information about Chicago than the *Post* will tell them; and it certainly makes everybody feel important.) The Source also includes price information on stocks, commodities, precious metals and foreign exchange, and tax data. There are a handful of educational programs for college, high school and elementary school students, wine and restaurant guides, games and horoscopes.

Response to The Source was enthusiastic, but in its first year of operation it experienced serious management problems that affected the quality of service. *Reader's Digest* bought a substantial interest in the company, which may provide a brighter future.

To people who have proved their receptiveness to electronic information by acquiring a computer, the service's appeal is undeniable; whether anyone would buy a machine just to get The Source is another question ("The fact that we exist pushes some people over the line," says one Source executive). In all the computer community there is no group more passionate than the personal-computer people: at the 1979 National Computer Conference their plenary sessions sounded like a revival meeting, with one believer after another rising to tell stories of civilians, mostly wives and children, who came to scoff and stayed to program. The preacher, a bubbly Texan named Dr. Portia Isaacson, asked the congregation whether it thought the personal computer was just "an electronic hula hoop"; most of the speakers cited useful or socially beneficial applications to show that it wasn't, while one man allowed that even if it was, what was wrong with that?

At present, zeal discounted, all these people are right: that is, anyone who cares enough about the computer to learn programming may find it invaluable in his work or hobby, but canned programs for novices restrict the user mostly to game playing and personal accounting chores that can be done as easily and much cheaper with pencil and paper and a $10 calculator. The shortage of useful software packages is the personal computer's current weakness; that should change soon. As content becomes richer—more programs that are attractive and easy to use, more services like The Source with cleverer types of information—more people will be willing to invest in computers.

Indeed, for all home information systems, the problem is getting people to buy the hardware; once they have the gear, if one kind of data doesn't hook them, another will. Vendors and market researchers embrace three theories about how consumers will come to purchase the necessary equipment: the "sidling-up" theory, the "demographic" theory, and the "new-generation" theory, which complement each other.

The sidling-up theory holds that people will buy computer-based equipment to extend something they are already spending money on: the television set, the stereo, the telephone, the thermostat, the burglar alarm. A leading proponent of this theory is Quantum Sciences, which in 1978 did a multiclient study of the market for electronics-based consumer entertainment and information systems. Among other research, the study included some two hundred interviews with consumers around the country, conducted mostly through panel discussions. While occupations varied—one panel included both an insurance underwriter and a chef—the panelists tended to be in their thirties and forties, with middle income and at least some college education, the sort of people one would expect to be receptive consumers but not trend-setters.

Quantum came up with several purchasing patterns, each of which would evolve into a home information system. A consumer might, for example, want better and more convenient television programming: he would then invest in a videotape recorder, a videodisc player, or cable TV (or several of these), then buy some package of information services using the TV set as a display unit, and finally perhaps attach a personal computer. Or he might follow the "controls" pattern: an automated thermostat, computer-based fire, smoke and burglar alarms, or security and emergency warning systems operated via cable television. Instead, he might spring for more elaborate telephone service—message-recording, call-forwarding, abbreviated dialing and so forth—which would lead to a push-button telephone and then a display telephone with a memory unit. And this would evolve to viewdata, a home printer and scanner, banking and shopping at home, and electronic mail.

Most people in the industry cite the energy problem as a catalyst for the spread of home information systems. While the study bears this out, it doesn't suggest an imminent fad for automated thermostats and home appliance controls; the panelists' first instinct was to save gas by investing in home entertainment products. Since videotape recorders were still expensive and several panelists criticized current network programming, the first step on the road appeared to be cable TV. Panelists wanted shopping and banking at home only if they could have paper receipts; this suggests a market for home printers.

The exemplar of the sidling-up theory is Warner Communications, whose two-way cable television system, Qube, has been operating in Columbus, Ohio, since December 1977. Interactive cable was the first technology touted for bringing computer power into the home; Qube received a lot of publicity, particularly during the summer of 1979, when the system supplied instant subscriber response to President Carter's energy speech. Qube provides thirty channels of which ten are regular television, ten are premium entertainment (movies and sports events, offered with a fee for each viewing), and ten are "community," carrying programs that range from local town meetings to a Columbus imitation of the "Today Show."

Each subscriber's television set is hooked up to the computer at Qube's studio, which pools subscribers for billing and Warner's own market research; more important, it receives and tallies viewers' responses to questions posed on the community television programs. The viewers respond by pressing one of five buttons on a keypad. Columbus viewers have been asked all sorts of questions: Do you want a copy of our free booklet? Do you want this comedian to continue his act? Are you more confident about the president's ability to lead the nation? Are you in favor of this revision of the zoning laws? Who should win the Oscar for supporting actor? Local colleges offer courses for credit, during which the professor can take attendance and ask questions of individual students.

Qube is a popular feature: within the first-year and a half, 29,000 of the 37,000 Columbus households receiving cable chose to pay the extra $3.45 a month for premium and interactive TV. The service includes shopping from the American Express catalog and an additional burglar-fire-medical alarm package, which warns both the residents and the appropriate authorities. What Qube didn't offer until recently, however, was a Prestel or Source-like information feature. "We find people like entertainment they can't get on regular television," says Gustave Hauser, chairman of Warner Amex Cable Communications, the joint venture of Warner and American Express which now provides Qube service. "Ohio State football games that aren't on television draw a fifty-five or sixty percent share. 'Adult' movies are popular, and action movies, and old movies. Culture is not an overwhelming winner. Voting on public issues is extremely popular; those who care are devoted. But information retrieval is complex. First you establish what they understand: movies, then sports, education, culture. You don't start with the exotic, you build a ladder with things people can relate to."

Both Quantum and AT&T advance the demographic theory, which points to the changing needs of a population in which, as AT&T's Sullivan notes, "Women make up forty-one percent of the labor force, fifty-one percent of wives work, and twelve percent of the households are headed by single people." This adds up to lots of well-heeled, educated people who aren't home very often, and thus need more elaborate security, more efficient ways to run their households, and better means of keeping in touch with each other— that is, remote-controlled ovens, extended telephone service and tax information on viewdata. The demographic trends that take some people out of the home could bring others back, however: thus the widely touted egalitarian married couples who each spend a few days at home working at their personal computer and minding their fewer and deferred children. This fits in with the need to save gas. As D. Weston Boyd, a marketing manager on Sullivan's staff, reports, "One concrete thing we've found in our market studies is this: the most precious commodity for people today is time, not money. People want ways of freeing up time."

The Quantum study conveys a strong impression of consumer ambivalence toward tomorrow's technology. The panelists find a number of conveniences appealing, and make wistful remarks like "I would like a sensor that would turn the lights off when you walked out of a room. That would be marvelous." On the other hand, the report on one panel notes, ". . . the concept of a totally automated home, including control of its heat and appliances was met with strong resistance. Dehumanization, distrust of electronic devices and possible system failure were cited. . . ."

While panelists were widely enthusiastic about educational applications, older parents wanted their children to learn to use the traditional library first, while younger parents weren't troubled by notions of electronic spoon-feeding. This encourages the "new-generation" theory, usually cited by more pessimistic industry people: home information systems won't catch on till the end of the decade, when a new generation of consumers comes of age, people who grew up with computers in school and aren't intimidated by them.

So we will probably sidle up and our children will plunge in. As for corporations, the older ones sidle up and the younger ones plunge in. Each sees the future in terms of its particular interests. In September 1979, for example, IBM launched a joint venture with MCA to make and sell videodiscs and disc players; the announced plans for DiscoVision, as the new venture was called, were somewhat vague, but Cary and MCA's chairman expressed interest in home entertainment as well as industrial education. IBM has had a hard time figuring out its niche in the home market, however. A technical man who is a long-time habitué of task forces on new technology says, "We've had innumerable task forces on home information systems. Each one comes up with a list of sixty applications and none of them would keep you awake at night. The equipment can be done cheaper and better by other companies; what could IBM offer that's unique? As for just selling data banks, the task forces disband on that one. It's not clear what will happen with the MCA venture. We started looking at the home market back in the doldrum days when there was idle capacity at the Fishkill plant, and whenever there's a recession we think about it again. Then business picks up, and we don't have the plant capacity to grind it all out, and we decide to stick to what we do best.

"While people are hung up on education for their kids, and will spend unreasonable amounts of money for it, the prime justification for information systems is business, and after that most other things fall out. I think companies will pay for equipment in employees' homes, so they commute less.

"All the big companies are looking at home information applications, but nobody has a real swinger. The one who makes it go is going to be some guy in a garage, not IBM."

It's no surprise that the IBM'er thinks working-at-home will be the wedge, an unpopular prediction among officials of consumer-minded companies. An AT&T man, however, is prey to surprisingly similar fears. "If people take the modular approach and start buying separate pieces of equipment, one gadget to turn off the oven, another for the burglar alarm, and a third to get information on the TV screen," he says, "and all the equipment works through the telephone, you're going to have electrical chaos. So you'll have to bring in some kind of microcomputer controller to sit between the telephone and the gadgets and act as a traffic cop. Perhaps we will make this. Besides controlling the gadgets it may do other kinds of computing.

"We've got all these different technologies that either compete with or complement each other. In the consumer goods business everything depends on the distribution channels, how products are priced and marketed. Videodiscs could go into libraries or be sold in supermarkets or by publishers. If someone gambled on the learning curve and decided to sell videodiscs for $1.75 it would change everything. So we're all whistling in the dark. Deep down we think it won't be IBM or AT&T that makes home systems go. It will be somebody like Finast supermarkets."

ELECTRONIC BANKING

Some years ago computer people and reporters used to talk about the "cashless, checkless society," a vigorous phrase which has been largely abandoned, partly because it was imprecise (we will never get rid of cash, most bankers avow, and checks will be around, in declining proportions, for many decades). Electronic Funds Transfer—shortened to EFT—is the new bland but accurate name for checkless banking. It means what it says—the substitution of an electronic impulse for a piece of paper as the instrument that moves money from debtor to creditor.

The information that John Jones has $3,000 in his checking account is stored in the bank's computer; via a terminal or a reel of magnetic tape the computer is told to deduct $20 from Jones's account and pay it to J. C. Penney's; the deduction is made, and the information travels over the communications lines to the computer in Penney's bank, which credits the store's account with Jones's $20. While there are many variations to this procedure, today's checks and tomorrow's EFT payment both represent the exchange of information. Bankers, legislators, regulatory agencies and consumer groups have been asking many questions about EFT. The questions concern how that information can be made secure and authoritative, what path the information will travel, and who will develop, own, pay for and profit from the systems that bear the information.

Batch-processing EFT applications stem from the banks' eagerness to eliminate the costly, labor-intensive job of processing checks. What James Jacquette, a vice-president of the Chase Manhattan Bank, calls "the applications that can go on while you're asleep" include automatic payroll deposit (instead of handing you your paycheck, your company instructs the bank to credit your account once a week) and preauthorized bill payment (instead of mailing a check to Con Edison, you tell the bank to credit the utility's account and debit yours). Because these transactions aren't instantaneous and the consumer doesn't come face-to-face with any machine more futuristic than his own telephone, they are a bit less intimidating than terminal-based EFT. Most of the benefits of this group of applications, however, accrue to banks and businesses, which can cut operating expenses. But since the new procedures had to be made palatable to the consumer to gain acceptance, the banks have come up with some attractive services.

The more visible brand of EFT involves banking through a computer terminal either after hours or off the premises or both. While the banks began installing the terminals primarily to woo the consumer, cost-saving motives have become increasingly important. Since this type of transaction is accomplished immediately and since consumers must deal directly with the eccentricities and impersonality of the equipment, it has met more resistance than the other kind of EFT. One group of applications can proceed without the other.

Banks have been heavy and often innovative users of computers and communications for nearly three decades. The distinctive magnetic ink identification numbers at the bottom of checks are the result of ERMA, a system for automated reading and sorting developed for the Bank of America by Stanford Research Institute and built by General Electric in 1956; ERMA, five years in the making, is considered a landmark in the history of computing. Banks have been transferring funds via telecommunications since 1950, when the Bank Wire System, a teletype link managed by Western Union, was established to join 142 institutions. In the sixties, however, many bankers felt that despite the efficiencies introduced by the use of computers in processing checks, the paper payment system would soon be overloaded and the banks would be faced with the same back office problems that were plaguing Wall Street. In 1968 banks in California began looking into the possibility of automated clearing houses, which would handle interbank funds transfer electronically. But EFT proceeded slowly at first, mostly under the aegis of operations executives. It was unclear whether their fears about the paper system were justified.

In 1970 the American Bankers Association hired Arthur D. Little, the Boston consulting firm, to investigate the sturdiness of the nation's checking procedures; ADL concluded that the paper system would hold up nicely until 1980, by which time the number of checks processed would double, reaching a volume of some $45 billion a year. From then on, its future was uncertain. Certainly the costs of the system would zoom, and ADL suggested that bankers make the most of the next ten years to experiment with EFT. Still, automated clearing house research continued to drag during the early seventies. Individual banks, however, were testing remote computer applications—the "wired nation" was a popular topic in the press. A service called In-Touch, offered by a subsidiary of Seattle– First National Bank, represented wired-nation banking at its most futuristic. For $6.50 a month, the subscriber could rent a template that fit over his Touch-tone telephone, through which he could key in checkless payment of bills to local retailers, utilities and fuel companies. The package included other services, too: there was a printout of household expenditures, a report of tax-deductible expenses, a retrievable file of insurance policy, credit card and household appliance numbers, and even a reminder service to warn the customer that his mother-in-law's birthday was coming up. The customer could use his Touch-tone phone as a calculator.

While droves of banks called Seattle-First to ask about licensing agreements, In-Touch was unable to attract enough customers or merchants to survive. In 1973 too few citizens of Seattle had Touch-tone telephones, and those who did found the system expensive and complicated.

Another remote banking service caused an even bigger sensation. In Lincoln, Nebraska, First Federal Savings and Loan—an institution of little renown in the banking community—installed IBM terminals in two Hinky Dinky supermarkets. The bank's depositors received a plastic card just like an ordinary credit card, with their identification numbers encoded on a magnetic stripe. They took the card to a special booth next to the checkout counter at the Hinky Dinky, filled out a ticket with the sum of money they wished to withdraw or deposit, handed the ticket and the plastic card to the Hinky Dinky clerk in the booth, and recited a memorized identification number which matched the number coded on the magnetic stripe. The clerk, as a further security measure, had a card of her own; she inserted both cards in the terminal and keyed in the amount of the transaction. After receiving verification from the bank's computer, the clerk opened the cash drawer and either gave the customer the money he needed—enough, perhaps, to buy groceries at Hinky Dinky and do the rest of the day's shopping—or accepted his deposit.

Was Hinky Dinky in the banking business? No, said First Federal, and the assertion was later upheld in court. When a customer withdrew $100 at the supermarket the bank's computer deducted it from the customer's account and paid it to Hinky Dinky's account; Hinky Dinky simply delivered the money to the customer. In case of a deposit, the savings and loan debited Hinky Dinky and credited the customer, who reimbursed the supermarket. A customer who wanted to open a new account had to travel to the bank. An official of First Federal later told a conference of the American Bankers Association that while a similar transaction at the teller's window inside First Federal cost $2.00 to process, the Hinky Dinky transaction cost the bank $.05. It was cheap because the bank already had an internal on-line computer system. The customer had the advantages of an interest-bearing account at a savings and loan combined with convenience that surpassed that of a checking account. The commercial banks were furious.

The Hinky Dinky project was temporarily shut down when the state attorney general, several commercial banks and competing savings and loans filed lawsuits; the lawsuits were unsuccessful and the terminals were turned on again to do a thriving business. The project had a dramatic effect on the banking community. The Nebraska Bankers Association, realizing that court challenges were futile, set out in short order to develop an EFT transmission and switching system which would enable commercial banks to compete with savings and loans. EFT became the subject of speeches, articles and conferences for bankers all over the country; competition between savings and commercial banks was a far more powerful spur than the prospect of operating economies. By the mid-seventies, it had become apparent that EFT presented a tangle of regulatory issues within the banking industry, in the intersection of communications and data processing, and in consumer protection. In 1974 Congress established a National Commission on Electronic Fund Transfers, but in the tradition of panels that study controversial matters it took two years to get it staffed and ready to work; the commission's report, delivered in October 1977, took a wait-and-see position on every issue except consumer protection, which it said required prompt lawmaking.

Two leading New York banks have been exploring EFT for some years, and the direction of their efforts sheds some light on the issues raised by electronic banking. "In 1966," says John Reed, the executive vice-president who heads Citicorp's consumer operations, "Walter Wriston had GE's think tank do a study of future developments that would affect the banking business. They said we should get into computers somehow. So we looked at the computer industry—it was back in the go-go days when anything seemed possible, and for about three hours we even talked about buying a computer manufacturer. We knew the computer would have a significant effect on the way we deal with customers, both corporate and consumer. But we came to believe that although computer networks would bring about fundamental changes in the way corporations move money, these changes wouldn't be important enough to the corporations to alter their relations with us: architecting loan agreements is what gets us the business of company X, not our computer network. A consumer, on the other hand, chooses a bank by the services it offers."

Unlike many smaller banks, whose more limited resources force them to embark on joint ventures, Citicorp believes in fierce competition in EFT technology as well as services. It walks alone; it can afford to. The bank formed its own research and development subsidiary, Transaction Technology, Inc., which began work on a terminal to automate credit card verification. When a pilot program led Citicorp management to doubt the security of the magnetic stripe used on credit cards, the chairman of TTI went to Cal Tech and offered $15,000 worth of prizes to students who could devise a technique for defrauding a magnetic stripe credit card system. The students found twenty-two ways to foil the mag stripe. While other banks were not amused and continued to work with magnetic stripe technology, Citicorp developed its own proprietary encoding technique. In all, the corporation has spent more than $150 million on hardware and software to improve its consumer services through electronic banking.

The rising costs of labor and real estate have made it increasingly difficult to make a profit from consumer banking, particularly in New York City. In 1977, Citibank stepped up its installation of automated teller machines through New York City and some of its suburbs. After a year's time Richard Kovacevich, the bank vice-president in charge of the program, was reporting that more than two-thirds of all cash withdrawals were made at the machines, and that while the terminals were open twenty-four hours a day (their main selling point), some 40 percent of usage occurred during normal banking hours; that means that a significant number of customers chose the machine over a human teller.

Citibank is also enthusiastic about a machine called the Universal Teller System, which speeds up business at the human teller's window. The terminal can handle more than a hundred different transactions: if, for example, a customer comes in with a check for $275 and asks to buy an $85 money order, make a $100 payment on a loan, deposit $10 in a checking account and $20 in a savings account, and take the balance in cash, the teller can do it all in a few seconds without getting up; the machine will figure out how much cash is due and spew it forth. This application, of course, is not EFT, but it fits into Citibank's policy of visibly using computers to streamline customer service while trimming labor costs.

Chase Manhattan Bank has also been active in EFT, but its attitudes and policies are quite different from those of Citibank. Chase was the initiator of the Bank Wire System in 1950 and remains its heaviest user; it was also instrumental in the development of the CHIPS computer system, through which New York Clearing House banks transfer large sums of money among themselves and internationally. Like Citibank, Chase also flirted with the idea of producing its own computers: back in the fifties, the bank was dissatisfied with the equipment the vendors were selling, and it began to work, in cooperation with MIT, on a computer system called "The Goddess of the Chase." "The Goddess never did get finished," says Donald Hollis, a bank vice-president. "We decided we were in the banking business, not the computer business. So we shifted our emphasis to preparing ourselves for automation."

In the early seventies Chase began to experiment with various types of EFT; it ended up with an opposite set of enthusiasms from Citibank's. An early experiment with automated teller machines in Grand Central Station aborted; the machines were expensive and didn't do enough business to make a profit. Recently the Chase has begun installing machines again; the hardware is cheaper now, but Hollis remains skeptical. "I still question the payback on these machines," he says. "But the competition has them, and there are some consumers who actually prefer using the machine. I personally doubt if we'd put them in otherwise."

Both Citibank and the Chase perform what is called "merchant services," which include leasing terminals to retailers for Master-Card, Visa and check authorization. In a credit card authorization, the data goes from the retailer to his bank to Visa and back again; Visa then bills the customer's bank, which bills the customer. For larger retailers, however, Chase has integrated this procedure with the store's own computer system, so that credit authorization can be performed through the same terminal and communications lines that do inventory control. This method is more efficient and reliable, and Chase officials believe that many merchants will not tolerate a bat-tery of terminals for different purposes; space is cramped and clerks balk at mastering the intricacies of several different kinds of equip-ment. Chase, then, sells the merchant custom-built software which connects him to the bank's computers. In this business it preceded Citibank.

Chase has also been active in developing preauthorized payments systems which aid corporations in trimming operating expenses. Since 1972, for example, the bank has enjoyed an arrangement with Equitable Life in which Equitable sends Chase a monthly tape con-taining the names of its policyholders. The bank weeds out the names of those who bank at Chase and electronically debits their accounts for the amount of the premium payment.

This kind of preauthorized payment, called a "standing order," originates with the company that's doing the billing. The reverse of that transaction, initiated by the customer, is telephone bill-paying, a service which has grown nicely since shorn of the expensive, compli-cated extras that marked its unsuccessful ancestor in Seattle. Accord-ing to James Jacquette, the Chase vice-president who deals with this application, two hundred financial institutions across the country were offering telephone bill-payment services by 1979, and that number would at least double by the end of 1980; there were some twenty million bill-payment transactions by telephone during 1979 (that's less than half of 1 percent of all consumer remittances). Since large companies are now getting quantities of incompatible data from different banks telling who paid what bills in Boston, New York and Chicago, Chase is selling them a middleman service to manage the data.

Many of today's batch EFT transactions, Jacquette says, are actu-ally hybrids of paper and electronics. If, for example, technical or legal roadblocks made it impossible to begin an Equitable-type transaction with a reel of tape, the consumer may authorize Equitable to make out a monthly payment check in his name. Chase also processes share drafts, the equivalent of checks for consumers who join credit unions; the consumer sends the draft to the electric company to pay his bill; the electric company deposits the draft in its own bank, which forwards it to the Chase; the Chase destroys the check and transfers its contents electronically to the credit union. Instead of a canceled check, the consumer gets back a descriptive statement with the serial number of his payment, which the IRS accepts as proof. Just truncating the paper payment process saves costs for the credit unions.

The hybrid nature of many EFT systems and the different approaches of Citibank and the Chase suggest that EFT will continue to develop piecemeal and coexist with checks for some time to come. While Arthur D. Little's estimate of the number of checks processed in 1980 was near-target, the system didn't break down. The government, through direct deposit of payroll and Social Security payments, converted a fair number of checks to EFT, and direct payroll deposit has begun to catch on among corporations, too. On the other hand, Dennis Opicka of the American Bankers Association says direct deposit of paychecks and Social Security has increased people's feeling of financial security, causing them to write more personal checks than before; so might EFT terminals for check authorization. In 1980 the paper system was still, as the bureaucreats say, viable, mostly because technology has given us better equipment for reading and sorting checks. "We won't wake up one day and find there are no checks," Opicka says. "But there has to be some saturation point. We want EFT to keep down the increase in check-writing."

At first the banks had installed automated teller or cash dispenser machines to gain competitive advantage; the pioneer's increase in market share, however, had dissipated promptly once other local banks followed suit. Now, according to several market studies, banks install the machines primarily to cut costs by off-loading expensive branch transactions. But despite Citibank's experience, most of the automated tellers are still used to withdraw cash after regular banking hours.

The main reason EFT in general has moved slowly is that consumers have had serious reservations about it; some of these have been answered by recent laws, while others haven't. In November 1978 Congress passed the Electronic Funds Transfer Act. According to this law, banks must inform consumers of their rights and responsibilities at the time they contract for EFT service. The consumer gets a receipt for every transaction he makes at an EFT terminal, and a monthly statement describing his EFT disbursements; like canceled checks, these documents are legal proof that he has paid a bill. The act specifies procedures for resolving errors, giving the consumer use of the disputed amount of money while the bank's investigation is under way. If the bank concludes it didn't make an error, it must give the consumer a copy of all the documents that influenced this decision.

Customers have been justifiably worried about their liability for unauthorized transfers; a thief who gets hold of his victim's EFT card and the personal identification number (PIN, in banking lingo) that activates it could drain a bank account in short order. The PIN is supposed to be a safety device; at the hearings on the EFT Act, bankers and consumer advocates differed over how safe it really is. The PIN is often a number or code name chosen by the consumer; to jog their memories, people pick a birthdate or some other item of personal significance, and then treat it like a citizen-band radio handle which they proudly disclose to neighbors and coworkers. When, on the other hand, the bank assigns a random combination of numbers with no convenient mnemonic, people tend to write it on a piece of paper they keep handy in their wallets with the card; some people even write the PIN directly on the card. The banks felt consumers who have been negligent should be fully liable for unauthorized transfers; the consumer advocates wanted the banks to find a better security device than the PIN. If, as a study made in Wisconsin suggested, half of all consumers disregard bank warnings and keep their PIN with their cards, this behavior no longer constitutes negligence. The reason banks like the PIN, of course, is that it's cheap.

Lawmakers wanted to balance the risks to move banks away from PINs and give consumers some reason, meanwhile, not to be careless. Thus the consumer's liability is limited to $50 unless he fails to report the loss or theft of the card within two days after he discovers it; after that he is liable for up to $500 unless he's been in hospital or on the road. In all cases the burden of proof is on the bank.

The act prohibits certain kinds of compulsory EFT and allows others. While it is illegal to condition the extension of credit on a consumer's repayment by preauthorized transfer, landlords and other businesses may require customers to pay their bills by EFT. A company may insist on paying its employees by direct-deposit EFT, but it can't tell them where to bank; the same conditions apply to government benefits.

The plastic card that activates automated tellers and check-guarantee terminals is commonly known as a debit card. A few years ago many people in the banking community believed the debit card would also replace checks as a means of paying stores for on-the-spot purchases. The customer wouldn't need cash when shopping out of the neighborhood, while the merchant wouldn't have to choose between taking a risk and losing a sale. The banks hoped to get consumers accustomed to the card by using it first in automated teller machines (where instantaneous debit yielded cash-on-the-spot) and check-authorization terminals in stores.

Consumers, however, didn't want to move to the next step: between checks—now more readily accepted with the authorization terminals—and credit cards, their shopping needs were satisfied. An important reason for their resistance was that debit cards lack some attractive features of the paper system. When the consumer gets a used car home and discovers it's a lemon, he wants to be able to stop payment. He has this leeway for a few days while his check is clearing; an EFT debit affords him just the rest of the day before the transfer is accomplished (real-time debiting is not yet technologically feasible). Consumer activists wanted a reversibility provision in the EFT Act, but they lost to the retailers and didn't get it.

Instantaneous debit also eliminates "float," the use of one's money while a check is clearing. Most consumers occasionally write a check exceeding their balance, knowing they can deposit funds to cover the check the next day (corporations manage their finances using sophisticated float optimization techniques that are sometimes ethically questionable). Float is costly to the banks and the Federal Reserve, and it is understandable that financial institutions want to reduce it; bankers pettishly but not inaccurately point out that float is a windfall benefit, not a consumer right. There are ways of building float and reversibility into an EFT system; it will be interesting to see whether bankers or consumers win this tug-of-war. The features might become a competitive device to attract business; they could be offered as an extra service, for a fee. The worst consumer fear is that depositors will be charged such high fees for choosing checks over EFT that the "choice" will be a sham. It seems unlikely that the price of checks will zoom until EFT is very widely accepted; in the more distant future, however, checks could become a luxury.

Security and privacy also worry consumers. Since EFT systems would contain considerable information about an individual's activities, privacy is a serious concern; it is part of the larger privacy problem that includes governmental, medical and educational information systems as well as the financial ones.

Most consumer security risks are addressed by the EFT Act's liability and error provision; the banks have to eat losses derived from embezzlement. Computer crime is a hierarchy that ranges from a teller's simple manipulation of small amounts of money to highly sophisticated capers requiring programming skill. Donn Parker, a senior management systems consultant at SRI International, is widely acknowledged to be the leading authority in the field; he has spent most of the last decade trying to alert citizens, particularly executives, to the seriousness of computer security problems. Parker is quite optimistic about security at the bottom of the hierarchy. "The more we automate banking," he says, "the safer it becomes for the consumer. I spoke to a prisoner who had been head teller at the Union Dime Bank in New York. He had manipulated up to fifty accounts through an on-line terminal to keep the shortages hidden. He'd have been caught sooner by a computer security system which had simple controls in it to analyze the pattern of transactions teller by teller. His activities would have stuck out like a sore thumb."

"The credit card companies are already using this kind of control," Parker says. "There are highly cost-effective solutions which use the power of the computer to detect deviations. The high incidence/low loss fraud cases are mainly a people problem. With more automation you give fewer people positions of trust and shine a brigher light on them. It's better than before, when we had rooms full of clerks."

For the next few years it will be difficult for banks to force EFT payment systems on reluctant consumers; they will have to persuade us all that EFT is more than a mixed blessing. If they are mostly successful, it may become difficult for the minority of consumers to hold out.

ARTIFICIAL INTELLIGENCE

"°(INTERPRET RIGHTWING)
INPUT TEXT: The United States Congress voted to fund the Trident submarine project.
(1) Q: What did the US Congress do this for?
    A: THE UNITED STATES CONGRESS WANTS THE UNITED STATES ARMED FORCES TO BE STRONGER.
(2) Q: Why should the US be stronger?
    A: THE UNITED STATES ARMED FORCES SHOULD BE STRONG TO STOP COMMUNIST EXPANSION.
(3) Q: What should the US do if Russia builds submarines?
    A: THE UNITED STATES SHOULD BUILD MORE SUBMARINES."

"°(INTERPRET LEFTWING)
INPUT TEXT: The United States Congress voted to fund the Trident submarine project.
(1) Q: What did the United States Congress do this for?
    A: THE UNITED STATES CONGRESS FEARED FALLING BEHIND IN THE ARMS RACE.
(2) Q: What will Russia do next?
    A: RUSSIA WILL PROBABLY BUILD MORE WEAPONS.
(3) Q: What should the US do if Russia builds submarines?
    A: THE UNITED STATES SHOULD NEGOTIATE WITH RUSSIA TO STOP THE ARMS RACE."

The dialogue above was produced by POLITICS, a product of the Yale Artificial Intelligence Project. POLITICS, as described by its author, Jaime Carbonell, Jr., is "a system of computer programs which simulate humans in comprehending and responding to world events from a given political or ideological perspective." Artificial intelligence research, the most exotic and controversial branch of computer science, attempts to duplicate human intellectual processes on computers in hopes of learning more about how people think. Not surprisingly, such work has been the target of criticism on both economic-intellectual grounds (AI will never achieve its goals, and is therefore wasting research dollars: machines can't think the way people do) and moral ones (even if AI could achieve its goals, it shouldn't; the better a system like POLITICS gets, the worse it gets).

Even if the researchers never fulfill their grandiose aspirations, they are beginning to produce practical and effective programs whose influence will be felt in the world at large; it is time to take them seriously. Some programs carry a frightening potential for misuse; others are benign and helpful; and still others suggest that AI techniques may bring computer systems a new humanity—in the better sense of the word. To approach computers rationally we must confront the Frankenstein issue, which strikes an emotional chord in laymen and computer people alike. Thinking is evidence of man's immortal soul; to design a thinking machine is to show a hubris that will be punished; we derive comfort from the thought of our own uniqueness. At the same time, being contradictory animals, we reach out for a way to explain it all: there is some security in being able to reduce the workings of the mind to predictable 1's and 0's. Thus many debates about artificial intelligence carry an undercurrent of hysteria.

Discussions of AI often begin with the question of how we can tell a machine is thinking. The best-known test was proposed in 1950, some five years before computer technology had proceeded far enough to make that question more academic; Alan Turing, the late British mathematician, suggested it in an essay called "Computing Machinery and Intelligence." Turing's test was a game which, however elegantly described, much resembles the familiar television panel show called "To Tell the Truth," in which three contestants, two of whom are ringers, try to convince Kitty Carlisle and other TV notables that they are the real intrepid deep-sea diver or expert on fifteenth-century Chinese art; the panelists, by clever questioning, try to trap the two ringers, who receive prize money if they can fool the panel. For the Turing version, imagine Carlisle sitting in a room isolated from the contestants, with a typewriter in front of her. There are two contestants, a computer and a human being; each wants Carlisle to think it (or he) is the human. Carlisle types out her questions and hands them to a courier, who delivers them to the contestants and returns with typed answers. Like Turing's interrogator, Carlisle might start by asking the contestants questions about mathematics and chess, but suppose she moved on to this question, suggested in Turing's essay:

> Q: Please write me a sonnet on the subject of the Forth Bridge. (Let literary license permit Carlisle this Anglicism.)
> A: Count me out on this one. I never could write poetry.

Did that answer come from a human or a computer?

MIT's Seymour Papert suggests that Turing's essay was "a serious joke. He was pulling people's leg. There's no simple answer to the question 'What is intelligence?' but there are no profound mysteries either; we have ways of finding out whether a person is intelligent, and we do the same thing with a computer. Certainly we can't poke it with a pin."

Papert and his colleagues bristle at what they call the "superhuman human fallacy"—the argument that a computer is not "thinking" unless it can best Bobby Fischer at chess, compose *The Rite of Spring*, or write a sonnet on the Forth Bridge. Most people can't do any of these things, and no one can do all of them; and since people often make mistakes of fact and errors of judgment, computers should be allowed to do the same.

The Turing test can sometimes prove misleading, as Dr. Joseph Weizenbaum, a former artificial intelligence researcher, found out. When Weizenbaum came to MIT in 1963, he was interested in the problem of communication between man and machine: the possibility of enabling laymen to query computers without learning a special programming language seemed (and still does seem) a worthy and useful goal. The ability to carry on a conversation with a human being would also be a hallmark of intelligent machine behavior.

Weizenbaum wanted to start simply, to see how far he could go in constructing a program that conversed in natural language without the complicated sentence-parsing that characterized most research in the field. To carry on an intelligent conversation in most subjects a computer would need a fund of information about the world, and Weizenbaum wanted to avoid the problems of feeding knowledge into the machine. There was one type of discourse in which one of the participants might claim to know nothing about the subject at hand without seeming unintelligent: the Rogerian psychiatric interview. If, as Weizenbaum noted later, the patient were to tell the psychiatrist, "I went for a long boat ride," and the psychiatrist answered, "Tell me about boats," the patient would not criticize his ignorance but assume there was a purpose to the query; this assumption, Weizenbaum was careful to point out, was entirely in the *speaker's* mind, but was highly useful to the programmer. There were further attractions to programming the computer to act as a psychiatrist. Other AI researchers spent years playing with sentences like "The boy hit the ball," a prospect Weizenbaum found utterly boring. The psychiatrist idea appealed to his puckish sense of humor. "There's a lot of the con man in me," he says. "Why not have some fun?"

So Weizenbaum designed a clever program called ELIZA, named after the heroine of Shaw's *Pygmalion*. Once ELIZA learned to impersonate the psychiatrist, Weizenbaum planned to teach her to simulate other occupations. ELIZA was designed to react to certain keywords that might be used by a psychiatric patient: the word "mother," for example, triggered the response, "Tell me more about your family." The program had a repertoire of psychiatric conversational techniques: it could transform the patient's statement into a question, and if keyword methods failed, it knew bluffing phrases that would move the conversation along. It performed impressively: here is a sample, taken from a paper of Weizenbaum's:

Patient: Men are all alike.
ELIZA: In what way
Patient: They're always bugging us about something or other.
ELIZA: Can you think of a specific example
Patient: Well, my boyfriend made me come here.
ELIZA: Your boyfriend made you come here
Patient: He says I'm depressed much of the time.
ELIZA: I am sorry to hear you are depressed
Patient: It's true. I am unhappy.
ELIZA: What would it mean to you if you got some help
Patient: Perhaps I could learn to get along with my mother.
ELIZA: Tell me more about your family

As Weizenbaum began to demonstrate his program, he encountered a frightening response. While he preceded every demonstration with an explanation that ELIZA was just an experiment in natural language communication, visitors often behaved as if the program were a real psychiatrist. One day Weizenbaum brought in a distinguished psychology professor, expecting the man to be amused by ELIZA's life-like response; within a few minutes, the psychologist had told the program of his grief at his father's death. Weizenbaum's secretary had watched the birth of the program and was fully aware of his goals; given a seat at the terminal, she asked her boss to leave her in privacy. "Sometimes people switched modes," Weizenbaum remembers. "They would start out in a spirit of fun, telling ELIZA that 'A little green man is following me.' Then suddenly they would change to 'I have always hated my sister.' "

Weizenbaum was even more disturbed by the irresponsible reactions of psychiatrists who came to see the program. "They told me that with ELIZA we could treat a hundred patients an hour at state hospitals," he says. "I concluded that many psychiatrists are doing no more than what ELIZA does. I was shocked at how easily people are fooled." While Weizenbaum's success encouraged other efforts in automated psychiatry, he himself has become AI's most eloquent critic. In 1976 he wrote a book entitled *Computer Power and Human Reason*, which called for an end to the glorification of technology in modern society, using AI research as an illustration of the moral dangers of scientism.

ELIZA was not a psychiatrist; it was a natural language program, and a highly primitive one at that, as Weizenbaum eagerly admits. Yet it played the Turing game most convincingly (a similar effort, designed at Stanford, is PARRY, which simulates paranoia; in competition with real paranoid patients, PARRY fooled 49 percent of the psychiatrists it was tested on). If the Turing game is partly a joke, and if, as Seymour Papert and his colleagues observe, computers should be granted the right to fallibility, how do we know a machine is thinking? Perhaps the best way is to look at recent work in the field, at the problems it has encountered and the likelihood that they will be solved.

An IBM'er, asked to map the AI community, said, "There's your problem-solving crowd, your vision crowd, your robotics crowd, your natural language crowd and your speech and pattern-recognition people." Sometimes, these categories overlap; other times, work in these areas is not considered artificial intelligence research at all. Corporations with research divisions (notably, IBM, Bell and Xerox) do work in several of these fields while claiming they wouldn't touch AI with a ten-foot pole (too blue-sky for the shareholders). And so most unabashed AI research is done at universities; its chief patron is ARPA, the Advanced Research Projects Agency of the Department of Defense, which is, indeed, the largest benefactor of all university research in information processing. In artificial intelligence, ARPA spends between $2 million and $8 million a year (the range comes from questions of what is and isn't AI) at some fifteen institutions around the country. As ordinary product development becomes more adventurous, it starts to impinge on AI; on the other hand, when government research funding gets tight, AI people begin to talk louder about practical applications.

The leading centers of AI research have been MIT, Stanford and Carnegie-Mellon; since the middle seventies, Yale has been doing important work; and two consulting research firms, Bolt Beranek and Newman and Stanford Research Institute, also have sizable projects. Each institution has a slightly different focus. Similar patterns of progress, however, have marked research in all branches of AI. If the latest work shows, at last, some promising computer applications, it is the failures which, perversely, have shed light on human thought processes, revealing unexpected complexity in the most prosaic mental activities.

At Carnegie-Mellon the chief AI experts are Nobel Laureate Herbert Simon and Allen Newell. Chess playing is a major pastime at Carnegie-Mellon. Researchers have called it the *drosophila* of cognitive psychology, offering a maximum of intellectual complexity for a minimum of computing facilities and man-hours. While computers can surpass humans in the brute-force calculation of possible moves, sheer brute force is an impossible method: an early estimate suggested that there are 10^{120} moves to be evaluated in a single game, with only 10^{16} microseconds in a century. Clearly, computers would need some powers of elimination and the ability to learn from past mistakes. Researchers began to devise *heuristics*, the rules-of-thumb people use to guide themselves through a vast maze of possibilities.

Early chess programs were given a set of goals—king safety, center control and so forth—and designed to use these criteria in evaluating moves to a certain depth. Gradually, the programs have improved, enabling the computer to play creditable tournament chess. But heuristics alone did not account for brilliance and imagination in chess playing. A psychologist in Amsterdam had compared the techniques of ordinary players, masters and grandmasters. As one Carnegie-Mellon paper reports,

> . . . none of the statistics he computed to characterize his subjects' search processes—number of moves examined, depth of search, speed of search—distinguished the grandmasters from the ordinary players. He could only separate them by the fact that the grandmasters usually chose the strongest move in the position, while ordinary players often chose weaker moves. Why were the grandmasters able to do this?

The Dutch professor set up chessboards in positions taken from actual master games. His subjects—who had never seen these particular games before—were shown the chessboards for a few seconds and then asked to reproduce them. Grandmasters and masters, it developed, could reproduce the positions with 93 percent accuracy, but between masters and experts and between experts and novices there was a 20 percent drop. Researchers then set up pieces at random and tried the same experiment, this time finding that players of every rank could reproduce only three or four positions. The masters did not, then, possess any innate perceptual superiority; rather they had learned to see the board in terms of remembered patterns instead of individual pieces, and thus could zero in on significant moves.

Programs had been developed to solve brain-teasers and to prove geometric theorems, but had yet to equal human skill in handling complex problems like chess, which required the player to draw upon a large vocabulary of patterns. The study of perception and the representation of knowledge offered a new focus for research at Carnegie-Mellon. Newell, Simon and their colleagues have expanded their studies to other domains that required a rich body of knowledge, contrasting the techniques of students and professors, for example, in solving physics problems.

MIT is well known for its work in vision and robotics; the co-director of the school's artificial intelligence laboratory, Marvin Minsky, was technical advisor to Stanley Kubrick's *2001*, and is thus partly responsible for Hal, the disturbingly intelligent computer. Seymour Papert, the other codirector, a disciple of Jean Piaget, has devised a system for teaching geometry and other subjects to elementary school children with the aid of computers; while the children study geometry, Papert studies the children. Minsky and Papert sometimes work together, hoping to produce a theory of thinking and learning that will prove equally effective for people and machines.

Progress in vision and robotics has followed the same pattern as the research in chess. AI researchers try to solve small, simple problems first and gradually move on to more elaborate situations. Some vision programs have simply studied different arrangements of blocks; others have controlled robots composed of a television camera "eye," an "arm" and a minicomputer. Difficulties in raising enough money to develop advanced robots led Minsky to give priority to solving the vision problems that are inherent—and perhaps primary—in robotics.

Originally, vision researchers programmed the computer to see shapes by compiling lists of simple features: it looked for edges and corners, and if it found four right angles it would label a shape square. These heuristics didn't help when the lines were fuzzy or part of the shape was obstructed. Rules that worked for flat drawings were ineffective for three-dimensional scenes. Texture and lighting were difficult to handle. "Seeing," it turned out, was a matter of making sense out of a welter of ambiguities, which involved complex perceptions fed by knowledge about the world in general. A small child can spot the relationship between an armchair, a rocker and a swivel chair; it knows that a chair remains a chair even if one leg is broken off, and that a toy chair is still a chair even if no human being can sit on it. Purely visual rules about lines and angles will not account for all the different types of chairs, nor enable the machine to distinguish a chair that is blocked by a desk.

If seeing entailed drawing on a fund of different types of knowledge, there must be a way of getting at all this information quickly, making tentative judgments, checking them out and revising them. Minsky steered a new course with his frame system theory, which suggested that when one encounters a new situation one selects from memory a structure called a frame, which is then adapted to fit reality by changing details as necessary. When we open a door on the twentieth floor of the Chrysler Building, we might choose an "office" frame, but if the details we see do not confirm our expectations, we would summon the frames for cafeterias, staircases or lavatories. The frame system theory operated on many levels and involved a complex network of interconnecting nodes and slots. There were, however, mental processes it didn't account for—reflection and emotion and the development of children's minds—and so its author has superseded it with other theories which are even more abstruse and bear only a slight family resemblance to their predecessors. In 1979 Minsky, who had not yet heard about Proust's experience with the madeleine, arrived at the hypothesis that knowledge is stored in terms of past experiences, which we evoke by duplicating the feelings that accompanied them.

The best illustration of the problems faced by AI researchers—and of recent progress toward solving them—comes from the field of natural language. During the fifties, enthusiastic computer people promised that fully automated, high-qualilty mechanical language translation was just around the corner, offering easy access to the enormous and rapidly proliferating body of technical information published in foreign languages. All you needed to do was feed the computer a dictionary and a list of grammar rules.

But translation programmers, financed by sizable amounts of government money, discovered a host of unforeseen linguistic quirks and ambiguities. One programmer gave his machine the phrase "The spirit is willing but the flesh is weak" for rendering into Russian. What he got back, retranslated from the Russian, was "The vodka is strong but the meat is rotten." How, with just a dictionary and the rules of grammar, could a computer render "The box was in the pen," a sentence which would present no problem to a human translator? The human would know immediately that the "pen" was an enclosure, not a writing instrument; the computer would have to be given information about the sizes and functions of objects. In a James Bond movie, as one critic of AI pointed out, the box in question might indeed be inside a writing instrument. A human translator could pick up eccentricities by understanding the context. Did "He follows Marx" mean "He shadows Groucho" or "He endorses Karl"? While the examples sound bizarre, ambiguities permeate everyday language: one researcher found it highly significant that his program could distinguish between two meanings of the verb "to have" in "John has ten fingers" and "John has three marbles."

The researchers set out to give computers common sense, to join semantics with syntax and to introduce knowledge, and they began to make dramatic progress. At MIT Terry Winograd produced a flamboyant program called SHRDLU, whose conversations about block-building exhibited a Talmudic complexity. SHRDLU, like the robot programs, busied itself with stacking blocks, not physically but via a terminal display. It adjusted the picture on the screen according to instructions and answered questions about the stack. "Does the shortest thing the tallest pyramid's support supports support anything green?" the interrogator asked. "Yes, the green pyramid," answered SHRDLU. SHRDLU's brilliance, however, was confined to a narrow and simple world. The information needed to answer questions about it was voluminous, and the interconnections were convoluted; another MIT language paper observed, "Winograd himself can barely understand the code he has written after being away from it for a while."

In light of past difficulties, the work done at Yale is particularly impressive. One winter afternoon in 1979, a program called FRUMP was busily scanning the UPI wire. FRUMP is interested in stories about international relations. When the UPI runs one of these, the program produces a one-line summary in four languages. FRUMP had received the following input:

> A BULGARIAN FISHING VESSEL WAS SEIZED BY THE COAST GUARD OFF THE OREGON COAST TODAY AND ACCUSED OF VIOLATING THE 12-MILE FISHING LIMIT OF THE UNITED STATES. A COAST GUARD SPOKESMAN SAID THAT THE 274-FOOT OFELIA, A COMBINATION STERN TRAWLER AND FACTORY SHIP, WAS SEIZED BY THE CUTTER VENTUROUS AND WAS BEING ESCORTED INTO COOS BAY, ORE.

Here is Frump's output:

ENGLISH:
> THE U.S. COAST GUARD HAS SEIZED A BULGARIAN BOAT NEAR OREGON.

FRENCH:
> LES GARDES-COTES US A ARRAISONNE BATEAU BULGARE AU LARGE DE L'OREGON.

CHINESE:
> MMEIGWO HAEANN JIINGWEY TZAY EHLEHGANG JUAJUHLE I JY BAOJIALIHYAH DE CHWAN

SPANISH:
> LA GUARDA-COSTA DE LOS ESTADOS UNIDOS CAPTURO UN BARCO BULGARO CERCO D'EL ESTADO DE OREGON.

"FRUMP is very close to working right," says Roger Schank, the thirty-three-year-old professor who runs the laboratory. "We've set up a company to sell it to the outside world. We have a small time-sharing service; by pulling off what each customer wants—crop failures or trucking strikes, for example—we can give him a personalized newspaper. I thought of this after reading my seventy-fifth Patty Hearst story, when all I really wanted to know was whether they'd found her."

In the AI community the entrepreneurial instinct, however well developed, is usually directed toward securing grant money. Schank's interest in setting up a business is unusual. "The only real way to know if the programs work is to test them in the outside world," he says, "to be sure they won't fall apart on new input. Besides, it's part of the fun." Even the more theoretical work at Yale has some practical bent. Many programs deal with current events, and most of the subject matter is of reasonable interest to adults.

Schank studied computer science at Carnegie Tech, and after several years of postgraduate work in linguistics and AI, he arrived at Yale in 1974. Fellow linguists had considered him unorthodox: as disciples of Noam Chomsky, they believed that the study of syntax and the grammatical structures common to different languages would ultimately reveal the capabilities of the human mind. Schank thought language study ought to focus on the representation of meaning. The sentences "I hit Fred on the nose" and "I hit Fred in the park," for example, were syntactically similar but conceptually different. Schank also wanted to develop a theory of thought that transcended language; if such a theory were applied to a computer program, then, as he later wrote, "any two inputs . . . no matter how constructed with respect to word choice or syntactic form, would have only one possible meaning representation if they had the same meaning." Many of the programs at Yale, therefore, while they have other purposes, also translate their output into several languages.

Schank and his assistants realized that a sentence was more than the sum of its parts: "He wrote a book" really meant "He created a book by writing it," and "He doubts his wife" meant "He doubts that what his wife is saying is true." The more you looked at any sentence, the more you found things that weren't there on the surface. Two sentences put together posed additional complications:

Q: Do you want a piece of chocolate?
A: I just had an ice cream cone.

To understand that the answer in this exchange meant "no," you would need to make elaborate inferences. The questioner was really saying, "Do you want me to transfer to you an object which is edible so you can eat it so that will make you feel some feeling (full, happy, etc.)?" and the respondent was saying, "I already have that feeling because I just did an action that resulted in that feeling." Five-year-old children can handle this unconsciously, while computers have to be given the necessary information. After reading many AI papers one looks at small children with new respect.

Schank evolved the notion of describing events through basic acts called primitives, and the states which result from the acts. Two primitives, for example, involve "transfer," which is represented as ATRANS for abstract transfer and PTRANS for physical transfer: when a junta executes a coup d'état, political power is ATRANSed from the ruler to the junta; when you visit London, you are PTRANSed from one city to another. Whether the input is some form of "buy" or of "acheter" or of "sell" or of "vendre," the Yale programs will map it into the combination of ATRANSes and PTRANSes that represents a financial transaction. Henceforward the programs will assume that A has B's money and B has A's car.

The next step was to study sentences in context, which eliminated some problems that had plagued computational linguists in the past. People don't misunderstand "He follows Marx," after all, because they know they are talking about either a political activist or a filmmaker. The computer could scour the text to illuminate many ambiguities.

Once Schank's computer started reading texts, it often found a series of events which could not be related by the simple causal chains he and his team had constructed before; the only reason people seemed to understand these sequences was that they had encountered them in the past (like the chess patterns at Carnegie-Mellon and the frame systems at MIT). The device Schank used to deal with this problem was called scripts; an example of it is this excerpt from a story read by SAM (for Script Applier Mechanism). Sam will read a story, produce longer and shorter paraphrases of it in five languages, and answer questions about it. Part of one input story reads like this:

He got off the train and entered Leone's. He had some lasagna. When the check came, he discovered he couldn't pay.

The long paraphrase of the lasagna sentence, an application of the restaurant script, runs this way:

HE ORDERED SOME LASAGNA. THE WAITER INDICATED TO THE CHEF JOHN WOULD LIKE HIM TO PREPARE SOMETHING. THE CHEF PREPARED THE LASAGNA. THE WAITER GOT IT FROM THE CHEF. THE WAITER WENT TO THE TABLE. HE SERVED THE LASAGNA TO JOHN. HE BECAME FULL.

Scripts, of course, explain only predictable events; to understand a real story one must know something about motivation, and several Yale programs face this problem. PAM interprets simple stories through the goals and plans of the general characters. One story, for example, tells PAM that "John wanted some money. John got a gun and walked into a liquor store. John told the owner he wanted some money. The owner gave John the money and John left." When PAM prints out the story from John's point of view, it says, "I told the shopkeeper that if he didn't let me have the money, I'd shoot him." The store owner, on the other hand, comes out saying, "He threatened me with a gun and demanded all the cash receipts. Well, I didn't want to get hurt, so I gave him the money."

The way we interpret information is, of course, colored by our personal beliefs. During the mid-sixties a Yale psychologist named Robert Abelson had set out to illustrate this by writing a program to simulate the responses of Barry Goldwater to questions about current events. In the ideology of its namesake, The Goldwater Machine would comment on the implications of any political development, predict its repercussions and make suggestions for appropriate governmental action. The program could not, however, handle mundane reality. It predicted that Castro would "build the Berlin wall," because Russia had just done so, and if Russia had done so, it must be the sort of bad thing that Communists like Castro would also want to do.

Schank and Abelson began to work at combining their theories; the application of goals, plans and scripts wedded to political belief systems was carried out by Schank's student in POLITICS, the program that led this section, which can now "personify" the ideologue of any political stripe. Students are now working on programs that argue their beliefs relentlessly, ruining any dinner party; other programs, in contrast, would modify those beliefs. Another type of com-munication that intrigues Schank and a colleague, Wendy Lehnert, is "a conversation between emotionally related people who share a great deal of background information"—that is, a marital quarrel. Schank and Lehnert's analysis of a stereotypical spat uncovers twelve levels of conversation and, drawing on the work with Abelson, sug-gests various belief systems the computer will need to hold its own: there is, for example, the love theme ("if X has free time then X will want to spend it with Y"), the husband role theme ("if X goes out at night X tells Y where and comes home on time") and social rules ("you may only love one person at at time").

One is bound to notice, after scanning the input given Schank's programs, that the marital quarrel is a far cry from Edward Albee and the stories aren't Tolstoi, either. Even on the most applied level, FRUMP and its peers have a way to go before they can deal ade-quately with the more sophisticated background articles and politi-cal analysis in *The New York Times*. Schank points out the unsolved problems that will keep him busy in the years to come and displays considerable admiration for the proficiency of man as an informa-tion-processing machine. Asked whether the decreasing price of memory circuits would speed the development of thinking ma-chines, Schank answers, "That's a layman's question. Our handicap has always been theory, not hardware. Space is secondary: engineers make the machines bigger, faster and cheaper before we can fill them up. It's useless to keep an encyclopedia stored in the computer if you can't get at the information you need."

Still, Schank has the gratified air of a man who has done at least some things that were thought to be impossible; thanks to his work and that of his peers the limits of computer capabilities seem much further out that they did even five years ago. The only thing cau-tious about Schank's optimism is the timetable he sets: "Sometime before my lifetime is finished computers will do all the neat things we can imagine," he says. "The computer will be a doctor, a lawyer and a friend who knows everything and tells us whatever we want to know."

MIT's Minsky, Carnegie-Mellon's Newell and Stanford's Edward Feigenbaum are equally optimistic—and equally long-range in their predictions. The question of what computers can be made to do, however, is no longer the province of academicians. Here are the stipulations of a pessimist, Joseph Weizenbaum, the ELIZA man from MIT. After observing that "intelligence" is a relative and thus unmeasurable quality, he writes:

> I accept the idea that a modern computer system is sufficiently complex and autonomous to warrant our talking about it as an organism. Given that it can both sense and affect its environment, I even grant that it can, in an extremely limited sense, be "socialized," that is, modified by its experiences with its world. I grant also that a suitably constructed robot can be made to develop a sense of itself, that it can, for example, learn to distinguish between parts of itself and objects outside of itself, that it can be made to assign a higher priority to guarding its own parts against physical damage than to similarly guarding objects external to itself, and that it can form a model of itself which could, in some sense, be considered a kind of self-consciousness. When I say therefore that I am willing to regard such a robot as an "organism," I declare my willingness to consider it a kind of animal. And I have already agreed that I see no way to put a bound on the degree of intelligence such an organism could, at least in principle, attain.

But Weizenbaum argues that there are "some things humans know by virtue of having a human body. No organism that does not have a human body can know these things in the same way humans know them" and that "there are some things people come to know only as a consequence of having been treated as human beings by other human beings." Accordingly, Weizenbaum writes, there are "appropriately human objectives that are inappropriate for machines," and these objectives govern "what machines ought and ought not to be put to doing."

The artificial intelligence researchers disagree with Weizenbaum, but point out that it will be some time before either view can be proved. Edward Feigenbaum of Stanford observes, "Either you believe that there is just an information processing machine in the skull or you believe that there is an information processing machine plus something else, the soul. The second belief is Joe Weizenbaum's religion; the first is mine. I believe that whatever is doable by the human information processing machine is doable by computer, and that includes having feelings. I think feelings are caused by mental states; even if the computer doesn't feel tension in the pit of the stomach, it can still say, 'You make me nervous.' My religion also says that a computer can create a great symphony. But I stress that this is a religious belief: there is no evidence either way."

Schank stops just short of Feigenbaum's position: "I have a belief in humanity," he says. "A computer will never feel love. But this distinction has no practical importance: you could tell the machine that when you are in love you act in a certain way, and its behavior would look like feelings to anyone. You could teach it to observe what's beautiful. Children are told what to feel. And there are certain people I know who don't have any feelings at all."

Computers will play the Turing game with increasing skill; some programs are already, within their limited domains, expert players. It is time, then, to start thinking about Weizenbaum's warning, ". . . since we do not now have any ways of making computers wise, we ought not now to give computers tasks that demand wisdom."

MEDICINE

Throughout its life, computer technology has advanced largely in response to the needs of the military; if, like Roger Schank, Marvin Minsky and their peers, you want to work at the frontier, you will more than likely have to accept the Defense Department as your benefactor. This historic alliance makes some computer people uncomfortable and thus eager to search out more humanitarian applications; even those who are untroubled by it take on beatific expressions when they discuss computers-in-medicine. Medicine offers computer people plenty of opportunity to do good. More efficient record-keeping might help contain spiraling medical costs. Imaginative methods of information retrieval could aid doctors in keeping pace with a rapidly growing and changing selection of tests, drugs and therapeutic choices (as one government study notes, "The quality of clinical care often depends on the accuracy and completeness of the physician's memory"). Used interactively, the computer is a unique and powerful educational tool. And the machine's ability to process large amounts of numerical data may bring us new kinds of knowledge in medicine as it has in other branches of science.

Despite the apparent wealth of opportunities and the indisputable cosmetic effect of hospital photographs on vendors' annual reports, the use of computers in medicine lags behind computer applications in both business and other branches of science. Most hospitals still use computers only for accounting. During the sixties, optimistic efforts by industry and government to develop applications useful to doctors led to expensive failures and attendant skepticism in the medical community. Many medical problems did not lend themselves readily to precise mathematical definition. Doctors and computer people, whose specialties require opposite types of mental discipline, had trouble understanding each other; the observations of Aran Safir, one member of the small fraternity of M.D.'s who work with computers, are interesting:

> I believe that there are important personality differences between the mathematical-physical types and physicians.... People who study mathematics and physics are, in general, those who are excited or pleased by the idea of learning a few basic principles and techniques and then using these to study a large discipline, most of which can be understood and predicted with the application of the few fundamentals.... Physicians commit to memory large masses of facts and observations that cannot be organized very satisfactorily.... Physicians are constantly forced to make decisions on the basis of inadequate data. ... Medical education is a long slow process of teaching an intelligent and discriminating person how to live with such a difficult situation day after day.... Mathematicians, physicists, and engineers rarely, if ever, are confronted with such forced decision-making.

Doctors interested in computing are considered offbeat by their colleagues, and since medical specialties are aligned in terms of organs or diseases, there is no clear constituency for the advancement of computer-aided medicine. Until recently, computer technology had not progressed far enough to accommodate sophisticated medical programs. Lately, however, some promising developments have appeared. Most are in the prototype or field trial stage and need more work to be marketable; even then, they will be first-generation programs and it will take three generations to win widespread acceptance. But they illustrate some directions that medical computing may take; each reflects the developer's philosophy of medicine and the computer's role in it.

Several universities have produced consultation programs in which the machine helps the doctor make decisions about diagnosis and therapy. They come from collaborations between doctors and artificial intelligence researchers who were drawn to the challenge of reproducing expert skills on the computer. At Stanford a program

called MYCIN, written by the computer science department and the
medical school, helps the doctor to diagnose and treat bacterial infections. Doctors must often start treating such infections when only
a sketchy preliminary laboratory report is available. MYCIN mobi-
lizes the knowledge of specialists at Stanford to help the doctor make
the best use of what information he has.

In AI style, MYCIN stores its knowledge in the form of "if . . .
then" rules. One rule, for example, looks like this:

IF:
 1) The site of the culture is blood, and
 2) The gram stain of the organism is gramneg, and
 3) The morphology of the organism is rod, and
 4) The patient is a compromised host

THEN:
 There is suggestive evidence (.6) that the identity
 of the organism is pseudomonas-aeruginosa.

The program applies these rules to laboratory and patient history
data fed in by the doctor, who spends an average of fifteen or twenty minutes at the terminal. MYCIN's sleuthing is highly sophisticated: it passed one Turing test with flying colors. The program was
given the case histories of ten patients with different types of infectious meningitis. Eight human physicians—five faculty specialists in
infectious diseases, a research fellow, a resident and a senior medical
student—also reviewed the histories. MYCIN's recommendations,
along with those of the human doctors and a record of the therapy
the patients actually received, were sent unidentified to eight specialists outside of Stanford, who were asked to compare each set of
recommendations with their own. The highest rating went to MY-
CIN, which nosed out all five of the faculty experts. (Is Stanford
specialist no. 5, whose credentials matched the examiners' but whose
decisions didn't, a dithering incompetent or a brilliant original
thinker, and what does *that* tell us about computers, human beings
and modern medicine?)

The program has an attribute more significant than all this cleverness, and that is what computer people call "human factors engineering." MYCIN's designers realized that doctors would never
place blind faith in a computer program; this one would have to
explain and defend its judgments "in terms that suggest to the physi-

cian that the program approaches problems in much the same way that he does." The doctor's conversation with MYCIN is a dialogue which looks very much like one he would have with a human specialist. To find out what MYCIN is driving at, he simply types in WHY, HOW or EXPLAIN. The program is also set up to let the doctor specify just how detailed he wants the explanation to be.

Without the aid of a programmer, specialists in hospitals could add new rules to MYCIN and correct those they disagree with. When the specialist has formulated a new rule, the program asks him, "On a scale of 1 to 10, how much certainty would you affix to this conclusion?" In its explanations, the program uses that number to suggest the force of the rule. Despite its obvious strength and promise MYCIN's future is uncertain. But whatever becomes of this program, its self-explanation features make it a model for humane partnership between man and machine, a partnership set up to afford man the maximum control.

Another medical consultation program that uses AI techniques is CADUCEUS (formerly INTERNIST), which models the diagnostic skills of Dr. Jack Myers of the University of Pittsburgh's School of Medicine; the program's coauthor is Harry Pople, Jr., an alumnus of the Carnegie-Mellon artificial intelligence group who now teaches at Pittsburgh. Myers's goal in conceiving CADUCEUS was to help doctors keep up with the medical information explosion; Pople, like the AI men at Stanford, was interested in the way experts solve complex problems.

CADUCEUS's knowledge is stored in two categories—diseases and "manifestations"—which must be matched with each other to get a diagnosis. In the fall of 1980, when the program contained three-quarters of the knowledge Myers considered adequate for clinical operation, it knew more than three thousand individual manifestations of disease—symptoms, laboratory data, and demographic and historical information about patients that might shed light on a disgnosis. "No physician could regurgitate that long a list on command," says Myers, "and you won't find the whole list in any textbook." In addition, CADUCEUS records some five hundred diseases. Stored with each disease is a list of manifestations that are known to occur in it; a separate list of manifestations is similarly keyed to possible diseases. Thus the program is set up to gauge both the likelihood that a patient with jaundice has hepatitis and the chance that a patient with hepatitis will be jaundiced. CADUCEUS uses AI problem-solving techniques to reach a diagnostic conclusion.

CADUCEUS acquitted itself well in diagnosing difficult cases published in medical journals. Pople says a number of good hospitals have shown interest in participating in field trials. "Our primary objective," he says, "is to provide something the physician would use instead of going to the library or consulting a specialist. There aren't that many experts available, even in major centers; Myers gets calls from all over the country, and he's not always around. But we're getting some pressure to apply the program for primary care— NASA is interested in it for space expeditions, and the Navy for nuclear submarine missions. State agencies may want it as backup for nurse-practitioners in rural health clinics. It could be useful for telling when to move a patient to a better-equipped clinic in a major center."

Assuming Harry Pople has done his work successfully, CADU-CEUS is equivalent to a session with Jack Myers. An examination of the patient by Dr. Myers himself might be better than the computer consultation, particularly if one agrees with AI's critics that there are intuitive aspects of medical diagnosis that can't be programmed (Myers himself does not believe this). But if the doctor and patient live in Tucson and must deal with Myers over the phone anyway, the program is probably better than Myers himself in that it is never tired, harried, sick or on vacation. It is not, however, more detached or unbiased than Myers; it is, indeed, a model of Myers's professional biases, just as the various AI programs at Yale model the beliefs given them by their authors. As the tests evaluating MYCIN showed, specialists frequently disagree. Since there is some evidence that computers carry a special *mana* and since programs don't have visible bylines, CADUCEUS requires a caveat that would be unnecessary if Dr. Myers simply wrote a textbook.

Both MYCIN and CADUCEUS were designed for a research environment in which cost-effectiveness was not paramount; the hardware and software are expensive to run, and it is uncertain how the programs would survive conversion to more economical media. A program at the frontier of computer technology may not solve the most pressing medical problem in the most practical way; MYCIN, for example, applies only to hospitalized patients with blood infections or meningitis. To adapt it to other specialties requires a new set of rules and data, and these are difficult to develop (a descendant of MYCIN, for diagnosing pulmonary disease, is now in routine use at a hospital in San Francisco; it is considered to be another program).

As for CADUCEUS, it is interesting to hear the comments of Aran Safir, an ophthalmologist at Louisiana State University Eye Center. In collaboration with an artificial intelligence researcher, Safir wrote a glaucoma consultation program; his remarks about his own experience seem *a propos* of CADUCEUS as well:

"Very little of medicine is a detective story. The Ellery Queen model of the learned professor making a diagnosis that's escaped everyone else is only for books, movies and television. Generally, if a diagnosis can be made at all the ordinary practitioner can make it; if he fails, it's because he's omitted some basic procedure. The expert gets the hopeless cases, and if he can help one patient in ten he's a hero.

"Why did we write the program? To see if we could do it, and with the pious hope that it might identify problems we'd failed to see ourselves and so teach us more about glaucoma. But that didn't happen; the program just answered the questions we asked it. As for the AI side of it, we made a good simulation of a glaucoma expert in the sense that the same inputs would get the same outputs, but the process wasn't the same; when experts try to explain how they reach a diagnosis it always reminds me of that essay of Poe's on how he wrote 'The Raven.' It's very clever, but it doesn't ring true."

Not all medical consultation programs are based on artificial intelligence techniques. Dr. John H. Siegel, a surgeon at Buffalo General Hospital, thinks the computer's greatest contribution to medicine will come, more traditionally, from exploiting the machine's power in number-crunching. "The big advances," he says, "will come from applying statistical and modeling techniques to data to understand how systems like the blood operate under interacting stresses. Then we will be able to predict the response to different types of therapy." Such applications would be the biological counterpart of the econometric models now in use, but Siegel says the medical models will work better than the economic ones because "the control through which biological systems maintain homeostasis has been developed over billions of years of evolution, while economic systems are terribly new."

Siegel's first step toward this goal is a program called CARE, for the management of critically ill surgical patients. CARE now stores a large fund of detailed cardiovascular, respiratory and metabolic information on previous patients; this data can be used to give the doctor a prototype recovery pattern against which he may gauge the progress of a patient and make appropriate decisions about therapy. The system also produces a daily patient record. The program will assess the patient's condition at any moment, and will warn the doctor of significant changes. CARE also applies standard equations for calculating the patient's fluid and metabolic requirements, which vary with age, sex, size and particular injury or disease; too often, doctors have relied on guesswork, educated or less so, because when a patient is fighting for his life and his condition is changing rapidly, there isn't enough time for careful mathematics. Between 1973 and 1978, CARE was phased into the surgical intensive care unit at Buffalo General. During this period, according to Siegel's report, there was a "steady and progressive drop in general surgical mortality from 18.8% to 10.5%; in trauma mortality from 33% to 7.5%; and in mortality from gastrointestinal complications from 24% to 5.6%." There are several other projects around the country in both patient-monitoring and the statistical analysis of disease patterns.

In describing an earlier version of CARE which was designed to improve surgical emergency care outside of big city hospitals, Siegel used the term "living textbook"; there is a high educational content in all medical consultation programs. If the computer can give helpful on-the-job training to practicing doctors, the role it can play in teaching medical students is unique. Much of the best work in computer-aided medical instruction uses the machine to simulate a patient; the student is responsible for diagnosing him and prescribing therapy.

In one program devised at Massachusetts General Hospital—which has been a leader in this and other applications of computers to medicine—the student is given a list of possible questions to ask a patient with abdominal pain and another list of lab tests that might be ordered. He is then presented with the "patient": "A 45-year-old white male used-car salesman is brought to the EW (Emergency Ward) by his anxious wife because he complains of moderate epigastric pain which started about a week ago after a night out with the boys playing poker." The student types in the number of the question he wants to ask ("#4 When do you first have this pain?") and gets an answer ("I've been having pains like this for a number of years. It seemed to start when I was in Korea. It gets particularly bad when the new model cars come out in the fall.") At any point in the questioning he may type in HELP and the computer will give him an estimated disease probability and offer suggestions for further workup. When the student arrives at a diagnosis, the program will comment on his diagnostic procedures; its purpose is to teach him a logical sequence for gathering information.

In another type of program in the Mass General series, the patient's condition changes as a result of the student's therapy. He tries to resuscitate a patient in cardiac arrest and prescribes various tests and drugs for another patient in diabetic ketoacidosis. Along the way the computer acts as a consultant ("You gave 1 L IV. This is not really adequate initial hydration. You will find that patients in ketoacidosis require large volumes of fluid. . . .").

Since 1972, the Mass General programs have been offered to medical schools and teaching hospitals over a time-sharing network dedicated to computer-aided instruction in medicine. One user is Downstate Medical Center in Brooklyn. Dr. Herbert Diamond, who has for some years been involved in the computer-aided instruction program at Downstate, observes, "This gives the student a chance to do decision-making he couldn't do otherwise. We can't produce a real diabetic in ketoacidosis on demand, and even if one were there, we wouldn't let a student make the decisions. We've offered the course as an elective to fourth-year students, in competition with other electives. About a sixth of the class have taken it and liked it, so by the marketplace measurement it works. Will it be valuable? I don't know. The students disperse, and we don't have grant money to do follow-up studies."

Unless they work at a leading-edge hospital or have a personal interest in computers, the average doctor and nurse don't get the opportunity to sit at a terminal and deal directly with the machine; all of the applications we've seen so far will, if they are successful, bring the computer that one step out of the back office. There is, however, a second step, the one in which the patient sits at the terminal. Programs that get their data directly from the patient have been on the research scene since the sixties. Lately researchers have recognized that the computer's usefulness in educating doctors might be applied to patients as well, and that give-and-take between the patient and the computer might add a valuable new dimension to medical care. A recent report from the National Center for Health Services Research, the Health and Human Services agency that doles out money for projects in health care delivery (as opposed to biomedical research), features a section on "patient self-help," noting that "the largest and least utilized provider of health care is the patient."

This echoes the phrase of Dr. Warner Slack, an associate professor at Harvard Medical School who also co-directs the computer medicine program at Beth Israel Hospital in Boston. Slack has been an enthusiastic and persevering advocate of patient-computer relationships since 1966, when he was a research fellow at the University of Wisconsin and devised one of the first automated medical history programs. His work is interesting because it plays right into people's resistance to the computer and tries, through an engaging showmanship, to turn the negatives into positives.

Recording medical histories is a time-consuming and unpopular activity for doctors, and when they are harried they do it sloppily. Some clinics have coped by giving patients questionnaires, but Slack found these rigid and impersonal: you couldn't follow up a significant answer with more detailed questions or clarify a question the patient didn't understand. Because of the computer's ability to branch, it could combine the thoroughness and economy of the questionnaire with the depth and flexibility of the human interviewer. Slack's first program contained five hundred questions on hives, hay fever and asthma; no one had to answer all of these, and the average patient spent fifteen or twenty minutes at the terminal. The program used a multiple-choice format: as each question appeared on the screen, the patient could key in "Yes," "No," "Don't Know," and "Don't Understand," the last choice being one Slack had never seen on a printed questionnaire, and which he programmed to bring on a few words of clarification.

When Slack began to test the program, he found an elderly patient talking back to the computer, cheerfully criticizing it for asking dumb questions. At least for some people, it seemed, the machine was less authoritarian than the human physician. Afterward, the patient asked to look at the printout, corrected the errors in his history and contributed some useful suggestions.

Slack's patients have edited their histories ever since, in accord with the underlying philosophy of his work—that the patient should be in control. An early addition Slack made to the history program was a fifth option on the multiple-choice sequence: "None of your damn business" (later changed to "Skip it" when Slack moved to Boston). In 1977, in an article in *The Lancet*, he wrote:

> For centuries, the medical profession has perpetuated paternalism as an essential component of medical care and thereby deprived patients of the self-esteem that comes from self-reliance. . . . If physicians were willing to let go of the notion that they are responsible for controlling their patients; if, like electricians, accountants and others with special knowledge, they were willing to present possible plans of action in a step-by-step manner, patients who wanted to could make informed decisions on the basis of their own values. . . . Self-reliant patients will be responsible for the consequences of their decisions, and their physicians will be freed from the inappropriate liability that accompanies medical paternalism.

Slack began to insert teaching sequences into the history programs, so that a patient complaining of hay fever might be asked, "Would you like to know something more about it?" Most often the patients did. Slack believes that interactive computing holds great promise for counseling patients, at first in the doctor's office and later, with personal computers and two-way television, in their own homes. "The most difficult diagnostic decision a patient makes," he says, "is whether to go to the doctor. A clinic or hospital is a terrible place for love and friendship. When possible, it's better for the patient to cure himself at home. With books and finally with computers we can help him to make that difficult decision better. Imagine what an interactive Benjamin Spock could do for worried parents at three o'clock in the morning!"

For several years Beth Israel has been using Slack's three-part program in diet counseling, which includes a general history of the patient and his habits, a session called "the usual-day interview" in which the patient, in response to multiple-choice branching sequences, records every morsel that would pass his lips on such a day, and a diet and menu planner. It would be hard to imagine a human nutritionist taking a more detailed history. The usual-day interview produces a printout with a calorie count for each item consumed; it makes a persuasive catalog of one's sins. But the menu planner is fairly prosaic and the program's general tips for weight-watching

("Take the stairs instead of the elevator"; "Better not to watch TV or read while eating") are as personal as a newspaper health column. Perhaps the only real way to lose weight is to eat less and exercise more, and the variations are limited; still, the custom-tailoring seems at least partly an illusion, like those children's birthday records in which the same song is addressed to Susie or Jimmy or Anne. That illusion may, however, be just enough to make the computer more effective than a diet book.

When Slack produces a new self-help program, he tries it out on a group of paid volunteers and calls for their comments and suggestions. The results are equivocal: in some areas the programs do better than humans, in others not so well. The very impersonality of the machine seems to be welcome for sensitive gynecological problems. These programs are not technologically adventurous; if hospitals find them useful and economical they will be picked up. Another of Slack's programs, however, is more controversial.

"Soliloquy therapy," a treatment promulgated by Slack and his brother Charles, now a psychologist at the University of Alabama, uses the machine to help people cope with emotional problems. While it sounds like just the sort of innovation that set MIT's Joseph Weizenbaum to reconsidering his life's work, the difference between the Slacks' approach and ELIZA and its descendants is that the Slacks' machines make a point of *not* understanding what the patient says.

The Slacks believe that "talking out loud and alone can be therapeutic," but most people are embarrassed about doing this and don't know how to start; the machine can give them the prodding they need. While the computer won't quite say, "Now vee may perhaps to begin," it does ask a few psychiatristlike questions just to get the patient in the mood; it doesn't give any direct feedback (some psychiatric patients make the same complaint about their human therapists). If it does help it will be much cheaper than a weekly session with a real psychiatrist.

The Slacks' computer is hooked up to a microphone and tape recorder. The patient sits down at the terminal, types in the basic name-age-sex information, and then answers, in multiple-choice form, thirteen history questions about common emotional problems. ("Have you been feeling sad or down in the dumps? Have you, within the last year, lost someone close to you? Are you a lonely person?") When the history is completed, the program asks, "You've indicated to us that you've been feeling sad or down in the dumps. Would you be willing to talk about this?" The patient hits the "yes" key, and the program says, "Fine, tell us about your sadness." The computer can detect whether the patient is talking at all, but can't understand what he's saying; if there's silence for twenty seconds, the program says, "Are you having trouble getting started?" and then recommends, "Well, begin by saying—'My sadness seems to stem from' . . ." Periodically the program offers words of encouragement, and when the initial monologue is finished, it poses discussion topics favored by the disciples of Freud, Ellis, Glassner and Rogers.

The Slacks have written several articles about soliloquy therapy since 1972, for publications ranging from *The New England Journal of Medicine* to *Psychology Today*. All of the articles cite the same experiment, in which thirty-two male volunteers aged eighteen to twenty-six, none of whom were currently receiving psychotherapy, had one session with the computer and another with one of the Slack brothers. While most people preferred talking to the doctor, a few favored the computer, and nearly everyone was willing to say something about intimate problems during his session with the machine. One problem with this study is that it samples a very small group; another is that in contrast to the usual financial arrangement between therapist and patient, the Slacks' subjects were paid to talk to the computer. Warner Slack says another study was done recently, but he has not yet tallied the results.

Whether anyone will pay to talk to a computer remains to be seen. People do, of course, buy quantities of books on emotional self-help, and the popularity of this technique will have much to do with its price and the way it is offered. The tape-recorded interview might be played by a human psychiatrist later (when he gets back from the Vineyard after Labor Day, for example) or erased or taken home by the patient. The technique could be integrated with personal computers or interactive TV; some observers have envisioned little kiosks like automated bank teller machines. Warner Slack says, "Psychotherapy is an elitist situation, and I'm skeptical about its value. You're paying for friendship, which is over when the hour is out, and it's more expensive than paying for love. I wouldn't charge anyone a hundred dollars an hour just to speak to me. If we're correct and just talking aloud is helpful, the price is right."

The Slacks' program raises moral questions pertaining to the overall role of computers in society. In none of the brothers' articles are grandiose claims made for curing serious mental disorders, nor does Warner, in conversation, imply such intentions; rather the program seems designed to help ordinary people cope with the usual bumps and bruises of life, the kind that have, as Slack notes, kept one celebrated entertainer supporting his psychiatrist for twenty-two years.

There are three possible objections to the program. The first—which Weizenbaum suggests in discussing programs of this type—is that despite the Slacks' assurances that the machine understands nothing, the program derives its efficacy from an aura of scientific competence falsely attributed to the computer; thus it is a con game. Using the computer this way is like paying your next-door neighbor twenty dollars to put on a white coat while listening to your troubles: not immoral, but a bit kinky. The Slacks compare their soliloquy therapy to Demosthenes proclaiming his anger to the lonely sea, which they consider perfectly normal, but their subjects are proclaiming to the sea *with props.* If that isn't kinky, perhaps it is due to that spurious aura of scientific competence Weizenbaum notes.

One might also object that many emotional problems involve difficulty in getting along with people. In seeking therapy, a patient commits himself to the risks and responsibilities of a continuing relationship with another human being, and that in itself may be therapeutic. To dodge this commitment in favor of machine-aided soliloquy may be taking a step in the wrong direction.

Finally there is the suggestion that even though what the Slacks are now doing seems fairly harmless and may even help some people, it is the sort of program that might be misused. One can object to some, but not all technology on the basis of potential misuse; whether soliloquy therapy is vulnerable requires consideration.

Programs that offer consultation or self-help in a narrow domain will be luxuries for some time; first the machine must be used for information-handling in medicine as it is in business. But medical information systems present special problems. To be useful, they must be on-line and immediately accessible in many locations to users—doctors, nurses, dietitians, pharmacists, laboratory technicians—with varied needs. This implies expensive hardware, large data bases and sophisticated software. But even the biggest hospitals are smaller than most corporations using computers extensively.

While the consequences of error can be serious, medical information is difficult for laymen to understand; when clerks do the input, they make mistakes, but doctors and nurses hate typing and haven't the patience for long sessions at the terminal. Natural language work in medical applications has not developed sufficiently for computers to understand the free-text notes that form an important part of the medical record; this limits the flexibility of the systems. Because record-keeping habits are notoriously quirky not only among institutions but from service to service and doctor to doctor within an institution, the systems are difficult to standardize and mass-produce.

Still, designers are beginning to come up with systems that get around the problems, and declining hardware prices will make automated record-keeping more attractive. An outpatient system called COSTAR, operating successfully at Boston's Harvard Community Health Plan for some years, has been adapted for wider use. Two hospital systems are also considered "leading-edge": the Technicon System in use at El Camino Hospital in Mountain View, California, since 1972; and PROMIS (for Problem-Oriented Medical System) a controversial design still in development at the University of Vermont.

Computerized medical records offer particular advantages. Because information can be summoned from terminals in several different places, they save the inconvenience of tracking down John Jones's manila file folder. Legibility is a boon. And while manual records tie the doctor to a chronological organization of data, the flexible computer system can retrieve information in more useful forms. If she is interested in Jones's ulcer she doesn't have to run through reports on his broken leg; if she wants the results of all lab tests on a patient and nothing else, she can summon them. The computer can notify the doctor of all patients who are receiving a certain drug which has been withdrawn because of undesirable side effects, or all patients who don't keep their appointments. It can cull the patients who qualify for flu shots and print postcards to them. One system routes drug orders from the nursing station to the hospital pharmacy and simultaneously prints labels for the medicines. Without wasteful duplication of data-gathering effort, computerized medical records can provide information for billing, administration, statistical research and peer review.

In the new systems, doctors and nurses don't have to do much typing. The two hospital systems offer multiple choices on the screen, and the user makes his selection by touch; COSTAR gives the professionals a coded form which is transcribed by clerks or secretaries. While COSTAR doesn't understand free text, it will store a few lines of it with the code number for the patient's problem.

COSTAR and the Technicon system were designed in consultation with doctors and nurses who would use them; they aim to accommodate wherever possible to the doctor's own habits. PROMIS, on the other hand, seeks to improve the doctor's thoroughness and logic and to enforce greater medical accountability. Practitioners must adhere to a strict format in which new frames of data automatically flash on the screen in response to the user's last answer; the doctors are obliged to supply goals and reasons for every action. PROMIS delivers medical information and therapeutic recommendations unbidden as the doctor enters data.

The system breaks down medical decisions into a series of small steps, each offering the doctor a choice of ways to accomplish his goal; he is free to differ from these suggestions provided he tells PROMIS why. One purpose of this method, according to Dr. Lawrence Weed, its developer, is to make sure treatment is tailored to the patient's individual needs. Like Harvard's Warner Slack, Weed laments medical paternalism and seeks to put the patient in control of his therapy; when the PROMIS patient is able, he even sits at the terminal with the doctor and helps devise a treatment plan, keeping a copy of the printout. Since colleagues, pharmacists, nurses, and other hospital staffers who participate in the treatment also get to look at the record, PROMIS ends doctors' arbitrariness. Dr. Weed's final and perhaps most important goal is to establish highly detailed national standards for the practice of medicine.

The problems Weed addresses are legitimate and serious. "There is disorder in the medical profession," he says. "Our auditing system is failing, and poor record-keeping doesn't let us grow wiser from what we do. We want more information about the effect of radiation, but people who live around Three Mile Island all go to different doctors who scribble on paper without any common system. Then someone from the government comes up later to pore over the hieroglyphics like an archaeologist. If you want to look at outputs you've got to control inputs. Patients are dependent on what's in the doctor's head, and what happens if he drops dead? We're not being authoritarian, just offering guidance. But there will be no more freedom without accountability."

The question remains whether these problems can and should be solved through a computer system like PROMIS. Despite the choices available along the way, it is PROMIS which defines the problem for the doctor, and the doctor who must defend variations from its regimen. Should medical practice be dictated beforehand by a central authority? "I'm concerned about the growth of predigested systems put out by anonymous academies," says LSU's Safir. "It's important to preserve pluralism in medicine." What happens when the individual practitioner no longer feels responsible for a medical decision? And what individuals are responsible for it?

The machine adds not only efficiency but its own authority. Weizenbaum has raised an objection to far gentler counseling systems than PROMIS (in particular to MYCIN, that model of automated humility). He notes that "following the computer's advice" makes a good defense in malpractice suits; differing from its suggestions gives ammunition to the prosecution; "very soon," he says, "doctors would set aside their judgment in favor of the machine's." The computer makes such a valuable memory aid that it would be a pity to restrict the use of consulting programs to medical schools, as Weizenbaum suggests. But vendors, hospital and public health officials must work on safeguards in the design and use of these systems to protect pluralism and independence.

The spread of medical information systems will depend on economics and sociology. There's not much data yet on whether they actually improve patient care, partly because such improvement is difficult to attribute and measure. Soft benefits aren't enough to sell cost-conscious hospital administrators, but as hardware gets cheaper the savings may be more clear-cut.

Even the most permissive medical information system requires some change in habits, which doctors may be reluctant to accept. Gerald Cohen, who heads the Medical Information Systems Cluster at the National Center for Health Services Research, points out that the doctors, nurses, hospital staff and administrators who must adjust to a system aren't the ones who benefit from cost savings. "A hospital information system saves money for third-party payers, not the hospital. If better information shortens the average hospital stay, that may give the hospital an occupancy problem."

Doctors and officials in the field think it will be some time before the computer makes its mark in the delivery of health care. The American health care system is now the subject of widespread debate and scrutiny. Its problems are social and beyond the scope of technology alone; technology must be fit to social objectives, not the other way around. "A lot of what we're doing now is thrashing, while technology and society grind to their goals," says Safir. "But if we thrash long enough, the solutions will get better, and then there'll be another generation of computers and a new generation of doctors who have grown up with them and understand their use."

PART VI
CONCLUSIONS

15

The Trial

IN NEW YORK'S Foley Square, near the scene of IBM's sempiternal antitrust trial, there is a building with the carved inscription, *Beati qui ambulant in lege Domini*—"Blessed are they who walk in the law of the Lord." The record on whether IBM walks in the law of the Lord consumed, as of October 1980, 103,041 pages of transcript, covering the questioning of 81 live (if not universally lively) witnesses; 928 depositions and 11,644 documents had been introduced in evidence.

The IBM trial has performed a slow-motion scan of three decades of computer history, which does injustice to a colorful industry. The outcome of the trial (still some years off, if it runs its course without settlement) will affect the industry's future. And while that future is itself a matter of social concern, the case has even wider significance, because it raises the questions of what we should expect of our businessmen, and how much or how little we should govern them. Insofar as the business of America is business, what sort of society are we?

The executives whose interoffice mail we read with wicked pleasure down in Foley Square do not stand accused of bribery, domestic or foreign, nor of fomenting revolution in distant lands; neither do they pollute the environment, nor profit from political crises. Their aggressive salesmen do not peddle lavish coffins to new widows, nor hawk artificially sweetened breakfast cereals to toddlers on daytime TV; their customers are, or ought to be, highly skilled, wary, hard-nosed professionals, practiced in the techniques of quantification. The company has a reputation for social responsibility which, at least in some ways and compared with many other corporations, it deserves. The sins condemned by Sherman 2—and "sins," as we will see, may not be the right word—are subtler, and difficult to define.

At the moment, it is unfashionable to call for vigorous enforcement of the antitrust laws; some lawyers and economists would like to scrap these laws altogether, and they use the IBM case to bolster their argument. Surely, the ungainliness of this lawsuit dictates that antitrust procedures need streamlining. Just as surely, a careful study of the IBM case suggests that the Sherman Act is as necessary now as it was in 1890, and we dismiss it at our peril.

The second section of the Sherman Act declares that "Every person who shall monopolize or attempt to monopolize . . . any part of the trade or commerce among the Several States, or with foreign nations, shall be deemed guilty of a misdemeanor. . . ." It is an older prohibition than many laymen realize. Jerrold G. Van Cise, in a law textbook for the general practitioner, notes that the Roman Emperor Zeno forbade price fixing and monopolizing. The direct ancestor of Sherman 2 was England's Statute of Monopolies, passed in 1623, by which time many merchants had secured patents of monopoly over a variety of products from salt to playing cards. The statute proclaimed that in the future patents would be awarded only to inventors (and the patent has remained a legal monopoly granted for a limited period to reward those who take the risks of innovation).

Van Cise observes, not originally, that "It has principally been selfishness—not selflessness—that has led explorers to open up new land to feed the hungry, inventors to discover new means to clothe the naked, and businessmen to develop new industries to serve the wants of society," and in judging IBM we ought to remember that the free enterprise system was never based on the assumption that businessmen are altruistic folk. When competition works properly, it serves the consumer, but the contest needs rules: "Uncontrolled," says Van Cise, "the energy of a self-interest may explode into an unfair competitive race in which the beast defeats the best."

The Sherman Act, passed in 1890, was a response to public outcry against the brutal tactics of railway and industrial trusts, giant, powerful organizations which combined to squeeze the farmer, bankrupt the small businessman and reap extortionate profits from the consumer. But the act was not a spontaneous gesture: English common law prohibitions of monopoly and trade restraint had been applied, in somewhat irregular fashion, since the early days of the republic, and some states had even buttressed these injunctions with antimonopoly statutes. The federal law only strengthened the enforcement of traditional sanctions.

In a murder trial, the jury knows a crime has been committed and can examine the murder weapon and photographs of the corpse. The antitrust judge must establish the crime, the corpse and the weapon as well as the defendant's guilt, applying the "rule of reason" to determine whether a corporation's conduct, delineated in hundreds of thousands of pages of documents and testimony, fits a legal definition of "monopolizing" or "attempting to monopolize" "any part of the trade or commerce." The language of the Sherman Act is broad and simple, and lends itself to changing interpretation according to the attitudes of both individual judges and the general public toward big business. This flexibility, while it allows antitrust enforcement to move properly with the times, also makes for long trials, rich lawyers and uneasy clients.

One important issue, for example, is the definition of the market a company is supposed to dominate. The classic defendant's strategy is to draw the market as large as possible, thus diminishing its own share. There is, it might say, a "nourishment" market, in which meat and vegetables and baked goods, wholesalers, supermarkets, butchers and restaurants all slug it out together, competing to fill the customer's stomach; when a man is hungry, after all, he must choose whether he wants a steak or a box of chocolate chip cookies. The plaintiff, on the other hand, tries to depict a narrow market: a man with a yen for chocolate chip cookies won't settle for ginger snaps, and when he reaches for chocolate chip cookies on the supermarket shelf, he finds nothing but Company X's.

The judge must study a business carefully to determine which products are in the same market: how easy is it for the customer to substitute one product for another and for the manufacturer, seeing a lucrative opportunity, to shift his production from widget A to widget B? In 1956 the Supreme Court dismissed the government's complaint that Du Pont had monopolized the market for cellophane. The relevant market, said the Court, was not all the cellophane sold in the United States, of which 75 percent had been produced by Du Pont, but all the "flexible packaging materials," a market in which cellophane competed with Pliofilm, glassine, Saran and a host of other products; Du Pont's share came to less than 20 percent. The Du Pont decision was not unanimous: Mr. Justice Warren, with two colleagues concurring, wrote a vigorous dissent. In scrutinizing another industry, the Court ruled that remote alarm systems which rang in the headquarters of a protection agency were in the same market whether they signaled for fire or burglary, but neither competed with night watchmen or the audible alarm systems that went ring-a-ling on site.

The IBM case follows this antitrust model: the government spent considerable trial time attempting to prove that the principal relevant market was "general purpose electronic digital computer systems," which in its most populous days consisted of IBM and the Seven Dwarfs and perhaps Digital Equipment, Scientific Data Systems and the Singer Company. Now, says the government, IBM's only real competitors are Univac, Burroughs and Honeywell. IBM claims the market is the entire electronic data processing industry, including several hundred firms that sell all sorts of computers, peripherals, terminals and software, as well as the independent lessors. Is the computer business like the cellophane business or the alarm business? It is like neither, of course; it is just like the computer business, and so precedents are of limited usefulness in monopoly cases.

Monopoly power is the power to control prices and exclude competitors. Some evidence of willfulness has been necessary to convict a defendant, and the stickiest job in antitrust law is to distinguish intent to monopolize from what one Chief Justice called "normal methods of industrial development." Among the many practices deemed anticompetitive in various antitrust cases are price discrimination among customers, price-cutting, tie-in sales, reciprocity, certain types of leasing, and horizontal and vertical integration. While some of these practices are more consistently censured than others, Van Cise points out that "every practice singled out for per se condemnation has nevertheless been upheld as lawful . . . in one or more cases." Although corporate lawyers try to be supercautious in counseling their clients, they do not always stand on firm ground, and company executives may gamble on disregarding their advice.

The narrowest margin for acceptable behavior was drawn in the Alcoa case. Lawyers have been debating that decision for thirty years. A brief look at Alcoa will shed some light on the issues; the decision, written by that most articulate of jurists, Learned Hand, is interesting because both IBM and the government can look to it for support.

Until 1909 Alcoa, through patents, held a lawful monopoly of the production of virgin aluminum ingot in the United States. For three years afterward, it maintained that monopoly through unlawful practices which were forbidden by a consent decree in 1912. Nonetheless, between 1912 and 1939 the company continued to be the single producer of virgin ingot in this country; its competitors in the American market, whose share amounted to 10 percent, were all foreign firms. Alcoa maintained that it had done nothing improper since 1912 and Judge Hand, in discussing the purpose of the antitrust laws, postulated that the company's claims were true. Even so, he said:

> Many people believe that possession of unchallenged economic power deadens initiative, discourages thrift and depresses energy; that immunity from competition is a narcotic, and rivalry a stimulant, to industrial progress; that the spur of constant stress is necessary to counteract an inevitable disposition to let well enough alone.

The antitrust laws, said Hand, had other purposes besides the economic: it was, he suggested,

> possible because of its indirect social or moral effect, to prefer a system of small producers, each dependent for his success upon his own skill and character, to one in which the great mass of those engaged must accept the direction of a few.

In establishing Alcoa's intent, Judge Hand went further than any jurist had done in the past. Alcoa's chief strategy had been to plan ahead, to anticipate increases in the demand for ingot and to make sure it was prepared to supply them. Hand asserted:

> Nothing compelled it to keep doubling and redoubling its capacity before others entered the field. It insists that it never excluded competitors: but we can think of no more effective exclusion than progressively to embrace each new opportunity as it opened and to face every newcomer with new capacity already geared into a great organization, having the advantages of experience, trade connections, and the elite of personnel.

"No monopolist," said Hand, "monopolizes unconscious of what he is doing"; Alcoa "meant to keep, and did keep, that complete and exclusive hold upon the ingot market with which it started. That was to monopolize, however innocently it otherwise proceeded."

Hand's strict interpretation of antitrust law can be used to bolster the government's case. He did, however, set limits on the definitions of monopoly and monopolizing, and these may give some support to IBM. First, there was difficulty defining the market in the Alcoa case, and three different definitions allotted Alcoa a share of 90 percent, 64 percent and 33 percent. Hand accepted the 90 percent definition, which gave the company a clear monopoly, but held it doubtful whether the 64 percent share, if accepted, could have sustained a monopoly charge. The most extravagant figures, those used in the government's pretrial brief, have awarded IBM, between 1961 and 1972, the last year covered in the brief, a share which ranged from 83 to 71 percent—higher than "doubtful" but lower than "enough" according to Hand's decision. The 75 percent share has been iffy in other antitrust cases, acquitting some defendants and convicting others. Perhaps a firm whose dominance is less flagrant than Alcoa's might not provoke so strict an interpretation of the antitrust laws.

Finally, Hand excluded from condemnation the firms possessing monopoly by accident, or merely by virtue of skill, foresight and industry. "The successful competitor," said Hand, "having been urged to compete, must not be turned upon when he wins." It is this notion upon which IBM has built its case.

The government charges IBM with monopolizing the market for "general-purpose electronic digital computer systems"—that is, the basic market for 360's, 370's, their direct descendants and Dwarf equivalents (there are separate monopoly claims in the submarkets for peripherals and terminals). This definition excludes military computers which are "ruggedized" to survive rough treatment in the air or at sea, special-purpose machines designed for a particular application such as typesetting, supercomputers, minis and micros. The government claims that Control Data and NCR don't really compete with IBM: CDC's mainframes are now aimed almost exclusively at the scientific customer, while NCR serves limited industrial markets; when the government's market-share witnesses testified, NCR was still making only small computers. The government claims that peripherals, terminals, programs supplied by software houses and service bureau offerings are augmentations of a system already in place, not a substitute for that system. Finally, the government insists that the defendant's market share includes products supplied by the leasing companies and plug-compatible manufacturers that IBM fought so hard.

IBM, on the other hand, asserts that products and services supplied by the independents displace its own offerings, and that their prices and technology affect both IBM's own business decisions and the customer's choice. It notes that a manufacturer of minis or special-purpose equipment can easily move into the 370-plus market (as some have), which makes him a competitor, too. Its share of this diverse and thriving agora, it says, decreased from 78 percent in 1952 to 33 percent in 1972, a period in which the number of companies earning edp revenue grew from nine to more than six hundred.

Which statistics are used in the daily operations of the computer industry? Market researchers like International Data Corporation and Quantum Sciences organize data to make their reports most useful to clients in the industry; should they set it up to prove some legal point they would soon go out of business. Figures on total edp revenues generally appear in surveys of user spending; they give businessmen and economists a feeling of whether the climate is favorable. Such figures might also be valuable to job applicants, publishers launching trade periodicals and journalists studying the industry. Companies that sell hardware, software and services, however, want more specific breakdowns focusing on their true competitors (or customers or suppliers). The market divisions that appear in leading research reports are largely similar to those the government makes. The report from IDC's 1981 Briefing Session, for example, lists revenue figures for "1980 General Purpose Computer Shipments." The companies it places in this market are IBM, five plug-compatible mainframe suppliers, Univac, Honeywell, Burroughs, NCR, CDC, DEC and Cray. IBM's share of this market amounts to 62.4 percent.

Even more interesting, however, is a subtotal of the list. IBM and the four plug-compatibles are separated from the others, and their shares, adding up to 70.1 percent, comprise what IDC calls the "IBM Base." Like the government, the IDC report also lists manufacturers by "installed base"—that is, all mainframes with the company's nameplate, including machines that were purchased or obtained from independent lessors and thus no longer earn money for the manufacturer (here IBM's worldwide share comes to 69.8 percent). Quantum Sciences also records a market for general-purpose computer systems; in 1979 IBM's share of its installed base by dollar value was between 65 and 70 percent.

The purpose of these classifications is to show the interested businessman how much of his market must adhere to technical standards set in Armonk. In this respect anyone who does business in the computer industry must acknowledge the paradox that IBM's most despised competitors sometimes form part of its market share; technologically speaking, there is an IBM world and a non-IBM world, and the company's power exceeds its share of revenues. Like the aluminum ingot, plastic-wrapping and burglar-alarm businesses, the computer industry has its quirks. The government, of course, has made its boundaries a bit too narrow. The IDC figures, citing manufacturers excluded by the government, mark the overlapping borders between scientific, mini and general-purpose computers.

Until 1968 IBM's own business decisions were based on market-share measurements similar to the government's. The Commercial Analysis department reported on market share via COMSTAT figures sent in by the salesmen. IBM has little praise for COMSTAT now. "Besides being the worst kind of hearsay," notes the company's pretrial brief, "it is grossly inaccurate and consistently underestimates competitive activity." The story of Project Yardstick, cited by the government, explains how the company came to lose faith in its own measurement methods.

Yardstick, an effort to revamp IBM's procedures for gauging market share, was launched in 1968 while the government was discussing market measurement with company lawyers. The new procedures counted only the equipment IBM was renting to customers, excluding the gear purchased outright by customers and leasing companies. The result was to lower IBM's share, the first step toward achieving the broad market definition the company now uses in court.

IBM avows that the impetus for the project came from management, which had long found COMSTAT inadequate for decision-making and wanted to add material from other sources. The government claims Project Yardstick was a lawyer-inspired gambit to cosmeticize IBM's monopoly position, and that marketing and forecasting people found it a nuisance. A document called "Share Measurement Change Why & Action" gives three reasons for the switch. Under "Business," it says, "The marketplace is changing. It is difficult for management to take the 'best action' without adequate data. ... We are hiding future market growth areas. ..." Under "Antitrust" it says, "We have told the Department of Justice how to measure the market. Our internal measurements do not agree with the above. . . . If IBM's internal measurements cover the Data Processing Industry in methodology and scope, then our share percentage borders on monopoly. . . . We must not put IBM's executives in an untenable legal position relative to market share data in their files if they were called to testify in the future." Finally, under "Legal," it says simply, "IBM's outside Legal Counsel has requested these changes."

The government cites the special combination of business practices peculiar to the computer industry—leasing, bundling, total systems selling and nonstandard software—as evidence of IBM's power to control prices and exclude competition. The government argues that while IBM had financial incentives to unbundle, and while bundled software put a heavy burden on the programming staff, its value as an anticompetitive marketing tool ensured its survival until legal and business pressures became insupportable.

The government cites many documents to show that the company, in Hand's phrase, did not monopolize unconscious of what it was doing; some excerpts from these give the flavor of management's thinking. In setting prices, IBM tried to balance the conflicting goals of high profit and a stable market share. In November 1963, as the announcement date for System 360 approached, Tom Watson wrote a memo to Kenneth Davis, the company's senior financial officer. IBM's prices were too far above the competition's, said the chief executive, and increasingly, the company had to promote its support services as the competitive advantage over less expensive hardware. Some of the problem, Watson felt, could be attributed to "a certain flabbiness in our development and production side," but the engineers oughtn't to bear all the burden; it was time to reconsider pricing policies. Characteristically, Watson was as worried about esprit de corps as he was concerned with cold numbers; he continued,

> To gain the profit positions that we want, we ask our engineers to do the impossible and we are building up a frustration in Engineering. We ask our sales force to appear with machines that are always higher than our competitors' and this doesn't help their morale. And so I think we must conclude that as our competitors drop their prices, we have a clear choice. We can either follow them, or we can maintain our very high margins, have a balance sheet that looks unusually good

for two, three, or even four years, and then reap what we have sown in the forms of substantially less markets, lowered prestige and even greater frustration.

Another memo, written in January 1966, tells much about the way Watson saw IBM's role in the industry. Here the chairman was stating, for the record, the corporate goals:

> The goal of the IBM Company is to keep the organization dynamic and growing, and moving ahead to the benefit of the three affected groups—the employees, the stockholders, and the customers and public . . . that IBM should attempt to maintain its market share in the immediate foreseeable future with the idea that with the industry growing as rapidly as it is, other companies can grow quite rapidly under this general mandate.

While there is a certain kingly elegance to Watson's *oeuvre*, his lieutenants could be a bit more crass; either way, the IBM spirit was giving H. Bartow Farr, Jr., the Data Processing Group legal counsel, a conniption fit. This memo, sent by Farr to fourteen DPG managers in October 1966, reads nicely to the sound of Alka-Seltzer fizzing in the glass:

> I would like to make a few suggestions on the recent strategy conference charts.
> 1. Try to avoid unnecessary militant language. Remember, your presentations may be read aloud in a courtroom some day and try to envisage their effect on a jury which is deciding whether IBM deliberately attempted to maintain a monopoly position. . . .
> 2. (Fairly lengthy suggestions for projecting market share.)
> 3. Avoid as a strategy objective maintaining or increasing market share or competitive position at least where the market share is currently in excess of 50%. Use the term market leadership which is sufficient to get the point across. Similarly, avoid such phrasing as "containment of competitive threats" and substitute instead "maintain position of leadership."
> 4. Avoid implying that you might suppress technological improvements unless competition forces your hand.
> 5. Never imply that we would be willing to sacrifice profit for market share.
> 6. Avoid expressing a strategy as designed solely to contain a competitive announcement. . . .
> 7. Avoid justifying a loss machine on the basis that it will help sell

more of something else. This is particularly true when there are separate competitors for the loss machine. Similarly, avoid implication of abnormal allocation of costs in related items in order to subsidize the one facing the most competition. . . .

8. Avoid forecasting a high market share for an unprofitable item. If such a situation occurs, just omit market share figures. Conversely, avoid forecasting greater than normal profit where we have an unusually high market share.

Perhaps the most incriminating document in the IBM Papers is the Faw memorandum, allegedly prepared to edify Cravath, Swaine & Moore, IBM's legal counsel, in November 1969, ten months after the Justice Department brought suit; the author is Hilary F. Faw, IBM Director of Business Practices. The memo, which received wide coverage in the trade press, summarizes the strategies of leasing, total systems selling, pricing and timing. The first paragraphs make fairly abstruse reading, but here are the conclusions:

> The key underpinnings to our control of price are interrelated and interdependent. One cannot be changed without impacting others.
>
> These interrelationships are not well or widely understood by IBM Management. Our price control has been sufficiently absolute to render unnecessary direct management involvement in the means . . . [the next five or so lines were deleted from document]
>
> The D.J. Complaint specifically covers varying profit margins and an intensive investigation of this issue would reveal the extent of our price control and its supporting practices. Such a revelation would not be helpful to our monopoly defense. . . .

If you ask me, says Mr. Faw, we are guilty as hell. But that is only one man's opinion.

The problem of assessing complex behavior and motivations becomes more difficult with the next batch of government charges. IBM is accused of selling "fighting machines," a phrase which harks back to the "fighting ships" charge in Thomsen v. Cayser, a 1917 case in which a combination of shipowners was charged with giving rebates to customers who remained exclusively loyal on routes which were vulnerable to lower-priced competition. In IBM's case, the fighting machine charge alleges "precipitous announcement or introduction by IBM of selected computer products, usually with low profit expectations, in those markets or segments of the markets where IBM's monopoly position had eroded or threatened to erode."

The "fighting machines" on the government's comprehensive list include the entire 360 series, the model 67 time-sharing machine, a small scientific computer called the 44, and the Mallard disc drives.

The designation of System 360—an entire product line—as a fighting machine is rather a surprise. The government doesn't claim that the 360 models had "unusually low profit expectations"; it does assert that the acceleration of the system's announcement, brought on by competitive pressure, was an abuse of monopoly power.

IBM doesn't deny that it announced the series earlier than it would have without competition. "True, undoubtedly true," says the defendant's brief, "but, so what? No violation of law can arise from such facts." The company maintains that the 360 was technologically advanced and required an enormous commitment and risk, that the "driving force behind . . . System 360 was a concern that if IBM was not best and first, it would lose out to competitors." This, says the brief, should be "the model of the best type of competitive conduct which our system can produce."

Certainly it is normal business behavior to push a product through when competition threatens. But the government points out that the speed-up required the waiver of certain product testing procedures. G. Berry McCarter, who headed the product testing department when System 360 was announced, testified that the main purpose of pre-announcement tests was to identify potential development and manufacturing problems; without the tests, he couldn't predict what complications would arise. But the hardware, software and manufacturing people said they could meet their commitments, so the product was announced. It took several years before the software worked well. In a properly operating competitive system, a company whose products don't perform adequately should suffer for it; IBM didn't suffer. System 360 doesn't fit the classical definition of a fighting machine, but its early success argues for monopoly power.

Except for the Mallard disc drive, IBM's other "fighting machines" were all notorious failures. At announcement time the models 90 and the 360/67 showed high risk of loss and very limited possibilities of profit. IBM asserts that these machines were a proper response to customer needs and competitive efforts—or as Learson put it in his deposition, that the company could "not be Packard or

Stutz and do nothing." And if IBM had monopoly power, it argues, how did the CDC supercomputer manage to outsell IBM's models 90 by about five to one? The string of financial disasters in the scientific market is a poor argument for IBM's omnipotence. But particularly in the case of the models 90, the company was both able and willing to take inordinate financial risks and continued to cut prices, possibly selling below cost (methods of accounting for advanced technology were the subject of some courtroom haggling). It is hard to imagine Burroughs or Univac shaking up the marketplace as IBM did with the announcements of the 90 and the 67.

Of all the business practices cited by the government, IBM's "educational allowance" poses the most interesting philosophical questions. As far back as the twenties, when the small company was trying to make its mark, it had donated machines to educational institutions, and Watson had believed ever afterward that if IBM showed kindness to universities, the world would look kindly on IBM. During the computer era, the cornerstone of the company's largesse was an equipment discount offered to universities, colleges and secondary schools: sometimes the discount mounted to 60 percent, and other times it descended to 10 percent. The basic allowance was supplemented by several kinds of selective subsidies: there were "value received" contracts, in which the university customer supplied research or consulting services in exchange for rental credits or cash payments; "buy-backs" of excess computer time which the university had and IBM needed; outright grants and contributions; and gratis machines.

The rewards IBM hoped would accrue from its educational support policies were greater than mere good will. Universities were prestigious installations which influenced the decisions of ordinary customers. Research done on an IBM machine would stretch the capabilities of that machine, making it more attractive in the marketplace. And most important was the way school experiences shaped the young computer expert's later life: a man who had learned his trade on IBM gear would go out into the world—to corporations, to other universities, to government jobs—with a predisposition toward that equipment.

During the early days of the trial one of the distinguished men of university computing, Dr. Alan J. Perlis, now of Yale and late of

Carnegie-Mellon, testifying for the government, described the effects of IBM's educational policies. Dr. Perlis's answer to cross-examination by defense counsel tells the story:

> The 60% discount IBM made available to universities opened up digital computing in universities in the sense that almost no university was able to afford . . . funds of the kind required to establish a digital computer lab until that discount became available, after which there were just a very large number of IBM computers . . . in the universities and forming the focus of computer centers.

Asked whether IBM educational allowance policy was one of the principal forces enabling universities to become competent in computing as soon as they did, Perlis answered, "Absolutely."

On direct examination, Perlis had described IBM's solid position in the university curriculum. While FORTRAN was an important IBM invention, before 1971, "85 to 99 percent of students were taught that programming and learning FORTRAN were synonymous . . . if they had been taught as most courses were organized in the U.S., they would tend to equate computing, programming, FORTRAN and IBM as all one ball of wax."

It was a sticky ball of wax in light of the 1967 report of the President's Science Advisory Committee on computers in higher education, which stated categorically:

> We believe that undergraduate college education without adequate computing is deficient education, just as undergraduate education without adequate library facilities would be deficient education.

The report argued for greater federal subsidies for computing in education; en route to its conclusions; it noted that "Great good has been done through donated computers, obsolescent computers, and the struggles of enthusiastic men with inadequate machines."

The story, then, is familiar: IBM developed the market, and so developed the art. The greatest beneficiary, perhaps, was IBM, but the universities and the entire field gained, too. The Dwarfs followed suit, offering educational discounts as they were able. It is difficult—seriously, not ironically difficult—to measure the price paid in intellectual freedom. If the benefits exceeded the price, the next question is whether doing good is enough, or whether one must also do good for the right reasons. How much altruism have we a right to expect from a corporation?

The government cites many documents that show how value-received contracts, grants and gratis machines were offered to accounts that looked in danger of going competitive. The haggling that goes on between universities and vendors in the computer industry would do credit to an Oriental bazaar. Dr. Perlis described the negotiations for a time-sharing machine at Carnegie Tech. GE had the most advanced time-sharing computer, but its main memory was too small. The CDC machine had the best raw speed, but it was not designed for time-sharing. IBM offered the model 67. Carnegie wasn't sure of its needs: the IBM and CDC systems seemed most capable of expansion, but IBM's price was $20,000 a month higher. The IBM system had more of what Carnegie wanted but not enough to justify the difference in rental.

Carnegie had heard IBM was giving a break to MIT and Stanford; Perlis thought Carnegie ought to be treated "likewise well." It was up to IBM to bring its system into line with the CDC price. IBM came back with a proposed two-year contract for $200,000 worth of research. It was, said Perlis, "quite clear to us that the tasks listed were ones we would ordinarily be doing anyhow, and it was also obvious that IBM's r and d program was not waiting with bated breath for us to accomplish these tasks. . . ." Perlis didn't want to be obligated to supply service to IBM, but "we signed the contract because we wanted to get the machine and get on with our work and not play games any more." Asked by the Court why he didn't want to sign the contract, Perlis replied that "in a very real sense it was a sham."

When the first contract expired. IBM came back to Carnegie with a more specific set of requirements, and "ultimately the dollar value of the contract was lessened. . . ." Perlis admitted Carnegie was to blame for signing the first contract, but now that work on the new machine was under way, the university had no recourse but to sign the second contract.

Cross-examination was designed to bring out that IBM was genuinely interested in Carnegie research, that the IBM machine was mostly superior for Carnegie's purposes, and that CDC had offered a discount and a research grant too. The story of IBM's dealings with universities elicits little sympathy for either side. The professors were hardly innocent victims; IBM and the other vendors were not noble philanthropists. The legal question is whether IBM's educational policies were discriminatory and constituted anticompetitive price-cutting; the moral questions are more interesting.

Among the government's other important claims are that the exit of GE, RCA and Xerox from the computer mainframe business— three companies which were highly successful in other endeavors— was evidence of IBM's monopoly power; and that IBM's actions against the leasing companies and the pcm's were monopolistic and anticompetitive. The flurry of new products and price changes during the past several years were an updating of IBM's traditional competitive strategies, aimed once more at pcm's and lessors. Itel, which was both a lessor and a pcm, left the business; like many of IBM's previous fallen competitors, it had operating problems of its own, but even stronger pcm's were tarnished on Wall Street. As for the Dwarfs, the case-by-case argument that each was put out of business directly by IBM is unconvincing, even though IBM knew its peripherals and 370 pricing actions, aimed at the pcm's, were also damaging RCA; the defunct Dwarfs made serious mistakes in judgment throughout their history. But cumulatively, their departures show a most disturbing pattern, which suggests that the margin for error among IBM's competitors is dangerously narrow; companies of distinguished reputation, including IBM, are eminently fallible and can survive many mistakes in a favorable business climate. The Dwarfs did not fail through inferior products; all made important contributions to computing, and their presence as an alternative to IBM has been missed.

After examining the government's claims, it is interesting to look at the industry through IBM's eyes. The tone of outrage in IBM's brief parallels the anger in the government's. The company observes:

> The electronic data processing industry and IBM have delivered greater product performance and price reduction to consumers, and have delivered them faster and more consistently, than any other industry or company in the history of this country. . . . In a period of rising prices and escalating costs, the EDP industry is virtually alone in giving consumers better products at lower prices. . . .

The extraordinary record of the computer industry is central to IBM's case.

Early in the brief there is a chart showing the legal precedent in six previous Sherman 2 antitrust cases, four in which the defendant was found guilty (Alcoa, United Shoe, American Tobacco and Grinnell) and two which resulted in exoneration (the Du Pont cellophane case and Hughes Tool). The monopolized industries were mostly over sixty years old and had little record of price and product improvements: United Shoe was selling twenty-eight-year-old machines, and American Tobacco's prices had gone up even during the Depression. The market share of three of the guilty defendants was over 80 percent, while American Tobacco had held 75 percent of the cigarette industry for forty years. According to IBM's chart, these defendants' competitors were few and insignificant. The innocent defendants, on the other hand, were in industries only a quarter-century old, not much younger than the computer industry, and had a record of lowered prices and improved products. Hughes Tool had kept a stable share of 75 percent of the rotary drilling bit industry, and had only four significant competitors. Under "reasons for success" IBM briefly lists various flagrant-sounding anticompetitive practices for the guilty defendants and benign, commendable behavior for the innocents; monopolistic tactics, however, are in the eye of the judicial beholder and, like the abuses of which IBM stands accused, are too complicated to analyze on a chart. But the listings do give a picture of four withering industries, an adjective inapplicable to the computer business.

The next batch of charts shows the remarkable improvements over four generations of computers introduced between 1952 and 1974, the year before the trial began (IBM uses its own equipment as a base, but the standard is general to the industry). Processor performance per dollar of rental is 85 times better; memories fit 43½ times the capacity into 800 times less space per rental dollar; price/performance of magnetic tape units is 158 times improved; and the total cost of performing 100,000 multiplications has dropped from $1.26 in 1952 to $.01 in 1974. Updated charts would be even more impressive.

All these figures have given the customer something to cheer about, but they are somewhat deceptive. More bang for the buck, which is what they add up to, has largely been the result of developments in component technology made by the semiconductor industry. And while IBM has been responsible for some important developments in computing, its record as a technological pioneer is not proportionate to its share of the market.

In a book entitled *The U.S. Computer Industry, A Study of Market Power*, which came out at the time the trial began, Gerald Brock, a University of Arizona economist, notes that neither IBM nor any other single firm has consistently led in technology. Moreover, no firm has made an important innovation that was not duplicated quickly by another firm. Brock observes:

> The rate of advance has been kept extremely high by the many opportunities for advance and the competitiveness of the industry. The rate of advance possible has been so high that no firm can maintain its market position without continual advance and reduction of prices. Innovative possibilities not used by the dominant firms are likely to cause new entry into the industry or expansion of the smaller established firms.

A tour of the exhibit floors at the National Computer Conference, the industry's annual fête and bazaar, is a dizzying, fatiguing experience. At booth after booth, nervy young salesmen in Captain Kangaroo haircuts and aviator glasses are demonstrating why this terminal or minicomputer or software package is a quantum jump ahead of the one next door; the spiels are infinite, the load of literature and souvenirs an invitation to bursitis. This is IBM's market for "electronic data processing," served from the ever-bubbling cauldron of technology and hope. There is no time, of course, to examine each company's financial history or the progress of its stock, nor to reflect on how many of these exhibitors were here five years ago, and which ones will be around five years—or even one year—from now. But the impression presented by the show is so powerful that one is tempted to imagine the Sunday afternoon when the exhibits were set up. A fleet of quite different-looking young men is bustling about, hammers in hand, nails in the mouth, building booths. They are wearing three-piece pin-striped Brooks Brothers suits, and their neckties are slung nonchalantly over the shoulder, Ivy-league fashion. They are all associates with Cravath, Swaine & Moore.

In a competitive industry IBM has, it asserts, done just what it was supposed to do: it has competed. As the brief notes,

> IBM was, in the early years of the EDP industry, a company of relatively moderate size compared to the giants in electronics, AT&T and GE, and substantially larger companies, such as RCA, Sperry Rand and Bendix Aviation, who entered the industry in the 1950's.

Yet IBM has become one of the most dramatic industrial success stories of the twentieth century, growing at a more rapid rate than either
GE or AT&T, although IBM is still not as large as either. IBM's explosive growth has resulted solely from internal expansion in response to
consumer demand for IBM's products and services—the procompeti-
tive and judicially approved "socially preferable" alternative to
growth by acquisition and merger. . . . IBM's success is the result of
skill, industry and foresight, *i.e.* better products, business acumen, and
risk-taking and overall superiority in satisfying customer demand.

Now, of course, IBM has passed GE; otherwise, about three-
quarters of that statement is undisputably true. Only the parts about
"better products" and "superiority in satisfying customer demand"
are debatable. As Judge Christensen, the only judge who ruled
against IBM, observed, the legal term "skill, industry and foresight"
is an odd one: surely monopolistic tactics are devised through foresight and practiced with skill and industry. The formula of leasing,
total systems selling and bundled pricing was the result of extraordinary business acumen.

The claim of "better products" doesn't jibe with IBM's Quarterly
Product Line Assessments, in which the Commercial Analysis Department rated the company's gear against the competition. In the
August 1971 QPLA, for example, seven IBM products were marked
"superior"; sixteen were "equal" and eighteen "deficient." The
QPLA's ought not to be used—as they are by IBM's more violent
critics—to suggest that the company sells shoddy equipment. They
show that IBM had the discipline to take a hard look at its products,
many of which had been in the field longer than the competitors'.
But they also demonstrate that the customer's interests are not best
served by dealing exclusively with IBM, nor are the failures and
difficulties of competitors the result of poor technology.

IBM argues with merit that unlike GE and RCA it made a commitment to electronic data processing and supported that commitment with "bold and resolute decisions" and great risks; among these
were the original decision to enter the computer industry over the
objections of the elder Watson, the undertaking of the Defense Department's SAGE contract, and System 360. There is a school of
opinion which says there were no risks, that IBM had the industry
sewed up from the start. That argument is unconvincing. IBM could
have lost the game in the early days, and GE or Sperry or RCA

could have won; whatever its mistakes, IBM generally had more nerve and savvy than its larger competitors.

IBM defends the bundling-leasing package as a response to customer needs in marketing a complex and unfamiliar product, a willingness to take the responsibility of making its products work and to absorb the risks of obsolescence in a fast-moving technology. That is true; it is equally true that the package became the means to secure and perpetuate the monopoly. Here, as in other aspects of the case, it is not simple to determine what the user has gained and lost.

In particular, IBM sees the antitrust suit as an attack on the process of competition. The very incidents that the government describes—the fighting machines, the action against the leasing companies and peripherals houses—and the documents that show IBM studying the competition and planning its response are proof that the company does lead what Judge Wyzanski, in the United Shoe case, called "the quiet life" of a monopolist:

> IBM innovates, competitors threaten, IBM reacts, competitors react in turn and IBM reacts again. Each action or reaction described is a better product or a lower price. This is not the "quiet life" of monopoly but the very essence of competition.

IBM does not, of course, mention the scenario which begins with competitors innovating.

The proceedings, even without the squabbling among the lawyers, make campy reading. The evidence falls into four categories: testimony of experts; testimony of users and competitors in various segments of the industry, with supporting documentation; testimony of IBM executives, present and former; and IBM's internal documents. Expert testimony is a war between "their" specialists and "our" specialists: the venture capitalists with impressive credentials who say small companies have trouble raising money because prospective patrons fear IBM's might and the venture capitalists with equally impressive credentials who swear that bright, competent people with a promising idea can always find a backer; and the distinguished economists presenting incontrovertible theories on either side.

Testimony of competitors presents a different problem: the competing executive is talking for his shareholders as well as the judge. The president of a large, substantial corporation may be reluctant to show himself at the mercy of IBM; the chief executive of a small, struggling company, on the other hand, may decide he has nothing to lose and everything to gain by blaming all his troubles on the giant. The weight of each witness's testimony will depend on the judge's subjective impressions and his ability to separate substance from hype.

Much of the government's case rests on IBM's internal documents, which are supposed to represent the smoking gun. IBM's executives who authored or received various memos and reports were shown the documents and asked to comment on them. Besides the expected "I don't recall this," there were several dominant themes. A senior executive writing a junior man in monopolistic vein was "playing the devil's advocate" or "giving him the needle." A junior executive addressing his boss with similar indiscretion was "overstating the case just to get management's attention." Sometimes a damaging document was written by a marketing man about engineering, in which case the author was obviously way out of his depth; other times a marketing man was writing about marketing, and thus speaking from a vested interest.

There is some truth in all of this: in any organization, most of the interoffice mail is hot air. But since almost all memos are written to advocate something, they compel the author to choose the arguments that seem most convincing, and so tell us something about him, the person he is writing to, and the company where they work. A company shouldn't be shot down for one impure thought expressed by George in the branch office in Sandusky, Ohio on the day he lost his best customer; but if lots of Georges in different parts of the corporation express the same impure thought, it becomes part of the corporate canon. By these standards, much of IBM's defense for its documents doesn't wash.

Two obvious questions arise from studying the industry and the issues in the case. The first is "What should one think of IBM?"—a question which is not just philosophically interesting but also bears on antitrust law in general; the second is "What ought to be done?"—which pertains to the future of the computer industry. The documents shed considerable light on question one.

There are three different batches of IBM Papers, each with a different character. The minutes of the management committee meetings were made public in 1973 during the Telex trial; they are cited frequently in earlier chapters. They show the complexity of running a large corporation, and the intricate balance of varied goals and interests; they illuminate the character of management, which, despite occasional arrogance and the expected gamut of human failings, displays an attitude toward issues and people that is generally intelligent and humane. All things considered, they enhance respect for the company. Then there are the routine reports and memos released in connection with this and other lawsuits; these invite a harsher view.

Finally, there is a group of memos admitted in evidence in the government case after IBM lost a claim of lawyer-client privilege; a couple have been cited here. They show the knowledge that some of IBM's practices were indefensible. In the case of unbundling in particular, they show the company finding the most convenient solutions first and devising glib rationales for competitors, customers and the Justice Department later. Among the "Alternatives Regarding Tie-In Problem," listed in one memo, is to maintain the bundle but turn the branch offices into franchised dealerships; the purpose is to "Throw sand in the eyes of D.J. Make D.J. . . . proceed against 100 to 150 independent dealers in order to break the tie." Also, the documents show an effort (not always successful) to sanitize the files, substituting legally acceptable motives for anticompetitive ones and replacing rough phrases with euphemisms. Nor was the problem simply one of restraining hot-blooded young men: several of Bartow Farr's "clean-up-your-act" memos were addressed to vice-presidents, including Cary, Opel and Beitzel.

These documents tarnish the veracity of entries in the minutes which show legitimate business motives and even, on occasion, statesmanlike concerns. IBM's management had been reminded, as far back as 1966, that it was talking for an audience. It would take an advanced case of paranoia to assume the minutes are totally fraudulent: they are a detailed four-year record of the management of a giant corporation, essential to its functioning. When the television cameras spend a day following some official around he does get some work done, even while turning his better profile to the viewers; this cleaner version of the official is the official nonetheless. In areas that don't directly concern the antitrust suit—policies toward personnel, for example, and social issues—the minutes are trustworthy. All the discussions in the minutes carry some weight. But there is no question that IBM's primary goal was to protect its turf, and toward this end it would do whatever it could get away with. It gave no quarter and deserves none in return.

IBM has a great reputation for social responsibility, and in assessing the company we ought to see if that reputation is justified; its bearing on antitrust issues will appear shortly. In 1968, IBM leased and renovated a warehouse in Brooklyn's Bedford-Stuyvesant ghetto, hired and trained a staff from the community and had a plant producing cables for computers in three months. Ten years later this successful venture moved into a newly built plant. The general manager and most of the other managers and employees are from ethnic minority groups. IBM has made numerous grants to black and women's colleges, and has supported programs for minority and women students in engineering and business schools. It does $40 million worth of business with 500 minority-owned suppliers. It has received awards from the National Urban League, the Interracial Council for Business Opportunity, the League of United Latin American Citizens and the New Rochelle NAACP, among other organizations.

Equal employment efforts, spearheaded by Watson in the 60's, seem—at least on paper—fairly impressive. Goals for hiring and promoting women and minorities are now incorporated in the operating plans. A manager's record on equal opportunity affects his promotion. There has been a large spurt in the number of women and minority managers. Measured against a broad sampling of companies with more than 100 employees taken by the Equal Employment Opportunity Commission, IBM's record for black managers—5½ percent of the managerial total—is slightly less dismal than the national average (below 4 percent). Its record for women is still relatively poor: in the EEOC's sampling, 17 percent of corporate managers are women, while in IBM the figure is less than 8 percent.

The computer industry's renown as an egalitarian paradise is misplaced: industry EEOC figures for black and women managers are below both IBM's and the national average. Some women have earned distinction in the industry but few have held positions of corporate power. As for blacks, in the course of research for this book I have interviewed several hundred members of the computer industry, chosen because they either held important jobs or had worked on significant projects; I have never interviewed a black person at IBM or anywhere else, and have heard of only one at a high level, a Xerox executive in California. Like most large industrial corporations in America, IBM remains in its senior ranks a white male preserve. The percentages for women and black salesmen, the chief resource for high positions in the company, are somewhat better, which suggests the company is trying, but it still has a long way to go.

When public concern for computers and the invasion of privacy began to heat up, IBM hired Alan Westin, the leading authority in the field, to help overhaul its own procedures for gathering information about employees. IBM'ers no longer take personality or general intelligence tests, and performance evaluations are removed from personnel files after three years. Much personal information about employees has been deemed irrelevant and either kept off applications or held off-limits to bosses. Employees are given a chance to correct factual errors in their files and to obtain a summary of evaluations used for promotion. The company won't give information about an employee to a credit bureau or government agency without his consent. It is, of course, enlightened self-interest for a computer company to clean its own house first; still, that enlightenment is to IBM's credit.

IBM is one of many corporations that have been criticized by the National Council of Churches for operating in South Africa. The company was among the first to endorse the "Sullivan principles" for equal treatment of all its employees, and contributed to various black education programs. Its South African business accounts for less than 1 percent of its gross revenues, and of this amount sales to the South African government make up less than one-fifth. Still, IBM is the dominant computer supplier, and there are few government agencies that don't use some of its equipment. The rumor that IBM equipment prints black citizens' passbooks is erroneous; it has been used, according to the National Council of Churches, to register coloreds and Asians.

The company states that "It is IBM's policy not to bid for business anywhere in the world where it believes its equipment would be used for repressive purposes and we know of no case where it is so used. However, it would be misleading to suggest that any manufacturer can control how its products are used." In a somewhat contradictory argument, it asserts that to withdraw from South Africa or refuse to sell to the South African government would set "a precedent of taking foreign policy out of the hands of government and putting it into the hands of corporations."

Whether American corporations should do business in South Africa is debatable; but computers aren't Coca-Cola, and their suppliers have responsibilities, at home and abroad, that don't apply to other companies; in the U.S., IBM has recognized these responsibilities in its policies on privacy protection. Despite IBM's questionable performance in South Africa, however, Timothy Smith of the National Council of Churches says, "On social issues in general, they are certainly not in the conservative wing of the business community, and they're positive performers on many issues. They're better than above average."

This bears out the conclusion that in social matters, IBM is usually (but not always) responsive, rarely (but on occasion) innovative. As a competitor, however, it has few scruples. The business conduct guidelines which IBM circulates among its employees—with strongly worded sections on "discussion of IBM's size," "taking 'direct aim' at competitors," and "obtaining competitive information" are certainly commendable, and Cary says, "We expect people to operate under these principles or we'd rather lose the business. You can't manage a business on a grey line." In a speech Cary once observed, "I think it is clear that if the chief executive winks, some of his employees will wink back." Still, these employees are under tremendous pressure to perform; there is no question that fear is a strong element in IBM's style of management. This affects the tone of many memos written by IBM's middle managers, which suggest that the eyes of the company's highest executives suffer a fearful tic.

There are, perhaps, a few gentlemanly companies. They are the ones that get written up on the front page of the *Wall Street Journal* for their leisurely manufacture of riding boots or Tabasco sauce. In testimony before the Senate Subcommittee on Antitrust and Monopoly several years ago, former Xerox executive Dan McGurk observed that "Monopoly or a significant power over the marketplace is the goal of all managers of free enterprises." It is silly to ask whether IBM "intends" or "attempts" to monopolize—of course it does. So do all companies—and IBM, after all, is in other matters of conscience "better than above average." At one time or another, the accusations of reciprocity, lavish promises and other sharp selling practices have been leveled against most of the Dwarfs and many of the independents. The computer business is cleaner than most others. Nor is ruthlessness the exclusive property of businessmen—it is also found among artists, writers and college professors. It would be nice to eliminate ruthlessness from American life, if someone could figure out how. Meanwhile, it seems more realistic to expect it and try to minimize its bad effects by setting clear limits on what sort of behavior we will tolerate.

Well over a decade has passed since the government brought suit against IBM. A good deal of that time will have been spent trying to prove IBM's intent—a charade which offends the spectator, corrupts the witness and wastes the taxpayers' money. If one accepts the premise that "intent to monopolize" is built into our system, it is foolish to waste time determining whether Company A has more intent than Company B. The only questions worth asking are "Has the company monopoly power?"; "If so, is it desirable to perpetuate that power?"; "If not, what is the best way to dissipate that power?" In 1972 the late Senator Philip Hart, who had come to similar conclusions, proposed the Industrial Reorganization Act, an extensive revision of antitrust policy; in 1976, when the chances of passage of that bill seemed slim, he introduced a more moderate bill to amend the Sherman Act. Both proposals, unfortunately, died with Hart; the bills and their author were believed, inaccurately, to be radical. It is time they were reconsidered. The procedural reforms that have been suggested since then don't really confront the problem.

The Hart amendment, sometimes known as "no-fault monopoly," eliminates the need to prove intent in a government antitrust suit; correspondingly, superior performance would no longer be an acceptable defense. A defendant could prevent divestiture by proving its monopoly is attributable to a lawful patent, or that divestiture would bring about the loss of substantial economies of scale. The amendment recognizes that a government suit aims to restore competition to an industry while the private plaintiff's goal is to recover damages. The private plaintiff, therefore, would be subject to the old requirement to prove wrongdoing; if his suit followed a successful government action, monopoly power would be established and the private plaintiff and the defendant would argue on the basis of wrongful conduct versus superior performance. The amended act would cut considerable time from discovery and trial and remove the unrealistic and unfair element of moral censure.

The Industrial Reorganization Act takes a more aggressive posture. It proclaims a rebuttable presumption of monopoly power when there has been no substantial price competition in a line of commerce in any section of the country for three consecutive years out of the preceding five, or when four or fewer corporations account for 50 percent of the sales in any of the preceding three years. The defenses against divestiture are the same as those in the amendment to the Sherman Act—lawful patents and economies of scale.

The act provides for an Industrial Reorganization Commission to study whether monopoly power exists in various industries and to propose reorganization and other relief to an Industrial Reorganization Court, which would hear the companies' defenses and enter a judgment.

As Senator Hart observed in Congress, there are precedents for legislative restructuring, most notably the Public Utility Holding Act and the Glass-Steagall Act, and his bill, in requiring monopoly power before divestiture, was more conservative than these. The act doesn't pursue large corporations with a meat cleaver: it maintains true economies of scale, but the burden of proof is with the company. Determining these economies would still be a complex job, and the sticky question of market definition would remain. Some observers have suggested tax incentives for corporations of a certain size to make divestitures; this policy could be coupled with one of Hart's measures.

Without considerations of intent, the IBM case is a difficult one: there are compelling arguments on either side, advanced both in court and in the industry at large. A prime concern should be the need to provide a healthy environment for small companies to compete in a vital technology. The subject is well analyzed by Gerald Brock in his study of the computer industry. Brock summarizes the most frequent arguments of economists who hold that innovation is better served by economic concentration and market power. Essentially, these arguments suggest that only large companies have adequate internal funds to finance big research projects; that the greater the company's market share, the more it has to gain from introducing new products (and the large company can sell the product faster and more widely than the small firm); that large companies can afford the "basic" research in many areas that leads to greater technological fallout. He notes, on the other hand, that many innovations aren't that expensive; that in a big company a new product must fight its way through many levels of management; and that high profits can insulate management from the need to innovate. To Brock's analysis it might be added that IBM took its greatest risks when it was smaller, thereby surpassing larger, more cautious rivals. Even System 360 was more the result of entrepreneurial instinct than the disciplined, scientific management for which the company is now famous, and the family entrepreneur responsible for these courageous moves retired long ago.

The conduct of AT & T before and after it was challenged by competition is a lesson to those who would trust the future of an important technology to one large company; nor does such a policy seem the best way to meet foreign competition, whatever that company's present success in foreign markets. As Brock observes—and as anyone who has studied the industry can see—technological progress in computers has been served by a combination of large and small firms. Besides contributing actual innovations, the small companies have been gadflies to the large corporations and have provided homes for many talented people who wouldn't work for a big company. Even if all the Dwarfs survive, the industry may grow stagnant without the small firms—and three Dwarfs have died since 1970. Predictions of their future health fluctuate over time from very optimistic to gloomy—but they are always pegged to IBM's behavior.

The question remains whether adequate competition will survive even if no action is taken. The story of Gene Amdahl's efforts to start his company shows the difficulty of this question. When Amdahl left IBM in 1970 to start a company making large plug-compatible mainframes, he figured he needed $33 million to $44 million to enter the market. Amdahl decided to try raising the money in small steps; after each he would have something to show prospective investors at the next level. It was the worst possible time to raise money; a recession was on and RCA's strategy of being nearly compatible with IBM was proving unsuccessful. The refusals Amdahl got were all tied to the difficulty of competing with IBM. Finally, when hope had almost run out, he managed to raise $2 million to get his company to the first level. The second-level financing, after months of fruitless searching across the country, was $5 million from Fujitsu. A third round of financing from Fujitsu and a German company enabled Amdahl to build a prototype and tool up; his luck in the American capital markets was next to nil.

The company experienced further delays in financing and had to redesign its machine in accord with IBM's newest announcement; what money it raised to tide it over came from Fujitsu. Once the company started showing a profit, it made a successful public stock offering; its growth for the next four years was extraordinary, until IBM's retaliation sent Amdahl's revenues, earnings and stock plummeting. Amdahl would be fighting for survival from then on. Its founder was not a parasite; he surpassed IBM in satisfying customer demand with an innovative product that IBM itself was unable to supply until forced to. His company was conservative and well managed; it offered good service and didn't depend on accounting gimmicks. The difficulties it encountered, from its inception, were beyond reasonable start-up problems; they were directly derived from IBM's dominance.

Amdahl himself retired as chief executive in September 1979, but announced nearly a year later—after Fujitsu had squelched the company's plan to merge with another pcm—that he was severing all ties with Amdahl Corporation and would found yet another company to compete with IBM's next product line. A chronic entrepreneur, he seemed to be having no trouble raising money for this second effort, but the fates of both Amdahl I and Acsys, the new company, were unpredictable.

People who say the glass is half full will argue that despite IBM's dominance Amdahl got financing, founded a company, sold a product, twisted the elephant's tail, brought on a barrage of improvements that benefited the customer, and lived to tell the story. Those who notice that it's half empty will observe that Amdahl almost had to pack it in several times, that the only backers he could find after the first $2 million were Japanese and German computer companies, and that both he and his original company will henceforward be dancing entirely to IBM's tune (and nobody else's). At present, the venture capital market is flourishing, but that business is volatile at best. If entrepreneurs face an IBM vindicated in the courts, an IBM which, if it maintains its traditional 15 percent growth rate, will reach $50 billion by 1986, an IBM which needs to maintain that growth rate as technology drives hardware prices down—by increasing aggressiveness? by the compulsion to enter and dominate innumerable other markets?—how many insurance companies are going to write a policy on even the sharpest entrepreneur's survival?

Economic issues, however, are always debatable, and each side commands a phalanx of learned men to advance its cause. The political argument against IBM's dominance seems even more compelling. In a widely esteemed study of the antitrust laws of the United States a British civil servant, A. D. Neale, observes:

> It seems likely that American distrust of all sources of unchecked power is a more deep-rooted and persistent motive behind the antitrust policy than any economic belief or any radical political trend. This distrust may be seen in many spheres of American life. . . . It is expressed in the theories of "checks and balances" and "separation of powers." In the United States the fact that some men possess power over the activities and fortunes of others is sometimes recognized as inevitable but never accepted as satisfactory. It is always hoped that any particular holder of power, whether political or economic, will be subject to the threat of encroachment by other authorities . . . and at the same time that any authority which seeks to encroach on another's power will be strenuously resisted and held in check. In large part antitrust is the projection of these traditional American beliefs into the economic sphere.

Today almost every decision made in every segment of the computer industry about what technology to adopt, what product or service to offer, how to price it and how and where to sell it is based at least in part on what IBM is doing now and how it may behave in the future. Nobody worries at all about Burroughs and Univac; in the mini-computer business, which IBM entered only recently, everybody worried equally about everybody else, which is how it ought to be. IBM's own decisions are guided by the balance sheet and naturally influenced by the advocacy skills and internal political interests of various scientists and executives. There is nothing improper in this system, but unless one believes that what's good for IBM is good for the country it is unsuitable as the sole determinant of how our computer technology develops.

Computing is a technology with many paths to follow; at each fork there is vigorous dissension among the brightest practitioners. We need to preserve that dissension, to offer scientists and businessmen a reasonable chance to pursue whatever goal seems promising and customers the greatest possible opportunity to choose their supplier. It is true that IBM is not a pure monopoly, that it feels competitive pressure even now; nor is it desirable to cosset incompetent companies. But a more equitable balance of power would be healthier.

Finally, IBM's political power is cause for concern. When the Carter administration took office, three IBM board members joined the Cabinet, and a host of other high government officials had IBM connections. It isn't news that there is an establishment in American politics (although even by establishment standards, the IBM jackpot in the Carter administration was disquieting); its relationship to industrial concentration is a subject for other books. But since the acceleration of computer technology will raise an increasing number of public issues, a concentration of power in the computer industry is far more alarming than similar dominance in other industries.

The conclusion that something must be done to balance the industry solves half the problem. The other half is deciding what. Many suggestions have been offered over the years, especially by IBM's competitors; these are often tinged with vested interest, great for the software houses and useless for the leasing companies or vice versa. Most solutions are imperfect; here are the three most workable possibilities.

A weak-medicine solution would give competitive forces a gentle push in the right direction. Such remedy would start with injunctive relief—the prohibition of anticompetitive practices. IBM would be required to disclose the specifications for functional interfaces and protocols—the information that allows a plug-compatible manufacturer or software house to design equipment or programs to run with IBM's—at the same time the company's systems architects supply it to the development engineers and programmers in IBM's own plants and labs. This is not crucial product design information that should be proprietary to IBM—it is like releasing the specifications of a plug or outlet—but with early disclosure it would permit other companies to produce compatible products in time to be competitive with IBM's equipment. Critics of this requirement have suggested that it only perpetuates IBM's authority to dictate standards. There is some truth in that, but while IBM survives it will do so anyway; disclosure at least gives the small companies an even break.

IBM might also be required to disclose more detailed statistics about its operation. In 1974, at hearings held by the Senate Subcommittee on Antitrust and Monopoly, Marilyn Walter-Carlson, an executive of an investment advisory firm, observed that "No reputable financial institution with a fiduciary responsibility, and acting on the prudent man theory, can support a new venture where there is no market information available." The market research companies get their data chiefly by polling users. Most industry observers think they do a good job under difficult circumstances, but the figures are not exact. IBM might be compelled to supply this information to independent accountants unless it could demonstrate that its competitors were not doing likewise; that would open up the whole industry.

Some competitors want IBM to leave the satellite business and not enter the services business for some period of time or forever. Prohibitions of certain unethical practices have also been suggested, but these are already violations of the antitrust laws and of IBM's own code, and insofar as it stands accused of them, it denies its guilt. The trouble with any sort of injunctive relief is that it has to be policed, a cumbersome, expensive, and sometimes ineffective process.

The injunctions might also be accompanied by structural relief. IBM might be required to divest itself of its non–data processing operations—the educational publishing subsidiary, the Office Products Division and perhaps the Federal Systems Division. The computer divisions could be aligned into three separate subsidiaries, for small medium and large computers, each with its own research labs and marketing organization, and Armonk as a holding company controlling everything and supervising the computer architecture to make it compatible. IBM's own reorganizations have gone part of this way already; Cary testified that he had rejected a spinoff of the office products and small computer divisions into a separate subsidiary because it was too expensive. This sort of restructuring, however, would not enhance competition because each segment would dominate its market; IBM would be the same powerful entity it has always been.

The strong-medicine solution has been favored by the government in the past and touted for some time by the Computer and Communications Industry Association. This solution would take IBM's customer base and count off by random nines (for the CCIA solution) or sixes (for the government's). Each customer would be assigned to one of these roughly equal Newcos which would design, develop, manufacture and market complete computer systems. The Newcos would start with $2 billion to $3 billion in annual sales—in a class with the Dwarfs. The CCIA's president, A. G. W. Biddle, often says that instead of having a race between Secretariat and five mules, you would have a slew of equal horses coming out of the starting gate. The Newcos would be big enough to compete well internationally, and could be as aggressive as their former parent, without its dominance.

The loudest criticism of this vertically integrated fission has come from several Dwarfs, in particular Control Data's William Norris. Norris prefers marine imagery to Biddle's horsey metaphors, and would rather be in a tank with one big whale than all those hungry sharks. Biddle replies that the sharks will go after each other because their equipment is compatible, giving the Dwarfs a grace period; then the Newcos will start to differentiate their products, and the field will be open. The Dwarfs have tended to favor limited divestitures combined with injunctive relief, in particular ordering IBM to reduce its market share by a specified percentage within five to ten years. Of all the proposed suggestions this is the least congenial: it discourages initiative by punishing success outright. It would produce a dreary, sluggish whale with several dreary, sluggish babies.

The critics of vigorous antitrust enforcement deplore it as more government intervention in the free enterprise system. But it is questionable whether a system of giant multinationals, each in its headquarters producing central five-year plans that involve millions of souls around the world, can properly be called free enterprise. Businessmen often complain about the vagueness of the antitrust laws (Van Cise suggests that they are less troubled by what they don't understand than by what they understand all too well). The unwieldy IBM case suggests that it is time to clarify our policy toward big business and strengthen the means of carrying it out.

16

Social Issues

Imagine a future cookie farm. The smart (computerized) planting machine loosens the land ultrasonically (or with short bursts of microwaves) and then sows rows of wheat, oats and sugar beets. The seeds will be specially encapsulated, containing moisturizers to face any drought situation but moisture-inhibited to withstand a downpour. When the field is full of reapable crops, along comes the computerized micro-factory machine (the seed capsules, incidentally, will be time-programmed so the diversified crop matures at the same time, making such a harvest possible). The crops pass through to the processing part of the machine where they are crushed, mixed and baked, chocolate chips are added and the cookies are then processed, packaged and palletized.
 —From "1990: A Vision of the Future," by Earl C. Joseph,
  Univac staff scientist, in *Computerworld*, December 31, 1979

There will be no conflict between television in the home and motion pictures in the theater. Each is a separate and distinct service. History confirms the fact that the creation of a new service for the public does not result in the elimination of an older service, provided each has something of its own to give. On the contrary, many examples might be cited to prove that the reverse is true. The telephone did not displace the telegraph. The radio did not displace the cable. The incandescent lamp did not displace the candle; more candles are being sold today than before the creation of the incandescent lamp. And television in the home will not displace the motion picture in the theater.

... When television has fulfilled its ultimate destiny, man's sense of physical limitation will be swept away and his boundaries of sight and hearing will be the limits of the earth itself. With this may come a new horizon, a new philosophy, a new sense of freedom, and greatest of all, perhaps, a finer and broader understanding between all the peoples of the world.
 —From "Television—Today and Tomorrow," Statement made
  by David Sarnoff in Hollywood, California, May 18, 1931

AUGURY is a growth industry. The technological revolution has spawned a ravenous demand for visions of the future, supplying jobs for a new class of professionals. The latest visions can be assembled quickly and cheaply from standard off-the-shelf components; new fabrication techniques offer an increasing density of complex words (or, as somebody is bound to call them, "word elements") in a single two-line sentence, thus providing, it is believed, more bang for the buck.

Two samples of the product appear above, one in the clotted style of modern corporate haruspices, the other, included for comparison, in the graceful construction of the Art Deco period. The seers differ in stature, but that is unimportant: Dr. Joseph and General Sarnoff have equal comprehension of what technology can do. Since Sarnoff is recalled as a virtual clairvoyant, it is useful to consider how well his predictions held up; this shows the limits of prophecy, even the best of it.

The errors in Sarnoff's speech illustrate some common obstacles to accurate prediction. Most reasonable people (including the chairman of Western Union) would admit that the telephone did displace the telegraph; it simply took several decades longer than Sarnoff expected. With the candles, Sarnoff was begging the question: the incandescent lamp made candles a decoration, not a necessity. One might as easily say that the hustle did not displace the waltz. As for the "finer and broader understanding," that would be true if the definition of "understanding" did not include "sympathy."

Overall, Sarnoff's predictions are colored by his purpose, to allay the movie people's fear of television; the purpose of Joseph's article, which views impending technological developments benignly, is to encourage the computer people's belief that they are working in an important and exciting industry. Futurists who are pessimistic, taking off from the same laboratory developments, might produce an entirely different set of assumptions. The truism that "technology is inexorable" means we can't put the genie back in the bottle; but how a society absorbs and applies technology is *not* inexorable, and is most difficult to predict. All technological odds-makers load the dice; they are useful to read as long as we delete the word "will" and substitute "might."

Current futurists arrive at their visions by pondering the implications of a few major developments: VLSI (for very-large-scale-integration), in particular the microprocessor; distributed data processing; and the whole package of advances in communications technology.

Today one can purchase microprocessors in quantity at about $1 a chip, each with the processing power of a computer that cost $100,000 twenty years ago. Today's microprocessor is one descendant of the old-fashioned (that is, late-sixties vintage) LSI circuit, which combined several thousand transistors on a chip. This high degree of miniaturization makes LSI an extremely sensitive, precise technology. Since the tiniest cinder can ruin a chip, the yield of satisfactory chips is relatively low; fabrication is governed by a learning curve through which costs come down by nearly a third when production doubles; and the investment required for new types of equipment to produce ever-denser chips has increased substantially. Thus the chips have always had to be produced in great volume to make a profit. But as the chips became more powerful their design grew more complex and their function more specialized, and suppliers had to bring out a variety of expensive designs, each with a limited market. Then semiconductor manufacturers came up with the idea of designing a general-purpose chip which could be programmed for different applications; this, the microprocessor, made LSI abundant. When microprocessors were grouped with the memory chips that store data and instructions, they gave birth to electronic cash registers, remote bank-teller machines, and other "smart terminals" that took computing out of its glass cocoon and into the purview of civilians.

Today, microprocessors go into microwave ovens, postal scales and taxi meters; they are beginning to show up in automobiles, telephones and television sets and will appear in dishwashers, vacuum cleaners and just about every other machine or appliance you can think of. In its own small way the microprocessor has become as remarkable a number-cruncher as any of the supercomputers at Livermore Laboratories, performing complex real-time calculations that couldn't be done any other way, that nobody ever thought of doing before. In cars, for example, the microprocessor controls the engine so as to reduce pollution and increase fuel efficiency. Microprocessors analyze stress to promote safety in equipment ranging from truck brakes to ski bindings. Trade and professional journals abound with ingenious new applications for the chips, including a host of extraordinary prostheses to help the blind see, the deaf hear and the crippled walk.

The following developments are sure. Microprocessors will make the machines we use more flexible, versatile and efficient. Lots of things will work better, thus removing many of the minor irritations of modern life. (From the user's point of view the importance of having chips in traditional consumer products can, however, be overblown. A vacuum cleaner with a small computer in it will never do anything but clean the house; since you can't get inside and program the computer to do something else, you will probably forget it's there.)

As they become ubiquitous and we grow to depend on them, the chips and the industry that produces them will become a critical national resource. Their use in machine tools will profoundly alter the nature of American manufacturing; specific industries whose products employ microprocessors will acquire a different pace and economic balance.

Since the advent of VLSI (which includes more sophisticated custom-designed chips as well as microprocessors) designers have begun to explore new forms of machine architecture that could divide and conquer ordinary problems with the brute force once reserved for supercomputers. With each job assigned to a tiny, inexpensive wafer one could assemble a truly modular, custom-built computer. Inexpensive duplicate chips could give computers fail-safe protection. But microcircuitry has not yet produced radical changes in computer architecture. Many mainframes do hold diagnostic chips which enable the service engineer to spot and sometimes repair malfunctions from his office, offering cheaper, faster maintenance for the user and lightening the vendors' burdens. Certainly the development of cheap memory chips (the newest products, for example, feature chips that store sixty-four thousand ones and zeros, and quarter-million-bit chips are not far off), combined with equally dramatic advances in auxiliary storage, diminishes the requirement for parsimonious programming. As *Spectrum*, the engineering society magazine, pointed out in January 1980, "Software development costs about $10 per written line of program, or several times the cost of an ic [for integrated circuit] chip"; programmers can now make freer use of higher-level languages that simplify writing and debugging at the expense of much memory space. And, of course, microcircuitry is making possible applications that once were too expensive to consider. While the engineers work on new architecture, conventional computers are becoming much more powerful.

By far the most significant contribution of VLSI, however, is in bringing about distributed data processing, both within organizations and throughout society.

A computer system equals a collection of bookkeepers, librarians and file cabinets. How a corporation distributes the latter depends on its own organizational convenience. A company couldn't operate comfortably keeping the whole lot in one central office: there is a separate bookkeeping department in the consumer products division, a set of file cabinets in each branch office, a library in every lab. No artificial barriers dictate the way a manual information processing system should be organized. But until recently the economics of computing ordained that the edp operation had to be at least fairly centralized: a company might have several computer centers, but individual departments could not do their own work. And this farming-out process led to either high telephone bills or inconvenient delivery arrangements with long waits or both; the edp department often specified how data should be supplied.

Now it is possible to disperse an electronic data processing system as if it really were a collection of bookkeepers, librarians and file cabinets. The scattered computers can—at least in theory—tap each other's information supply in real time. Bell and its competitors are already providing transmission better suited to data needs (that's the third major development), and more innovation lies ahead.

A distributed network can be laid out as a hierarchy from the desktop terminal to the home-office giant, or many computers of different sizes can tap each others' data; this is the layout of the Arpanet, a pioneering research network launched by the Defense Department a decade ago, which links various universities. Also, distributed data processing is allied to the "office of the future," in which computers, word-processing equipment, facsimile transmission machines, sophisticated telephones and switchboards, and advanced communication networks may combine to banish unsightly paper as St. Patrick chased the snakes from Ireland.

Hardware has always moved faster than software, and distributed networks; like the other engineering advances we've noted, still present challenges in systems design and programming. What information is held and processed locally and what gets sent to the home office is both a technical and organizational (or political) problem. Programming for data security is still an infant technology, and few designers know how to schedule access to a data base among mini-computers without a nasty traffic snarl. If, for example, Smith borrows a manila folder containing the history of the Excedrin account, he knows no one is going to fiddle with that information while he is reading and updating it. But if Excedrin is on line to twelve departments, each planning to add and change and delete snippets of material, nobody will be sure of what he is reading unless some system of priorities is worked out; that is the software man's headache, with management supplying the pecking order. The user may be patient when a manila folder is out of the cabinet, but a real-time system is supposed to be, well, real-time. The bigger the network, the worse it can get.

Charles Lecht, the consultant, who sees computers ultimately scattered "like radios," notes some reasons to look at distributed processing with caution. "While the vendors protest otherwise," he says, "most dispersed computers need specialists to attend them." One of the industry's more serious problems is the shortage of good programmers; another is the spiraling cost of labor. As Lecht observes, "It's hard enough to control costs in one dp shop. It will be a lot tougher with many computer rooms."

As for the office of the future, the new equipment calls for as many changes in working procedures and habits as the first computers required two or three decades ago. "The more people are involved the slower the rate of change," remarks one veteran IBM'er. "Traditions are slow to change. Nothing happens that fast."

We can be cautious and skeptical up to a point. But we do know that the computer will become—at whatever rate—an increasingly flexible and pervasive tool. We ought to assume the day will come when computers can do just about anything we want them to do, that software difficulties, shortages of specialists and capital, and bureaucratic inertia will give us a means of buying time, and that we should use that time thinking about how we want to use the computer. The spread of computer technology raises a number of social questions that want public discussion.

The privacy issue has received increasing coverage by magazines, newspapers and television; of some fifteen hundred citizens interviewed by Louis Harris and Associates in 1978, more than half believed that present uses of computers were an actual threat to privacy in the United States, and this figure represented a 20 percent rise in the amount of citizen concern reflected in a similar poll done two years earlier.

Better record-keeping is an obvious dividend, if not the prime purpose, of most computer applications. To receive many of the benefits of a complex society—credit and scholarships, jobs and insurance, health and safety—we must surrender to some organization the details of how we lead our lives. Frequently the information we gave turns up in unexpected places; often the data organizations gather is inaccurate or obsolete; sometimes it is used against us without our knowledge. The questions of what obligations we should impose on those who collect personal data and whether, indeed, we can control information-gathering practices in an age of apparently runaway technology are both complicated and urgent.

Privacy is a civil-liberties problem, which applies to manual as well as computer systems: who has the right to gather what data on which individuals, and with whom can it be shared? and what right has the individual to see, challenge and correct the information in his files? *Security* is the technical problem that accompanies privacy: how should data about individuals be protected?

These issues are complicated because the responsibility for privacy protection is divided among the three branches of the government, commercial users of computers, and the vendors of equipment and software, and because security devices are not a standard item like seatbelts in cars: protection measures include guards with guns, plastic identification badges, passwords and built-in locks on hardware and software, and depend on how the system itself is laid out. A distributed network requires a different type of protection from a purely local computer file; as the prices of security devices vary, so does the sensitivity of different types of information.

To understand the computer's role in privacy problems, some historical perspective is useful. In books and interviews, Dr. Alan Westin, a professor of public law and government at Columbia University and the country's leading authority on information technology and the right to privacy, supplies a long view. "The McCarthy era," he observes, "was the apex of American Puritanism and hostility to dissent. It was also the high point of credentialism, of systematically excluding people because of information in their records." Written records, held and shared by various "gatekeepers," affected the citizen's rights and opportunities in education, employment, credit and social services. By the mid-sixties, however, a general challenge to the authority of all our institutions brought about widespread questioning of the gatekeepers' criteria for making decisions about individuals; records of political dissent and cultural nonconformity, intelligence and personality tests, questionnaires and applications that called for information on race, marital status and personal beliefs all came under attack. Westin points out that "debates over the uses of records and manual data banks would have become a major issue in American society even if computers had never been invented."

Computer people sometimes remark that the Gestapo did a fine job of invading privacy before computers were invented. Westin agrees, but adds, "Think of what they'd have done *with* computers." His own experience bears this out. At the time people began challenging the gatekeepers computer technology was burgeoning. Early articles on the electronic brain were followed by business pieces touting computer stocks and announcements of ambitious information systems being developed by government and industry. In 1969 Westin, sponsored by the Computer Science and Engineering Board of the National Academy of Sciences, began a two-year study of how public and private organizations gathered, stored, used, shared and protected personal information. Among the subjects were the FBI, the Social Security Administration, the Bank of America, MIT, the Kaiser-Permanente Medical Care Program and the Church of the Latter-day Saints. The result, a book called *Data Banks in a Free Society*, was published in 1972; despite subsequent technological changes which have affected Westin's views, it is still worth reading.

As investors and as citizens, we were gullible about computers; in those days many complex systems aborted. When Westin and his staff went out to examine how organizations were actually using the machines, they found that computer usage in itself had not "created the revolutionary new powers of data surveillance predicted by some commentators." In general, organizations were not collecting or sharing more personal information than they did in the precomputer era. Still, many fears about surveillance were justified by manual record-keeping policies; civil-liberties law had lagged seriously behind changing attitudes toward privacy.

By the seventies the courts had begun to define the individual's rights of privacy and due process in record-keeping matters, and the federal and state governments were applying these to new laws. The Privacy Act of 1974 covered federal record-keeping practices and created a commission to suggest policies for the states and private industry; the commission recommended that a series of laws be passed to apply to different industries.

Privacy legislation has been designed to carry out broad principles of fair information practice suggested by Westin and other specialists in the field. As Westin has written, "matters that ought not to be considered in making decisions about individuals do not become part of the formal records at all." A corollary to this is that any such information gathered in the past should be stricken from the records. A second set of principles dictates that the individual should know what records he appears in and have the to right to see, challenge and correct his records. A third principle requires controls on data sharing, and a fourth makes organizations legally responsible for pursuing fair information practices. The legislators have not set up enforcement agencies, finding it more practical to afford relief in the courts.

All of this might lead people to believe that the privacy problem is under control. They would be wrong. As Westin says, "Solving privacy problems is not like neutering a cat; there isn't any one step you can take so your worries are over. Every time there's a change in technology, in information-gathering practices, in the balance of power we have to ask the privacy questions again."

As Westin points out, we are beginning to gather more sensitive information for employee health records because of industrial dangers from radiation and from pesticides and other chemicals. To shoulder their responsibilities for workers' safety, employers will have to ask a lot of highly intrusive questions—"Have you had trouble conceiving?" "Are you impotent?" "Have your sex drives diminished lately?" Since chemicals may have delayed effects, the records will have to follow the employee from job to job for the rest of his life. "This information is not being collected out of willful intrusion but for the health of the employee and the tort liability of the employer," Westin says. "It's a change in the balance between privacy and other social needs. So now we have to determine who has access to these records—the union? OSHA? the boss?—and how to keep them from getting into the wrong hands."

In *Data Banks*, Westin concluded—based on the technology of the time—that there were serendipitous privacy protections in the high cost of memory and data conversion. "Managers used to say 'Do we need all this information in the computer file?'" he observes. "Now, with machine costs down and labor costs up, there may be as much economic pressure to say 'Throw it all in.'"

In the past, organizations regarded their data as a valuable resource they weren't about to share; now, Westin says, both government and industry have new incentives for sharing and the technology to make it easy. Electronic funds transfer links banks, retailers, credit bureaus and communications carriers, and all sorts of consortia are appearing to provide home information systems. EFT, Westin says, could actually furnish more protection than the check system if banks were required to erase all transaction records after a short contest period; the parties to the transaction, of course, would have paper statements. "When the records are sitting there," Westin feels, "law enforcement sees them as a resource."

As for government, Westin fears the massive data banks that were squelched by technology and citizen protest in the sixties and early seventies will rise again in the eighties. A national health insurance plan, for example, might make it useful to maintain a social services profile of each person, listing all the services Jane Smith uses, so the agencies can plan their needs; technology has made this practical. There are "matching programs" that track down fathers who don't support their children and that compare welfare rolls with employment records to flush out the cheaters. The Harris poll of attitudes toward computers and privacy, sponsored by Sentry Insurance with Westin as academic advisor, drew responses from many demographic groups. While these groups differed over other technology and privacy issues, 85 percent of the respondents favored welfare-matching data banks; when taxpayers feel affronted, civil liberties go by the board.

"For all personal data systems there should be a heavy burden of proof on the planners that the system is necessary and will deliver the benefits it promises," says Westin. "I'm for epidemiological systems, for example: to my knowledge there's no other way to keep track of who's taken a drug that may later prove injurious. And the taxpayers seem to want welfare reform. So then you have to apply fair information practices—notice and the right to challenge. And a 'hit' in the matching system should be used as the start of an investigation, not proof of guilt."

If Westin is the *doyen* of privacy crusaders, Robert Ellis Smith is the young Turk. Smith, a former American Civil Liberties Union lawyer, edits a newsletter, *Privacy Journal*, and wrote a book entitled *Privacy: How to Protect What's Left of It*. In both the book and the newsletter Smith delineates the areas that privacy legislation hasn't covered yet, the compromises and loopholes that weaken existing laws, and the inadequacies of privacy law enforcement. He depicts a society already close to the one Orwell envisioned, with one important difference: Orwell's people knew about the surveillance and adjusted their behavior accordingly, while we don't know and pursue our business as usual. One might add that Orwell's surveillance was monolithic, while ours comes from both public and private sources only some of whom are linked to one another. Even the best public policy isn't completely effective, and when it fails the individual must protect himself; Smith's writings provide a guerrilla handbook for citizens. Both Smith and Westin make clear that the privacy problem will be with us forever, and we must learn to live with that; we do so not by accepting surveillance, but by continually fighting back.

The attitudes of computer people vary: the hardware companies recognize that facing the privacy issue squarely (and selling security devices) will further the use of computers in the end, while companies that gather, sell and use personal data are antagonistic, because privacy regulations increase their costs and cramp their style. Other industries have battled the end of their freewheeling days and learned to put up with rules society deemed necessary. As consumers have accepted, within reason, that society's need for more information than they would like to divulge, so companies in the data business will have to live with the fact that government regulation comes with the territory.

We can't protect privacy without effective security techniques, so the security and privacy problems are closely allied; tighter security measures are needed to guard us from criminals as well as snoopers, so computer crime is linked to security; and as Smith points out (and anyone who has boarded a plane in the past ten years must have noticed) strict security measures often intrude upon privacy. "The computer has become our vault, which holds more and more of our money and documents of record," says Donn Parker, the expert on computer crime. "Now we are running a race: will we make the technology safe as quickly as we're hooking up our valuable assets to it? I don't know if we're winning; it's a close race."

Parker is optimistic about protection from small theft and embezzlement, in which old-fashioned criminal methods are updated with more ingenuity than technological sophistication. The passage of a federal computer crime bill will ease the job of prosecutors hamstrung by laws inadequate for modern technology. Companies reluctant to prosecute computer criminals for fear of unfavorable publicity are beginning to recognize the danger of their position.

It is the other end of the criminal spectrum—the low-incidence/big-loss heist pulled off by programmers—that worries Parker. Designers haven't yet learned how to protect a system from the more exotic dodges which may be hidden in a dozen out of six million instructions. The criminals tend to be staff programmers who know how to find and exploit the bugs that always exist in large systems. "The newspapers say how easy it is to engage in computer crime," says Parker. "While systems are vulnerable, mostly it's not easy, it's complicated and difficult. There are hazards for the outside criminal because he may not know all the controls that are in the system. And it's hard enough to make a system work correctly, let alone diddle with it. There have been very few cases in which the criminals were outside people. Usually it's someone in a position of trust with the access and the skills."

Granted these, however, the enterprising criminal can break into any system operating today. For some years the ultimate in computer security was represented by Multics, a system designed at MIT and sold by Honeywell to the wealthiest of customers. Two specialists commissioned by the Air Force to test the vulnerability of Multics cracked the system in two and one-half hours. Researchers at Parker's company, SRI, and elsewhere are working hard to improve security techniques. "We're playing a one-upmanship game with the enemy," Parker says. "We think of better safeguards, and they think of more ingenious crimes. I believe we can make business safer with computers than it was before, but the time gap is uncertain. Maybe it will be the end of the eighties before we have adequate computer security. So today technical stuff isn't the main problem because the experts are working on it but won't succeed for a while. Meanwhile the rest of us should concentrate on people problems, where we can do more in the short term."

It's important, Parker says, to "sensitize computer people to be mutually suspicious like people in the accounting profession, where they've developed a code of ethics and professional responsibility over hundreds of years. The medical and legal professions have ethical codes, too. You hear about the people that break them, but tens of thousands of doctors, lawyers and accountants are ethical because there's a code. Data processing developed in a benign environment, and the computer science teachers never thought there was any need for ethical training. There was more encouragement of the game in computer science, but you don't play games in vaults. You have to get people to accept the need for security procedures. They're not used to it, and it constrains them, so they'll beat your safeguards."

Security itself raises complex political issues, as the recent affair of the data encryption standard illustrates. Commercial users seeking protection when sending data are turning increasingly toward encryption, a technique formerly the province of military and intelligence agencies. Encryption is the same camouflage familiar to readers of spy novels: it takes the letters or numbers of the original message, called the "plaintext," and either transposes them or substitutes other letters, according to some rule, to produce a gibberish known as "ciphertext." An encryption technique, or algorithm, can be mass-produced on LSI chips programmed to alter data according to a general plan; this is like mass-producing padlocks. What is individual is the combination, or "key," which specifies how each bit is to be altered. Encryption and decryption are done automatically by chips in terminals that communicate with each other.

Several years ago, the National Bureau of Standards asked vendors to propose an algorithm which might become a data encryption standard, thus encouraging the sale of inexpensive, compatible security devices (once the standard was adopted, all encryption equipment sold to the federal government would have to employ it, and since the government is the largest computer customer, vendors would be more or less compelled to adopt it for the rest of their gear). The standard would be in the public domain, and the vendor would not receive royalties from competitors who used it. In its usual spirit of pragmatism IBM submitted an entry, which won (had IBM chosen to keep its algorithm proprietary or collect royalties, it would have risked antitrust prosecution; had the company done nothing, it would have had to endure the inconvenience of accepting someone else's design). The data encryption standard (or DES, as it's familiarly known) is now available in a host of different vendors' equipment, and most experts agree that the standard makes data transmission a whole lot safer than it used to be.

The meaning of "a whole lot," however, is something about which they heartily disagree. There are two things encryption can do to a binary 1: it can change it to a 0 or leave it alone. The encryption key is simply another string of 1's and 0's which the sender adds to each bit of plaintext to produce the ciphertext; the receiver's terminal uses the key to subtract, yielding plaintext once more. With this scheme, the longer the key, the tougher the spy's job. If the key is 8 bits long, for example, a spy might have to test 2^8 or 512 possible combinations of 1's and 0's to decipher the message The DES key is 56 bits long—2^{56} or seventy-two quadrillion combinations—but Professor Martin Hellman, a cryptography specialist at Stanford, considers that inadequate. In 1975, when the Bureau of Standards called for comments on the DES, Hellman asserted that for $20 million someone could build a machine that would take an average of twelve hours—at a cost of $5,000—to crack the cipher by trying all the possible combinations of 1's and 0's. This would be too high for ordinary corporate spies, but well within the means of the National Security Agency, the Onassis of cryptographers. A longer key—particularly the 128-bit size that Hellman recommended—would be impregnable even to NSA.

Since American products are exported worldwide, a 128-bit key would, for the first time, equip many potential enemies or intelligence targets with ciphers that NSA couldn't break. NSA might understandably be unwilling to permit this, but the price of giving suspicious foreigners less security is that American citizens have less security, too; NSA might decide to vet our messages. NBS admits getting help from NSA in "evaluating all submitted algorithms." The Senate Select Committee on Intelligence established that while the security agency didn't tamper with the actual algorithm, "NSA convinced IBM that a reduced key size was sufficient." Still, the committee did conclude that DES is "more than adequate for its intended purpose."

The debate between Hellman, NBS, NSA and IBM raged for four years, in letters, at meetings, in the trade and professional journals, and even in a few newspaper articles. Hellman further pointed out that the way circuit costs were coming down, by 1985 a machine costing $200,000 could crack the DES for $50 worth of computer time; even if all his calculations were off by a factor of ten, the declining cost of chips would take up the slack within five years. NBS has argued that the cost of the additional memory needed for the larger key is significant for a user with many terminals, and that there had been some pressure from banks to approve an even shorter key; that it would take two thousand years to crack the cipher using the "most powerful computers" of 1976, and advances in technology and computer architecture wouldn't change that situation much before 1982, when NBS policy dictated a review of the DES. The DES is approved for sensitive but not classified military information.

Much of the dispute is highly technical, dealing with cryptographic techniques, computer architecture and systems design schemes for networks that use encryption; it is beyond the layman's comprehension. Some academic and industrial cryptographers with impressive credentials have supported Hellman; in a letter sent to Hellman and to Dr. David Kahn, author of "The Code-Breakers," Dr. Robert Morris of AT & T wrote:

> The encryption scheme is more than proof against casual snooping. However . . . I suppose that the cipher is intended to be resistant to fairly determined attack by persons with large resources. Measured against this standard of performance, the proposed scheme is ludicrous.

Hellman sums up the affair this way, "I understand that there's a tradeoff between the requirements of the codebreaking part of the government and the need for privacy and security of civilians' data. But there ought to be an open public discussion of which of these needs takes precedence."

The acceleration of computer use and the exacerbation of international tensions happen to be occurring at the same time; we can expect more conflicts between defense and civil liberties (in 1980, for example, the National Security Agency moved to preempt academic research in cryptography previously sponsored by the National Science Foundation). If, on the other hand, the DES decision was economic it is fair to ask how much the guardians of our data should be required to spend on its protection. The freedom to conduct open public debate on this issue is, presumably, why American democracy is worth defending.

The problems of privacy and security, however urgent, are well understood. The explosion of computer technology raises a number of other issues that we know less about. The more reflective members of the computer community have been discussing them for years; it is now time for the public to join in. Since a revolution may be upon us soon, we had best prepare for it.

The invention of the computer revived arguments about automation and employment that have flared up and subsided ever since the beginning of the Industrial Revolution. Early fears were calmed when people saw that advanced computer applications were difficult and slow to develop, and that computing seemed to create more jobs than it eliminated. Now, however, as the technology becomes more sophisticated and the use of computers spreads to new fields and penetrates the old ones more deeply, these worries are returning. In the automobile industry, for example, robots are handling an increasing number of assembly-line jobs; back in November 1979 *The New York Times* pointed out that the hourly cost of a robot came to $4.50, while the human he replaced made $15 an hour and would soon be getting $20. The market for industrial robots is growing rapidly, and research projects to improve their skills are proliferating. Japan is the world's leader in robot use, but the technology is spreading in Europe, too. Businessmen fear that without the efficiencies offered by robotics, American products will lose ground in international markets.

Past and future trends in the telephone and insurance industries, two of the heaviest users of computer technology, suggest some of the patterns we may see as other industries and jobs become automated. While technological changes have made these industries much less labor-intensive, a dramatic increase in demand for the services rendered has kept employment growing; other businesses may not be so fortunate. The telephone industry's employment needs have fluctuated sharply; so have the distribution of jobs and the skills required for them. During the eighties, the communications industry will grow faster than any other, but employment, according to Labor Department projections, will increase by only 1 percent a year. The insurance industry will continue to grow and will gobble up data processing managers, programmers, systems analysts and computer operators, but as the Bureau of Labor Statistics points out,

> Although the insurance industry will continue to employ substantial numbers of young high school graduates, many of them women, computerization of practically every mechanical operation is expected to reduce the availability of low-skilled, entry-level clerical positions.

If automation creates new jobs while doing away with old ones we will, at the very least, have to retrain and possibly move around large numbers of people; even so, how many potential keypunchers can be turned into systems designers? What degree of central planning is consistent with a free enterprise society? Some wise men doubt that growth will compensate for job displacement. Wassily Leontief, the Nobel Prize–winning economist, has written:

> "Stepped-up investment can certainly provide additional jobs for people who otherwise would be unemployed. However, under conditions of labor-saving technological advance, creation of one additional job 20 years ago might have required $10,000; today $20,000; and 20 years from now easily $50,000 or more, even if inflation is controlled. A high rate of investment is indispensable to satisfy the expanding needs of a growing society. But it can make only a limited contribution to solution of the problem of involuntary technological unemployment, particularly since the greater the rate of capital investment, the higher the rate of introduction of new labor-saving technology.

Leontief states firmly that Luddite cures are worse than the disease, and favors "supplemental benefits to wage earners who work less than the normal number of hours per week." Whether or not one agrees with Leontief, the problem certainly deserves more interest than it has received in the United States. There is much worry about this issue in Europe, as Philip Dorn, a consultant with international ties, pointed out in an article in *Datamation*. Dorn is worried, too: what he sees on the far horizon is "drastic population bipolarization . . . a small minority of technologically oriented elitists against a vast majority of unskilled, nearly unemployable workers."

What computer and communications companies like to call their "major competitive thrust" is in bringing about the "office of the future"; it is actually a broad horizontal sweep across industry borders. Office workers now outnumber factory workers. The average factory worker, according to figures widely used in the computer industry, has $25,000 to $35,000 worth of equipment supporting him, while his white-collar counterpart commands a capital investment of only one or two thousand. Employers haven't yet given at the office, and when they do there will be significant changes.

As distributed processing networks become widespread, they will compel organizations to define themselves politically. A real-time computer network, for example, might be designed to give the chairman greater access to raw data instead of reports filtered up through several levels of bureaucracy. This may be a highly desirable end, but what would it do to the middle manager's sense of autonomy and importance? Would problems that should be solved at a lower level come too quickly to the attention of top management? How much "information float" should be built into a system?

As Anthony Oettinger of Harvard has pointed out, a real-time information system might also be designed as a force for greater democracy in an organization, giving the Indians as well as the chiefs data from other levels and departments that might help them do their job better. Computer-based information systems can be a catalyst for beneficial or dangerous social change in organizations; while we worry, quite properly, about personal privacy we may be underestimating this equally serious problem, in which many fears of computer technology are rooted.

The computer can improve quality control in the workplace, to the workers' displeasure. The *Wall Street Journal* recently told of an executive vice-president at AT & T who had an electronic calendar remind him every single time a subordinate missed a deadline. The subordinates—corporate vice-presidents—complained of the pressure, and the feature was taken out. Frederick Weingarten, while studying electronic mail and funds transfer systems for the Office of Technology Assessment, visited supermarkets that employed electronic checkout systems. Many of them were using the computer to monitor employees' transaction rates. "In an automated workplace management can keep closer tabs on productivity," he says. "You are working in a fishbowl, and you never realize you're being monitored until you ask for a raise. There was the same battle back in the twenties, when people rebelled against the time-study man with the stopwatch. Automation encourages employers to impose specific performance criteria, and then they substitute these numbers for judg-ment." The use of computers for quality control can, as Weingarten says, "upset the uneasy balance between labor and management," with serious repercussions.

The issue presents further complications. It is easy to sympathize with a human being's right to do his work without the surveillance of Big Brother when he works in a supermarket or a factory; what if the human being is your cardiologist? Are the doctors' objections to medical record systems like PROMIS, which perform quality con-trol, any different than those of the auto workers? When, and in what form, is automated auditing acceptable? What are its limita-tions? Does noblesse oblige in the case of doctors and others with responsibilities we deem crucial, or do we take an across-the-board position on privacy and dignity?

Futurists love to speculate on—and then to deplore or applaud—the way home information systems will alter the texture of our lives. We ought to be particularly skeptical of predictions in this area, in which the future is still mysterious but well within our control. Technology will, for example, enable people to work at home, but it isn't clear whether they will want to do so. One school of prediction shows Ma and Pa sitting at their respective terminals pursuing meaningful careers and watching their kids romp around the media room; the second imagines working at home will never play because people need to press the flesh, and because there are either too many distractions at home or too few. Similar forecasts are applied to our private lives, based on the notion that we will stop going to the store, we will stop going to the bank, we will stop going to the movies and the library, we will stop reading books and newspapers, and all this will turn us into a society of passive, antisocial button-pushers; a small number of gurus suggest we will reject some or all of these innovations.

The trouble with these visions of the future is their rigidity. It is probably true that few people are suited to work at home every day for a significant period of time; some people believe, as a matter of principle, that home and office should be kept utterly separate; and most jobs require at least some gathering with colleagues. Still, for many workers the home terminal hooked up to the office can be a regular twice-a-week boon and at some times of life a daily godsend; adapted to the needs of the company and the individual it can save energy, relieve stress and increase productivity.

Browsing in a bookstore or a library, reading a good book on a snowy night, spending a lazy Sunday with the paper are sensual pleasures we will never give up and can pass on to our children, but sometimes we are harried and just need to get information fast, without savoring it. The only difference between doing research on viewdata and doing it at the library is we save travel time and time spent waiting for our number to come up; we must still look something up in an index and read the material we summon. Going to the bank, the supermarket, the appliance store and the airline office are hardly rewarding human experiences; the less time we spend at these tedious chores, the more we can give to the kind of shopping that's intimate and fun. If we see all our movies at home, perhaps we'll go to restaurants more often, get into amateur theatricals or give wonderful parties. It is useful, once again, to look at General Sarnoff's predictions about television. He said:

> Man is a gregarious creature. Granting that we can develop 26 million potential theaters in the homes of America, public theaters will continue to operate because people will go there in response to the instinct for group emotions and to see artists in the flesh. These are human demands which television in the home cannot satisfy.

This Sarnoff prediction has been right so far. The influence of technology on the quality of life—the spiritual, not public policy issues—is fascinating to talk about but highly complex. As a more familiar example, there are children today who have never had a meal that wasn't cooked by a conglomerate; there are other children who, thanks to food processors, have tasted home-baked bread and a host of other old-fashioned dishes their grandmothers never made; and there are still some children who go to bed hungry.

The proliferation of computers does not in itself dictate a depersonalized society. One of the conveniences the technology promises is an abundance of custom-tailored products, from automobiles to computers themselves (as artificial intelligence techniques improve, computers might be programmed to "learn" and respond to the idiosyncrasies of their users). Indeed, computerized snooping is frightening for being personal, not impersonal.

The more available and inexpensive computers are, however, the more we tend to rely on them to solve problems without questioning whether the mechanical (or information-gathering) solution is suitable. Even if it's possible to write a computer program that simulates paranoid behavior well enough to fool many psychiatrists, that may still be a superficial way to learn about paranoia.

One of the joys of any métier is the belief that one is doing work that may serve humanity. Computer people are exuberant in proposing solutions to urban problems and to the dilemmas of inadequate medical care and educational facilities. The solutions tend to be machine solutions, because that is what computer people know about, and because human labor is expensive and error-prone and unpredictable; as they observe every day, it is people who drop paper clips, chewing gum and cigarette ashes into machines, who make mistakes in coding and keypunching, who hit the wrong buttons, who get irrational about technology. It would probably be impossible to find a computer expert who wants a controlled, mechanistic, Orwellian society, but there are plenty who want to save labor costs and design people-proof systems, goals which are commendable only up to a point.

In discussing computer security, Donn Parker has said we are "putting more and more of our assets in a fragile container"; the comment has even broader applications than Parker intended. In 1979, for example, several near-collisions in mid-air provoked a fierce dispute between the air traffic controllers' organization and the FAA. The incidents occurred following computer breakdowns at the control centers; the task of converting from computer to manual methods was complicated and stressful, and controllers lost track of planes in the confusion of the shift. The controllers, besides criticizing the FAA for delays in replacing obsolete computers they considered inadequate to handle current traffic, for lax maintenance and for short staffing, sought more backup equipment and better training for their younger colleagues, who had not been taught the manual methods; the FAA, besides defending its equipment and procurement policies, charged featherbedding and interunion squabbles.

There are several things to be alarmed about in this story. First, the truisms that machines are fallible and people are fallible miss the point, which is that machines and people are fallible in different ways; if one is to cover for the other, the systems designer must consider two separate sets of weaknesses. Operations in which life-

or-death responsibility is shared by people and machines are becoming more common: two other examples are nuclear power plants and patient-monitoring systems. What is the background and training of the people who are expected to wing it when the machines break down, and how is the environment suited to their skills? What effect do the pace and demands of the job—long periods of boredom peppered by short crises, for example—have on an employee's judgment and indeed on the sort of employee the job attracts? Moreover, other human failings may *indirectly* affect the safety of a system: bureaucracy, venality and political pressure can weaken quality control despite the designer's best efforts. These questions will have varying effects on the decision to install a particular system, but they should be asked.

Another computer application which carries some risks is model building, in which the machine is used to simulate some real-life environment. Models are used in training when it is dangerous to give the student a crack at the real thing: the Massachusetts General programs for medical schools, in which the computer simulates a patient with a heart attack or diabetic coma, are a kind of model, and so was the Whirlwind computer built at MIT for aircraft simulation. The other use of modeling is to predict the behavior of some complex system—the human body, the body politic, the economy— when various events befall it, by calculating the way the system's many components act upon one another. If the interactions can be described in equations, the computer will solve high numbers of equations with human-mind-boggling speed; all the human mind has to do is set up the equations, which, of course, is where the catch lies.

A model is in every respect the product of human knowledge, judgment and bias. All models are simplifications of the real thing, and the builder must decide what features are worth including. The staffs of nuclear reactor plants are trained partly by working at a model of a control room. As the Kemeny Commission reported, "Simulator training did not include preparation of the operators for multiple-failure accidents. Indeed, the B & W simulator was not, prior to March 28, programmed to reproduce the conditions that confronted the operators during the "accident" at Three Mile Island.

Models can be extremely useful: the builder gains a powerful tool for clarifying, examining and testing his theories, and the student acquires some experience he could never get otherwise. A model certainly can alert the mind to some unexpected consequences. The danger is in the showmanship, the aura of precision and complexity, the soothing abundance of equations. All that glitz is highly seductive; one tends to assume the model has covered all contingencies, and one forgets to question either the assumptions or the data. Moreover, as Roger Schank's work illustrates, prejudice is eminently programmable, but arguments framed in statistical terms often carry a weight they don't deserve; as a corollary, moral and philosophical arguments, however, precisely stated, tend to fall into disfavor when a society is too enamored of "science."

With the model comes the expert to interpret it; no matter how widespread personal computers become, we won't all be huddled over our TRS 80's forecasting the rate of oil depletion. On either side of every public policy issue stands a battery of experts dueling with data at a hundred paces. The more deeply computer (and other) technology becomes enmeshed in operating our society, the more the average citizen may believe he is no longer qualified to hold opinions on important social and political questions. This would be a perilous belief.

There is no significant issue pertaining to computer technology that cannot be described clearly in plain English and understood by real estate brokers, sculptors and teachers of nineteenth-century French literature; moreover, democracy assumes that janitors and taxi drivers can comprehend important political questions, and computer technology does not present any compelling reason to abandon that assumption. It takes some extra effort for computer people to talk exclusively in layman's language; they must be required to make that effort. Laymen, on the other hand, have the responsibility of meeting them halfway: that is, of listening when English is spoken.

It is also important that we recognize at what point the expert stops being an expert and stands on equal footing with the layman. A lawyer may tell his client, "If you do that you'll probably have a lawsuit on your hands, but you stand a pretty fair chance of winning"; computer people (or doctors or economists using computer projections) might offer the same sort of advice in numerical terms: "The following data suggest to us that if A and B are true, there is about a 60 percent chance that C will also be true." Like the lawyer, the expert is there to show us the tradeoffs; after he has done this, he is supposed to sit down among us once again. Subjective words like "safe," "feasible," "economical" and "worthwhile" are part of the language of judgment, not counsel, and the informed layman is as qualified to use them as the expert.

The responsible expert has an obligation to point out problems that merit public attention. In periods of technological ferment, some scientists and laymen ask whether certain types of research and applications of technology ought not to be pursued because they might lead to abuse or undesirable consequences or because they are simply morally repugnant. Joseph Weizenbaum, in thus criticizing artificial intelligence work, has been called Luddite and anti-intellectual; his response is persuasive. Weizenbaum argues that we haven't the money and talent to explore every possible line of research: for various reasons (often insufficient interest in the problem) grants are denied and projects are killed. Since every society must decide on the wisest use of its scientific resources, and in an open society this must be a matter for public debate, "why are ethics to be excluded from the discussion?" Everyone, of course, has different ethical criteria—and a consensus will have to evolve over time. But our society, in its laws and in its products, reflects the values and choices of its citizens; the application of technology ought not to be mindless or soulless.

Besides the ethical issues, there are political ones. Alan Westin has described computing as a power-reinforcing technology (as opposed to the Molotov cocktail, which he calls a power-redistributing technology). What he means is that computers are expensive and not available to everybody, and their use helps the rich get richer. Large corporations can afford sophisticated computer-based market studies and forecasting techniques that are beyond the reach of small competitors; wealthy participants in court cases can affort computer-aided jury selection and other legal services unavailable to poorer adversaries; incumbent congressmen benefit from publicly funded research and record-keeping services while their challengers must go it alone; and Congress, in turn, is an impoverished computer-user compared to the Defense Department, which it is supposed to monitor.

Here technology presents some good news. In 1979 a tiny weekly newspaper called the *Point Reyes Light* won the Pulitzer Prize for public service, honoring its investigation of cultism at Synanon, the therapeutic community for drug addicts. The *Point Reyes Light,* it turned out, was a Mom-and-Pop store made possible by computer technology. Computer-aided photocomposition methods enabled the owners and their reportorial staff of one to prepare their own layouts and deliver them to a printing shop, dispensing with the need for an expensive old-fashioned linotype operation. The opportunity to start a newspaper is now, as James Reston pointed out, open to "any group of people, of whatever political, economic, social or religious persuasion . . . even with limited finances in these inflationary times."

The benefits of computer technology will be increasingly available to small businessmen and organizations in many fields. Certainly the minicomputer will not even the score. But there are a few races in which the competitor who is small and fast on his feet gains some advantage over the lumbering monster, and the new technology can help him exploit it. Insofar as the computer allows a business to run more efficiently, that efficiency and its contribution to success will be available to the corner bookstore and the community action group, thus providing some counterweight to the trend toward concentration of power. Likewise, it will be there for the small political movements that claim, sometimes for good and sometimes for ill, that—in the words of some supporters of the Ayatollah Khomeini, the ascetic who mobilized his followers with cassettes and copiers— "We are struggling against autocracy, for democracy, by means of xerocracy." And it will be there for the Red Brigades and the Symbionese Liberation Army. There is no way to gauge the effects of all this, to predict how it will change the world.

We must still find ways to deal with traditional issues of power. Who, for example, will be allowed to provide information for the new viewdata systems? Should editorial or financial criteria prevail, and should there also be rules of "public access" or "equal space" to be sure the systems aren't dominated by rich organizations? How can wired nation services like EFT be provided to the poor, so that the information society does not become hopelessly elitist? Will bank-supplied financial services, tied into EFT, drive single practitioners out of business?

We have many choices to make over the next few decades. Certainly we can no longer afford to be a two-culture society. It is fairly obvious that every literate citizen, even real estate brokers, sculptors and teachers of nineteenth-century French literature, even janitors and taxi drivers, ought to have some knowledge of how computers work and what, in current technology, they can and can't do; economics and the rudiments of computer-aided decision-making should also be as basic as reading. Educators seem to be aware of the need for computer literacy, and more and more of our children will acquire it in their schooling, especially as hardware costs come down; we elders will have to educate ourselves. What is less obvious, however, is the need for more humanities courses in engineering curriculums (this assumes that scientists, mathematicians, economists and sociologists attend liberal arts colleges where an encouraging trend toward wider course distribution requirements seems to be under way). Such courses should not be considered a frill, aimed at helping engineers make fruitful use of increased leisure time; their purpose is to produce better engineers. Our technology ought not to be applied by people who believe that the scientist's way of observing the world is more serious than the poet's.

As Weizenbaum urges, we must learn the limits of our tools; often we must find the courage to say no. But we must also learn to use those tools humanely and imaginatively. As the technology develops, so will it raise many new social questions; the answers will be slow in coming. But man is in control, and lay man must not abdicate that control to an aristocracy of experts. It is our responsibility to keep our hands on the button, because we are going to get what we deserve.

Postscript

This book was first published in October 1981. Like most books, it had gone into production a year earlier. During the past few years computer technology has been most volatile. Today's buzzword is forgotten in a few months; promising trends die a-borning; hot entrepreneurs emerge as *dei ex machina* in every sense, only to vanish tomorrow. While all technology-watchers must make a pass at predicting the future, security analysts and magazine and newspaper reporters write for immediate publication, weighing the odds as they look at the moment, relatively secure in the knowledge that their predictions have a short life. Authors of books, on the other hand, must commit themselves irrevocably for a dim hereafter; moreover, what they write must have reasonable validity through what they hope will be a decent shelf-life for their books.

Perforce, then, we take the long view, withholding lengthy comment on the fragile trend that hasn't yet become an onslaught. Some developments I scanned with a wary eye in October 1980 were viewdata/videotex, videodiscs, personal computers, the impending shift of major profits from hardware to software, and the increasingly successful Japanese assault on computer and communications technology. Except for viewdata—a service I thought would not change much in the near future—I covered each in a few cautious sentences.

The greatest exposure was the IBM antitrust case. There was a good chance the suit would be settled before publication date or shortly thereafter. The trial had gone on way too long and IBM seemed besieged on all sides by new competitors, and so there was little sympathy in the press for the government's position; even if the case ran its course, the smart money favored IBM, at least on appeal. I had three choices: to cut out the antitrust chapter, to state the facts but remove the opinions, or to write what I believed. But the case was too important to ignore, and it provided an opportunity to sum up and interpret information on IBM and the competitive situation in the industry as laid out in earlier chapters. To come to no conclusions appeared cowardly. The third choice, then, was the only choice, and I remained with the position my research seemed to dictate, one narrowly in the government's favor.

On January 7, 1982, the government dropped its lawsuit against IBM, claiming the suit was "without merit and should be dismissed." This action represented the anticipated and entirely normal swing of the antitrust pendulum (although the government's total capitulation was a surprise). The press sought out the usual parade of experts, almost all of whom supported dismissal (only antitrust officials of previous administrations criticized it). At the same time, many observers pointed out that IBM would increase its market share in mainframes and become more aggressive in other areas of the computer business. It still dominated the mainframe sector and was now a significant presence in small computers; it had brought out a highly competitive personal computer in August 1981 and reentered the services business shortly after the antitrust dismissal.

As I write in the spring of 1982, what other conditions may affect IBM's role in the industry? The ascendance of small computers has dictated important changes in marketing and manufacturing for both IBM and its competitors. It is uneconomic to sell a $5000 machine through a personal sales call, so IBM now offers its personal computers through Sears and ComputerLand. Small computers need greater volume to make a profit, and so the Dwarfs, following IBM's lead, have had to retool for mass production. All of these developments require profound alterations of ingrained attitudes. It is uncertain how well each company will adjust to the changes.

Since the hardcover edition of this book went to press, legions of corporate executives have acquired desktop computers. Industry people suggest that mainframes will become giant libraries of data for individual machines to process, and they are probably right; the mainframe business is mature, and the real growth will occur in other sectors. But the smaller machines, whether mini or micro, must talk to the mainframes, and communications compatibility with IBM equipment has become an increasingly important requirement in the design of small machines. The Dwarfs, sorely squeezed by the price war between IBM and the plug-compatible manufacturers, are also offering this feature. The trade press still divides the computer systems market into "the IBM world" (meaning IBM and its plug-compatible competitors) and "the non-IBM world." In sum, not only is IBM positioned for future dominance of every segment of the computer industry but it now continues to set technological standards, exercising a power far broader than that suggested by its market share.

Accordingly, I have left Chapter 15 exactly as I wrote it. Which brings me to a few remarks on the purpose and value of history in a volatile technology. Certainly a corporate executive who plans his business according to the strategies of the 360 era will soon be out of a job; nor is a history book an intelligent source for investors searching out the latest growth stocks. The analysts' reports and the newspaper and magazine articles are daily operating tools for managing and investing, but their strength is also a weakness. Reporters and analysts must keep barreling ahead; they haven't the time to reflect or to fit current events into the pattern of what's gone before. That's a job for the historian, who knows that technology may change but human nature doesn't. IBM's corporate values and past behavior supply useful clues to what it will do in the future. This was the value of the government's antitrust suit, and it is part of the purpose of this book.

In the past few years, a new segment of the industry has sprung up: the microcomputer companies and the software houses that serve them. These are receiving constant vigorous press coverage, as they should, but they are still too raw to go into history books. Anything I say on the subject now I may want to recant in a few months. So I have decided to leave well enough alone, and this book remains a history of the computer industry from the late thirties through 1980, with some speculation on the future. I hope it will give readers a perspective on the complexities of the business, the patterns and the swings of the pendulum, and the different factors that make the technology race or dawdle, and that this understanding will help them to evaluate tomorrow's news.

New York, May 1982.

Notes on Sources

Interviews were the prime source of information for this book. Often, for reasons obvious or less obvious, the speaker asked to remain anonymous; when possible I've tried to supply some useful characterization, although some details have been altered for protective purposes.

I also read many books, academic papers, speeches, articles, and corporate and legal documents and testimony made public through the various lawsuits that have engaged computer companies over the years. Both limited space and common sense preclude my listing everything I've read over the past decade, so I will simply cite specific references and mention literature I found particularly helpful. To sample the range of contemporary opinion I regularly followed industry coverage in *Computerworld, Datamation, Business Week, The Wall Street Journal,* and *The New York Times* from 1970 to the present.

I read a good number of IBM's internal papers over a seven-year period. The same memo, of course, often crops up in several different lawsuits; I note where I happened to find it. The most abundant source of documents is *United States of America* v. *International Business Machines Corporation,* United States District Court, Southern District of New York, 69 Civ. 200. For papers I read during the discovery period before they were introduced in court, I've used deposition numbers; a Justice Department aide assures me these will be adequate to trace the documents.

Chapter 1

page

4   "It was Pascal . . . tax system." See Goldstine, Herman H., *The Computer from Pascal to von Neumann,* Princeton University Press, 1972, pp. 7–8.

4   "when *Fortune* . . . understandably humbled," Wise, T. A., "Control Data's Magnificent Fumble," *Fortune,* April 1966.

7   "a roomful of light bulbs . . . change the message," and

8   "series of mailboxes . . . mailbox 14." The best simple explanations of how computers work appear in booklets given away by the mainframe manufacturers. For the light bulb image I am indebted to IBM's "What Is a Computer" and Univac's "Mighty New Servant to the Mind of Man"; for the mailbox image to "You and the Computer" from GE, whose own computers, alas, you can no longer buy.

9   "a program developed at MIT . . . Else return 'Yes.'" *New Progress in Artificial Intelligence,* 1974 annual report of The Artificial Intelligence Laboratory, MIT.

page

13   "in 1980 . . . other supplies." Figures from International Data Corporation.

14   "In 1980 . . . around the world." Figures from International Data Corporation.

CHAPTER 2

The books I found most useful on the origins of computer technology were:

Bernstein, Jeremy, *The Analytical Engine*, Vintage Books, 1966.

Goldstine, Herman, op. cit.

Randell, Brian (ed.), *The Origins of Digital Computers—Selected Papers*,
Springer-Verlag, 1975.

20   "One scholar notes . . . Babbage's engine." Randell, p. 12.

23   "In late 1940 . . . foundation." The paper Atanasoff wrote to secure this
money is included in Randell's anthology.

25–   "A number of . . . 'Atanasoff calculator' . . . here?" *Honeywell Inc.* v.
26   *Sperry Rand Corp. and Illinois Scientific Developments, Inc.*, U.S. District Court, District of Minnesota, Fourth Division, Civil Action File No. 4-
67 Civ. 138. October 19, 1973. *Findings of Fact, Conclusions of Law and
Order of Judgment.* This account of the dealings between Atanasoff and
Mauchly follows the judge's findings, with comments supplied by the two
men in interviews with the author.

27   "According to Goldstine's . . . $486,804.22." Goldstine, pp. 150 and 154.

27   "we should realize . . . so great." Goldstine, p. 153.

27   "If you have . . . left-wing idea." See Eckert's testimony, *United States of
America* v. *International Business Machines Corporation.*

28   "the whole atmosphere . . . mathematics." Goldstine, p. 182.

28   "First Draft of a Report on EDVAC" is reprinted in Randell.

29   "all members . . . publication." Goldstine, p. 197.

33   "The judge ruled . . . to the other." *Honeywell* v. *Sperry Rand, Findings
of Fact, etc.*

35–   "Most IBM plants . . . problem." IBM, *Time to Know: A Brief History of
36   IBM*, 1967; distributed by IBM.

36   "Most dramatically . . . Great Britain.)" See Kahn, David, *The Code-
breakers*, Weidenfeld and Nicholson, 1967, pp. 562 ff., and Belden, Thomas Graham and Belden, Marva Robins, *The Lengthening Shadow*, Little,
Brown, 1962, p. 209.

37   "The Selective . . . $300 an hour." See Rodgers, William, *Think*, Stein and
Day, 1969, p. 177.

39–   "Every day or two . . . were important." From a tape-recorded interview
40   done for the Smithsonian Institution's computer history project.

40   "We spent . . . go in." See Hurd's Smithsonian tape.

41   "the meeting . . . obsolete." From transcript of SHARE meeting for pio-
neers, March 8, 1972, San Francisco.

44   "Univac had . . . in the field." "Tom Jr.'s IBM," *Fortune*, September 1956.

44   "That year . . . 9.9 percent." See *Honeywell* v. *Sperry Rand, Findings of
Fact.*

44   "The first Univac . . . competitors." Rosen, Saul, "Electronic Computers: A
Historical Survey," *Computing Surveys*, March 1969.

Chapter 3

page

52   "My affinity . . . enjoy either." Belden and Belden, p. 222.

53   "During that first . . . thousand of them." From "Tom Jr.'s IBM," *Fortune*, September 1956, which provides generally useful background on TJW Jr.'s early life.

54–   "His accession . . . and love.)" See Belden and Belden, p. 311, and Rodgers,
55   p. 227.

Chapter 4

66   "I believe . . . another?" Watson, Thomas J., Jr., *A Business and Its Beliefs*, McKinsey Foundation Lecture Series, Graduate School of Business, Columbia University. McGraw-Hill, 1963, p. 4.

70   "I understand . . . junior programmer." This memo has been widely reproduced. The full text appears in the Government's pretrial brief for its antitrust suit against IBM—among other places.

70   "memo to the chairman." I found the Clementi memo (March 14, 1969) with Watson's deposition in *U.S.* v. *IBM*.

72   "His hat . . . hopeless." *The Stories of F. Scott Fitzgerald*, Charles Scribner's Sons, 1951.

73ff.   Information on Thomas J. Watson, Sr. and on IBM in the precomputer era came mostly from Belden and Belden and from Rodgers. Also see T. J. Watson, Jr.'s reminiscences in *A Business and Its Beliefs*.

73   "why did . . . its growth." T. J. Watson, Jr., speech to Public Relations Society of America, November 6, 1958.

74   "From his own boss . . . done at IBM." T. J. Watson, Jr. himself cites this technique in *A Business and Its Beliefs*, p. 18.

77   "IBM's employee . . . estimate." "How IBM Avoids Layoffs Through Retraining," *Business Week*, November 10, 1975.

79   "In the elder . . . mature corporations." See *A Business and Its Beliefs*, p. 66.

81   Belden and Belden, p. 138.

86–   "The final word . . . many names to these." *U.S.* v. *IBM*, plaintiff's exhibit
87   1630.

88   "The Management Review . . . the business." MRC minutes, January 11 and November 27, 1968; February 26 and April 7, 1969.

89–
90   "What is most . . . spirit." see MC minutes, October 31, 1968.

Chapter 5

"IBM's $5,000,000,000 Gamble" and "The Rocky Road to the Marketplace" by T. A. Wise, two articles which ran in *Fortune* in September and October 1966, formed the definitive contemporary account of the 360 project; they are still a most useful source of information on System 360. I have also drawn on the reminiscences of IBM'ers at different levels who worked on the project; and finally, documents in *U.S.* v. *IBM* include much material on System 360 which, of course, was not publicly available in 1966.

page

94 "The SPREAD report" is defendant's exhibit 1404 in *U.S.* v. *IBM*.

96 "In December 1962 . . . through 1970." Exhibit 76-36 with deposition of Emanuel Piore.

96 "A month later . . . eloquence." Exhibit 76-42-B with deposition of Piore.

96 Tucker memo, April 16, 1963. Piore deposition exhibit 76-51.

98 "Tom Watson . . . general managers." Plaintiff's exhibit 1630.

99 "As Learson . . . March 1964." Plaintiff's exhibit 1079.

99 "Tom Watson . . . the system." Plaintiff's exhibits 4005, 1085, 1237 and 1107.

99–
100 "Product Test historically . . . difficult." This comment comes from the IBM lawyers' objection sheet attached to plaintiff's exhibit 1107.

100 "Corporate finance . . . presentation." Plaintiff's exhibit 3923.

100–
101 "The first crises . . . immediately." Exhibits 108 and 111 with the deposition of Emanuel Piore.

101 "A post-mortem task force . . . underestimated." Plaintiff's exhibit 3647.

101 "A Watson memo." Plaintiff's exhibit 1630.

102 "The programming slippages . . . criticized." Plaintiff's exhibit 1367.

102 "Dean Phypers . . . done." Plaintiff's exhibit 3645.

102–
103 "And a memo . . . time." Exhibit 035 with deposition of Thomas J. Watson, Jr.

103 "I think . . . people do." Plaintiff's exhibit 1630.

105 "We want . . . assessment." Exhibit 104-035 with deposition of David Allen.

107 "IBM could never . . . solution." The minutes of IBM's management committees show many discussions of what to do with ASDD. The early months of 1968 are particularly rich in such deliberations, which culminated in a task force report to the MRC delivered on July 15, 1968.

110–
111 "MIT's Project MAC . . . won the MIT contract." See these exhibits with the deposition of Emanuel Piore: 76-142 and 142A; 76-219; 76-148.

111–
112 "The dissenters . . . change." Plaintiff's exhibits 2811, 1194 and 3500.

112 "Because of . . . problem." Plaintiff's exhibit 1205.

113 "The strategy . . . systems." Document dated November 15, 1964, with deposition of Louis Robinson.

114 On segmentation, see plaintiff's exhibit 1349.

114 "Documents suggest . . . control." Plaintiff's exhibit 1360.

115 "In May . . . and 1967." Plaintiff's exhibit 1492.

115 "The 360 model 67 . . . customers." Financial figures on the model 67 come from its Greybook, April 1968, which, when I read it, carried the number P-IBM-680430-008.

116 "One report . . . approval." Exhibit 76-204 to deposition of Emanuel Piore.

117 "a 1969 forecast . . . program." Plaintiff's exhibit 2418.

120 "in all the program lost about $20 million." See *Fortune*, September 1966.

120 "The supercomputer's . . . withdrawn." See report of Special Machine Task Force, exhibit 64-054A to deposition of Louis Robinson.

121 "in a heated memo . . . of the Government)." Exhibit 001 to deposition of Harwood Kolsky.

122 The plan to negotiate with two customers comes from a confidential memo to the files from O. M. Scott, September 23, 1963, cited in the

page

Government's pretrial brief. Opel's memo, written to Dr. Louis Robinson, was among the documents attached to Robinson's deposition. The quotation from IBM's 360 announcement appears in the Government's pretrial brief.

122– "Documents from . . . state of the art." See Kennard to Gibson, June 5,
123   1964, cited in Government pretrial brief; exhibits 64-024, 034 to Robinson's deposition; exhibits 282-485 and 488 to T. V. Learson's deposition.

123   "This 'reach' . . . justify it." Exhibit 64-050 to Robinson's deposition.

123   "The company finally . . . project." Plaintiff's exhibit 2880.

123   Sales estimate on CDC model 6600 from Control Data.

CHAPTER 6

125   Galbraith, John Kenneth, *The New Industrial State*, Signet Books, 1968, p. 73.

131   Galbraith, p. 82.

134   "COMSTAT . . . antitrust case." Exhibits 104-008 and 009 with the deposition of David Allen.

136   "a 1965 corporate study": a well-known document known as the "Maurer report," exhibit 118-063 with deposition of H. G. Figueroa.

137   "Why do we . . . forced to!" Plaintiff's exhibit 2400.

137   "In the spring . . . lawsuits." See *Greyhound Computer Corporation* v. *IBM*, Appendix of Plaintiff-Appellant, United States Court of Appeals for the Ninth Circuit, No. 72-2553: plaintiff's exhibit 189.

138   "consider software as a product." Testimony of Larry Welke, president of International Computer Programs, Inc. See *Computerworld*, May 3 and June 7, 1976.

141   Bylinsky, Gene, "Vincent Learson Didn't Plan It That Way, But IBM's Toughest Competitor Is—IBM," *Fortune*, March 1972.

142   "The activities . . . 1970." See MC minutes, July 23, 24, 31, August 1, September 9, 13, October 31, 1968; May 8, 1969; also *Greyhound* v. *IBM*, plaintiff's exhibit 118.

142   "underestimated . . . recession." On February 25, 1970, the Management Review Committee received a forecast that "the probability of a recession in 1970 is 45% and of a moderate to severe recession 10%." By the July 2, 1970 MRC meeting, Cary was complaining about a misreading of the economy.

148   "A 1973 . . . effective.)" McLaughlin, Richard A., "Monopoly Is Not a Game," *Datamation*, September 1973.

CHAPTER 7

155   "Ranked . . . Burroughs." See *Findings of Fact, etc., Honeywell* v. *Sperry Rand Corp.*

155   "(In 1952 . . . IBM's.)" See IBM's pretrial brief in *U.S.* v. *IBM*, p. 24.

161   "Raytheon Corporation . . . patron." See Rosen, Saul, "Electronic Computers: A Historical Survey," *Computing Surveys*, March 1969.

163   "Honeywell replaced . . . 1401's." See Brock, Gerald, *The U.S. Computer*

page

Industry: A Study of Market Power, Ballinger Publishing Company, 1975, p. 94.

163   "In that decade... equipment." See *Findings of Fact, Honeywell* v. *Sperry Rand;* compare 1957 with 1966.

163–   "Binger... numbers-oriented." Levy, Robert, "The Heat's On at Hon-
164   eywell," *Dun's Review,* June 1969.

164   "Arthur D. Little... survival." See *U.S.* v. *IBM,* Binger's deposition; Spangle's testimony.

164ff. "In March 1970." In *U.S.* v. *IBM,* the Binger deposition contains a good account of the merger decision from Honeywell's point of view. For the story of GE's exit, see testimony of Reginald H. Jones. A good summary of the GE story as told during the Government-IBM trial ran in *The Wall Street Journal,* January 12, 1976 (Scott R. Schmedel). Spangle's testimony in *U.S.* v. *IBM* discusses the effects of the merger on Honeywell.

166   "a study done in 1970." See *EDP Industry Report,* May 4, 1970.

167   For early discussions of the B5000: See Lonergan, William and King, Paul, "Design of the B5000 System," *Datamation,* May 1961; and "The Generation Gap," *Computerworld,* April 23 and May 7, 1969.

170   "The vital... ahead." Allyn, Stanley C., *My Half Century With NCR,* McGraw-Hill, 1967, pp. 158–59.

171   "One of ... era." Allyn, pp. 165–66.

CHAPTER 8

177   "A. J. Liebling ... reporting)." Liebling, A. J., *The Press,* Ballantine Books, 1961, p. 240.

188   "When a man gets... salesmen.)" Belden and Belden, p. 169.

193   "Richard Sonnenfeldt... divesture [*sic*]." *U.S.* v. *IBM,* plaintiff's exhibit 199.

193   "Another staff report." *U.S.* v. *IBM,* plaintiff's exhibit 349.

194   "Sometime during... materialized." Demaree, Allan T., "RCA After the Bath," *Fortune,* September 1972.

195   "The report Morsey delivered." *U.S.* v. *IBM,* plaintiff's exhibit 208.

CHAPTER 9

199   "We... sufferance." Wierzynski, Gregory H., "Control Data's Newest Cliffhanger," *Fortune,* February 1968.

200   "We moved... enterprise." See Houston, Robert, "Nebraskan's Success Story," Omaha *Sunday World-Herald Magazine,* December 22, 1963.

200–   "When the war ... turkey." This account is based on a letter from Control
201   Data vice-president John W. Lacey to W. W. Jackson, May 22, 1969; and on an interview with Univac's Arthur Draper.

201ff. A good account of Control Data's original financing appeared in a report called "Moneymaking in the Twin Cities Local Over-the-Counter Marketplace," by James R. Ullyot, published by Economic Information, Inc. of St. Paul in 1972. *Fortune* covered the origins of Control Data in April 1966 ("Control Data's Magnificent Fumble" by T. A. Wise); so did *The Upper* page

Midwest Investor in November 1961 ("Control Data, From Mystery to Legend," by Roy Wirtzfeld).

203–   "In 1963 . . . on order." For a contemporary account of the 6600, see the
204   two *Fortune* articles mentioned above.

204   "The experiences . . . sued IBM." See testimony of Hugh P. Donahue, Assistant to the Chairman of the Board, Control Data Corporation, before the Senate Subcommittee on Antitrust and Monopoly, July 26, 1974.

205–   "In 1971 . . . indiscreet." United States District Court, District of Minnesota: Third Division. Civil Action No. 3-68-312. *Amended Answer and Counterclaim.*
206

209   "In 1972 . . . $350 million." "A Risk Capitalist Bids a Golden Adieu," *Business Week*, January 22, 1972.

210   "machine tool of the future." See Smith, William D., "A Small Computer Giant Welcomes IBM," *The New York Times*, August 3, 1969.

210   "In a system . . . emergency." Everett, R. R., "The Whirlwind Computer," in Bell, C. Gordon and Newell, Allen, *Computer Structures: Readings and Examples*, McGraw-Hill, 1971, p. 138.

222   "observers have questioned . . . for himself." For a good contemporary expression of skepticism about the Xerox-SDS merger, see Welles, Chris, "Xerox: Whatever Happened to Act II?" *Corporate Financing*, July/August 1971.

CHAPTER 10

231   "In 1979 . . . $7½ million." Market data from International Data Corporation.

233   "the number one problem in our business today." United States District Court for the Northern District of Oklahoma, *The Telex Corporation and Telex Computer Products, Inc.* v. *International Business Machines Corporation*, No. 72-C-89. Plaintiff's exhibit 103.

233–
234   "By the end . . . gloomy." *Telex* v. *IBM*, plaintiff's exhibit 162.

235   "The freight . . . cut." Brock, op. cit., p. 133.

236   "As one IBM . . . company!" *Telex* v. *IBM*, plaintiff's exhibit 141A.

237   "TJW . . . accordingly." See MRC minutes, April 23, 1971.

237   "The plan . . . 1972." See *Telex* v. *IBM*, *Findings of Fact*, p. 71.

237   "the net effects . . . concerned." *Telex* v. *IBM*, plaintiff's exhibit 152.

237   "In the fall . . . competition." *U.S.* v. *IBM*, plaintiff's exhibit 3852A.

238–   "In 1969 and 1970 . . . financing." *Telex* v. *IBM*, *Findings of Fact*, pp.
239   92–93.

239   "one of . . . history." "Inside IBM's Management," *Business Week*, July 14, 1973.

239–   "There was a . . . information." See *Telex* v. *IBM*, *Findings of Fact*; the
240   section on Telex's behavior begins on page 105.

242   "in 1972 . . . as sales." See American Institute of Certified Public Accountants, Accounting Principles Board Opinions No. 7 and 27. A clear and fairly entertaining analysis of creative accounting in several branches of the computer industry appears in Briloff, Abraham I., *Unaccountable Accounting*, Harper & Row, 1972.

page

243– My chief source of information for the Amdahl story was Amdahl's own
244 account, which ran in the February 1979 issue of *Datamation*. I also drew
on a piece by Scott R. Schmedel in *The Wall Street Journal*, July 14, 1976
("David vs. Goliath: Small Computer Firm Challenges Big IBM—To a
Certain Extent"). The problems of the new pcm's in general have been
covered extensively in the trade and business press; in particular, see Ippo-
lito, Stephen J., "Measure for Countermeasure," and Solomon, Laurence,
"IBM Versus the PCM's," in *Datamation*, February 1979; and Cornell,
Charles A., "Microcode: IBM Market Tool?" in *Computerworld*, August
28 and September 4, 1978.

Chapter 11

258 "a 'fandangle'... said Briloff." Briloff's *Barrons* articles were collected in
the book *Unaccountable Accounting*. See pp. 135–36.

259 "In all... purchasers." See plaintiff's exhibits 97 and 328, *Greyhound
Computer Corporation* v. *IBM*.

259 "In 1966... higher costs." See *U.S.* v. *IBM*, plaintiff's exhibit 035 with
deposition of Thomas J. Watson, Jr.

259 "By 1967... competitor." *Greyhound* v. *IBM*, plaintiff's exhibit 664
(MRC minutes, September 6, 1967).

259 "A purchasing binge... growth chart." See *Greyhound* v. *IBM*, plaintiff's
exhibits 124, 111 and 118.

260 "The 'control'... unionism." See *U.S.* v. *IBM*, plaintiff's exhibit 5153.

260 "cheap second-hand 360's." See plaintiff's economic brief, *U.S.* v. *IBM*,
which notes the dangers of the lessors' second-hand equipment market to
IBM.

260 "whose financial problems... pcm's." See *Greyhound* v. *IBM*, plaintiff's
exhibit 94.

262– "Howard Levin... Rockwood Computer Corporation." For contemporary
263 accounts of Levin-Townsend's woes, see "A $900 Attache Case Is Issue in
Struggle for Levin-Townsend," *The Wall Street Journal*, February 25,
1970; and *Time*, February 2, 1970.

Chapter 12

273 "the arteries... business." See Diebold, John, "ADP—The Still-Sleeping
Giant," *Harvard Business Review*, September/October 1964.

274 "Just as there... companies." This account of the pattern for software
houses draws heavily on an article called "The Computer Software Companies: How Much Can They Really Grow?" by L. Robert Johnson, *The
Institutional Investor*, March 1970. For other useful insights into the problems of setting up a consulting business, see Wittreich, Warren J., "How
To Buy/Sell Professional Services," *Harvard Business Review*, March-
April 1966. The observations of Johnson and Wittreich were echoed by
many software entrepreneurs and employees in interviews with the author.

282 "Computers at the time... properly." Lautenberg, Frank, speech to First
World Computing Conference, Barcelona, June 1978.

286 "All you have... business." "A New Industry's Wild Ride," *Business
Week*, May 24, 1969.

CHAPTER **13**

Preparation of this chapter required considerable basic background reading to understand a new technology and an unfamiliar economic climate. Among the books, reports and articles I found particularly helpful were:

Martin, James, *Telecommunications and the Computer,* Prentice-Hall, 1969. Martin is a prolific and widely respected author of textbooks in this field; by now, I assume, this one has either been updated or superseded by a newer work.

Phillips, Charles F., Jr., *The Economics of Regulation,* Richard D. Irwin, Inc., revised edition, 1969.

Stanford Research Institute, Report No. 7379B, vols. I and II, *Policy Issues Presented by the Interdependence of Computer and Communications Services.* This is SRI's analysis and digest of the responses to the FCC's first computer inquiry, which is mentioned in the chapter.

In the early seventies Salomon Brothers issued two useful reports, "A Data Communications Primer" and "Data Communications Primer II," which explain basic terms and concepts. The authors were Robert E. La Blanc and Winston E. Himsworth.

Business Week has done an excellent job of covering communications since the late sixties. Two early pieces on the technology and the management of the Bell System were especially helpful: "Why Ma Bell Chops Up the Signals," January 13, 1968; and "Why You Hear a Busy Signal at AT&T," December 27, 1969.

page

297– "IBM was not . . . division." See MC minutes, April 3, 1970, for discussion
298   of communications policy issues, noting "Knaplund [Paul Knaplund, a vice-president] agreed that we would ultimately come in conflict with ATT but prefers to do it in private rather than public."

306   "sophisticated lobbying skills." A fascinating article on Bell's lobbying operation ran in *The Wall Street Journal,* April 16, 1975 ("On the Job or Off, A T & T People Polish the Company Image," by Sanford L. Jacobs). Articles on Bell's lobbying for this bill in particular ran in *Datamation,* April and November 1976; *Computerworld,* May 24 and 31, 1976; *Business Week,* March 15, 1976; and *The New York Times,* June 14, 1976.

310   "IBM was concluding . . . communications." See MC minutes, 8/2/68, 4/2/69 and 10/21/71 on Carnation, IBM's European switchboard; 4/3/70 and 11/25/70 on public policy issues and satellites; 7/21/70 on providing communications products. See MRC 8/4/71 on remote computing, 8/13/71 on Carnation.

312– "SBS's market studies . . . grow." A good contemporary analysis of SBS
313   prospects appears in Research Bulletin #1846, February 1978, by Computer Industry Planning Service, a joint undertaking of International Data Corporation and Hoenig & Strock, Inc.

313– "In 1974 . . . inevitable." On mixed reactions to SNA, see IDC's *Distribut-*
314   *ed Processing Newsletter,* November 1978, Special Report, "SNA and the User . . . A Troubled Marriage?"; *Datamation,* March 1977, "Another Look at SNA," by P. D. Moulton and Ronald C. Sander; and February 1978, "IBM's Offering of SNA: Some Find It a Success," by Edward K. Yasaki.

320   "Unexpected success . . . time?" Schon, Donald A., *Technology and Change,* A Seymour Lawrence Book, Delacorte Press, 1967, p. 65.

CHAPTER 14

ELECTRONIC BANKING

The following publications provided particularly useful information on Electronic Funds Transfer:

EFT in the United States, The Final Report of the National Commission on Electronic Fund Transfers, October 28, 1977.

The Economics of a National Electronic Funds Transfer System, Proceedings of a conference held in October 1974, sponsored by the Federal Reserve Bank of Boston.

Hearings before the Subcommittee on Consumer Affairs, House of Representatives on H.R. 8753, The Consumer Credit Protection Act Amendments of 1977, Part 1, September 1977.

Zimmer, Linda Fenner, "Cash Dispensers, Automated Tellers Come of Age," *Bank Administration,* May 1978.

Zimmer, Linda Fenner, "Cash Dispensing Equipment and Automatic Tellers," *Bank Administration,* May 1977.

Payment Systems, Inc. Reports: Crooks, Jean H., "The Debit Card as a Third-Party Payments Mechanism," February 8, 1979; Zimmer, Linda Fenner, "Locating ATM's and Cash Dispensers," February 1977; Adcock, William O., Jr., "New Perspectives on the ATM Bottom Line," November 16, 1978.

"A Retreat from the Cashless Society," *Business Week,* April 18, 1977.

"Consumer Banking: Why Everyone Wants a Piece of the Business," *Business Week,* April 23, 1979.

Greenwood, Harold W., Jr., "Electronic Funds Transfer: An Edsel?" *The New York Times,* January 8, 1978.

Flint, Jerry, "Quick Electronic Banking Slowed by the Public's Habits and Fears," *The New York Times,* May 31, 1977.

Blumenthal, Ralph, "Electronic Fraud Accompanies Move Toward Tellerless Banking," *The New York Times,* March 26, 1978.

Lublin, Joann S., " 'Checkless' Banking Is Available, but Public Sees Few Advantages," *The Wall Street Journal,* November 18, 1975.

Laing, Jonathan R., "Courts and the Public Slow Up the Advance of Electronic Banking, *The Wall Street Journal,* January 6, 1977.

Portway, Patrick S., "EFT Systems? No Thanks, Not Yet," *Computerworld,* January 9, 1978.

ARTIFICIAL INTELLIGENCE

This section required considerable general background reading, which included all or part of the following books:

Dreyfus, Hubert L., *What Computers Can't Do,* Harper & Row, 1972.

Feigenbaum, Edward A. and Feldman, Julian (eds.), *Computers and Thought,* McGraw-Hill, 1963.

Jackson, Philip C., *Introduction to Artificial Intelligence,* Petrocelli Books, 1974.

Newell, Allen and Simon, Herbert A., *Human Problem Solving,* Prentice-Hall, 1972.

Weizenbaum, Joseph, *Computer Power and Human Reason,* W. H. Freeman and Company, 1976.

Wiener, Norbert, *Cybernetics,* second ed., MIT Press, 1961 (paperback, 1965).

Wiener, Norbert, *The Human Use of Human Beings*, Avon Books, 1969.
Wiener, Norbert, *God and Golem, Inc.*, MIT Press, 1966.

Among the many academic papers I read, these proved particularly helpful:

CARNEGIE MELLON UNIVERSITY

CMU Computer Science Speech Group, "Working Papers in Speech Recognition," April 1974.

Chase, William G. and Simon, Herbert, "Perception in Chess," *Cognitive Psychology*, January 1973.

Newell, Allen, "Remarks on the relationship between artificial intelligence and cognitive psychology," in Banerji, R. and Mesarovic, M.D. (eds.), *Theoretical Approaches to Non-Numerical Problem-Solving*, Springer-Verlag, 1970.

Reddy, R. and Newell, A., "Knowledge and its Representation in a Speech Understanding System," in Gregg, L. (ed.), *Knowledge and Cognition*, Lawrence Erlbaum Associates, 1974.

Simon, Herbert A. and Gilmartin, Kevin, "A Simulation of Memory for Chess Positions," *Cognitive Psychology* 5, 29–46 (1973).

Simon, Herbert A. and Chase, William G., "Skill in Chess," *American Scientist*, July-August 1973.

MIT

Artificial Intelligence Laboratory, "Proposal to ARPA for Research on Intelligent Automata and Micro-Automation, 1974–1976," *Memo No. 299*, September 1973.

Artificial Intelligence Laboratory, "New Progress in Artificial Intelligence," *Annual Progress Report*, June 1974.

Minsky, Marvin, "Steps Toward Artificial Intelligence," in *Proceedings of the IRE*, January 1961.

Minsky, Marvin, "A Framework for Representing Knowledge," *Memo No. 306*, June 1974.

Minsky, Marvin, "Plain Talk About Neurodevelopmental Epistemology," *Memo No. 430*, June 1977.

Minsky, Marvin, "K-Lines: A Theory of Memory," *Draft*, March 28, 1979.

Papert, Seymour, "The Artificial Intelligence of Hubert L. Dreyfus," *Memo No. 154*, January 1968.

Weizenbaum, Joseph, "ELIZA—A Computer Program for the Study of Natural Language Communication Between Man and Machine," in *Communications of the ACM*, January 1966.

Winograd, Terry, *Understanding Natural Language*, Academic Press, 1972.

HARVARD

Oettinger, Anthony G., "The State of the Art of Automatic Language Translation: An Appraisal," *Beitrage zur Sprachkunde und Informationsverarbeitung*, Oldenbourg Verlag (Munich), 1963.

YALE

Carbonell, Jaime G., Jr., "Ideological Belief System Simulation," Research Report #111, May 1977.

Schank, Roger C., "Computer Understanding of Natural Language," *Behavior Research Methods & Instrumentation*, 1978. Vol. 10 (2).

Schank, Roger C., "Inference in the Conceptual Dependency Paradigm: A Personal History," *Research Report #141*, September 1978.

Schank, Roger C.; Lebowitz, Michael; Birnbaum, Lawrence A., "Integrated Partial Parsing," *Research Report #143*, December 1978.

Schank, Roger C., "Interestingness: Controlling Inferences," *Research Report #145*, October 1978.

Schank, Roger C., and Lehnert, Wendy, "The Conceptual Content of Conversation," *Research Report #160*, 1979.

Kolodner, Janet L., "Memory Organization for Natural Language Data-Base Inquiry," *Research Report #142*, September 1978.

Wilensky, Robert, "Understanding Goal-Based Stories, *Research Report #140*, September 1978.

Magazine and Newspaper Articles

Cerf, Vinton, "Parry Encounters the Doctor," *Datamation*, July 1973.

Brand, David, "Latest Machines See, Hear, Speak and Sing—And May Outthink Man," *The Wall Street Journal*, June 28, 1973.

page

346 "Computing Machinery and Intelligence" appears in the Feigenbaum and Feldman anthology.

351 "none of . . . do this?" See Simon and Chase, "Skill in Chess."

353 "In a James Bond movie." See Dreyfus, p. 128.

354 "Winograd himself . . . while." *MIT Progress Report*, p. 78.

359 "I accept . . . attain." Weizenbaum, *Computer Power and Human Reason*, pp. 209–10.

359 "But Weizenbaum . . . doing." Ibid., pp. 193, 198, 208–9.

360 "since . . . wisdom." Weizenbaum, ibid., p. 227.

MEDICINE

Institutional Reports

Laboratory of Computer Science, Massachusetts General Hospital, Harvard Medical School, "Computers in Patient Care and Medical Education," *Status Report*, 1974.

Laboratory of Computer Science (Massachusetts General Hospital), National Center for Health Services Research, Digital Equipment Corporation, "COSTAR: Functional Specifications (Version 5.6)," 1979.

National Center for Health Services Research, *Research Digest Series:* "Automation of the Problem-Oriented Medical Record," April 1977; "Computer-Stored Ambulatory Record (COSTAR)"; "Evaluation of a Medical Information System in a Community Hospital."

National Center for Health Services Research, "Computer Applications in Health Care," September 25, 1978.

National Center for Health Services Research, "Medical Information Systems," Draft, 1979.

Office of Technology Assessment, "Policy Implications of Medical Information Systems," November 1977.

SUMEX (Stanford University Medical Experimental Computer Resource), *An-*

nual Report—Year 05, Submitted to Biotechnology Resources Program, National Institutes of Health, May 1978.

Academic Papers and Articles

Feigenbaum, Edward A., "The art of artificial intelligence—Themes and case studies of knowledge engineering," *National Computer Conference*, 1978.

Pople, Harry E., Jr.; Myers, Jack D.; and Miller, Randolph, "Dialog: A Model of Diagnostic Logic for Internal Medicine," *Fourth International Joint Conference on Artificial Intelligence, Volume Two*, September 1975.

Pople, Harry E., Jr., "The Formation of Composite Hypotheses in Diagnostic Problem Solving: An Exercise in Synthetic Reasoning," *Fifth International Joint Conference on Artificial Intelligence, Volume Two*, August 1977.

Rockoff, Maxine L., "Medical Considerations: Telecommunications Technology: Can It Lead to Health Care Delivery Reform?" *HERMES (The Communications Technology Satellite) Its Performance and Applications*, Proceedings of a Conference Sponsored by the Royal Society of Canada, the Department of Communications Canada, and the National Aeronautics and Space Administration, November-December 1977.

Safir, Aran, "Optics and the Physician," *Survey of Ophthalmology*, vol. 18, no. 6, 1974.

Safir, Aran, "Computers in Ophthalmology," *Investigative Ophthalmology*, March 1976.

Shortliffe, Edward, "MYCIN: A Knowledge-Based Computer Program Applied to Infectious Diseases," *First Annual Symposium on Computer Application in Medical Care*, October 1977.

Shortliffe, Davis, Axline, Buchanan, Green and Cohen, "Computer-Based Consultations in Clinical Therapeutics: Explanation and Rule Acquisition Capabilities of the MYCIN System," *Computers and Biomedical Research*, vol. 8/3, 1975.

Kunz, Fallat, McClung, Osborn, Votteri, Nii, Aikins, Fagan and Feigenbaum, "A Physiological Rule-Based System for Interpreting Pulmonary Function Test Results," Stanford Heuristic Programming Project, *HPP-78-19 (working paper)*, November 1978.

Siegel, Shetye, Moody, Keane, Carr and Cerra, "An Integrated Computer-Based Care System for the Organization of Clinical Data and the Quantification and Prediction of Physiological Recovery of the Critically Ill Patient," from *Computers in Cardiology*, IEEE Proceedings, September 1978.

Siegel, John J. and Strom, Brian L., "The Computer as a 'Living Textbook' Applied to the Care of the Critically Injured Patient," *The Journal of Trauma*, vol. 12, no. 9, 1972.

Siegel, John H., "Computers and Mathematical Techniques in Surgery," in Sabiston, David C. (ed.), *Davis-Christopher Textbook of Surgery*, 11th ed. W. B. Saunders, 1980.

Slack, Warner V., "The Patient's Right to Decide," *The Lancet*, July 30, 1977.

Slack, Warner V. and Slack, Charles W., "Talking to a Computer About Emotional Problems: A Comparative Study," *Psychotherapy: Theory, Research and Practice*, Summer 1977.

Slack, Charles W. and Slack, Warner V., "Computer as Therapist," *Psychology Today*, January 1974.

Slack, Warner V. and Van Cura, Lawrence J., "Patient Reaction to Computer-Based Medical Interviewing," *Computers and Biomedical Research*, I (1968).

Slack, Warner, "Computer-Based Interviewing System Dealing with Nonverbal Behavior as well as Keyboard Responses," *Science*, January 8, 1971.

Slack, Warner V. and Slack, Charles W., "Patient-Computer Dialogue," *New England Journal of Medicine*, June 15, 1972.

Slack, Warner, "Patient Counseling by Computer," *The Changing Health Care Team*, MCSA, Seattle, Washington.

Witschi, Porter, Vogel, Buxbaum, Stare, and Slack, "A Computer-based Dietary Counseling System," *Journal of the American Dietetic Association*, October 1976.

Weed, Lawrence L., "Your Health Care and How to Manage It," PROMIS Laboratory, University of Vermont, Burlington, Vermont.

page

360   "The quality . . . memory." OTA, "Policy Implications of Medical Information Systems," p. 42.

361   "I believe . . . decision-making." Safir, "Optics and the Physician."

CHAPTER 15

380   "Jerrold G. Van Cise . . . innovation)." Van Cise, Jerrold G., *Understanding the Antitrust Laws*, 1970 ed., Corporate Law and Practice, Practice Handbook Series, Number 3, Practicing Law Institute, pp. 4, 7–8.

380   "It has . . . of society." Van Cise, p. 3.

380   "Uncontrolled . . . the best." Van Cise, p. 2.

381   "In 1956 . . . dissent." *U.S.* v. *E. I. du Pont de Nemours & Co.*, 351 U.S. 377 (1956).

381–
382   "In scrutinizing . . . site." *U.S.* v. *Grinnell Corp.*, 384 U.S. 563 (1966).

382   "every practice . . . cases." Van Cise, pp. 120–21.

382–
384   "The narrowest . . . Hand's decision." *U.S.* v. *Aluminum Co. of America*, 148 F. 2d 416 (2d Cir. 1945).

386   "Share Measurement Change." Plaintiff's exhibit 4790.

387–
388   "In November 1963 . . . frustration." This memo is cited in the Government's pretrial brief.

388   "The goal of . . . mandate." My own copy of this particular memo, dated January 3, 1966, is in *Greyhound* v. *IBM*, Appendix of Plaintiff-Appellant; it is plaintiff's exhibit 654 in that case.

388–
389   "I would like . . . market share." *U.S.* v. *IBM*, plaintiff's exhibit 4794.

389   "The key underpinnings . . . defense." My copy of this memo appears on p. 5113 of the transcript of hearings before the Senate Subcommittee on Antitrust and Monopoly on S. 1167, The Industrial Reorganization Act, July 23–26, 1974.

389   *Thomsen* v. *Cayser*, 243 U.S. 66 (1917).

396   "The rate . . . firms." Brock, p. 205. Brock's chapter 11, in which this paragraph appears, contains an interesting discussion of innovation in the computer industry.

page

397 "As Judge . . . acumen." What Judge Christensen said, precisely, was ". . . it must be recognized that [IBM's] diligence and foresight have included the competitive studies and the anti-competitive objectives and intent heretofore found, and that particularly as applied to this case have included an attempt to substantially constrain or destroy its plug compatible peripheral competition by predatory pricing actions and by market strategy bearing no relationship to technological skill, industry, appropriate foresight or customer benefit." *Telex* v. *IBM, Findings of Fact*, pp. 89–90.

397 "August 1971 QPLA." My copy of this particular QPLA is in the transcript of the Senate Antitrust and Monopoly Subcommittee hearings, cited earlier. It appears on pages 5110–12, and was plaintiff's exhibit 128 in the Telex case.

400 "Among the . . . tie." *U.S.* v. *IBM*, plaintiff's exhibit 5260.

400 "several of . . . Beitzel." See plaintiff's exhibits 4795, 5053, 5054, 4822.

404 "In 1972 . . . Sherman Act." The two Hart measures, with the late senator's views on them, appear in the Congressional Record for June 17, 1975 and May 13, 1976.

405 "The subject . . . industry." See Brock, chapter 11.

408 "It seems . . . economic sphere." Neale, A. D., *The Anti-Trust Laws of the United States of America, A Study of Competition Enforced By Law*, Cambridge University Press, 2nd ed., 1970 (paperback), p. 443.

410 "Cary . . . expensive." "Cary: IBM Vetoed Spinoff for Small Machines," *Computerworld*, April 23, 1979.

411 "(Van Cise . . . too well)." Van Cise, p. 263.

Chapter 16

412 "There will . . . world." Published in Sarnoff, David, *Looking Ahead*, McGraw-Hill, 1968, pp. 95–97.

419 "In 1969 . . . reading." Westin, Alan F. (Project Director) and Baker, Michael A. (Assistant Project Director), *Data Banks in a Free Society*, Quadrangle Books, 1972.

419 "created the . . . commentators." Westin and Baker, p. 341.

420 "matters . . . at all." Westin and Baker, p. 348.

422 Smith, Robert Ellis, *Privacy: How to Protect What's Left of It*, Anchor Press/Doubleday, 1979.

423 "Multics . . . hours." This story was told in Whiteside, Thomas, "Dead Souls in the Computer," *The New Yorker*, August 22 and 29, 1977, later published in hardcover.

424 "the recent affair of the data encryption standard." The account of the controversy over the data encryption standard has drawn on the following sources:

From Martin Hellman

Diffie, Whitfield and Hellman, Martin E., "Exhaustive Cryptanalysis of the NBS Data Encryption Standard," *Computer Magazine*, June 1977. Summary of NBS Workshop on Cryptography 9/21–9/22/76 as seen by Martin Hellman.

"Statement to Participants at NBS Workshop on Cryptography in Support of Computer Security," 9/21/76, from Martin E. Hellman.

Letters: To Dennis Branstad from Martin Hellman, October 22, 1975; to Hellman from S. Jeffery, National Bureau of Standards, January 6, 1976; to Hellman from Ernest Ambler of NBS, March 31, 1976; several letters between Rep. Charles A. Mosher and Dr. Ruth M. Davis of NBS, exchanged in 1976; from Hellman to David Kahn, January 16, 1976; from Richard Curtis of Alcoa to Hellman, April 14, 1976; from Robert Morris of AT&T to Hellman and David Kahn, June 17, 1976; from Keith Uncapher to Hellman, February 13, 1976.

From IBM

Feistel, Horst; Notz, William A.; and Smith, J. Lynn, "Some Cryptographic Techniques for Machine-to-Machine Data Communications," *Proceedings of the IEEE*, November 1975.

Feistel, Horst, "Cryptography and Computer Privacy," *Scientific American*, May 1973.

IBM Research Reports, vol. 7, no. 4, 1971, "Data Privacy."

Letter to the author from Daniel M. Burnham, then Director of Information, December 2, 1976.

Miscellaneous Articles

Sugarman, Robert, "On Foiling Computer Crime," *IEEE Spectrum*, July 1979.

"The Cryptography Affair," *IEEE Information Theory Group Newsletter*, December 1977.

Kahn, David, "Tapping Computers," *The New York Times* (Op Ed), April 3, 1976.

Yasaki, Edward, "Encryption Algorithm: Key Size is the Thing," *Datamation*, March 1976.

page

427   "in November 1979 . . . $20." Serrin, William, "New Auto Industry Technology: A Source of Wonder and Anxiety," *The New York Times*, November 5, 1979.

427–   "Past and . . . positions." "Technology and Labor in Five Industries," U.S.
428   Department of Labor, *Bureau of Labor Statistics Bulletin 2033*, 1979.

428   "Stepped-up . . . technology." Leontief, Wassily, "Newer and Newer and Newer Technology, With Little Unemployment," *The New York Times*, March 6, 1979.

428   "drastic population . . . workers." Dorn, Philip, "The Automated Office: The Road to Disaster?" *Datamation*, November 15, 1978.

429   "As Anthony Oettinger . . . out." "Communications in the National Decision-Making Process," in *Computers, Communications and the Public Interest*, M. Greenburger (ed.), Johns Hopkins University Press, 1971 (with discussion by Ithiel Pool, Alain Enthoven, David Packard).

429   "The *Wall Street Journal* . . . out." Wysocki, Bernard, Jr., "Executives Discover Computers Can Help Them in Daily Routine," *WSJ*, July 6, 1979.

431   "Man is . . . satisfy." Sarnoff, p. 95.

432   "In 1979 . . . squabbles." This dispute was well covered in *The New York Times* and *Computerworld*. A detailed article by John Noble Wilford,

page

"Air Control Technology Refined to Meet Hazards," ran in the science section of *The Times*, January 1980.

433   "As the Kemeny . . . Island." *Report of the President's Commission on the Accident at Three Mile Island*, October 1979.

435   "Joseph Weizenbaum . . . discussion?" *Computer Power and Human Reason*, p. 265.

436   "any group . . . times." Reston, James, "How to Win the *Pulitzer*," *The New York Times*, April 18, 1979.

436   "How can . . . business?" See Hiltz, Starr Roxanne and Turoff, Murray, "EFT and Social Stratification in the USA," *Telecommunications Policy*, March 1978.

Index